Brief Therapies

Community Mental Health Series

Sheldon R. Roen, Editor

Research Contributions from Psychology to Community Mental Health
Edited by Jerry W. Carter, Jr.

From Dependency to Dignity: Individual and Social Consequences of a Neighborhood House
Louis A. Zurcher and Alvin E. Green with Edward Johnson and Samuel Patton

Coordinate Index Reference Guide to Community Mental Health
Stuart E. Golann

Mental Health and the Community: Problems, Programs, and Strategies
Edited by Milton F. Shore and Fortune V. Mannino

Children of Mentally Ill Parents: Problems in Child Care
Elizabeth P. Rice, Miriam C. Ekdahl, and Leo Miller

Mental Health Related Activities of Companies and Unions: A Survey Based on the Metropolitan Chicago Area
Elizabeth J. Slotkin, Leo Levy, Edwin Wetmore, and Ferdinand N. Funk

Brief Therapies
Edited by Harvey H. Barten

Issues in Community Psychology and Preventive Mental Health
Division 27 of the American Psychological Association

Brief Therapies

Harvey H. Barten, M.D., Editor

Behavioral Publications, Inc.   **New York, New York**

Library of Congress Catalog Card Number 78-140053
Standard Book Number 87705-017-1
Copyright © 1971 by Behavioral Publications

BEHAVIORAL PUBLICATIONS, 2852 Broadway—Morningside
Heights, New York, New York 10025

Printed in the United States of America

To Sybil

Contents

PART II.   BRIEF THERAPY IN THE CONTEXT OF COMMUNITY MENTAL HEALTH

PART III.   TECHNIQUES AND PROGRAMS FOR SPECIFIC PATIENT POPULATIONS

Acknowledgements

I should like to express my appreciation to all of the authors and publishers who generously consented to have their articles reprinted. My interest in brief therapy was sparked and encouraged by Leopold Bellak, to whom I owe a special debt. Sheldon Roen, who suggested that I undertake this volume, offered constant support and many useful suggestions. Herbert Rothman contributed helpful criticism of parts of the manuscript. Betty Atkins and Ann Noll provided excellent secretarial assistance.

I am particularly grateful to my wife, Sybil Barten, for her unflagging patience and good humor during the months of my preoccupation with getting the manuscript assembled; and for her fresh ideas, critical scrutiny, and invaluable editorial judgment.

H. H. B.

Introduction

Chapter 1

The Expanding Spectrum
of the Brief Therapies

Harvey H. Barten, M.D.

The brief therapies are certain to become a major treatment modality in the next decade. Although some of the concepts and techniques originated many years ago, their widespread acceptance by the mental health professions has occurred only in the last few years. It had awaited the convergence of a number of historical developments:

(1) A growing professional commitment to provide immediate treatment, relevant and practical, to all segments of the community. The Community Mental Health Movement embodies this philosophy and has particularly stimulated its implementation.

(2) An increasing shift within the mental health professions from psychoanalytic techniques to ego-oriented psychotherapy.

(3) A new emphasis upon preventive and emergency therapeutic measures in addition to corrective ones.

(4) A changing philosophy of treatment that often accepts limited therapeutic goals as a sufficient answer to the patient's needs and sometimes as the treatment of choice.

(5) A broadening and redefining of professional roles which has enlisted as therapeutic agents a diversity of medical professionals, allied professionals in other helping disciplines, paraprofessionals and nonprofessionals, increasing the need for uncumbersome, practical but specific counseling techniques.

(6) Long overdue recognition of the special needs of the poor and lower socio-cultural groups, for whom traditional techniques often have been unsuitable and ineffective.

(7) Increasing consumer demand for economically feasible services. The growth of prepaid, limited outpatient psychiatric insurance coverage has been a reflection of this.

In this volume, I have attempted to gather together some important theoretical underpinnings and some provocative innovative experiments from the rapidly growing number of articles which are appearing in the literature. It is a sampling rather than a compendium. Many of the papers provide illus-

trative case material. I hope that these presentations will be
useful not only to mental health professionals, but also to
nonpsychiatric physicians, medical students, students in the
counseling disciplines, and allied helping professionals.
While I attempted to present diverse points of view, some
repetition and overlap was inevitable. At the same time, space
being limited, some valuable papers had to be omitted.

In a complex field such as brief therapy which is rapidly
evolving and changing, a volume of readings cannot provide a
unified conception. Indeed, the thrust of this presentation is to
demonstrate that the brief therapies are a spectrum of approaches
which will if anything become more heterogeneous in answer
to changing needs. The range of problems which we as psychotherapists encounter is itself so great, and the opportunities for
interventive measures so varied, that the hope for a single approach would be specious and indeed undesirable. Moreover, we
must reluctantly acknowledge that there are many intangibles in
the practice of psychotherapy, and that its essential qualities are
still in dispute. Beliefs about therapy tend to reflect therapists'
personalities and their involvement in different therapeutic settings where they treat patients of diverse social class or illness
distributions. From the sampling of papers in this volume, the
reader can abstract some basic principles of brief therapy and
select those approaches that best relate to his own professional
activities as well as temperament. Hopefully these examples
can serve as useful models and perhaps as a stimulus for
further innovative efforts.

While the many voices of the authors can speak for themselves, I shall in this introduction present an overview in the
hope that it will provide a framework for examining somewhat
diverse opinions and techniques. There are many possible ways
of rationing out scarce therapeutic resources, stemming from
both pragmatic and theoretical concerns. Some brief therapies,
particularly crisis intervention, have evolved from a point of
view which describes the balance between stress and coping
ability. I shall try to expand this adaptational frame of reference, which is helpful in looking at all of the brief therapies.

As I shall discuss later, the brief therapies can be defined by
other attributes than their brevity, and not all therapies can
be easily abbreviated. Since psychotherapy has become extra-
ordinarily heterogeneous, it was necessary to concentrate on
verbal therapies to keep the size of this volume within manageable proportions. Behavior therapies and drug therapies receive
little attention. The obvious suitability of brief therapy vehi-
cles for the drug therapies does not require much discussion. Abbreviated forms of behavior therapy (such as implosive therapy)
are being increasingly described, but they embody markedly
different concepts.

It should be emphasized at the start that shortened treatment must not be equated with nonspecific treatment. In recent years, a number of authors have raised questions about the specificity of psychotherapy in general. Influenced by studies of persuasion and placebo effects, as well as the "spontaneous recoveries" of patients on waiting lists, some have gone so far as to assert that it makes little difference what the therapist says, does, or indeed thinks, provided that he conduct himself in a warm, understanding, helpful manner. One can hardly deny that these attitudes often contribute to successful outcome, particularly in brief therapy. Their advocates are in part reacting to the old, not always accurate stereotype of the passive, remote psychoanalyst. But empathy and positive regard should be seen as the leavening of psychotherapy rather than the substance. As knowledge of maladaptive behavior patterns becomes more precise, and as therapists develop an increasingly rich repertoire of behavior-modifying strategies, they must venture towards a range of carefully determined goals, rather than merely cashing in on nonspecific effects. Psychotherapy, however condensed, can in many cases provide patients with a learning experience. Questions about behavioral styles or motivations which are raised in the course of a few sessions can sometimes be productively pursued after their conclusion. While the results of brief therapy will in some cases reflect only nonspecific factors, this is hardly a sufficient objective. If our aims are minimal, our results will be likewise.

THE ROOTS OF BRIEF THERAPY

There has been a general acceptance and utilization of brief psychotherapy in the last decade, but many of the ideas were originally propounded thirty or forty years before (9, 10, 12, 17). Indeed, some of Freud's early patients were not extensively treated. Malan (22), in reviewing the earlier literature, reminds us that psychoanalysis began as a brief procedure, which lengthened as it evolved and assigned an increasingly passive role to the therapist. "This is not so much that each new technique is eventually proved unreliable as that before this happens, it apparently gives good results. Therapeutic currency, so to speak, is subject to a continuous depreciation or inflation. . . .the early analysts seem to have possessed the secret of brief psychotherapy, and with increasing experience to have lost it" (22).

Extensive work in this area was done under the leadership of Franz Alexander between 1942 and 1946, at the Chicago Institute for Psychoanalysis, reflected in three volumes of Proceedings of the Brief Psychotherapy Council (26-28). *Psychoanalytic Therapy* (1), written by Alexander and French in 1946, is a landmark which should be read by everyone interested in brief therapy. The authors reiterated Ferenczi's and Rank's beliefs that the patient's emotional experience in therapy was more crucial than the genetic reconstruction of the past. Alexander and French focused on present life problems, emphasized the importance of the patient's actions, and tried to prevent regression and dependency. Treatment promoted more productive efforts at problem-solving. The patient's ability to handle new experience was a crucial measure of treatment outcome. Manipulation of the transference relationship was a central therapeutic strategy. The therapist ascertained how earlier experience had distorted the patient's expectations of interpersonal relationships and attempted to disconfirm these by acting in a markedly different way from what the patient's persisting distortions would have led him to expect. This was intended to produce a corrective emotional experience, enabling the patient to see the present for what it was, rather than maintaining outdated, inappropriate attitudes. Currently, the focus in short-term therapy has shifted away from transference distortions as a central issue, though Malan (22) still maintains that it is important to deal with them.

THE NEED FOR NEW THERAPEUTIC APPROACHES

Until the last decade, the vast majority of psychiatrists and members of the other counseling professions were handicapped by the lack of technical versatility in practicing psychotherapy. Most training institutions provided a thorough grounding in only one or two psychotherapeutic techniques. These usually emphasized the detailed exploration of memories and feelings through the use of free association and other relatively unstructured procedures. The process was frequently lengthy and costly, and it did not promise immediate benefits. It was generally most suitable for verbal, well motivated, middle-class patients who could accept its premises, learn its language, and persist through periods of modest return, maintaining a belief in its ultimate rewards, which were sometimes considerable. The treatment of large numbers of patients was impossible, particularly in geographical areas where the shortage of professionals was acute. Moreover, these techniques had not been designed for the patients who are generally seen in low-cost clinics. Many of the patients who sought help in these clinics were inappropriately served, if served at all. Unconscionable waiting lists, selective admission practices, and large numbers of early dropouts were accepted as inevitable.

In recent years, there has been a growing sense of dissatisfaction with these outmoded practices. Epidemiologic studies have documented vast needs, particularly in the lower socioeconomic groups which receive the least psychotherapeutic services. The Community Mental Health Movement has crystallized these emerging concerns and has provided much of the impetus for the development and implementation of new therapeutic strategies. There has been a growing interest in the prevention of illness through study and change of the social system, and the utilization of early interventive strategies to discover and contain emotional disequilibrium at a time when relatively modest treatment can restore health. In the space of a few short years, the mental health professions have found themselves committed to the treatment of large numbers of patients, many of whom they had never previously endeavored to serve, except perhaps in token fashion in wholly inadequate, regressive state hospitals.

Once we redefine our task as the provision of treatment services to patients in all classes with all kinds of problems, traditional, slow-paced techniques become obviously insufficient. These techniques were unwieldy, impractical, and often excessive in treating emergency or crisis situations, adjustment problems of recent origin, and uncomplicated anxiety and depressive reactions. They were equally unsuitable for long-standing disease processes at the other end of the illness spectrum, such as alcoholism, chronic schizophrenia, or organic brain disorder. Even in the treatment of classical neurotic illnesses, results were sometimes disappointing and could not justify the continuance of expensive treatment over many years. Poor and uneducated patients in particular seemed unreached by sophisticated techniques which they found alien and esoteric, assuming that they were even available. As a rule these patients want therapists who are warmly supportive and who provide concrete help rather than an opportunity to examine feelings (6, 37), though some of them can be taught how to utilize the latter approach (19, 25).

Short-term therapies were inevitably rediscovered as psychiatry embraced a growing eclecticism. They have become a vital part of our vastly enlarged armamentarium of treatment modalities. Traditional techniques have by no means been discarded, but they have come to be used more judiciously. In some cases, more economical alternatives have worked as well. In others, they have worked better. Brief techniques themselves have expanded to include brief group and family therapies, behavior therapies, drug therapies, suggestive therapies such as hypnosis, re-educative therapies, and role-induction therapies.

The traditional psychotherapist may view this as a regrettable compromise, an ignoble surrender to the pressures of circumstance which produces transient, superficial, or token results. To the eclectic, brief therapies are innovative, pragmatic, developing approaches which may change our conception of the nature, objectives, possibilities and limitations of psychotherapy. We should neither exaggerate the results of short-term therapy nor deprecate the rationale and objectives of long-term therapy. The brief therapies are a distillation based upon the understanding of personality dynamics and patterns of illness which traditional techniques delineated, and the latter of course are sometimes indispensible. It is their indiscriminate application which is at issue.

A PLEA FOR THERAPEUTIC PARSIMONY

Unlike physicians in other fields, psychiatrists have been surprisingly disinclined to try simple procedures before committing themselves to more complex ones. Perhaps this is a reflection of their pessimism about the capacity of individuals with diagnosed emotional problems to regain a reasonable level of health without major corrective measures. Too often it is stated that an alarming dynamic picture has been discerned, foreboding disaster unless corrected by extensive psychotherapy. Our training predisposes us to describe areas of illness rather than areas of health, and this illness orientation can make the prognosis of a great many people appear rather bleak. At times, however, limited supportive treatment is more appropriate than an extensive or more radical procedure. Thus the nonpsychiatric physician is often conservative in treating symptoms, hopeful that modest intervention will be sufficient. When more drastic measures are considered, the patient often is permitted, indeed expected, to participate in the decision. Perhaps this philosophy is pertinent to many of the psychiatric reactions whose investigation does not provide evidence of profound underlying difficulties. If indicated, periodic re-evaluations, at intervals of three to six months, can modify or enlarge initially modest goals when the situation demands. With this flexibility in mind, the initial treatment approach need not be comprehensive and definitive.

THE NATURE OF BRIEF THERAPY

Since the brief therapies are still very much evolving, efforts at a current definition must be tentative and exploratory. Brief therapy is characteristically a technique which is active, focused, goal-oriented, circumscribed, warmly supportive, action-oriented, and concerned with present adaptation. Traditional therapy tends to be more passive, reflective, open-ended, and patient steered; it is oriented toward feelings, self-understanding as a prerequisite to action, and the reflections of the past in the present, with the hope that enduring behavioral modifications will emerge as a result of the prolonged exploratory collaboration of patient and therapist. In contrast, brief therapy deals with a specific problem constellation. It may aim for the resolution of a present conflict or discomfort, and its objectives indeed may be of an emergency or stopgap nature.

The articles reprinted in this volume exemplify a growing diversity of techniques. Basic principles which are generally adhered to include early formulation of the problem, focusing, bypassing areas of resistance, and accepting, indeed sometimes strengthening defenses rather than challenging them. More uncertain are the criteria for selecting suitable patients, the kinds of issues which ought to be discussed or avoided, and the time limits which must be established.

One can hardly question the need for the therapist to assume an active, empathic role in therapy to establish a rapid working relationship which will fully exploit the available time. It is equally clear that the scope of treatment must be delimited to keep it within manageable proportions. What material is actually examined is a more open question. Many brief therapists confine therapeutic discussions to the present problem. Some, however, do not eschew focused probing of the past, examination of characterological problems, or interpretation of transference distortions. It is useful to apply Sarvis, Dewees, and Johnson's dictum that one deals with whatever will facilitate adaptation, beginning our enquiry with the presenting difficulty and using this as a point of reference (32).

Considerable discussion in the literature has been devoted to selection criteria (5). Diverse opinions attempt to describe patients who are suitable for particular brief techniques, with differing selection criteria sometimes determined by different therapeutic objectives. This question, however, is by no means a simple one. Some therapists feel that the response of the patient to test interpretations is more prognostically significant than such commonly mentioned factors as acuteness of onset, adequacy of previous adjustment, circumscribed complaints, environmental stability, favorable diagnosis, and degree of precipitating stress. Other therapists emphasize the adaptability and potential resources of the patient rather than the nature and severity of the illness. Pumpian-Mindlin (29), for example, states that brief therapy with more than supportive objectives has been successful with patients who manifest severe psychopathology, providing that there is sufficient ego strength, some adequate coping techniques, some capacity to obtain gratification, some degree of frustration tolerance, and some flexibility in interpersonal relationships. Certainly we have all had cases who seemed to be poor prognostic risks, but who sought therapy at a time when they very much wanted to change and were particularly motivated to discover dormant coping resources. One can be much less hopeful with stubbornly resistive patients, patients who deny the existence of any problems, patients who reject any kind of therapeutic alliance, and patients who cannot sustain any degree of independent functioning.

From a logistical point of view, it is more advantageous to regard the brief therapies as a range of procedures, including potentially long-term brief-contact therapy, which can accommodate a great variety of patients, rather than narrowly defining brief therapy and thereby limiting its use to patients who are suitable for one particular technique. Bellak's suggestion (7) is that we utilize trial brief therapy instead of an intake procedure and offer more where necessary.

Some limitation of time or objectives, most therapists would agree, should be established at the start of treatment. The majority of those who practice brief therapy, particularly when facing heavy demands for service, would set a limit of six to twenty sessions. On the other hand, some therapists prefer defining the end point of treatment in terms of limited *objectives*, rather than any particular number of sessions, with the expectation that twenty sessions would generally be an outer limit. Whatever the limit established, it is essential that both patient and therapist are aware that it exists. The duration of treatment often seems to expand to fill the available time, as though in observance of one of Parkinson's Laws. Patients who expect therapy to be an open-ended, slowly evolving process, tend, as indeed do their therapists, to move slowly in defining problems and goals. Dependent patients are particularly inclined to make the therapeutic process drag on as long as possible. Several studies have shown that patients respond much more quickly when they know in advance that time is limited (11, 33, 34), and therapists tend to adjust their expectations in a similar manner (14).

The process of delimiting a problem area which is to be the major focus of treatment is one of the most critical operations of brief therapy. Clearly the complexity of a life experience cannot be reconstructed in a few hours. Even when an individual enters treatment with a specific problem in mind, the feelings which are rekindled in the intimate sharing of emotionally charged material may unleash a flood of associations or forgotten memories which obscure the central issue. However enticed by this, the therapist must be careful to maintain a realistic focus so that he and the patient are not inundated with material. Information which falls outside of the area delimited for discussion may enhance the therapist's overall understanding of the patient, and certainly it should not be ignored, but its incorporation into the therapeutic dialogue risks diffusion of the treatment process. Even in long-term therapy, of course, material must be discussed in an orderly fashion to avoid wild analysis. In long-term therapy, many of the issues which arise can be resolved eventually, while in short-term treatment they are passed over.

PROBLEM SOLVING

Confusion about the nature of the problem and the precipitating events is often a major factor in escalating dysfunction and symptoms. The manifestations of many psychiatric illnesses, unlike relatively uniform medical illnesses, vary with the patient's preconceptions, the flux of events, and the vagaries of environmental reinforcement. The acutely anxious patient, for example, suddenly may become overwhelmed by such a diversity of physical and psychological symptoms that the precipitating event is obscured. In his desperate search for an explanation, he may fasten upon an element which is comprehensible within the range of his experience. He may, for example, become preoccupied with chest pain and erroneously label what is going on as a heart ailment. On the other hand, his cognitions may remain excessively fluid or diffuse. In either case, the patient cannot address himself to the essential tasks which will restore health. The longer this process smolders on, the greater the possibilities for growing confusion, mislabeling, and the elaboration of further dysfunction and debilitation. Therapy, particularly when it is instituted early, can clarify what is happening, redirecting the patient's cognitions and actions to the most critical or at least the most malleable elements. Recognition and realistic response to the precipitating stress is more productive than preoccupation with the symptoms it has created. Thus, the therapist labels symptoms as such, reduces their threat by restoring a more accurate perspective, minimizes ambiguity, and helps the patient to set up feasible problem-solving tasks which can handle the previously overwhelming flux of disruptive experience in a more systematic and effective manner. This clarifying and ordering function of therapy reduces problems to manageable proportions. If the patient is successful in devising new problem-solving strategies, these may have useful subsequent applications.

Sifneos (35) has been one of the first to document how the problem-solving techniques which patients learn in therapy can be employed later. In a particularly interesting study, one group of patients was untreated for several months. During this period some of them experienced spontaneous symptom relief, but it occurred without their learning anything about the process which had created their symptoms. Only after they were subsequently treated was there evidence that they had acquired new problem-solving skills. Sifneos describes this treatment as "concentrating on a circumscribed area of unresolved emotional conflicts such as are usually associated with the patient's symptoms. . . .the therapist helps the patient to identify an emotional conflict which becomes the problem to be solved. The therapist encourages its solution and in so doing helps the patient to develop new problem-solving techniques which can effectively be utilized by him in the future" (35).

Brief therapy thus helps patients look beyond the symptom to the conflict. Even though symptom relief or conflict resolution without insight is sometimes all that the situation will permit, the possibilities for generating limited insight or cognitive restructuring should not be overlooked. Removing symptoms may relieve the patient of a painful or even crushing burden, and this is not to be minimized, but it is not the only option in brief therapy. When possible, we can try to help patients to become less vulnerable to subsequent stresses. Malan regards this as a more stringent measure of treatment outcome (23).

AN ADAPTATIONAL FRAMEWORK

Short-term therapies are best understood within ego-oriented, adaptational conceptual contexts. For both practical and theoretical reasons, psychotherapists within the mental health professions have gradually placed less emphasis upon the uncovering of primitive instinctual drives and the explication of their transmutations. Many adaptationally oriented therapists concentrate upon the individual's present coping style and repertoire of adaptive skills (indeed, solving problems is itself seen as a basic need). Others seek a more longitudinal view of the evolution of adaptational mechanisms in the process of growth and differentiation, or their stunting in the slump toward stagnation and adaptational impoverishment.

Discussions of crisis intervention frequently refer to states of adaptational equilibrium and disequilibrium (31). A schematic developmental model is a useful frame of reference for the discussion of other brief therapies as well. Perhaps it is helpful in understanding the diversity of therapies to think of patients not in terms of a dichotomy of "well" versus "sick" but in terms of an adaptive-maladaptive continuum (32), within which there are both transient and more lasting fluctuations and shifts. Along this dimension, maladaptive behavior can reflect disturbances at varying levels, requiring different kinds of treatment.

Theorists such as Erikson regard the developmental process as a hierarchy of challenges whose mastery generates an increasingly complex repertoire of coping skills. These are reflected in a more differentiated sense of identity and a growing sense of self-worth. The healthy individual evolves throughout his life, acquiring new skills, developing new awarenesses, enhancing or replenishing feelings of self-esteem, mastering new tasks with minimal ego attrition, successfully weathering periods of danger, and at times discovering and prizing unsuspected potential. This process of growth and self-enrichment can continue throughout life, perhaps decelerating with advancing age. This dynamism enhances adaptive resilience. A fluid, expansive adaptational system is well suited for mastering adversity, novelty, or even monotony when it becomes burdensome. If development is arrested, the individual gradually becomes a prisoner of habit, circumscribed in experience, stereotyped in response, and handicapped in dealing with new or unfamiliar internal or external demands. During periods of equilibrium, this may cause no conscious hardship. However, when there is dissonance between the demands of the inner or outer apperceptive world and the capacity to meet them, the unequipped individual is more likely to falter. When defensive or avoiding maneuvers fail, decompensation may result. The individual may seek professional assistance immediately, he may wait until there has been an accumulation of adaptive failures, or indeed he may never seek help.

The growth process is discontinuous. As people reach new developmental stages, or as new opportunities or demands arise, there begins a process of unsettlement, aspiration, planning, rehearsal, and action which may lead to the discovery of new perceptions, behavior patterns, roles, values, etc. Following this period of movement, a new equilibrium is attained, during which the individual ascertains, codifies, and celebrates his new position. He integrates new attainments with existing experience and rests for a time at a plateau of relative contentment and constancy. In time, his developmental chronometer, external circumstances, or internal drives will stimulate another excursion. Individuals, of course, differ in their sensitivity to internal and external proddings, and they vary in their need for further stimulation, challenge, or reconfirmation of identity. Disequilibrium is created by factors which have specific impact, such as demands of significant others, labile hostile or sexual impulses, or vulnerable belief systems.

For some, periods of growth cease early in life, perhaps even in childhood. Living becomes defensive, the preservation of the status quo, often by blind instinct. The confrontation with unfamiliar internal or environmental demands may be a dangerous threat, and coping efforts aim at containment and preservation of sameness rather than exploration, discovery, and growth. Adaptive capacities are limited and sometimes overtaxed, leading to periods of decompensation manifested by impaired functioning, uncomfortable feeling, or both. When this occurs insidiously the slow erosion of competence and self-esteem may obscure the process and camouflage the need for help.

There is a growing literature on normal coping mechanisms (18, 24), from which we can draw implications for brief therapy. Studies of individuals who have successfully mastered the challenges of transitions such as college entry have defined some of the elements of successful coping. Among these are anticipatory preparation, development of alternative plans, role rehearsal, realistic assessment of the tasks which will be faced based upon adequate advance information, and an orderly sequencing of intermediate, stepwise objectives leading to the eventual goal. When the individual is aware of his capabilities as well as his limitations, and reinforces his strengths by utilizing appropriate role identifications, existing models, and other available sources of assistance, he is better equipped to deal effectively with expected and unexpected events. There is a sense of active striving with the expectation that solutions can eventually be found, even if multiple efforts are required. Indeed, multiple efforts of an orderly kind enhance chances for success, enrich experience, and enlarge the repertoire of behavioral strategies. Such a positive, active, flexible experimental approach maximizes chances for mastery. (In fact, inflexibility is one of the common denominators of emotionally impaired people.) When obstacles and setbacks are anticipated, they do not create undue frustration or discouragement, or the deflation of self-esteem. Coping reserve enlarges as the individual develops an increasingly versatile repertoire of coping skills. A vitalizing circle is developed, where heightened self-esteem provides the confidence to experiment and undertake new endeavors which, when successful, further increase self-valuation.

During transitional periods such as puberty, early adulthood, marriage, childbirth, career changes, menopause, or retirement, problem-solving strategies must be developed or reactivated. At other times, one may have to contend with unexpected stressful events such as physical illness, financial setbacks, difficult geographical relocations, loss of or rejection by valued persons, thwarted hopes, etc. An adequate level of self-esteem and a varied repertoire of coping techniques greatly enhance the individual's capacity to accept and master new challenges. The less well-equipped individual is more likely to be temporarily overwhelmed, and this may lead to dysphoria, dysfunction, or even decompensation. If problems are pathologically solved, progressive constriction multiplies his vulnerabilities, leading to chronic dysfunction, depression, impaired interpersonal relationships, and other signs of mental illness.

This admittedly oversimplified adaptational model provides a useful frame of reference in developing a broad range of therapeutic interventions. Some patients with relatively normal behavioral patterns and an untraumatized developmental history seem to have been temporarily overwhelmed by a major stress or a rapid sequence of misfortunes. Restoration of equilibrium, perhaps via crisis intervention, may be a sufficient though minimal objective, and it often will avert more serious consequences. The therapist attempts to reduce symptoms, strengthen ego defenses, and prevent an escalation of dysfunction. In some cases, he helps the patient to discover dormant coping capacities or to amplify or rechannel weak, diffuse coping efforts. In others, he may concentrate more upon a modification of external threats. Limited experience with novelty or adversity may create vulnerability in some individuals, if their coping potential has previously not been sufficiently developed. In the process of treatment, they may incorporate some of the new mechanisms for mastering stress which they discover, so that they are better prepared for future eventualities.

Sometimes the therapist may go even further in clarifying operational styles, generating limited insight about characterological problems, interrupting vicious circles and helping the patient to find alternatives to neurotic, self-defeating, stereotyped behavioral patterns.

Sometimes individuals are naive in approaching transitional life tasks, not having acquired those coping mechanisms which the more successful employ. Instructional or re-educative counseling techniques, which teach coping strategies such as anticipatory preparation, are particularly appropriate for some beleaguered younger people, such as college students, army inductees, or foundering married couples.

On the other hand, when there is evidence of rigidification and regression, the therapist must decide whether reconstructive efforts are possible and desirable, and whether prolonged multiple-focus therapy or brief, limited-goal therapy is mandated.

THE SPECTRUM OF INTERVENTIONS

A range of brief intervention techniques has emerged to meet the varied needs of patients and treatment settings. The determination of specific therapeutic objectives is a complex decisional process. In addition to taking into account the nature and setting of the problem, the wishes of the patient, and the therapist's versatility, we must also consider the mission of the agency, available resources within it, community needs or demands, and alternative forms of help. As Community Mental Health objectives carry increasing weight within this system, efforts will be geared toward providing assistance within practical dimensions to increasingly large numbers of patients, for many of whom services might otherwise not be available at all.

The brief therapies constitute an increasing variety of contexts of therapeutic intervention. Illness can be viewed in terms of many dimensions and theoretical systems. Multidimensional evaluations, which reconnoiter the individual's developmental history, key relationships, ego strengths, pattern of strivings and successes, and repertoire of coping skills, as well as genetic and metabolic factors, suggest many possible levels of intervention. A hierarchy of treatment goals is essential when the determinants of a feasible therapeutic approach are complex and shifting.

Since therapeutic decisions must be made rapidly on the basis of limited information, it is expedient for the therapist to have a knowledge of *patterns* of illness and intervention. Much as a skillful chess player attempts to discern patterns on his board and to consider multiple strategies, the experienced therapist searches for illness patterns and their corresponding intervention strategies.

Lindemann's (21) description of the symptomatology and management of grief is a classic example of an effective interventive schema. Lindemann shows how morbid grief reactions can be challenged by brief interventions which encourage the patient to confront and resolve feelings and discover ways of constructing a new life after having achieved "emancipation from the bondage to the deceased." The practice of brief therapy is facilitated by the knowledge of concise, action-oriented schemata such as this.

Different therapeutic strategies require appropriate *brief therapy contexts,* such as: (1) A single interview, "the briefest psychiatric encounter" (20), which not only can produce a therapeutic blueprint but sometimes provides sufficient clarification or affective discharge to suggest or reinforce a constructive course of action. (2) Crisis intervention, usually limited to six sessions, and concerned with restoring homeostasis during a period of acute disequilibrium. (3) Brief therapies encompassing more varied goals, ranging in length from three to twenty sessions, and dealing with a wide range of both acute and even long-standing problems, such as psychoneuroses, psychosomatic disorders, and character disorders. In some cases the therapeutic goal is insight-oriented, within a circumscribed focus. (4) Re-educative techniques, such as assertive therapy, aimed at correcting specific behavioral handicaps through retraining or role rehearsal. (5) Brief contact therapy, such as fifteen-minute sessions, which not only can sustain patients with chronic symptoms and limited responsiveness, but also may be used as an alternative to brief therapies with other objectives. Short sessions are particularly suited for pharmacotherapy. (6) Suggestive therapies, such as hypnosis. (7) Short-term group and family approaches. (8) Brief hospitalization. (9) Primary preventive approaches, such as anticipatory preparation, role clarification prior to marriage, etc. (10) Periodic reassessment of recovered patients, or therapy dropouts.

Many of these approaches are illustrated in the articles in this volume. What follows is both an elaboration of several methods which received less attention and a discussion of relative indications.

There is a tendency to overlook the fact that a *single interview* can have beneficial therapeutic consequences. Even when interviews have been utilized as research instruments, it has been serendipitously noted that some of the subjects profited from this experience (30). Perhaps their attention is directed to problems or attitudes they had previously overlooked, catalyzing the search for new behaviors. In a therapeutically oriented interview, provocative questions are raised about the nature and precipitants of a problem. The therapist can provide reassurance that the symptoms will be limited in magnitude or duration, mitigate fears of severe mental illness, underscore reality factors, promote more positive expectations, or suggest alternative courses of action. Even when further interviews are available, they may not be needed or wanted. Many of us have had the experience of contacting patients who had failed to return for the therapy we had prescribed, only to be told that the initial interview had sufficiently met their needs. They were pursuing a more productive course of action and saw no reason for additional contacts. However limited our resources, we can try to provide something meaningful to most patients we see, regarding every encounter as potentially therapeutic.

The *crisis intervention* approach concentrates specifically upon the restoration of adaptive equilibrium. According to Caplan (8), the patient is particularly receptive to therapeutic influence during the period of turmoil generated by the disbalance between life stresses and coping resources. This fluid state is said to last about six weeks. Crisis intervention therapy focuses the patient's attention upon a crucial problem area, perhaps the precipitating stress, which may have become obscured in the flux of emotional distress and compromised coping efforts. By placing the problem in bold relief, crisis therapy reveals possible solutions which the patient may have overlooked, and thus averts further recourse to pathological solutions. This technique has been employed with notable success in walk-in clinics serving the poor, and for emergency therapy such as that which has been used in preventing hospitalization. Relatively uncomplicated, quite specific, and easily taught, it is a particularly suitable model for training paraprofessionals.

It must be emphasized, however, that crisis intervention is but one of many brief therapies, others of which need not be limited to crisis situations. Furthermore, there are alternative methods of treating reactions triggered by crisis. Indeed, many patients seen in crisis clinics are referred for further therapy after the *status quo ante* has been restored. Other practical techniques are needed to treat neurotic symptoms and character problems, often more insidious in origin. *Flexible brief therapies,* with a range of three to twenty sessions, permit more diversified or complicated therapeutic objectives. Under suitable circumstances, brief therapy can modify some of the manifestations of character disorders, such as dependency, impulsivity, or aggression. Recurrent, self-defeating behavior patterns can be identified. Reconnaissance of the past may reveal the origin of interpersonal attitudes which have perseverated in subsequent relationships. The pursuit of such diverse therapeutic objectives is illustrated in a number of the papers in this volume.

Since some patients with characterological problems respond poorly to insight-oriented techniques, other brief approaches enlarge the therapist's capacity to offer something meaningful. *Brief re-educative therapy* is sometimes a more productive choice for patients with long-standing marital or family maladjustments, and for some passive and socially withdrawn patients. Their maladaptive patterns may have been perpetuated by habit, inexperience, or resignation, and they welcome the opportunity for experimentation with different kinds of behavior. Indeed, our educational system is remarkably deficient in teaching youth about adult roles and the multiplicity of their behavioral options, the models for which often do not exist in their families. Re-educative therapy is sometimes indicated, for example, for alienated married couples. After years of mutually provocative hostility, they can forget that any other scenario exists, and they require outside help to break the vicious cycle.

Brief contact treatment is particularly useful for supportive purposes, when patients require continuing treatment, and traditional modalities are unavailable or unnecessary. Since there are increasing numbers of chronic patients who need long-term care, economical techniques such as the "fifteen minute hour" (4) are an important part of the therapeutic repertoire. Clearly, they must be employed thoughtfully to avoid the tokenism of stereotyped, mechanical sessions which attempt no more than refilling prescriptions. It is this practice which has given aftercare clinics their negative reputation as a dumping ground for patients with the poorest prognoses, certainly a handicap for staff as well as patients. Short interviews do not preclude a thorough, dynamic evaluation which can be extended over the course of many weekly, fifteen-minute sessions. Guided by a careful initial formulation, the therapist attempts to maintain continuity from one short session to the next. He encourages modification of maladaptive patterns and supports and encourages healthier behavior as it emerges. I have often thought that the number of contacts with the patient might be as important a determinant of the therapeutic relationship as the length of the sessions. In fact, patients have become accustomed to short contacts with nonpsychiatric physicians. Indeed, fifteen-minute sessions are a realistic psychotherapeutic device for the busy internist or general practitioner.

Brief contact therapy is useful in treating patients who require prolonged re-learning, in which the therapist reinforces their tentative, uncertain steps toward improved functioning. Multiphobic housewives, somatically preoccupied patients, hysterics, and alcoholics, to mention a few, often fluctuate markedly in the severity of their symptoms and the adequacy of their functioning. Undiscouraged by relapses, the therapist attempts to enlarge the islands of health which he occasionally glimpses even within a markedly impaired personality structure. Brief contact sessions can also be utilized for suggestive therapies such as hypnosis and for drug therapies. Moreover, they can be employed for the periodic re-evaluation of patients who have recovered from illnesses which tend to relapse, such as manic-depressive psychosis or drug dependence.

Brief group and family approaches incorporate many of the techniques discussed above in different contexts, and some innovative approaches have been included in the articles in this volume.

THE CARE-GIVING SYSTEM

The components of this spectrum of brief therapy contexts, described in detail in subsequent articles, will have varying degrees of usefulness within different care-giving systems. This will depend upon other system variables, such as the training, experience, and temperament of psychotherapists and the mission of their institutions. The therapeutic setting, whether a Community Mental Health Clinic or a general practitioner's office, permits or indeed urges differing therapeutic objectives, depending upon such factors as staffing adequacies or fluctuating seasonal demand for service. Clinics in congested urban areas, usually understaffed, often can provide little more than six session, crisis oriented therapy aimed primarily at the rapid resolution of the presenting problem. Mobile clinics, hopping around states with limited mental health manpower, can offer even less, if they attempt to provide direct service at all. On the other hand, some more adequately staffed clinics can comfortably offer therapy of fifteen, twenty, or more sessions for some of their clients, when indicated. This allows greater flexibility in technique and provides a more varied experience to staff members. Many programs for university students employ the latter approach. Most insurance plans which offer outpatient psychiatric coverage specify a limit of fifteen to twenty sessions (2, 13, 15). As these programs increase, they will undoubtedly influence the development of the brief therapies, particularly in private settings.

Other community resources must also be considered. However efficient the utilization of brief therapies, it may never be possible to train enough counselors within the mental health disciplines to serve all those in need. If the goals of the Community Mental Health Movement are to become a reality, we must develop and effectively utilize the counseling skills of clergymen, teachers, nonpsychiatric physicians, probation officers, nurses, rehabilitation workers, and other helping agents. We must strive to develop a network of counseling services, using the concepts of brief therapy, and practiced by professionals in different disciplines and paraprofessionals with varying skills.

The articles in this volume provide examples of a broad scope of therapeutic objectives, ranging from treatment of the relatively well-integrated college student who requires limited assistance during an isolated period of crisis in his life, to the chronically disturbed patient who requires more probing therapy or periodic therapy. To meet these heterogeneous needs, techniques of varying impact and complexity are required. However taxed our resources, we ought to provide something meaningful to everyone who seeks help, even if it can only be a few therapeutic interviews. Brief therapy may sometimes be the treatment of choice, particularly when the patient seems ready to assume new responsibilities and might otherwise become too dependent upon the therapist or indeed fall back into his sick role. In other cases, apparently promising candidates for brief therapy will subsequently require referral for more extensive treatment.

CONCLUSION

It is estimated that there are millions of individuals in the United States who are severely disturbed (36), and countless others who experience periods of unmanageable or extremely painful emotional distress. Among the latter, when adaptive reserves are limited, acute suffering can be escalated into chronic incapacity by vicious circles which are accentuated by negative family or community expectations. The external reinforcement of distorted self-perceptions can ultimately lead to more extreme coping failures such as the social breakdown syndrome (16). Many of these malignant consequences can be averted by well-timed therapeutic interventions which interrupt the spiraling system at a number of accessible points. The brief therapies are efforts to define an increasing number of such points of possible therapeutic influence. Thus a spectrum of practical interventive strategies is emerging, with varying specificities ranging from prevention to resolution to containment. Depending upon their point of entry and the receptivity of the clients, these therapies stimulate varied kinds of learning, shore up weakened defenses, or modify unmanageable environmental demands.

There are many differences in technique, based upon both realistic concerns, such as differing treatment settings and patient populations, and philosophical viewpoints about how and how much human beings can change in a short period of time. Despite these differences, brief therapists share a commitment to provide something meaningful to all those who seek or should be seeking help, in terms that are acceptable and relevant to the patients. These therapists recognize that they must answer some of the patient's needs quickly, and that at times simple, perhaps superficial solutions are more cogent than profound but unduly delayed ones. Simple solutions often have profound preventive consequences. Although the objectives are pragmatic, the therapist need not eschew a dynamic, multifaceted scrutiny of whatever material emerges, selectively sharing with the patient what is germane and usable.

Although results are sometimes of pivotal significance, generally they are more limited in their effects. When brief therapy fails, other approaches may have to be explored, and some patients will require more than one period of brief therapy. Above all, brief therapies should be regarded as a diversity of possible interventions which permit different options under varying circumstances, and which provide practical alternative approaches when initially chosen ones fail. Delivery of services occurs within a complex, changing system so that a treatment choice which is appropriate at a given time may become unsuitable under differing circumstances. Patients must therefore be evaluated not only in terms of their individual problems, but in terms of community priorities, availability of services, and other system variables. Indeed, Community Mental Health considerations will increasingly influence the development of the brief therapies.

REFERENCES

1. Alexander, F., & French, T. M. *Psychoanalytic therapy*. New York: Ronald Press, 1946.
2. Avnet, H. H. Psychiatric insurance—Ten years later. *American Journal of Psychiatry*, 1969, **126**, 667-674.
3. Bandler, B. Health oriented psychotherapy. *Psychosomatic Medicine*, 1959, **21**, 177-181.
4. Barten, H. H. The 15-minute hour: brief therapy in a military setting. *American Journal of Psychiatry*, 1965, **122**, 565-567.
5. Barten, H. H. The coming of age of the brief psychotherapies. In L. Bellak and H. H. Barten (Eds.), *Progress in community mental health*, Volume I, New York: Grune and Stratton, 1969.
6. Baum, O. E., & Felzer, S. B. Activity in initial interviews with lower-class patients. *Archives of General Psychiatry*, 1964, **10**, 345-353.
7. Bellak, L., & Small, L. *Emergency psychotherapy and brief psychotherapy*. New York: Grune and Stratton, 1965.
8. Caplan, G. *An approach to community mental health*. New York: Grune and Stratton, 1961.
9. Ferenczi, S. *Further contributions to the theory and technique of psychoanalysis*. London: Hogarth Press, 1926.
10. Ferenczi, S., & Rank, O. *Development of psychoanalysis*. Nervous and Mental Disease Monograph Series Number 40. New York and Washington, Nervous and Mental Disease Publishing Co., 1925.
11. Frank, J. D. The dynamics of the psychotherapeutic relationship. *Psychiatry*, 1959, **22**, 17-39.
12. Fuerst, R. A. Problems of short time psychotherapy. *American Journal of Orthopsychiatry*, 1938, **8**, 260-264.
13. Glasser, M. A., & Duggan, T. Prepaid psychiatric care experience with UAW members. *American Journal of Psychiatry*, 1969, **126**, 675-681.
14. Gottschalk, L. A., Mayerson, P., & Gottlieb, A. A. Prediction and evaluation of outcome in an emergency brief psychotherapy clinic. *Journal of Nervous and Mental Diseases*, 1967, **144**, 77-96.
15. Green, E. L. Psychiatric services in a California group health plan. *American Journal of Psychiatry*, 1969, **126**, 681-688.
16. Gruenberg, E. M. The social breakdown syndrome—some origins. *American Journal of Psychiatry*, 1967, **123**, 1481-1489.
17. Gutheil, E. Basic outline of the active analytic technique (Stekel). *Psychoanalytic Review*, 1933, **20**, 53-72.
18. Hamburg, D. A., & Adams, J.E. A perspective on coping behavior: seeking and utilizing information in major transitions. *Archives of General Psychiatry*, 1967, **17**, 277-284.

19. Hoehn-Saric, R., Frank, J. D., Imber, S. D., Nash, E. H., Stone, A. R., & Battle, C. C. Systematic preparation of patients for psychotherapy. I: Effects on therapy behavior and outcome. *Journal of Psychiatric Research*, 1964, **2**, 267-281.

20. Jacobson, G. The briefest psychiatric encounter—acute effects of evaluation. *Archives of General Psychiatry*, 1968, **18**, 718-724.

21. Lindemann, E. Symptomatology and management of acute grief. *American Journal of Psychiatry*, 1944, **101**, 141-148.

22. Malan, D. H. *A study of brief psychotherapy*. London: Tavistock Publications, 1963.

23. Malan, D. H., Bacal, H. A., Heath, E. S., & Balfour, F.H.G. A study of psychodynamic changes in untreated neurotic patients. I. Improvements that are questionable on dynamic criteria. *British Journal of Psychiatry*, 1968, **114**, 525-551.

24. Offer, D. *The psychological world of the teen-ager*. New York: Basic Books, 1969.

25. Orne, M. T., & Wender, P. H. Anticipatory socialization for psychotherapy: methods and rationale. *American Journal of Psychiatry*, 1968, **124**, 1202-1212.

26. *Proceedings of the Brief Psychotherapy Council*. Chicago: Institute for Psychoanalysis, 1942.

27. *Proceedings of the Second Brief Psychotherapy Council*. Chicago: Institute for Psychoanalysis, 1944.

28. *Proceedings of the Third Psychotherapy Council*. Chicago: Institute for Psychoanalysis, 1946.

29. Pumpian-Mindlin, E. Considerations in the selection of patients for short-term therapy. *American Journal of Psychotherapy*, 1953, **7**, 641-652.

30. Rae-Grant, Q., & Stringer, L. A. Mental health programs in schools. In M. F. Shore and F. V. Mannino (Eds.), *Mental health and the community*. New York: Behavioral Publications, 1969.

31. Rapaport, L. The state of crisis: some theoretical considerations. *Social Service Review*, 1962, **36**, 211-217.

32. Sarvis, M. A., Dewees, S., & Johnson, R. F. A concept of ego-oriented psychotherapy. *Psychiatry*, 1958, **22**, 277-287.

33. Shlien, J. M. Cross-theoretical criteria in time-limited therapy. In *Sixth International Congress of Psychotherapy, London, 1964: Selected Lectures*. Basel: S. Karger, 1965.

34. Shlien, J. M., Mosak, H. H., & Dreikurs, R. Effect of time limits: a comparison of client-centered and Adlerian psychotherapy. *Journal of Counseling Psychology*, 1962, **9**, 31-34.

35. Sifneos, P. E. Learning to solve emotional problems: a controlled study of short-term anxiety-provoking psychotherapy. In R. Porter (Ed.) *The role of learning in psychotherapy. International Psychiatry Clinics*, Vol. 6, No. 1. Boston: Little Brown, 1969.

36. Srole, L., Langner, T. S., Michael, S. T., Opler, M. K., & Rennie, T. A. C. *Mental health in the metropolis*. New York: McGraw-Hill, 1962.

37. Yamamoto, J., & Goin, M. K. On the treatment of the poor. *American Journal of Psychiatry*, 1965, **122**, 267-271.

I. Concepts and Strategies

This first section deals with major theoretical and technical issues. The chapter by Alexander is taken from *Psychoanalytic Therapy*, referred to earlier as a milestone in the evolution of the brief therapies. Although in some respects rather dated (Alexander was questioning the classical analytic method of daily interviews), this paper was included for more than its historical interest. It defines some of the key elements of brief therapy: relating therapeutic discussions to the solution of present life problems, reinstituting an active process of systematic trial and error attempts by the patient to overcome difficulties, underscoring small successes to restore confidence and encourage further efforts, thus generating a vitalizing circle and a more optimistic experimental approach to life situations.

Bellak and Small's discussion is excerpted from their book, *Emergency Psychotherapy and Brief Psychotherapy*, which has been very influential in stimulating present-day utilization of these techniques. (Bellak's Trouble Shooting Clinic was one of the first to provide prevention-oriented services of a practical nature to large numbers of patients from a low socioeconomic population, usually without appointments.) A major contribution of these authors has been the development of a systematic method of assessing ego functions, to determine what relatively intact elements can be reinforced. Therapy based upon specific evaluation thus can be tailor-made to the individualized needs of the patient. Bellak and Small discuss interventions in terms of the patient's readiness, and they strive to make the learning experience of therapy a vivid, maximally effective one. They caution a healthy respect for the potential dangers of potent psychotherapeutic interpretations, which often must be tempered in accordance with the patient's ego strengths. Threatening catharses must be foregone when repression is more prudent. The rationale for sometimes buttressing rather than exploding defenses is examined.

Short-term therapy, in skilled hands, permits a great range of strategies and maneuvers which can promote many kinds of learning. Wolberg's writings lucidly demonstrate the possibilities for therapeutic versatility. In the article reprinted in this book, he describes how the therapist must strike a delicate balance between providing needed support and discouraging dependency which will aggravate the patient's compromised self-image. He considers elements in the therapist's approach to the patient which promote the rapid development of a therapeutic alliance. He categorizes the subsequent stages of the brief treatment process as the apperceptive phase, the action phase, and the integrative phase.

Rosenbaum urges that the patient be given a major say about what he expects to gain from therapy. In this spirit, the patient's request for early termination should be respectfully considered, rather than viewed with suspicion. Rosenbaum observes that the therapist is most effective in brief therapy when he is a spontaneous, compassionate human being, sharing his innate resourcefulness rather than concealing it. A number of mechanisms which produce symptom relief early in the course of treatment are considered, such as allowing patients to identify with the therapist and borrow from his strengths.

Sifneos is presently engaged in important research on the problem-solving aspects of brief therapy mentioned previously. Another of his contributions has been to emphasize the need for developing different approaches related to varying patient characteristics. It is sometimes forgotten that short-term psychotherapy, in suitable patients, can and should generate some anxiety to increase motivation for self-understanding and change, rather than being uniformly supportive. Sifneos outlines his criteria for anxiety-provoking and anxiety-suppressive therapy and describes a crisis intervention form of each where the goal is one of prevention.

Sarvis, Dewees, and Johnson view "the lifelong process of adaptive-maladaptive integration" as a more useful conceptualization for the brief therapies than the infectious disease model. Contrasting the goals and techniques of psychoanalysis with those of limited therapy, they show how the latter approach organizes and interprets material in terms of present adaptations. These authors do not believe that there are adequate selection criteria for determining whether patients are suitable for ego-oriented psychotherapy. Response to the initial therapeutic transactions seems to be the best indicator. At times, treatment goals are modified as new patterns emerge from the therapeutic process. Time limits are determined by therapeutic objectives and vary considerably. Sometimes interruptions of treatment are planned to permit working through by the patient. Utilizing flexible methods which balance intake and discharge rates, the authors have been able to handle large numbers of patients in a student health clinic.

Establishing a focus is fundamental in conducting brief therapy. Contrasted with more traditional psychotherapy, which follows the patient's associations at many levels, the therapist quickly targets a particular aspect, based upon a rapid formulation, and attempts to stay within this area. Swartz shows how different possibilities for a focus are weighed. Among the guidelines he suggests are choosing a focus that has immediate relevance and that provides therapeutic leverage. Preference is given to a potentially progressive rather than regressive area. This emphasis has been described by others as "health-oriented psychotherapy."

The precipitating stress is often a major consideration in determining a focus, particularly in crisis intervention therapy. Harris, Kalis, and Freeman, in a frequently cited paper, describe an approach in which clarification and resolution of the precipitating stress is the sole objective of therapy. Even when patients remember the events which evoked the conflict, they often do not associate these with psychological distress. The authors feel that the ease with which homeostasis can be restored depends upon the complexity of old, repressed conflicts which are reactivated when equilibrium is disrupted.

Rapoport discusses crisis theory as it has been developed by Lindemann and Caplan, who have formulated some of the basic tenets. She describes the characteristics of a state of crisis and the ways it can be resolved. Crisis can be an opportunity for growth as well as a threat to the individual's integrity. These concepts have had a great impact on the fields of psychiatry, psychology, and social work, with the result that crisis intervention is presently the most commonly employed form of brief therapy. In the succeeding sections of this book, crisis intervention techniques are discussed by Jacobson et al., Gerber, and Pittman et al.

Chapter 2

The Principle of Flexibility

Franz Alexander, M.D.

As long as the psychoanalytic method of treatment was considered a single procedure, the analyst—whether he was aware of it or not—selected his patient to fit his technique; only a few tried to adapt the procedure to the diversity of cases they encountered. Such a state of affairs is far from satisfactory. In all medicine there are very few instances in which the therapeutic tool is rigidly fixed and the patients made to conform. The logical solution to the problems of therapy is rather the converse. Not only do their ailments differ greatly, but the patients themselves present many physical and psychological differences. In psychotherapy, as in all therapy, the physician must adapt his technique to the needs of the patient.

Today the tendency among psychoanalysts is to be less rigid in matters of technique. In the research cases described in this volume, the psychoanalytic method has been used in a flexible manner. We have experimented with frequency of interview, the use of chair or couch as the situation required, interruptions of long or short duration in preparation for terminating the treatment, and the combination of psychotherapy with drug or other treatment. Above all, we have sought to learn how to control and manipulate the transference relationship so as to achieve the specific goal and fit the particular psychodynamics of each case.

When a patient consults us, we do not accept him for any specific method of psychotherapy; the procedure is based upon diagnostic opinion. Yet, not even after the initial diagnostic appraisal can we foretell what technique will be necessary for a later phase of the treatment. As we now practice psychoanalytic therapy, we seldom use one and the same method of approach from the first to the last day of treatment.

The number and variety of psychotherapeutic techniques will probably continue to multiply. Our aim, however, is always the same: to increase the patient's ability to find gratifications for his

Reprinted from *Psychoanalytic Therapy*, by Franz Alexander and Thomas M. French, pp. 25-41. Copyright 1946, The Ronald Press Company, New York.

subjective needs in ways acceptable both to himself and to the world he lives in, and thus to free him to develop his capacities.

This therapeutic aim can be achieved by the use of various therapeutic techniques. Only the nature of the individual case can determine which technique is best suited to bring about the curative processes of emotional discharge, insight, and a thorough assimilation of the significance of the recovered unconcious material, and, above all, the corrective emotional experiences necessary to break up the old reaction pattern. Whether the abreaction and the corrective experience take place on the couch during free assocation or in direct conversation between patient and therapist sitting vis-à-vis, whether it is effected through narcosis, or whether it occurs outside the analytic interview in actual life situations while the patient is still under the influence of the psychoanalytic interview—all these are technical details determined by the nature of the individual case. In some cases the development of a full-fledged transference neurosis may be desirable; in others it should perhaps he avoided altogether. In some it is imperative that emotional discharge and insight take place very gradually; in others with patients whose ego strength is greater, interviews with great emotional tension may be not only harmless but highly desirable. All this depends upon the needs of the patient in a particular phase of the therapeutic procedure.

Is Such a Psychotherapy Psychoanalytic?

Some psychoanalysts who have used the standard method exclusively may feel we are not justified in calling all these different techniques "psychoanalytic." They may argue that the expression should be reserved for the procedure developed by Freud and practiced by his followers for the last forty years.

Whether the designation "psychoanalytic therapy" is justified depends upon one's definition of psychoanalysis. That concept of psychoanalysis which is based on superficial conformity to the requirements of daily interviews, uninterrupted free association, and the use of a couch, and which regards the transference neurosis as inevitable, obviously does not include the flexibility we advocate. However, if one defines psychoanalysis by more essential criteria as any therapy *based on psychodynamic principles* which attempts to bring the patient into a *more satisfactory adjustment to his environment* and to assist *the harmonious development of his capacities,* then all forms of therapy, however flexible, having this basis and this goal, may be considered psychoanalytic.

Yet even the so-called standard psychoanalytic therapy does

not consist merely in the patient's dreams, fantasies, free associations, and the analyst's interpretations thereof. Even this technique often entails direct questioning by the analyst, steering the material in the direction which seems most significant to the course of the analysis. It may require advice to the patient concerning the conduct of his affairs outside the treatment; it may even, in some instances, demand active interference by the analyst.

Then too, assimilation of newly acquired insight cannot be credited to the analyst's skillful interpretations alone, any more than the healing of an incision can be said to result solely from the surgeon's skillful suture. Just as the healing of a wound is a natural function of the human body, so the integration of new insight is a normal function of the ego. The surgeon endeavors to create the best possible conditions for the healing of the wound; the psychoanalyst tries to create the most favorable conditions for the integration, by the ego, of its recently liberated psychic energy. Integration is the ego's main function; the psychoanalyst merely supports it by proper management of the transference relationship.

And finally, the analytic process if not confined to the analytic interview. Abreaction and the development of new emotional reaction patterns take place not only in the presence of the therapist but throughout the rest of the day or week—at home, at the club, in the office. The importance of this fact has been gradually impressed upon us and we have become progressively aware that what transpires during this interval between the therapeutic sessions is of tremendous significance to the patient's progress toward health. Moreover, actual events within the family life or in business or other pursuits may help or hinder therapeutic progress. The careful analyst, therefore, is actively concerned not only with the analytic situation but also with the patient's other relationships, how they are affected by the analysis and how they in turn affect the analytic work.

FREQUENCY OF INTERVIEW

Procrastination: Regression

The standard procedure of daily interviews tends, in general, to gratify the patient's dependent needs more than is desirable. In a large number of cases the same results—emotional insight and relief of anxieties—could have been achieved with fewer interviews and less time if a technique of changing the frequency of interview according to need had been used from the very beginning of the treatment. Just as a person who is fed every half-hour never becomes conscious of the feeling of hunger, so the analytic patient whose needs for dependence are continually gratified never becomes emotionally aware of them. In such a situation, reducing the frequency of interview will suddenly bring into consciousness the dependent needs, together with all the reactive resentments for their frustration.

One should not forget that daily interviews exercise a seductive influence on a patient's regressive and procrastinating tendencies. The neurotic's proneness to evasion (after all, the most fundamental factor in his withdrawal from the actual life situation) is favored by the expectation of an almost infinite number of interviews. "If not today, tomorrow we will solve the problem—or next month, in the next half-year, the next two or three years."

This expectation of a protracted treatment has its therapeutic value, of course, in a patient who comes to the analyst in despair, sensing his utter incapacity to endure his given life situation. The initial improvement in severe neurotics is, to a large degree, due to the soothing effect of the procrastination sanctioned by the psychoanalytic technique. One relieves the patient by allowing him to evade the pressing issues of his life and to regress to a more comfortable infantile position, not only in fantasy but in reality, in the real relationship between patient and analyst.

By allowing such an actual regression, however, we later find ourselves involved in new difficulties. The initial soothing effect of the prolonged outlook gradually becomes corruptive and the therapist, faced with the task of driving the patient from his comfortable infantile position, realizes anew how difficult it is to force anyone to give up acquired rights.

When pregenital material (that which applies to sensations experienced in early infancy) appears in psychotherapy, it is frequently considered significant traumatic material when it may actually be merely an escape back to the early pretraumatic, highly dependent emotional state in which the patient felt safe and contented. Although it is true the deeper a patient sinks into a dependent transference neurosis the more regressive pregenital material he will produce, it is a fallacy to consider an analysis in which the patient brings up much regressive material as more thorough than one primarily centered around the actual life conflict. Regressive material is a sign not of the depth of the analysis but of the extent of the strategic withdrawal of the ego —a neurotic withdrawal from a difficult life situation back to childhood longings for dependence gratifiable only in fantasy.

In every neurosis we look for that time in the patient's life when he refused to yield to the ever-changing requirements of the process of maturation, to "grow up." This refusal may take place in almost any phase of life from early infancy through adulthood, and the severity of the neurosis is determined in part by how early in life the individual set himself against growing up. This point marks the beginning of the neurosis. When regressive material is brought which antedates this point, it should be evaluated, therefore, as a sign of resistance and not as deep penetration into the sources of the neurosis.

The more skillfully a treatment is conducted, the less time will be spent with such regressive material. It is the therapist's duty to lead the patient from his retreat back into the present, and to induce him to make new attempts to solve the problem from which he fled into the past. With the correct interpretation and handling of the transference relationship, the need for such deep regressions can be almost entirely avoided.

It should, therefore, be a general principle in all psychotherapy to attempt to check this regressive tendency from the very beginning of the treatment, allowing no more procrastination and regression than is absolutely necessary to calm panic, anxiety, and despair.

Intensity: Emotional Level

An extreme generosity with interviews is not only uneconomical but, in many cases, makes the analysis emotionally less penetrating. Daily interviews often tend to reduce the patient's emotional participation in the therapy; they become routine, and prevent the development of strong emotions by allowing the patient to verbalize his transference feelings as they emerge. This is particularly the case with aggressive impulses felt toward the analyst, for if the patient can give vent to them daily in small amounts he never becomes aware of them in a convincing manner. When the intensity of such hostile impulses is too low, it may be well to let it increase by lessening the frequency of interviews; when it is very great, more frequent interviews become imperative.

It is a common experience that an analysis in which the emotional level is low progresses extremely slowly. The whole procedure becomes intellectualized, without the real emotional participation of the patient. In general, stronger emotional participation brings the issues more clearly to the foreground and makes insight more vivid, thereby speeding up the progress of the treatment. Consequently, every analysis should be conducted on as high an emotional level as the patient's ego can stand without diminishing its capacity for insight.

This level, of course, varies from case to case. Roughly speaking, in patients with a so-called "weak ego" (poor integrative power), the emotional discharge and accompanying insight must take place very gradually. Such severely neurotic individuals cannot tolerate intense emotional participation and require small abreactions in almost daily interviews over a long period. Patients with good integrative faculty ("strong ego"), who can endure more intense sessions without developing too strong defenses, often need relatively infrequent interviews. With many such patients, as soon as a fairly good rapport has developed—which in some cases may require only a few interviews—the entire treatment may be carried out in infrequent interviews. These are apt to become more dramatic and of greater emotional intensity than the psychoanalytic interviews in the standard technique.

Manipulation of Frequency

Every psychoanalyst must at some time have unwittingly frustrated a patient—when circumstances forced him to cancel an appointment or when, for some reason, the patient had to leave without seeing the physician—and found that association material which had seemed meaningless or obscure because of the small amount of emotion involved, had suddenly become crystal clear. Vacations which were not intended to be technically indicated interruptions of treatment but were solely to refresh the analyst, have often had a similar vitalizing effect upon a treatment become stale in the routine of daily interviews. Many psychoanalytic treatments owe their progress to such an accident which precipitates more relevant material than can the most astute interpretations on material devoid of emotion.

The point to be considered, then, is how to use such incidents intentionally as an integral part of the therapeutic procedure, how to manipulate the frequency of interview so as to secure the patient's emotional participation and to maintain it at the desired level.

Frequency of interview must be regarded as a relative affair. Weekly interviews in some instances may be regarded as the normal frequency, in others constitute a drastic reduction, in still others take on the character of an interruption of treatment. For instance, a patient who has been seeing the physician five times a week might find three times a week a radical reduction, whereas an interval of an entire week might be tantamount to an interruption of treatment.

When the therapeutic relationship has become well established and the patient's ego defenses have been sufficiently analyzed, the patient reaches a fairly stable equilibrium. In this equilibrium—which, in standard psychoanalysis, may develop in some patients after three or four months—the patient feels much as if he were to say, "Yes, I am acting like a child—but what of it? This is not real life anyway." This partial insight into his dependence retains a kind of theoretical quality since it has been gained on the basis of relatively unimportant matters. It therefore becomes almost imperative to increase the emotional intensity in order to make the patient's insight more realistic and convincing. In this phase of the treatment, a radical curtailing of the frequency of interview (from five a week to two or even one) tends to make the emotional insight much deeper and speeds up the analytic process.

It must be borne in mind, however, that reducing the frequency of the interviews can cause stronger emotional participation only if the patient has already developed a fairly intense transference relationship. A patient who is not yet interested in the analysis will not react to the reduction of interviews by developing more intense transference feelings. In most cases, therefore, it is advisable to ensure interest by a series of interviews before reduction of frequency can serve as a method of intensifying the emotional participation.

The opposite procedure of shifting from infrequent interviews to more frequent ones may become necessary in other emotional situations. It is a common observation that in some patients accustomed to daily interviews, a few days' intermission may increase the resistance to such an extent that the patient becomes unable to continue the treatment, may never return to it. This is true of the resistance which develops from repressed hostile impulses, from intense feelings of dependent coloring incompatible with the patient's self-esteem and pride, or from erotic feelings toward the analyst which produce anxiety. In such situations, an intellectual check of the too-strong emotions is needed. More frequent interviews at this point allow a gradual discharge of the emotional tension which has accumulated during the intermission. (Occasionally the opposite technique can be used with success.)

The "acting-out" character also benefits from careful manipulation of the frequency of interview. Since these individuals (feeling no restraint within themselves) tend to act on their impulses without regard for social standards, they frequently clash not only with convention but with the law. The psychiatrist must represent prohibition in his own person and must anticipate his patient's impulses in order to help him by restraint. It is obvious that such patients will at times require almost constant contact with the therapist.

Another important reason for manipulating the frequency of interview lies in the tendency of psychoneurotic patients (with the exception of the "acting-out" character) to substitute experiences of the analysis for life experiences. The transference neurosis comes to serve the purpose of the original neurosis: withdrawal from real participation in life. The original neurosis was a withdrawal into fantasy; the transference neurosis is a withdrawal into the relatively harmless realm of the therapeutic relationship. When the frequency of interview is reduced, the patient is given less opportunity to substitute these safe analytic experiences for life experiences. The sooner a patient can translate what he learns during the treatment into actual life experiences, the faster the analysis will progress.

Economical Psychotherapy

From the beginning, the therapist must persist in trying to counteract the patient's tendency to sink himself into a safe, comfortable transference neurosis (1). Without this continuous, alert pressure from the analyst, even relatively mild neurotic disturbances may lead to a disproportionately prolonged treatment. A correct evaluation of how fast an analysis can progress, how intense an emotional strain the patient can stand, will decide whether the procedure will assume the character of the standard psychoanalysis or that of so-called brief psychotherapy.

The nearer the analyst can keep the patient to his actual life problems, the more intensive and effective the therapeutic process is. From the point of view of genetic research, it might be advisable to encourage the patient to wander way back into the Garden of Eden of his early youth; therapeutically, however, such a retreat is valuable only insofar as it sheds light upon the present. Memory material must always be correlated with the present life situation, and the patient must never be allowed to forget that he came to the physician not for an academic understanding of the etiology of his condition, but for help in solving his actual life problems.

The therapeutic maxim of an economical psychotherapy, therefore, must be to allow as little regression as the patient can stand, only that procrastination which is unavoidable, and as little substitution as possible of transference gratifications for life experiences.

Preparation for Interruptions

In most cases of standard psychoanalysis, the neurotic gratifications of the transference relationship sooner or later outweigh the patient's therapeutic desire for recovery. Freud expressed this as follows: "This transference soon replaces in the patient's mind the desire to be cured." The reason for this is that after the resistance against the emotions in relation to the therapist has been analyzed, the transference neurosis loses much of its painful aspect and the patient's shame for his dependence upon the analyst, his guilt for his hostile impulses, diminishes. The original neurosis was a combination of gratification, conflicts, and suffering; the transference neurosis repeats all these features but, with progressive analysis of the ego's defenses, the conflictful elements diminish and its gratifications increase.

No wonder the patient is not inclined to give it up if he can afford to continue treatment. It is naive to think that most patients stick to their prolonged treatments so consistently, often year after year, only because of their desperate desire to be cured. This may be true in the first phase of the treatment, but later they cling to it because it gives them neurotic gratification without much suffering. It is, nevertheless, true that the patient can frequently be observed behaving more normally in his daily life during this phase because, in a sense, the transference situation serves as a crutch and at the same time lessens his neurotic needs.

As the patient has no emotional need for a change, it may be extremely difficult to break up this inertia—particularly if there are no external inconveniences connected with the analysis, such as an excessive fi ancial burden or awkward time arrangements. Freud was aware of this impasse in standard psychoanalysis when he stated that in the early years of his practice he had difficulty in persuading his patients to continue their treatment; later he had difficulty in inducing them to give it up. Today an efficiently handled psychotherapy does not allow such a dilemma to occur but combats the growing inertia while still in an incipient stage.

The status quo can now be disturbed only by diminishing the gratifications of the transference neurosis through as radical a reduction of interviews as is at all tolerable for the patient, leading up to an interruption of the treatment which will serve as a test of his capacity to use in his daily life the new reaction patterns acquired in the therapy.

INTERRUPTIONS AND TERMINATIONS
OF TREATMENT

Many patients in this phase, having instinctively learned their therapist's predilections, bring seemingly interesting material to allay the analyst's impatience and give an impression of steady progress and deepening of analytic insight. While the analyst may believe that they are engaged in a thorough "working-through," in reality the procedure has become a farce, a clever technique of procrastination on the part of the patient. Or a patient may reach that place in treatment where he merely repeats material he has brought many times before, in order to avoid opening up other conflicts. Or again, a patient may make a "flight into health" in order to avoid painful insight. The genuineness of these attitudes is not always easy to divine. The therapist may take them for indications that the patient is ready to leave treatment and to meet life entirely on his own, or he may realize that the patient is employing unconscious subterfuge. In either case, an interruption will show whether the patient is able to lead a normal life without his regular interviews.

During an interruption the patient learns which of his previous difficulties he still retains, and the following interviews usually center around those emotional problems in which he needs further help. The author of this section has used the method of one or more preparatory interruptions almost exclusively during the last twelve years (the interruptions varying in length from one to eighteen months) and has found that the analysis after interruption has, without exception, become much more intensive, accomplishing more in the following few weeks than had been achieved in months before.

At first, the interruption may have to be imposed by decree and the patient forced to rely on his own strength and judgment. Soon, however, he may recognize that he actually does not need the therapist as much as before. This diminishes the resentment brought on by the patient's feeling of helplessness and increases his confidence in his own powers.

It is advisable to make the interruption not too short. The patient should have an opportunity to struggle with his problems alone and should not be encouraged to turn to the analyst at the first hint of relapse. On the other hand, he should have the assurance that if he really needs his therapist, he can always return to him. We thus avoid recrudescence of the patient's resistance to giving up his neurotic escape reactions and the panic reactions which have been observed in experiments with the termination technique developed by Ferenczi and Rank.

Termination of treatment, if the method of preparatory interruptions is used, will not be artificial but will become a natural ending to the therapy. Experience—how the patient actually reacted to previous interruptions—will determine when the therapy should be brought to a close, not such theoretical criteria as the filling in of memory gaps and complete understanding of the etiological factors, nor even the depth of intellectual insight. In some cases, the patient will be capable of completely changing the life situation in which he failed before and which precipitated his neurosis, adapting it to his needs and to his capacity for gratifying them. In all cases, the patient will have given actual, tested proof of his ability to find ego-syntonic gratification for his needs.

At the present state of our knowledge, it is difficult to make precise predictions concerning the length of a treatment or the number of interviews required in any given case. Our task is to make the patient self-reliant by exerting a constant but not excessive pressure, blocking the patient's neurotic retreat into fantasy and into the past, and urging him toward the actual difficulties of his current life situation. The intensity of this pressure—upon which the rate of progress, and thus the length of treatment, depends—can be determined only through repeated testing during the treatment, observing the patient's reactions as they manifest themselves either in recrudescence of resistance, or in progressive efforts in his everyday life.

How much preparatory experience in the transference relationship a patient needs before he becomes capable of handling the corresponding interpersonal situations in real life, depends upon the nature of the case. With patients whose ego's functional capacity is only temporarily impaired under trying life conditions, a few interviews to relieve acute anxiety may suffice. The intensity of the neurotic regressive trends in the different patients, however, is of such extreme variety that the length of treatment may be anything from a few isolated interviews to the standard technique of daily interviews extending over several years.

EXTRA-THERAPEUTIC EXPERIENCES

The so-called normal individual, when he fails in a life situation and has suffered a serious setback, will make new attempts to solve his actual problem instead of having recourse to the substitutive solutions of neurotic regression. An essential feature of neurosis is the giving up of systematic efforts of trial and error to overcome those difficulties which precipitated the neurotic breakdown. This neurotic reaction to traumatic experiences appears in all degrees of intensity. In some cases, no more help is needed than temporary support to enable the patient's ego to make new attempts at finding gratifications for its needs, even in the new baffling situation. At the other extreme are patients who react to almost every change in their life situation with neurotic escapes into fantasy and regressive behavior. Between these two extremes, there is a continuous gradation from the more acute to chronic types of neurosis.

The degree to which one should rely upon the therapeutic effect of the patient's experiences in life depends upon the nature of the case and the phase of the treatment. In general, a greater part of the therapy may take place outside the sessions with the less severe cases, in which an interview a week or every other week may have enough influence on the patient's daily life to insure progress. At the other extreme is the patient who must be hospitalized and under constant supervision. Another generalization of approximate validity is that, with the progress of treatment, one can rely more and more on the beneficent effect of actual experiences in life; these experiences, of course, have been made possible by the preparatory interviews in which the patient has learned to handle certain emotional situations in his relationship to the analyst.

It is important to keep in mind that the patient will finally have to solve his problems in actual life, in his relationships to his wife and his children, his superiors and his competitors, his friends and his enemies. The experiences in the transference relationship are only preparations, a training for the real battle. The sooner the patient can be led against those real obstacles in life from which he retreated and can be induced to engage in new experimentation, the more quickly can satisfactory therapeutic results be achieved.

In every psychotherapy, therefore, whether it takes the form of the standard technique or that of some briefer method, an integral part of the treatment consists in observing and systematically influencing the patient's experiences in life.

The attitude has been overstressed that a "real psycho-analyst"—in contrast to the "practical psychotherapist" who might give advice and directives to the patient—should not try to guide the patient in his daily life and should encourage or discourage his activities as little as possible. It was formerly felt (and sometimes still is) that during treatment the patient really need not do much concerning his practical problems, and that in any case to influence his daily activities was not the concern of the therapist. This assumption that the interviews will solve everything as if by magic has prolonged many treatments unduly. Freud himself came to the conclusion that in the treatment of some cases, phobias for example, a time arrives when the analyst must encourage the patient to engage in those activities he avoided in the past. (A patient who retreats into isolation, for instance, should in the different phases of the treatment try again and again to have human contacts.) This is a fundamental principle of every treatment, an intrinsic part of the therapy.

Even more generally accepted than the motto "As little interference in the patient's daily life as possible" is another rule all students of psychoanalysis were formerly taught: "No important changes in the life situation until after the completion of treatment." Back of this rule was the sound observation that some patients were inclined to act out in life their ever-changing trends as they became liberated during the treatment. For example, a formerly very cautious, intimidated patient, when he becomes aware of the dependent attitude responsible for his former habit of never standing up for his rights, may impulsively give up a good job just to prove his independence and courage. Or a patient whose sexual repressions have been relieved, may impulsively rush into promiscuous activities.

And yet, in a certain phase of the treatment the patient may be ready to marry, for instance, even though he still needs further treatment. Serious delay of therapeutic progress may result from adherence to the rule of "no important, irreversible changes during treatment." Marriage, change of occupation, even change of profession, may be indispensable to the therapeutic success of a case, and waiting for the end of treatment before such a change may destroy all possibility of success. The advice not to make important decisions during treatment, therefore, should be given the patient in a modified, more flexible form: "No important, irreversible changes in the life situation, *unless both therapist and patient agree.*"

First Attempts

The therapeutic process must at no time be thought of as restricted to the emotional experiences within the transference relationship. Too often it is forgotten that transference experiences and life experiences take place simultaneously and parallel to each other. Having learned to handle hitherto-conflictful emotional constellations in the transference relationship, the patient must then be helped to experiment with the same type of constellation in real life.

Like the adage "Nothing succeeds like success," there is no more powerful therapeutic factor than the performance of activities which were formerly neurotically impaired or inhibited. No insight, no emotional discharge, no recollection can be as reassuring as accomplishment in the actual life situation in which the individual failed. Thus the ego regains that confidence which is the fundamental condition, the prerequisite, of mental health. Every success encourages new trials and decreases inferiority feelings, resentments, and their sequelae—fear, guilt, and resulting inhibitions. Successful attempts at productive work, love, self-assertion, or competition will change the vicious circle to a benign one; as they are repeated, they become habitual and thus eventually bring about a complete change in the personality.

The chief therapeutic value of the transference situation lies in the fact that it allows the patient to experience this feeling of success in rehearsal, a rehearsal which must then be followed by actual performance. And curbing the patient's tendency to procrastinate and to substitute analytic experience for reality (by careful manipulation of the transference relationship, by timely directives and encouragement) is one of the most effective means of shortening treatment. Fostering favorable experiences in the actual life situation at the right moment in the treatment tends to make for economical psychotherapy, bringing it to an earlier conclusion than otherwise. The therapist need not wait until the end of treatment but, at the right moment, should encourage the patient (or even require him) to do those things which he avoided in the past, to experiment in that activity in which he had failed before.

While it is important not to urge the patient prematurely, the therapist's fear that his patient will fail is usually stronger than it should be. The therapist must prepare the patient for failures, explaining that they are unavoidable and that the most important thing for him is to be always ready to try new experiments. Moreover, failures can be turned to advantage when they are carefully analyzed and their cause thoroughly understood by the patient.

REFERENCE

1. Rado, S. The relationship of patient to therapist. *American Journal of Orthopsychiatry*, 1942, **12,** No. (3).

Chapter 3

The Choice of Intervention

Leopold Bellak, M.D., and Leonard Small, Ph.D.

Having determined the causes of symptoms, the therapist is led to the task of undoing. In brief psychotherapy specifically, he must establish those factors which require change or lend themselves most readily to it. These in turn lead to the choice of intervention, which may be verbal operations or selected from among the adjunctive measures available to the psychotherapist. In the case of panic described earlier in this chapter, the reader will note that both verbal and environmental interventions were employed.

In this section we shall describe the interventions based essentially upon oral communication between patient and therapist, and conclude with suggestions for ego-function assessment as a guide to the choice of interventions. Of necessity, we shall allude here and there to adjunctive measures, but these await fuller description in the next chapter.

IMPARTIAL INSIGHT— THE TRADITIONAL INTERVENTION

Traditionally, psychotherapy has sought to cure or ameliorate by conveying insight to the patient about the nature and causes of his fears and concerns, his impulses and his defenses against them, his preconscious and unconscious motivations.

The rationale of this treatment approach rests upon the observable effect of insight, in many cases, of bringing about a dynamic realignment of the personality which results in a stronger ego and more effective ego functioning. With patients for whom psychoanalysis or intensive psychotherapy are

Reprinted from *Emergency Psychotherapy and Brief Psychotherapy*, New York, Grune and Stratton, 1965, pp. 52-63, 68-72, by permission of the publisher and the authors. Dr. Bellak is Visiting Professor of Psychiatry, Postgraduate Training Program in Psychotherapy, New York University. Dr. Small is Chief Consultant Psychologist, Altro Health and Rehabilitation Services and Adjunct Assistant Professor, Graduate School of Arts and Sciences, New York University.

suitable, insight therapy is the treatment of choice. The treatment of the psychotic, the person with a character disorder, the acting-out person, and the patient in an emergency situation require other interventions from the therapist's armamentarium. Insight therapy, however, remains a crucially important technique in brief psychotherapy; because of time limitations the therapist must use it judiciously here.

The therapist, through the interpretation, imparts insight which, along with the aptness of diagnostic formulation and choice of intervention, is one of his greatest skills.

The Interpretation

Success in psychotherapy usually requires simultaneous change in several vectors or variables. At the same time that a patient gains insight into the causes of his symptoms, he must develop a sense of alienation from them. In some circumstances the drive must be made ego-syntonic in one respect and ego-alien in another; intra-aggression in the depressed patient must often be converted into extra-aggression, while cautions are taken that the latter does not become excessive or inappropriate. With some patients, the task may involve de-emphasizing one defense and increasing reliance upon another, minimizing one role while encouraging another, fostering his hating one parent less and disliking the other more.

A first and major concern with interpretation, therefore, is that it avoid the danger of oversimplification through singleness of purpose. The therapist must try to predict the effect of his interpretation and build in safeguards if he judges them necessary. This requirement should prevent some widespread confusion about the imparting of insight through interpretation. Uncritically to pursue the uncovering of instinctual urges is a misapplication of psychoanalytic practice. Psychotherapy must simultaneously strengthen as it uncovers, if indeed, it must uncover. Another misapplication often arises from the time-tested observation that the insight which is accompanied by an affective change is most effective in achieving the desired therapeutic results. The danger arises from attempts to induce the most intense affect possible on the premise, no doubt, that if affect is good, the more the better. The unitary striving to uncover or produce affect leads to the device of "confrontation" in which the therapist directly, baldly, interprets the drive which the patient has been denying or repressing.

The least dangerous consequences of confrontation are increased denial or repression. More serious possibilities are the eruptions of panic, deep depression, serious acting-out, even suicide. Consider the treatment of symptoms arising from repression of an aggressive impulse or drive. Confrontation in such cases may create havoc. The danger is that it will make the drive even less tolerable for the individual, increase intra-aggression, and result in a suicidal venture. The nature of the patient's symptoms very often is in itself a clue to the ego's ability to tolerate confrontation. Thus, in one instance an adolescent boy jumped out of a car which his father was driving, and quickly developed the delusion that he had destroyed the world. It became quite clear that he had wanted to kill his father, and had to jump out of the car to remove himself as a danger. By secondary elaboration it became acceptable to him that he had destroyed the world, rather than he had had an impulse to destroy his father. In confrontation, often mistaken for the cathartic interpretation, one might say, "Look, what really ails you is that you wanted to kill your father." This interpretation might lead immediately to a suicidal attempt.

Imparting insight through interpretation must take into account the patient's ability or readiness to accept and use the insight. To use the interpretation of an impulse properly, for example, the patient must be ready to accept the drive as a component of his personality, experience it, discharge it in a nondestructive fashion along with the anxiety and tension that have accompanied its repression, and achieve an active reorganization of his defenses with a resulting realignment of forces in his personality.

Therefore, we must guard against stressing the primitive qualities of a drive until, if ever, the patient is prepared through ego strengthening to accept them without feeling undue threat. Care must be taken to assure that the patient recognizes that he has adequate defenses against the drive to replace those more pathological defenses associated with his symptoms.

Facilitating Insight

We believe that many of the formal aspects of learning theory have been neglected in therapeutic application, and that their adoption would enhance psychotherapeutic learning.

Many therapists have commented upon the importance of timing of the interpretation in facilitating its acceptance. Couched in learning terms, timing involves the readiness or set of the patient. Thus, if the patient is concerned about some visible neglect on the part of the therapist, an interpretation that the patient is dependent and wishes to be supported is inappropriately timed. R. Löwenstein, we believe, tells the story of the analyst who falls asleep and drops his cigar, which rolls into the patient's view. Looking behind him the patient remonstrates with the analyst, who then interprets, "You always want to be the center of attention." Löwenstein comments: the interpretation is correct, the timing is not.

Another important aspect in facilitating learning is economy in presentation of the interpretation. Short, direct, pithy statements are more effective than wordy, literary allusions. An amusing story illustrates the point. Hitler's car broke down in a small Polish village, and all the assembled Nazi big-wigs and engineers could not make it move again. Finally, a little old Polish mechanic was brought up. He took one look, struck part of the engine a hard blow, and the motor sprang to life. When the astonished Hitler asked how much he owed him, the man requested one thousand zloti. "One thousand zloti for one whack?" Hitler asked in astonishment. The mechanic shook his head, "Only ten zloti for the whack; 990 for knowing where to whack."

Colorful language has a heightening effect which will long be remembered by the patient, and subsequently continue to serve as a guide or example. It is more effective to say "You think he is a son-of-a-bitch" than "You are angry with him."

The use of stories with pregnant, vivid illustrations is an excellent means of fostering learning through verbal communication. The great teachers used parables for good reasons! As an example, we have found the following gentle story particularly useful in helping patients overcome feelings of passivity and in encouraging self-assertion. The story concerns a discussion of the emotional aspects of juvenile delinquency with a group which ranged in experience from young, eager teachers to older, more sophisticated, somewhat disillusioned principals of schools. The lecturer took the point of view that the delinquent was a disturbed individual who required psychotherapy. One of the young teachers protested, "But, Doctor, what do you do when a boy tells you to go to hell?" While the lecturer fumbled for an appropriate response, one of the older men spoke up. "Don't go," he said. There is greater likelihood that the patient will remember this story, and perhaps even repeat it socially, so that it will serve as an ongoing guide for him; more so than some abstract advice from the therapist to the effect that he does not have to do what people tell him to.

Another formal aspect of learning methodology applicable in psychotherapy is the dictum that active learning is more effective than passive learning. At one level this would mean that the patient should discover for himself as many of the necessary insights as he can. In brief psychotherapy this is seldom possible, but the patient may be encouraged to learn actively. He may then be asked to formulate certain propositions, to repeat them, and to integrate them with other facets under consideration.

Switching roles in the session may facilitate insight with some patients. One patient may be asked, "Pretend you are the therapist. A man tells you he is always finding a repelling blemish, even in the most beautiful girl—her teeth are a little crooked, she has a mole on her cheek, her jokes fall flat. What would you say is bothering him?" It is well to start with some uncomplicated dynamic not likely to arouse resistance, or even one taken from the life of another patient.

An established principle of learning theory involves spacing or dispersal of training. Periods of learning interrupted by pauses are often more effective than a continuous effort. The concept of "silent learning" has been used as an explanation for this phenomenon. Very often the regressive effect of the therapy itself and the secondary gains from dependency upon the therapist may be minimized by spacing of treatment. In addition, this allows for "silent" integration and working-through during the intervals between treatment sessions. The experience of the llateau, typical for every learning curve, often has a retarding effect on the psychotherapeutic process, if not an altogether disruptive one. A hiatus in treatment may prove more fruitful than prolonged and discouraging efforts to work-through "resistance." We shall return to this principle in a further discussion of working-through.

Learning by repetition is perhaps the most widely understood of the formal applications of learning theory. In psychotherapy repetition is utilized when a dynamic is interpreted in various aspects and time phases of a patient's life.

The Thematic Apperception Test may be used in application of the repetition and the active learning principles. The therapist may take the stories which the patient has given in response to the pictures and read them back to him. Then the patient may be asked, "Well, what do you think the stories were about?" This procedure often has the effect of increasing the patient's awareness, especially of preconscious feelings and thoughts.

The psychotropic drugs have permitted us to carry on learning by insight with many patients who would otherwise not be amenable to the process. Overwhelming anxiety or lack of frustration tolerance and of impulse control sometimes make the therapeutic process unbearable. Drugs have helped to ameliorate these aspects so that the learning process may establish a new structure well enough automatized and integrated so as not to require prolonged use of the drugs. The psychotropic drugs resemble the aid which suppportive physiological measures give during a surgical intervention, in the sense that they seem able to increase the synthetic functioning of the ego. Dissociation seems decreased and learning becomes possible in cases where without the drugs the primary process abounds to the extent that secondary-process activity is disrupted.

Obstacles to Insight Learning

Repression and denial, involved as they are in symptom formation, are the most widely encountered obstacles to the learning effects of interpretation. The presence of repression, however, does not mean that the brief intervention is predictably inadequate. Continued repression naturally implies that the therapeutic process must go on for a longer period of time. Denial, like all other human behavior, is observable along a continuum. Essentially, it is a preconscious process which means that we are dealing with variables which can relatively easily be made conscious, in contrast to those resulting from repression.

Insight may be impossible for some patients because they do not have the logical equipment for the syllogistic thinking required. This may be due to a failure to acquire enough of the secondary process and of the hierarchal relationships of cause and effect, time, place, and person.

Overconcreteness of thinking is another problem. Verbal therapy and the use of interpretation and insight may be impossible in some such instances, though Arieti has suggested ways of dealing with this problem.

In these situations particularly, adjunctive measures are of critical importance when brief psychotherapy is attempted.

INCREASING SELF-ESTEEM

One technique which has a role in the psychotherapy of nearly all patients who come for treatment, especially in emergency situations, is that of strengthening the ego by increasing the patient's self-esteem. Counteracting the traumatic impact of the very necessity to seek help for an emotional or mental problem is often indicated. For many people, the need for psychotherapy is a blow to self-esteem and a stigma. The patient feels that he must be seriously deficient, and this notion adds to the feeling of lowered self-esteem. In addition, there are associated feelings of rejection and failure. The positive features in his life must be pointed out to such a patient, who, in addition, may suffer feelings of oral deprivation, projection, and regressive phenomena. The therapist must express recognition that the patient has accomplished something, that he has been able to tolerate many difficulties, and especially that he has been willing to do something rational about his condition. One must impart to the patient the feeling that his situation is understood and that he can be helped because of this understanding.

Being on fairly familiar terms with the patient (contrary to usual psychotherapeutic practice) may be useful in order to increase his feelings of self-worth. Although the therapist is necessarily the authority, the latient must be led to feel that he is on the same level with the therapist and that the therapist has no contempt for him. The patient should be helped to see that all human beings suffer from the same things, that there is nothing small or mean about the patient, or especially large and awesome about the therapist, and that both of them can talk over things together.

Yet above all, one must be careful not to overdo this approach, or to be insincere in its application. The therapist may choose to personalize the situation by bringing himself into the picture, indicating that he, too, at one time was in a situation comparable to the patient's, or had feelings comparable to the patient's. Here we should repeat that this approach to raising self-esteem must have a realistic basis, and not arise either out of the therapist's own anxieties, unitary approach, or simple desire to be kind and helpful to a distressed person.

CATHARSIS

The cathartic interpretation concerns itself with transposing an unconscious drive or thought into consciousness. All of the cautions necessary in the interpretation of a drive must be exercised. In effect, the cathartic interpretation may be best defined as confrontation with optimal safeguards practiced, which derive either from the patient's present ego strength, from a therapeutic process of ego-strengthening, or from modifications of the cathartic interpretations.

With a reasonably strong personality suffering a neurotic disturbance, the therapist may go directly to the core of the symbolic content (aggressive, sexual, exhibitionistic, etc.) of the disturbing sentiment. Consider, for example, the relatively intact adolescent who suffers panic accompanied by a fear of having an epileptic seizure. His concept of the seizure is that one becomes excited, loses control, and behaves in a wild, animalistic fashion. In the absence of neurological findings, the seizure symbolizes an aggressive sexual act. This conceptualization is reinforced when the boy relates that the fear of seizure is with him particularly on dates. He has never had a sexual experience and doesn't know what really happens during intercourse. His fantasy is that the quantity of excitement during intercourse is uniquely greater than during masturbation or petting. One might say to this boy:

> "You must have felt an impulse to grab this girl and really let yourself go. You were afraid of what you might do because you don't know really what happens in sex between a man and a woman. You were afraid you might lose control, hurt her, and hurt yourself. In other words, you were afraid you would behave like an epileptic."

Following this, real information would be necessary to replace his distorted notion about sexual behavior.

As intensive psychotherapy proceeds, the opportuneness of the cathartic interpretation increases: with time the patient gains gradual insight and acquires greater ego strength. Obviously in brief psychotherapy, this long, slow conditioning process is not available; consequently, the interpretation and its effects must be geared to the prevailing circumstances. Modifications of the cathartic interpretation are required to protect the patient from the full impact of repressed drives and ideas. As a rule, except for the truly "ready" patient, in brief psychotherapy it is best to err on the side of caution and to dilute the cathartic interpretation.

"MEDIATE" CATHARSIS

The desired effect of the interpretation in mediate catharsis may be: (1) to temper its uncovering potential, (2) to offer reassurance along with the uncovering, (3) to provide an acceptable outlet for the drive so that it will not be dammed up, (4) to alienate the patient from the drive at the same time as it is made more ego-syntonic, (5) or to "lend" the patient the ego strength of the therapist for combatting his own punitive superego.

In tempering the uncovering effect of an interpretation we substitute more "civilized" words for primitive ones: "That made you *damned* angry," or "You must have thought he was a bastard," rather than "You must have wanted to *kill* him." The words used are usually geared to be somewhat stronger than the patient would use in social exchange, hence pungent and carrying some affective charge.

Reassurance may be offered along with uncovering for the mediating effect.

> "You are so damned angry at your sister that you wish she would *drop dead* (note: *not kill*). But because you are so conscientious that you couldn't harm a fly this idea upset you very much. You were really angry at yourself for having such a thought and that is how you became depressed."

Too often a therapist attempts to convince a patient that all his troubles will be ended if the patient will only permit himself to experience the rage which the therapist correctly perceives is unconsciously seething in the patient. If the therapist is successful, the patient is left with an open cauldron of hate against which he has little defense, and which spreads through all his object relations, alienating family and friends and leaving the patient with overwhelming feelings of isolation and danger. The borderline paranoid psychotic is a notable example: the unwitting therapist may find intensely disturbing phobic symptoms emerging as he pushes the patient to a presumably cathartic experience of anger. Yet—since even without the pressure from the therapist the patient is uncomfortably angry much of the time—the drive must somehow be recognized and mitigated. The patient feels endangered because the impulse is ego-alien, yet the danger is that interpretation will make it ego-syntonic. The therapeutic task is to steer a middle course that seeks simultaneously to make the drive more syntonic and yet preserve the ego's feeling of alienation. This multiple goal will seem less contradictory when we realize that the patient's anxiety about the impulse is derived from the superego pressures upon the ego; hence, the task becomes one of simultaneously lessening superego pressures and increasing the ego's capacity for both recognizing the impulse as an acceptable human feeling and realizing that its expression must be limited.

A young woman very clearly displays a borderline paranoid personality. A highly competent factory worker, she is ceaselessly moving from job to job. At first on a job she is content, but soon dissatisfaction and anger with peers and supervisors emerge. With this, and usually preceding the anger, she experiences disturbing phobic reactions to vermin (in her dynamics, siblings). She has been maintained in yearly brief contacts by mediate catharsis. First efforts are made to achieve acceptance of her rage with colleagues and bosses by recognizing it, discussing it around the specific issues she perceives as being at stake, and by identifying her angry response as a rather universal one that most people in her situation experience. Then come efforts to preserve alienation: All people get angry in such situations but accept it as part of the job; her anger often arises from fear that a criticism or correction will lead to her dismissal so she quits rather than be fired; her fear of dismissal is somewhat exaggerated; other workers in the department are criticized and corrected without dismissal.

The ego-strengthening effects of mediate catharsis are often facilitated and reinforced by "lending" the therapist's ego to the patient: "If I were in your place I would be furious," then, ". . . *but* I'd clear the air by talking it over with her," or "*but* I'd decide that's just her way of doing things and I'd get used to it," or . . . "*but* I'd decide I needed my job more right now than to rub her face in the dirt."

When, in brief psychotherapy, "cathartic" insight into an impulse is desired, the brevity of the therapeutic contacts dictates that mediate catharsis be the approach of choice. The patient cannot be left "holding the bag," or holding an open Pandora's box of much impulse and little defense.

DRIVE REPRESSION AND RESTRAINT

With many patients the necessity to restrain or repress a drive becomes the important therapeutic task. A patient, under pressure from his peer culture, may be engaging in sex, stealing, or destructive behavior that is resulting in extreme anxiety or depression. A wife and mother may be leading a promiscuous life without feeling any concern for the effects of her behavior upon her children and marriage. A husband and wife may engage in savage battles in the presence of their two-year-old child without thought or perception of the child's reactions. A young man may be struggling with powerful but latent homosexual impulses that appear repeatedly in dreams that awake him and make him fearful of sleep.

To interpret the impulse or drive in many such cases may produce increased anxiety and psychotic regression (as with the latent homosexual) where the ego is weak, or an attitude of "So what do you think I've been after?" (as with the philandering wife) where the superego is lax. In some cases, the task is to increase the operative force of the superego, in others to strengthen the ego, and in still others to increase both simultaneously.

One might delineate for the quarreling husband and wife the predictable and dire consequences for their child. We could appeal to the philandering wife's narcissism by the threat of venereal disease, her unfavorable position in a divorce action, and the effect of both these upon her children. With the young adult or adolescent we may appeal to reason and judgment in suggesting delay of gratification until such time as they are more mature and can lermit themselves libidinal gratification under more sanctioned circumstances. At the same time, predicting future effects of present behavior can reinforce the suggestion of delay.

Where drive repression is the effort in therapy, repeated dreams may nonetheless keep pressure upon the patient and threaten to emerge into consciousness. The therapist cannot ignore these dreams; he must deal with them therapeutically. He may decide to work only with the manifest content and relate it only to contemporaneous events in the patient's life: a quarrel with the boss over the work schedule rather than the patient's wish for a sexual connection with his father. Or he may choose to deal with fear of the counterdrive rather than with the wish for gratification of the pressuring drive. Thus one might stress the fear of aggressivity rather than the wish for passivity.

Another technique is to encourage defenses against the eruption of a drive. One may detect in a patient's history the former operation of a moderate obsessive-compulsive component and elect to encourage its return by praise for this kind of behavior, while at the same time showing the patient areas of his life where it may be applied. A young man was successfully encouraged to devote his evenings to compiling statistics about stocks instead of spending them in depressed isolation in bars. By way of additional benefit, his research led to careful investments, and his increased income permitted him libidinal discharge in travel.

Still another approach is to provide substitute or sublimated outlets. An angry, hostile man may be encouraged to punch bags, sculpt stone, or chop wood. A mild, passive person may be supported in his feminine attitude without danger by encouraging him to contribute his services to the care of the elderly.

REALITY TESTING

Even among neurotic patients perception both of the external world and internal strivings may be distorted or warded off in order to avoid painful wishes and fears. Denial as in children, of unpleasant realities may be the defense employed. Projection of internal wishes and reactions may be resorted to by others. The mild paranoid reaction, often in the service of masochism, is found in many people who are not psychotic.

Memory and learning are fundamental to the development of reality testing, and become the techniques in the treatment of impaired functioning in this area. Memory of former, more appropriate responses may be elicited and contrasted with the present maladaptive distortion. The therapist may teach reality testing by suggesting outcomes of behavior, alternative interpretations of a situation, or a third person's comments, or by ascribing alternative motivations to the behavior of another that the patient may be misinterpreting.

Many people have simply not learned the appropriate pressures upon or emanating from a role, position, or status they occupy. A youth, newly employed, may not know that it is appropriate for him to be sent out for coffee by the older workers, or that he in turn may request another to do something.

SENSITIZATION TO SIGNALS

Perception of both internal and external signals might well be classified under the rubric of reality testing but merit special comment as a therapeutic intervention. Pointing out to patients that they have not been heeding warning signals from themselves or others is often helpful. We are reminded of a young girl who broke into tears of shame when her date proposed sexual intercourse, and to his amazement and hers then blurted, "Mary told me you would do this if I went out with you."

Requesting a patient to go over a situation or event in minute detail often supplies the data needed to show the patient that he had indeed received a signal but ignored it. This intervention may then provide the necessary receptiveness for an insight interpretation.

INTELLECTUALIZATION

The development of psychoanalytic practice has resulted in a degree of condescension toward the use of intellectualization as a therapeutic device, if not outright disapproval of it. The emphasis upon the cathartic experience, with insight accompanied by affective changes, undoubtedly is responsible for intellectualization being relegated to a position of disrepute. Nonetheless, as a practical matter, if the development of a defense, previously slightly used by the patient, results in a decrease in use of a more pathological defense, then a psychotherapeutic change has been brought about. The effect of intellectualization, therefore, has a proper place in the practice of psychotherapy. Knowledge where there has been misinformation, reality where there has been fantasy, often go a long way toward relieving the anxiety patients experience as a result of lack of information. Every psychotherapist has had the experience of immediate amelioration of anxiety when a patient has learned that his symptoms are, for example, not unique, but are rather widely experienced. Combatting distortions attendant to masturbation is perhaps a prime example. In cases where anger is generated in a relationship, we have effectively stated that many people respond with anger to situations in which they actually experience fear. This idea has been helpful in enabling the patient to contain the reaction based on rage, while intellectually he searches for those aspects of the relationship which may be generating anxiety. The effect of intellectualization is often the cutting through of denial, to assist in making that which is preconscious conscious, in turn permitting eventually a more insightful type of learning.

Much of the pain of anxiety and other symptoms derives from the feeling of helplessness *vis-à-vis* the symptoms. The patient feels attacked by an unseen antagonist or force. Intellectual presentation of the cause of depression, of displacement and somatization in hysteria, for example, can impart optimism and motivation to cooperate in psychotherapy.

Intellectualization is most useful in giving the patient a new way of looking at his behavior. It provides a start on a new approach to his problems, an approach that might never occur to him spontaneously.

REASSURANCE AND SUPPORT

The psychotherapeutic technique of reassurance lends either implicit or explicit support to the patient. A good example of implicit support and reassurance is a therapist's statement of his availability 24 hours a day to the panicky or suicidal patient. Through this statement of availability, which, of course, must be substantiated in practice, the therapist tells the patient: You are not alone; I am here as a source of help whenever you might need me. Most patients use this proffer judiciously; some even must be reassured several times that the proffer is a sincere one. They come to a therapeutic session reporting panic in a sharply conflicting situation which occurred in the interim between sessions; they had not called upon the therapist by telephone. In these circumstances, a therapist should repeat his offer and indicate how it might have helped. A very small number of patients exploit the proffer of availability, either to test the therapist's sincerity or perhaps to tax him to the point where he is inclined to withdraw the offer, therefore proving the patient's contention that he is rejected by everyone. These latter patients can often be helped by interpreting their testing of the therapist or their excessive passive needs. Still others can be helped by preventive predictive measures, indicating that sometimes the offer may seem so tempting that the patient will invent a conflict situation in order to justify his use of the therapist's assistance; then, abuse of the offer must be clearly delineated.

Implicit support and reassurance may also involve feeding the patient a variety of possible oral gifts: cigarettes, coffee, cookies, fruit, etc. This technique fosters the incorporation of the therapist as a benign introject and is a useful approach with the "depleted" personality observable in depressions, especially those of a depth which involves suicidal risks.

Explicit support and reassurance are manifest in expressions by the therapist of approval or of his own identification with the patient's emotions, utterances, and behavior. In these statements, the therapist is in effect, lending the patient his own stronger ego and less severe superego. Thus, he may say to the patient, "If I were in your position, I would have been angry too." Or, "You were right to be angry." The therapist may support and reassure the patient in requesting a raise in salary, in standing up to an overbearing parent, in moving away from the family home, and through a host of similar and related situations. Many patients need support and reassurance through what might be called "vestibule" anxiety: anxiety experienced on the threshold of a new situation but which the therapist is reasonably sure will disappear, or be mitigated once the patient has acted. This is often true of patients who need support while they are being pushed into involvement with a phobic situation.

On the other hand, in some situations the patient must be supported and reassured against certain feelings he experiences. Perhaps most prominent in clinical experience are those feelings which terrify a patient because he feels that they mean he is crazy or homosexual. With such patients, the therapist may offer direct reassurance, indicating that in his opinion they are neither crazy nor homosexual. He may also generalize or universalize the feelings, indicating that the patient is not unique in having experienced them, that they are phenomena characteristic of large numbers of people.

COUNSELING AND GUIDANCE

Counseling and guidance techniques are employed when the patient should be moved along a path of behavior which, the therapist has determined dynamically, will be beneficial for the patient. Directions for behavior may be required in the patient's interpersonal relationships, but most often will require use of environmental interventions which are treated more fully in a subsequent chapter.

The therapist may be nondirective, in a sense, in his approach to counseling and guidance with patients whom he feels have sufficient capacity for insight and reality perception to make their own decisions on the basis of data which he provides. In these situations, the therapist's statements usually fall short of being recommendations; they more often are posed as alternatives to a situation with predictions of the consequences involved in the alternatives. On the basis of these, some patients may be expected to arrive at decisions which foster the progress of their therapy.

With the acting-out patient, the therapist may find it necessary to make a flat, direct statement of desired action. With a very few such patients, adherence to or compliance with the recommendations may sometimes be a necessary concomitant of the therapist's willingness to assume or continue therapeutic responsibility.

A GUIDE TO THE CHOICE OF
INTERVENTION—ASSESSMENT
OF EGO FUNCTIONS

Among the first tasks of ego assessment is the identification of the "intact residue" (as Katan first called it). The intact residue, the healthy portion of the ego, becomes an ally in the psychotherapeutic effort with the weaker portion of the ego. The therapist must appraise overall ego functioning, to identify both strength and weaknesses of individual functions, and to enlist those which can facilitate the therapeutic goal. The employment of the intact residue may be illustrated by a few examples. In a very disturbed person we may note a tendency towards stabilization by obsessive-compulsive involvement with work, and support such activity. With another individual, improvement in reality testing may be possible by utilizing the patient's excellent intelligence to increase defense by intellectualization. In still another person, good object relations in the face of other impairment may be used to bolster the patient. In contrast, relative isolation may be recommended for someone for whom close interactions might lead to paranoid ideation.

A primary value of an assessment of ego functions is its capacity to prevent oversimplification, or the reliance upon a unitary approach. Not all patients benefit from uncovering of drives, impulses, and affects. Not all individuals are affected by neurosis or psychosis in the same manner. In emergency psychotherapy, particularly, the ability of the therapist to address himself to an intact portion of the ego and to utilize it in the management of crisis is of extreme importance. Appraisal of a large number of individuals with the same diagnosis will reveal that different ego functions may be disturbed or remain intact. For example, not all schizophrenics suffer primarily from a disturbance of object relations. Relatively good object relations can be identified in some schizophrenics whose primary disturbance is of the thought process. Narcissism was once seen as the outstanding characteristic of the schizophrenic. As we have indicated in our theoretical discussion of the subject, many individuals with character disorders have more narcissism of the self than many schizophrenics. (Hartmann notes that schizophrenics narcissistically cathect various ego functions rather than the self.)

Thus, many schizophrenics do not need relationship therapy. The schizophrenic who primarily suffers from a thought disturbance in that he has not yet acquired the structure of time and space may never benefit from any amount of good relationship or from the most loving mother or mother-substitute in the world. What he requires is the development of adequate secondary-thought processes.

With other individuals the outstanding problem may be a lack of impulse control. The therapeutic task is to help the patient acquire such control rather than to stimulate acting-out through cathartic interpretation.

We may lend further clarity to our point by presenting a catalog of therapeutic interventions in relation to the schema of ego functions and their disturbances. In this formulation, we allude briefly to various adjunctive measures.

Adaptation to Reality

Disturbances of adaptation to reality make up a large category of which we will mention a few topics. Inappropriateness of behavior, for example, will demand reality testing with an analysis of the apperceptive distortions. Insight therapy is exceptionally valuable here, with its tendency to facilitate the restructuring of the apperceptive mass. Disturbances in the sense of reality need insight therapy, but often must also be supported with drug treatment to allay both the anxiety and aggressiveness which tend to precipitate disturbances of the body image and body boundaries. Intellectualization can be useful in cases like the latter. Sometimes overbreathing in excessive anxiety produces feelings of faintness which in turn cause feelings of unreality. Teaching a new breathing technique is useful in such cases.

Insight treatment in reality disturbances must be directed cautiously to their relationship with disturbances in drive control and regulation. Reality testing plays an important role in the treatment of reality disturbances where repeated and careful re-education is necessary as treatment progresses.

Conjoint consultation with parents or spouse is useful where the patient needs the therapist's direct support in evolving a new role with either of these figures.

Regulation of Drives

Diagnostically, the concern in disturbances of drive regulation must be with whether control is too little or too much. Where control is exaggeratedly tight, the patient may benefit from an approach based upon mediate catharsis. However, with many patients, the therapist must consider the necessity for drive repression, in contradistinction to the cathartic or interpretive method. This is illustrated by an eighteen-year-old girl who is panicked by aroused sexual feelings. A great deal of petting goes on in her social group; she has been participating for competitive reasons, feeling obliged to do so in order to be popular. At the same time, she is in conflict with another part of her environment which does not sanction this behavior. Her intense anxiety arises from the conflict between the wish to compete and her severe superego. The therapist may choose, in such a situation, to help by supporting her superego but at the same time making it less punitive. Thus, he may caution,

> "Don't do this now; you don't need to. It is quite understandable that you feel badly about it. You need to sort out your feelings first and decide just what you want to do. You can go about it differently than your friends. You can approach it more slowly; perhaps even at a later time."

At the same time, one may explain that she needs to understand more about what is happening, and she can be enlightened tactfully and helped to dispel any distortions she may have about sexual behavior.

Another example involves a young man who refuses to use contraceptive procedures. He is unable to identify the source of his anxiety. One can tell this young man that he has enough trouble without being responsible for a girl's pregnancy, and that to practice contraception or forego relations would be best for him at this time. Another example is the man who is having an affair with a married woman and at the same time socializing with her husband. His anxiety can be alleviated by restraining his urge to continue the affair, pointing out that it places him in danger of incurring the wrath of the woman's husband whose relationship he values.

Inherent in these examples is the fact that the patient does not recognize internal signals of danger and anxiety and continues in a situation which produces the anxiety. These patients need to be educated to the signals which they are refusing through denial to perceive. Only through sensitization and reality testing are they able to comprehend the situation in which they find themselves. A woman who had been living with a much younger man, a severe alcoholic, found that their relationship had become intolerable for her. It was possible to point out to her that she had forgotten a number of similar earlier episodes which involved variations on a similar theme. It was also possible to show her that she had denied to herself the severity of her friend's behavior; she had earlier referred him to a psychiatrist, who had actually told her that her friend was schizophrenic.

Drive restraint often goes hand in hand with reality testing—for example, the "he-man" who suffers from panic when he is clearly engaged in manifestly dangerous and destructive behavior. The task becomes that of indicating to him point by point how much trouble he is likely to get into because of his drive to prove to himself that he is strong and courageous, and to indicate quite clearly that his panic is based on reality because he is doing things that should frighten him.

The use of energizers and tranquilizers has an important function in the control of drives and impulses.

Object Relations

Disturbances in object relations usually are not easily treated in brief psychotherapy, since they respond best via the transference relationship and interpretation of the defensive nature of secondary narcissism if it is involved. Nonetheless, brief psychotherapy may be helpful in some instances of disturbed object relations if the therapist is able to prescribe situations for the patient which take into account both the nature of the object relations and the intensity of relationship which the patient is able to tolerate. The parable of two porcupines is especially illuminating here: the two porcupines who meet on a cold night and elect to huddle together in an effort to obtain warmth. As they do, their spines hurt each other and they draw apart, only to suffer again from the cold. Gradually, however, they work out the optimal degree of closeness which permits them the greatest warmth with the least pain.

Individuals with a real yearning for closeness may find the ability to approach others when their impulse control has been improved either through insight treatment or drive repression. Still others may be advised to join certain social or athletic clubs where the relationship is diluted through the presence of large numbers of people with none of whom they need to come into close personal contact. And still others may have to be counseled into rather isolated activities which permit them the greatest degree of freedom from closeness.

One may observe, for example, the continuum along which intensity of object relations are spread among taxi drivers. Some drivers obviously find their work lonely, and if they detect the slightest willingness in their passenger, will engage him in conversation throughout the passage. Their conversation very often discloses intimate details, the expression of values and opinions shared usually only between close friends. At the opposite end of the pole is the driver who will not even repeat the destination asked for by the passenger and remains silent throughout the drive.

Group therapy, judiciously prescribed, can help illuminate object relations and their disturbances and produce therapeutic changes by "learning" in the group experience.

Thought Processes

When disturbances of the thought processes involve evidences of primary-process thinking such as contaminations, to use Rorschach terminology, treatment can be extremely difficult and time consuming. If the thinking disturbances are relatively circumscribed, as in an intelligent, otherwise intact paranoid, the problem may be handled with relative ease through reality testing in specific situations which are causing difficulty. Very often too, such people can be helped by adjusting the degree of object relationship, or by controlling impulses which are producing the disturbances in the thought processes. One must make sure, however, before attempting brief psychotherapy with such an individual that a reasonable degree of the secondary thought process has been acquired. When it has, the technique of choice may be to utilize the psychotropic drugs in controlling the tide of impulses which are stimulating the primary-process thinking.

Group psychotherapy involving a reward-and-punishment system may lead to a reinforcement of secondary process in thinking.

Defensive Functions

Very often the task in disturbances of the defensive functions is to assess the superego for its degree of integration. One must assure that the superego is neither too strict in some areas nor too lenient in others. This may require judicious firmness and permissiveness at different times in relationship to different sets of problems as they are indicated.

The problems in treating the defensive functions are very similar to those encountered in the treatment of impulse control. The inquiry must be directed toward assessing whether there is too much or too little of the defense. Mediate catharsis or drive restraint may be necessary in different cases. Secondary measures involving manipulation of the environment in order to decrease the pressure of stimuli are often essential. The administration of drugs, changes in vocation, habitation, and habits may be necessary. It is especially important that the therapist be able to conceptualize the dynamics correctly and clearly, and that he insist without hesitation even upon drastic changes, rather than maintain an analytic aloofness from decisions which involve reality.

Autonomous Functions

Very often the autonomous functions are part of the intact residue and become a psychotherapeutic ally, heavily drawn upon in restructuring the disturbed areas of the personality. A firmly established work habit of a high intelligence may be an invaluable asset in the treatment of an otherwise severely disturbed person.

Increasingly, in practice, one sees disturbances of the autonomous functions among married women whose children have grown and moved out of the home. If such a person has not become involved in other activities which occupy her time and energies in an interesting way, she is likely to become disturbed. In many such instances, the prescription of genuinely meaningful activities, particularly paid work, with its structured demands and rewards, is a helpful device.

The Synthetic Function

The synthetic function is usually only strengthened as a result of the improvement in other ego functions. However, the psychotropic drugs, for example those of the phenothiazine variety, seem to counteract dissociation directly, thus having a synthesizing and integrative effect. Perhaps they accomplish this feat indirectly by achieving drive control, or by action upon some organic substratum.

Chapter 4

Methodology in Short-Term Therapy

Lewis Wolberg, M.D.

The advantages of short-term over long-term therapy may be debated on various grounds. Financial savings, more efficient employment of psychotherapeutic resources, opportunities to reduce waiting lists—these and other expediencies are often presented as justification for short-term programs. Admitting that there may be pragmatic reasons for abbreviating treatment, we may ask a crucial question: "How truly effective are short-term approaches in modifying disturbed neurotic patterns?"

In a study of the results of patients treated by a team of psychoanalytically trained therapists from the Tavistock Clinic and Cassel Hospital, Malan (1) concludes that long-lasting "depth" changes are possible even in severely ill patients treated on a short-term basis. The findings in this study are similar in some respects to those I have observed among a large group of patients with whom I have worked briefly over the past 25 years. Follow-up visits persuade that not only have symptoms been controlled, but in a considerable number of patients reconstructive personality changes have been brought about. The rationale for short-term therapy and a detailed delineation of techniques have been elaborated elsewhere (2). In this paper, some stratagems I have found helpful that may possibly be adaptable to the style of other therapists will be outlined.

The psychotherapeutic process in short-term treatment may descriptively be broken down into four phases: a supportive phase, an apperceptive phase, an action phase, and an integrative phase.

THE SUPPORTIVE PHASE OF THERAPY

Turning to another human being for help is an inevitable consequence of feelings of helplessness, bewilderment and anxiety. It represents a final acknowledgment by the individual

Reprinted from *American Journal of Psychiatry*, 1965, **122**, 135-140, by permission of the publisher and the author. Copyright 1965, the American Psy-

that he is unable to cope with his difficulty through his own resources. More or less every emotionally ill patient overtly or covertly regards the helping authority as a source of inspiration from whom infusions of wisdom must flow that will heal his wounds and lead him to health and self-fulfillment. Such credences are powered by the helplessness that inevitably accompanies a shattering of the sense of mastery. Because his habitual coping mechanisms have failed him, the patient believes himself incapable of independent judgments and he delivers himself body and soul to the powerful therapeutic agent whose education and experience promise to take over the direction of his life.

This design is obviously unwholesome if it is permitted to continue, for elements will be released that undermine the patient's independence, inspire infantility, and mobilize anachronistic hopes and demands that superimpose themselves on the patient's other troubles, further complicating his existence.

Knowing that the patient covets a scheme to enmesh himself in a passive role with an omniscient deity, beneficent protector, and idealized parent, the therapist may plan his strategy.

First, it is essential to establish as rapidly as possible a working relationship with the patient. This can often be done by a skilled therapist in the initial interview. It is difficult, however, to designate any unalterable rules for the establishing of contact with a patient. Variable factors apply in one case that are not applicable in a second. However, there are certain general principles that are useful to observe within the bounds of which one may operate flexibly. For instance, the expression on meeting the patient of a sympathetic and friendly attitude is remarkably helpful in relaxing him sufficiently to tell his story. As obvious as this may seem, many therapists greet a new patient with a detached and passive attitude in the effort to be objective and non-directive. This can freeze the patient in a resistive bind from which he may not recover during the span of his contact with the therapist.

Second, it is important to treat the patient no matter how upset he seems as a worthwhile individual who has somehow blundered into a neurotic impasse from which he will be able to extricate himself. Neurotic difficulties influence feelings in the direction of being unloved and unlovable. The patient may harbor doubts that he can be accepted or understood. Irrespective of denial mechanisms, he will crave extraordinary reassurance that the therapist is interested in him and cares about what

chiatric Association. Dr. Wolberg is Director of the Postgraduate Center for Mental Health, New York City, and Clinical Professor of Psychiatry, New York Medical College.

happens to him. This obviously cannot be communicated verbally, but it may be expressed through a manner of respect, considerateness, tact, solicitude, and compassion.

Third, the patient must be inspired to verbalize as much as possible, while the therapist attends to what he is saying, encouraging him by facial expressions, gestures, utterances, and comments that reflect an interest in the patient and an understanding of what he is trying to say. The patient is constantly drawn out to express his problems, pointed questions being phrased to facilitate the flow of ideas and feelings.

Fourth, it is vital to avoid arguing or quarreling with the patient no matter how provocative he may be. The available time for therapy is so limited that one cannot indulge in the challenges and confrontations possible in long-term therapy. The therapist may not agree with what the patient says, but he should convey a respect for the patient's right to express his irritations and misconceptions.

Fifth, empathy is the keynote in establishing contact. Understandably one may not be able to sympathize with some of the attitudes, feelings, and behavior of the patient. It may also be difficult to put oneself in his place. Yet the therapist may be able to detect an essential dignity in the patient, considering that his problems, destructive to him and to other people, have deviated him away from creative and humanistic aims. While it is inexpedient therapeutically to reassure too readily or to praise, it is essential in the early stages of treatment not to underestimate the patient's constructive qualities. In concentrating his attention on his bad points, the patient will tend to minimize his worthwhile characteristics which may lend themselves to a recounting by the therapist after he has gathered sufficient data.

Sixth, the therapist may by his verbal and nonverbal behavior signal confidence in his ability to help the patient without promising him a cure. This presupposes that the therapist has faith in what he is doing and a conviction that all people, given even a minimal chance, have the capacity to develop.

Seventh, even in the first interview, the patient may be told that the rapidity of his recovery will depend on his willingness to cooperate in working on his problems. The therapist will show him how he can do this and will help him to help himself.

THE APPERCEPTIVE PHASE

If we are to proceed beyond the supportive phase toward an attempt at reconstruction of personality, we must strive to bring the individual to some recognition of what is behind his disorder. The power of "insight" has, of course, been greatly exaggerated, but irrespective of how valid or invalid an "insight" may be, it constitutes, when it is accepted, a significant means of alleviating tension and of restoring to the individual his habitual sense of mastery. The fact that we couch our "insights" in scientific terminology, being assured that they validate our theoretical preconceptions, does not make them accurate, even though the patient responds to them with relief, hope, and abatement of his complaints.

Yet the principle is a correct one. Some explanation for his trouble is essential and we must give our patient one that is as close to our current scientific understanding of human nature as possible, always mindful of the fact that as behavioral scientists we are balanced precariously on the pinnacle of profound ambiguities. What seems like the truth of today may be the exploded myth of tomorrow.

But myth though it be, we have no other more tenable explanation; so we make it, hopeful that it will find its mark. The most effective vehicle that we have for this is the unique relationship that is set up between the patient and therapist which acts as a corrective experience for the patient. The patient may project into the relationship the same kinds of irrational demands, hopes and fears such as have shadowed his attitudes toward early authorities and other significant people in his past. But instead of meeting indignation, rejection, ridicule, or hostility—the usual and expected rebuttals—the therapist interprets the patient's reactions with sympathy and understanding. Bringing these, if they are apparent, to his attention in a noncondemning manner helps the patient to arrive at an understanding of the meaning and possible origin of his drives while actually reexperiencing them in the protective relationship with the therapist. Under these circumstances, the patient may come to realize that his responses toward the therapist are the product, not of any realistic situation that exists, but rather of what he anticipates or imagines must be as a result of past relationships. He may then appreciate that what is happening with the therapist also happens under some circumstances with other people. Thus varied defensive reactions become apparent to the patient, not as theories, but as real experiences.

In short-term therapy, time prevents the employment of the conventional tools of free association, extensive dream interpretation, and the building up of a transference neurosis. However, an experienced therapist will be able, perhaps even in the first session, to gain knowledge of the operative dynamics from the history given by the patient, particularly the quality of his relationship with his parents and siblings, from one or two dreams, from the nature of the symptomatology, and from the patient's behavior with the therapist during the interview. He may then present at a propitious moment a cautious but firm explanation to the patient of the impact on him and his personality of some of the experiences and deprivations in his childhood, of the defenses he has developed, of how environmental precipitating factors have operated to bring his conflicts to a head and how these are registered in his immediate symptoms and sufferings. Only a fragment of the existing conflicts may lend itself to such exploration and interpretation in short-term therapy, but this can be like a biopsy of the total psychodynamic picture. If the patient grasps the significance of an interpretation and sees the continuity between problems in his development, their crystallizations in his general personality structure and their relation to the current complaint factor, a deep penetration will have been achieved. By concerted self-examination, the patient may thereafter progressively widen his own insights. In any equation the shifting of one factor will bring other elements into realignment.

Obviously, interpretations will have to be made that coordinate with the patient's capacities for understanding. The therapist will need to employ language comprehensible to the patient, encouraging the patient to restate what has been expressed to test his comprehension. It is surprising how patients, even those without an extensive education, can grasp the meaning of relatively complex psychological concepts if these are presented in terms of the patient's own experience. When a good relationship exists between the therapist and patient, even unconscious repudiated aspects may be explored without provoking too severe reactions of resistance. If the patient is unable to acknowledge the accuracy of an interpretation, the therapist may ask him to consider it nevertheless before discarding it entirely. The patient may also be encouraged to alert himself to factors that stir up his tensions, to work on connections between these provocative factors and what is being mobilized inside himself. Are his reactions habitual ones and if so how far back do they go? Are they related to important experiences in his childhood? Some patients may be able to get considerable understanding through the discipline of searching within themselves. Some may even learn to interpret their dreams in line with such percipience.

Sometimes the patient will, due to resistance or the lack of time, fail to arrive at any basic realizations in the course of short-term therapy. This need not deter the therapist from encouraging the patient to work on himself toward self-understanding after the treatment period is over. It is quite rewarding to observe how many patients, some months and even years later, arrive at insights which strike them with a dramatic force and which they can utilize constructively. Examining these one may recognize them as patterned after some of the therapist's original interpretations, which could not be accepted during the short treatment phase, but which were subjected to spontaneous "working-through" following treatment.

THE ACTION PHASE

The acid test of therapy lies in the patient's capacity to put his acquired new comprehensions into definitive action. This means that he must challenge conceptions that have up to this time ruled his life. A symptom may rapidly be overcome in the supportive phase of therapy; but a personality pattern, one that disorganizes relationships with other human beings, will scarcely be altered except after a period of resistance.

In short-term therapy even the tiniest action opposing neurotic misconceptions can be scored as a gain. The therapist may actively invite the patient to challenge his fears and engage in actions that hold promise of rewards. Discussion of the consequences of his movements may then prove fruitful. I have found several tactics of importance here. First, I actively outline specific courses of action hoping that the patient, prompted to act on my suggestion, will achieve a small success which will reinforce his determination to try again. Even after a signal success, patients will need further urging. Having escaped hurt by the skin of their teeth, they may feel that their luck will collapse the next time they engage in an experience that threatens to set off anxiety. Second, a tranquilizer or a barbiturate taken prior to a challenge may reduce anxiety sufficiently so that the patient may allow himself to enter into a fearsome situation and see it through. As soon as possible, a repetition of this action with reduced and finally no drug will be indicated. In borderline patients, a phenothiazine derivative like trifluoperazine appears to work better than the tranquilizing drugs. Third, I sometimes teach the patient self-hypnosis (3). In the trance, the patient is trained to visualize himself successfully mastering situations that upset him. The patient may phantasy an overcoming of progressively challenging difficulties, gradually working himself up to more fearsome ones. Suggestions made to himself in the trance that he will have the desire to tackle his problems may enable him to handle these with greater and greater ease.

THE INTEGRATIVE PHASE

Consolidating therapeutic gains will require practice the remainder of the individual's life. The chinks in the patient's defensive armor must be widened by constant challenges and

repetitive salutary actions. Complacency, riding on the notion
that one feels better and hence can remain at a standstill, invites a
recrudescence of symptoms once stress exceeds existent coping
capacities. Constant alertness to what is happening within onself
and a resisting of subversive neurotic temptations are mandatory.

In short-term therapy one must depend on the posttherapeutic
period to harden what has been molded during the active
treatment phases and to restructure into new patterns aspects that
were only casually perceived before. Encouraging is the fact that
once the old way of life has been unbalanced in one dimension,
new zones of activity and more wholesome modes of being and
feeling may present themselves.

Before therapy is terminated, the patient may realize that it is
possible to control tension and anxiety once it starts by making
connections between symptomatic upsets, precipitating factors
in his environment, and his operative personality forces; and by
recognizing that he is capable of developing a different
philosophy that can lend to his life a salutary meaning.

In some cases I encourage the patient to employ the technique
of self-hypnosis or self-relaxation periodically when he is upset,
both to resolve his tensions and to explore reasons for the revi-
val of his symptoms (3). Patients can easily learn to apply this
two-fold tactic by giving themselves the assignment to figure
out the aspects within their environment and within themselves
that have precipitated their anxiety. This may result in direct
understanding, or stimulated phantasies and dreams may yield
some leads. A helpful course of action may then spontaneously
be evolved. No more than a few sessions are usually required to
restore equilibrium.

The patient may also be counseled temporarily to employ a
mild tranquilizing drug if his tensions do not resolve after a
while. He must be cautioned, however, that drugs, while
provisionally useful, cannot constitute a way of life. The basic
therapeutic factor at all times is greater self-understanding.
Drugs cannot and must not replace such self-directed efforts.

Finally, the patient is exhorted to adopt a few basic
philosophical principles. Superficial as they sound, they
sometimes make a profound impact on him. In long-term
therapy, the patient is expected to develop new values through
his own spontaneous efforts. In short-term therapy a different
way of looking at things may be presented in an active
educational effort. For example, the following principle may be
proferred: "It is useful to remember at all times that while you are
not responsible for what happened to you in your childhood, and
the faulty ideas and fears you learned in your past, you are
responsible for carrying them over into your adult life." This
principle, if accepted, may block the patient from making a

career out of blaming his parents and crediting to past unfortunate episodes all of his current problems, justifying his neurotic carryings-on by the terrible things done to him as a child over which he had no control.

Another principle is: "No matter what troubles or terrible scrapes you have gotten yourself into in the past, you can rise above these in the future with the knowledge you now have. You need not indulge in patterns which you know you should be able to control, and really want to control." This precept, if incorporated, may help some patients control certain neurotic patterns, realizing that they have powers to inhibit them. The putting together of certain persuasive formulations in this way can be useful to patients who are unable to structure a philosophic formula by themselves. This may help consolidate the gains they have made in therapy.

Within this broad framework, then, the therapist may apply himself flexibly to the problems of his patients, utilizing techniques from various fields blended in an eclectic approach. Hopefully out of the experiences of workers from the various fields of human relationships there will eventually emerge a more scientific methodology in short-term psychotherapy that will enable us to help the greatest numbers of patients in the shortest possible time.

SUMMARY

Short-term therapy has more than utilitarian value. There are indications that it will, as its methodology becomes elaborated, develop into the treatment of choice for a considerable number of patients. This conviction is supported by observations from a variety of sources to the effect that patients suffering from a wide spectrum of emotional problems, treated over a short period of time, may obtain not only sustained relief, but also, in some cases, personality changes of a reconstructive nature that would have been considered significant had long-term treatment been employed. Four stages in the course of short-term therapy seem apparent: (1) a supportive phase during which homeostasis is brought about through the healing influences of the relationship with the therapist, the placebo effect of the therapeutic process, and the decompressive impact of emotional catharsis; (2) an apperceptive phase, characterized by the ability to understand, even minimally, the meaning of the complaint factor in terms of some of the operative conflicts and basic personality needs and defenses; (3) an action phase distinguished by a challenging of certain habitual neurotic patterns, facing them from a somewhat different perspective; and (4) an integrative relearning and reconditioning phase which continues after termination on the basis of the chain reaction started during the brief treatment period.

The specific techniques that are outlined in the paper are contingent, first, on the acceptance of eclecticism, adopting procedures from every field of psychiatry, psychology, sociology, education, and even philosophy, that may be of help in the total treatment effort; second, on the existence of flexibility in the therapist that enables him to adjust his stratagems to the immediate needs of the patient and therapeutic situation; and third, on the studied employment of activity in the relationship. All modalities are employed in those combinations that may be of value, including psychoanalytic techniques, interviewing procedures, drugs, hypnosis, reconditioning, and group therapy.

Among the procedures that may expedite treatment are the following: (1) establishing a rapid working relationship (rapport); (2) circumscribing the problem area as a focus for exploration; (3) evolving with the patient a working hypothesis of the psychodynamics of his difficulty; (4) employing dream interpretation where the therapist is analytically trained; (5) alerting oneself to resistances and resolving these as rapidly as possible; (6) dealing with target symptoms like excessive tension, anxiety, and depression, through the careful use of drugs; phobic phenomena by conditioning techniques; obsessive-compulsive manifestations by persuasive tactics, etc.; (7) teaching the patient how to employ insight as a corrective force; (8) outlining with the patient a definite plan of action by which he can use his understanding in the direction of change; (9) searching for transference elements and resolving these quickly before they build up to destroy the relationship; (10) encouraging the development of a proper life philosophy.

REFERENCES

1. Malan, D. H. A study of brief psychotherapy. Springfield, Ill.: Thomas, 1963.
2. Wolberg, L. R. The technic of short-term psychotherapy. In L. R. Wolberg (Ed.), *Short-term psychotherapy*. New York: Grune and Stratton, 1965.
3. Wolberg, L. R. Hypnosis in short-term psychotherapy. In L. R. Wolberg (Ed.), *Short-term psychotherapy*. New York: Grune and Stratton, 1965.

Chapter 5

Events of Early Therapy and Brief Therapy

C. Peter Rosenbaum, M.D.

Patients starting psychotherapy frequently feel well enough after several sessions that the goals of therapy deserve reformulation. Patient and therapist may agree that the patient has learned a lot about the circumstances which brought him into treatment, that the patient can now work competently on his own, and that this episode of therapy can end. The patient leaves, knowing he can return to a meaningful relationship with his therapist should future problems arise. Likewise, the patient's relief of distress may be sufficient so that he does not see the need to continue therapy now or in the future; the present gains are enough. Such outcomes are termed "brief therapy." Finally, even though the current distress is greatly relieved, the patient may wish to pursue a prolonged investigation of his life style in hopes of improving his future ability to handle similar circumstances more successfully.

This paper examines in detail many of the factors which facilitate the early relief of symptoms and the possibility of an early satisfying end to a given episode of treatment. Examples are drawn from my own experience and from cases presented in supervision. The numerous factors influencing events of early therapy are discussed in four categories: (1) certain attitudes and techniques of the therapist; (2) some mechanisms in the relief of symptoms; (3) frequent outcomes of the presenting complaints; and (4) common decisions necessitated by changes.

CERTAIN ATTITUDES AND TECHNIQUES OF THE THERAPIST

Therapists' widely differing attitudes about how one does psychotherapy, and the way in which these attitudes are

Reprinted from *Archives of General Psychiatry*, 1964, **10**, 506-512, by permission of the publisher and the author. Dr. Rosenbaum is Associate Professor of Psychiatry and Director, Adult Psychiatry Clinic, Stanford University School of Medicine, Palo Alto, California.

translated into techniques, depending on their training programs, can profoundly enhance or discourage brief therapy. Some attitudes which can enhance brief psychotherapy follow.

One must assume that, whatever the patient's life-long style of living has been, certain recent events have upset his inner and outer equilibrium sufficiently for him to seek help. Some understanding of these events and their meaning to the patient can greatly help him to restore the upset balance. Thus, the first attitude in the therapist which can enhance brief therapy is an almost monotonous preoccupation with the questions: "Why now? Why does this person come for help at this time; what recent set of stresses have interfered with the patient's previous equilibrium that he now seeks help?" The answers given by Kalis et al. (1) included recent disruption of object relationships, binds with previous sources of help, identification with another person followed by disequilibrium, surge of unmanageable (and possibly unfamiliar) impulses, and threat to current adjustment because of changes in the environment. Curiosity about these current events should be at least as important to the therapist as knowledge of early life events and their influence on character. Recent changes in the life situation furnish an obvious starting point; curiosity about them should not be delayed pending knowledge of childhood and adolescence.

Secondly, the therapist should let the patient define mental health, improvement, or relief in his own terms. The therapist must respect the patient's ability to formulate his own expectations and goals. All too often a therapist considers his job not done until a patient understands the origin and meaning of his symptoms. But such understanding, if it comes at all, may lag months behind the early relief of symptoms. To be sure, the patient's statement, "I don't know why you think I should come, now that I'm feeling so well," may be his resistance to engaging in an intensive psychotherapeutic effort. But it can also express bewilderment in the sufficiently and successfully treated truckdriver, housewife, bookie, or student.

A third attitude is the therapist's willingness to hear of termination early, or even his willingness to bring it up himself when he senses it in the air.* Patients often feel shy about mentioning this, sometimes because the popular media have taught them that therapy is lengthy and dramatic, and to talk of termination after six undramatic but productive sessions indicts themselves and their therapist, whom they have come to like; or it would be presumptuous to broach to a doctor when his treatment should end. Whatever the reason, a statement by the therapist to the improved patient such as, "It looks to me like you may not

---

* Neal Blumenfeld, M.D., has emphasized this point.

have to be coming for a great deal longer; does it look this way to you?'' may bring willing consent. If not, it is an excellent entree into discussion of future goals of therapy.

Some attitudes of the therapist, however, may work against an early, mutual consideration of termination, despite the patient's substantial symptomatic improvement.

The psychotherapist, because the fruits of his work are less easy to assess than those of an internist or surgeon, may nurture and tenaciously hold to certain attitudes about himself and his work that will insure his doing right by his patients. He may well see himself as a very accepting, persevering person; and, indeed, some measure of these qualities is essential. Thus, to speak early of termination may sound to him like rejection and uninterest, and he may hesitate to broach the topic, however appropriate. Likewise, if he is uncertain of helping the patient, he may ease his conscience by encouraging the patient to continue taking the two things the therapist knows he can offer: his time and his attention.

If the therapist believes that hours spent in therapy and weeks spent in personal growth change are necessarily proportional, he may encourage the patient to remain in treatment after the patient is capable of consolidating his gains on his own. These considerations include, for young therapists in private practice, the simple need to make a living.

The standards of residency and psychoanalytic training programs may obstruct early termination. Patients whose cases are being presented week after week to consultants in continuous case seminars become valuable possessions of the resident and his group. The patient who quits is frequently spoken of as "lost," and the resident has to endure the implication of some malfeasance on his part. Psychoanalytically oriented programs implicitly value long-term therapy with extensive investigations of unconscious processes and character structure; at the same time, cases of quick relief of symptoms are seldom presented, sometimes termed "just a transference cure that won't last," and made to seem inferior efforts. In a field where the criteria of superiority are frequently difficult to discern, who wants to have his efforts regarded as inferior? On the other hand, arbitrary limits of six to eight appointments to a patient are the basis of successful brief therapy programs in some clinics.

Another attitude of the therapist which may impede his letting go of the patient at a propitious time is his reluctance to let the patient use him primarily as an incorporation or as a transference object, with this as the therapist's main contribution. Such use may seem too much like abetting the magical thinking of the patient's unconscious—the same unconscious that helped him to get into trouble in the first place—and so a lengthy but sometimes only mildly productive analysis of the transference can result.

Several uses of technique may enhance brief therapy.

The therapist should be willing to bring a variety of the abilities which enable him to be a reasonably successful person in his nonprofessional life into the treatment situation. For instance, the therapist should be as spontaneous and flexible as his temperament allows, though not more. Different patients respond to different approaches: a chronically masochistic, anxious patient who gets into one self-defeating situation after another may well find that a therapist who can be direct, active, and sometimes bantering, can make the therapy situation rewarding. A patient with low self-esteem who has his fair share of appeal and wit may be helped by a therapist who can smile and laugh.

Example 1: A young woman in her first session protested conventionally her guilt and immorality for her sexual affair with a close relative, albeit with a cat-that-ate-the-canary smile. The therapist therefore suggested that she might also be enjoying the affair. When she berated him for his lack of compassion, he commented that it was just her luck to meet another nasty man. At the close of the session, when she suddenly and demurely apologized for her attack, he laughed, saying he did not believe a word of it, both had enjoyed it, and he would see her next week. Thus began an enjoyable relationship in which the patient's need to enmesh the therapist in her troubles diminished as her willingness to examine her own role in the affair increased.

Some patients may need an impassive therapist, but not every patient every session; and the therapist might well reserve his impassivity for periods of good, hard listening.

A therapist can also postpone taking a detailed history, inquiring instead about what springs spontaneously from his interaction with the patient and about details as they are relevant. Again, the therapist should allow himself to be used as a transference object, let the patient set the goals of therapy, and hear early about termination.

SOME MECHANISMS IN THE
RELIEF OF SYMPTOMS

A number of psychodynamic mechanisms are involved in the early relief of symptoms. Some of the more common mechanisms include primitive incorporation and identification, transference, object substitution, and diminishing the importance of the symptoms.

In primitive incorporation, seen frequently in schizophrenic or borderline patients, the patient takes part of the psychiatrist into his own psychic apparatus. If the psychiatrist has confidence that his devoured body part will regenerate, thus sanctioning the cannibalistic component of the act, he can be free to be repeatedly incorporated, as shown in the next two examples.

Example 2: A married artist of 27 complained of peculiar sudden "panic attacks" (they later proved to be displacements of anger from his job). He also became unbearably anxious whenever he had to leave the city limits for any reason. After eight sessions his panic attacks had virtually gone, but leaving the city was still difficult. Shortly thereafter, he reported that he had gone on a day's outing and had overcome his fear at the Golden Gate Bridge approach by conjuring up the image of a "portable psychiatrist"—his therapist—carried in his car trunk, to be consulted if he had to.

Example 3: A handyman, aged 45, a long-term ambulatory schizophrenic, said, with a peculiar smile, to his therapist that he "admired her brains." She had the distinct impression that he had pre-empted her cortex as his personal property and that this feeling was instrumental in the improvement he subsequently felt in his life and work.

In the category of the transference mechanisms, I place those unconsciously determined aspects of benevolence that the patient attributes to the therapist and the fostering institution. In many respects, such expectations may be a more sophisticated version of incorporation. Such trust may allow the patient to look into himself and learn about himself in a way he had never been able to do previously.

Through the transference, a patient may be able to borrow power and security to make decisions he could not previously make.

Example 4: A married housepainter of 28 sought therapy at the suggestion of a therapist in the state hospital where he had committed himself for exhibitionism. Before his hospitalization he had wanted to sell paint instead of going out on jobs, but had been too shy to ask for the change. After three sessions, he has asked for and obtained the store job, although this move had barely been touched on in the sessions. That he could do, after three sessions, what had been impossible for two years can be attributed to his positive transference.

His exhibitionistic impulses diminished greatly in three more sessions: he dropped out of therapy at that point, probably having got a good measure of what he came for.

The fact that the therapist accepts and likes a patient frequently makes it possible for the patient to use the therapist as a substitute object, to accept himself more, and thus to restore disrupted object relationships. Stories of middle-aged, depressed women who come to look on young psychiatrists as their good sons (that never were) and as doctors (who will take care of them in their old age) are legion. If the therapist can let himself be so used, he can often help the patient restore her real life object relationships.

The last main category of mechanisms is a diverse one of

diminishing the importance of the symptoms, i.e., detoxifying them somehow.

Intellectual insight, wherein a patient names a previously unnamed source of fear, may look animistic, but it often helps to lower anxiety and discomfort.

Superficial insight (unfortunately used too often in the pejorative sense), with an affective component, is illustrated in Example 5; in this case, it obviously benefited the patient.

Example 5: A housewife of 32 and mother 2 children—the younger of whom was possibly retarded—had made two half-hearted suicidal attempts and was rescued both times by her husband. She considered her husband, in the five years of their marriage, arrogantly authoritarian and constantly critical of her intelligence, femininity, and abilities as a mother. He blamed her for their younger child's so-called retardation, although the child was too young for evaluation. She wilted, becoming moody and depressed, and later making the attempts at suicide in reproach.

In the third session, I remarked that although obviously her husband had a low opinion of her, why did she agree with him, and had others in her life told her she would never amount to much? Her father had done so, it turned out.

(When a patient presents a depreciated opinion of himself without good reason, questions like "Whoever told you that you were such a no good?" may first make the patient aware that he has been living out a significant other's opinion.) The next session she exulted over how, the previous Saturday, her husband had started in on her again when she had just returned from the grocery store. Thereupon she took out each piece from the bag and hurled it against the wall, not too far from her husband. Three of the first depression-free days she had enjoyed in years followed. Of course she could not hurl groceries every time she got upset, but the escape was there if needed. In short, she no longer had to accept her husband's low opinion of her. A session later she discussed separating from him, and felt "right about it inside"; nor did she want any more therapy. We arranged a final session a month later; at that time, her good spirits and determination persisted, and therapy ended.

Sometimes the therapist can aid in the separation of the symptom per se and its implications of personal unworthiness and hopelessness.

Example 6: A cook, aged 54, a lifelong homosexual, had recently been left by his partner of several years. He had afterwards been picked up by the police on one of his very infrequent so-called cruises in a public lavatory. His stay in jail and the judge's lecture in court had stirred up in him fearful memories of his father's vindictive attacks (against which his homosexuality was a reaction-formation) and left him feeling most anxious, depressed, hopeless, a little less than human because of his homosexuality. The therapy was aimed at finding the causes of the break with his partner, how his partner could be approached to return or a new partner sought out, and the like. The therapist thus respected the patient's homosexual relationship and tried to help him find ways of increasing its satisfactions. After 12 sessions, the patient felt added security about his way of life and had made efforts to reestablish the liaison whose disruption had caused his cruise in the first place.

The strength of unacceptable impulses can be weakened through verbalization; the errant wish disappears.

Example 7: A woman, recovering from a florid post partum psychosis, told about forgetting several days in a row to pick up some duplicate car keys at the locksmith's. The original set may have been lost in a tussle to get her to the hospital when she became psychotic. Although no important material emerged, she picked the keys up the next day. Talking about forgetting them removed the inhibition.

Finally, the strength of the impulse's unacceptability can likewise be weakened through verbalization; a previously unacceptable impulse now becomes acceptable.

Example 8: A talented college student of 19 had twice attempted suicide because of feelings of futility, emptiness, and isolation. It soon emerged that his personal standards, despite his impressive talent and intellect, were impossibly high and admitted of no childishness or weakness. Any dependent gratification or close personal relationships were firmly forbidden. No wonder he felt his life futile. After two months of therapy, he began to see how his scorn of childishness concealed considerable wishes in that direction. As a result he considerably softened his standards for himself, though concurrently he noted an increasing productivity in his intellectual and artistic efforts. Most importantly, he took increased satisfaction in his interpersonal relationships. Therapy has continued for a year; he has consolidated and expanded many of the gains of the first two months.

FREQUENT OUTCOMES OF THE PRESENTING COMPLAINTS

In the early period of therapy, the patient's symptoms often change in intensity, quality, or importance. Five of the more common outcomes—transformations, if you will—of the presenting symptoms follow: (1) the symptom persists, but its importance changes; (2) the symptom disappears, without particular insight or affective discharge; (3) numerous symptoms diminish after common, underlying causes are found; (4) superficial insight and affective discharge occur; and (5) the symptom disappears, to reappear later in better perspective.

The original symptom may doggedly persist but therapy focuses on something else. Such a shift should be openly remarked upon.

Example 9: An obese married woman at the encouragement of an endocrinologist sought psychiatric help regarding her weight after failure of treatment at an endocrinology clinic. When, after several weeks, she began to dwell on a difficult marital situation, her husband was brought in. The marriage was slightly improved after several interviews. The wife's weight remained unchanged.

Symptoms frequently diminish without evidence of insight or affective discharge, especially in patients who have established transferences to therapists or institutions (2, 3). The passage of time, coupled with supportive measures, promotes the improvement.

Example 10: A widow of 57 was known to generations of residents of the psychiatric clinic. Every two years or so, she would become depressed and lose interest in her work, her reading, her friends, and her tennis. A supervisor, who had treated her several years before, advised a careful hearing of her story followed by kind but firm advice for her to keep up her apartment, her typing, and her tennis. He predicted that amidst considerable complaints that things still were not what they used to be, and with no insight whatsoever, she would return to her former level of functioning. His prediction was borne out in ten sessions.

Patients may come with several complaints that seem to them discrete, isolated, mystifying, and unpleasant occurrences in their emotional lives. After a few sessions these symptoms may emerge as superficial manifestations of current, unrecognized stresses (phenotypic), which in turn derive from nuclear, childhood conflicts (genotypic), as the following diagram and example illustrate. Furthermore, as recognition of the relationship of the symptoms to the current stresses and past conflicts burgeons, the symptoms and distress may recede spontaneously.

Example 11: A thrice-married secretary, aged 41, reported increasing nervousness, short-temperedness, crying spells, aches and pains in her head, neck, and pelvis, awkwardness ("arthritis") of her fingers, insomnia, and unwarranted anxiety about recurrence of a cervical carcinoma successfully treated eight years before. She came for evaluation and probable private referral.

The two major current stresses were her impending promotion as head secretary in her office and her relationship with her mother. She feared she could not assign work to the other women there without incurring their resentment, and she could not stand up to her boss, known to be a driver, whenever he was overdemanding. At home, her mother was becoming increasingly intrusive and demanding of the patient and her husband; the patient felt helpless to cope with her.

Her past included desertion by her father when she was young and by her first husband when she delivered her first child; a miserable second marriage for several years to an alcoholic, and the treated cervical carcinoma. At times of crisis, she turned to her mother, with whom she had always had a dependent ambivalent relationship. Yet she was a personable, intelligent woman, highly competent in her work.

The relationship between her current fears of abuse at the hands of a man (her boss) and of resentment from women whom she must supervise (the other secretaries and her intrusive mother), and her past experiences of desertion and abuse by men (father and husbands) and need to maintain a dependent relationship with women (mother) came out in the first three sessions, and her symptoms greatly diminished.

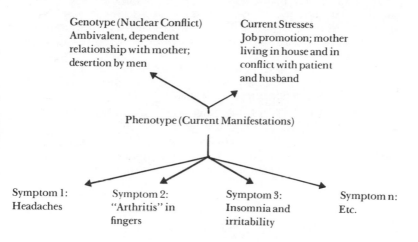

In the fourth session, while proudly telling how she had recently quietly refused her mother's suggestion of the proper perfume to use, she had a sudden twinge of pain in her neck—an anatomical pun that did not go unnoticed. Her therapist suggested "Step on a crack and break your mother's back?" She nodded, saying it was hard escaping from the feelings of a lifetime. Nevertheless, she felt she had by the end of the fifth session a great deal of understanding and mastery of the conflicts beneath her symptoms, which were almost gone. When she suggested stopping treatment, her therapist concurred.

Four months later she called to report the return of some symptoms. An appointment was scheduled. After the session had gone 20 minutes, her worry came out that her therapist would not be available if all her symptoms returned. The appointment was visible proof to the contrary and ended ten minutes later. Again, five months later, she feared a recurrence of her anxieties; another appointment quieted those fears.

A single, superficial insight coupled with an affective discharge—an emotional realization of the insight—may bring such improvement that the patient functions at a pre-symptom level and feels equal to meeting the challenges of his existence again. This is shown in Example 5, symbolized in the throwing of the groceries, and in Example 12.

Example 12: An unmarried nurse was referred by her supervisor to the employee health service for psychiatric evaluation because when working the midnight shift, she would call in sick at least once a week at 11:30 P.M., necessitating the supervisor's last minute search for a substitute. The illnesses, usually respiratory, were confirmed by physician's notes. On duty she worked well.

During her single session with the psychiatrist, it came out that the patient lived a lonely life, had few friends beyond her TV set, and felt close only to the grandparents who had raised her; they lived several hundred miles away. The psychiatrist asked her, "Who would take care of you if you really got seriously ill?" "No one," she replied sadly.

Her loneliness was discussed as was the idea that the frequent illnesses and trips to the doctor were the ways that she took care of herself as she wished someone else would. The patient's work record improved remarkably after this interview, though six months later she again began to miss work.

For the patient who feels deprived of dependent gratification, the acknowledgment of the deprivation and the awareness of the psychiatrist's compassion can prove beneficial.

The presenting symptoms may also disappear quickly, to reappear later in better perspective.

Example 13: A married woman aged 22 explained on her first visit that her worries about frigidity were dubbed minor by her gynecologist because "over 80% of all women have some degree of frigidity." No more was heard of this for six weeks, when in discussion of her marriage, the patient told of how she got sick every time her husband laid his hands upon her. Her original complaint thus was labeled as a ticket by which she entered therapy, so that she could talk about her marriage, and thereby paradoxically, discuss what she had only been able to hint at earlier, her abhorrence of sexuality.

This is an example of a symptom being used as a symbol for itself—frigidity as a symbol of sexual conflict.

COMMON DECISIONS NECESSITATED
BY CHANGES

These early transformations of symptoms can be handled by patient and therapist in several ways.

As symptoms disappear further search for their origins may be dropped, as in several examples. If the patient has re-established his equilibrium and wishes to terminate, therapy should be ended for the time being, provided his wish reveals no near-psychotic portions of denial, repression, or self-destruction. The therapist may indeed help re-enforce adaptive denial mechanisms (the denial of rage through homosexual acts, as in Example 6), and couple these with his expectation that the patient can indeed meet future situations more constructively. The patient's knowledge that the therapist has confidence in his ability to meet new situations successfully can measurably enhance the resources the patient brings to them.

Sometimes the patient will have a new perspective on his life and a burgeoning awareness of inner forces that precipitated his difficulty. He may wish to work primarily on his own, seeing the therapist now and then, to discuss how he has been doing. He may wish to return for brief episodes of active treatment when new and troublesome circumstances arise. Such visits provide a place to facilitate progress and maintain contact with the therapist.

In a few cases the patient may be ready for a more comprehensive, prolonged investigation of his life, as in Examples 1, 8, and 9. The goals shift from simple relief of symptoms or sharply focused attention on a single problem to broad self-knowledge. The shift should be made clear as it takes place so that both therapist and patient know why the patient is still coming, and further questions can be treated as true resistance.

SUMMARY

Relief of distress early in therapy allows patient and therapist to decide whether to continue therapy or to end, at least temporarily, with a sense of accomplishment. Therapists can enhance such brief therapy by the following: pursuing the question of why the patient comes for help now; allowing the patient to define his own needs for mental health; being active, spontaneous, and flexible as well as quiet and reflective; being willing to be used as a transference object; and being willing to terminate early. Attitudes counter to these, sometimes aided by difficulty in determining the worth of psychotherapeutic work, may impede brief therapy.

Psychodynamic mechanisms important in such symptom relief, and common shifts, transformations, or redefinitions of symptoms, are described. Therapy may end then, at least for the time being; future periods of therapy may be anticipated; or intensive, uncovering therapy may be started.

REFERENCES

1. Kalis, B., et al. Precipitating stress as a focus in psychotherapy. *Arch. Gen. Psychiat. (Chicago)*, 1961, 5, 219-226.
2. Reider, N. A type of transference to institutions. *Bull. Menninger Clin.*, 1953, 17, 58-63.
3. Wilmer, H. A. Transference to a medical center, *Calif. Med.*, 1962, 96, 173-180.

Chapter 6

Two Different Kinds of Psychotherapy of Short Duration

Peter E. Sifneos, M.D.

Misunderstandings and confusion have marked the use of the terms "brief" and "short-term" psychotherapy. A variety of therapeutic techniques which have little or nothing in common with each other except the short time interval have been treated as identical with no attempt to define and describe the specialized features of each type.

This attitude may be due to the preference of most psychiatrists for long-term psychotherapy. It may be true that long-term psychotherapy is a useful psychiatric treatment and, in certain instances, the only way to help a few seriously disturbed patients, but it is not true that it is invariably the psychotherapy of choice.

Against this trend there are a few notable exceptions (4-9, 13, 24, 25), and among these in my opinion the work of Alexander (1-3), Malan (10-12), and McGuire (14, 15) stands out.

The purpose of this paper, which is based on nine years of experience with patients treated in the Psychiatry Clinic of the Massachusetts General Hospital, is to present a conceptual frame of reference for two different kinds of short-term psychotherapy. The criteria for selection of patients, the specialized techniques utilized, and the follow-up findings will be discussed briefly.

It must be emphasized, first of all, that shortening the period of psychotherapy should not be an economic expedient to meet the growing demands for psychotherapeutic services in many communities, nor should it be viewed as a second-best alternative which aims at replacing long-term psychotherapy or circumventing psychoanalysis. Various kinds of short-term psychotherapy should be an addition to the psychiatrist's

Reprinted from *American Journal of Psychiatry*, 1967, **123**, 1069-1074, by permission of the publisher and the author. Copyright 1967, the American Psychiatric Association. Dr. Sifneos is Associate Director, Psychiatry Department, Beth Israel Hospital, Boston, Massachusetts, and Associate Clinical Professor of Psychiatry, Harvard Medical School.

armamentarium and should be offered to patients suffering from a variety of mild emotional illnesses, as well as to certain patients with more severe and protracted types of psychiatric disorders (11).

Because they are offered to different types of patients and are technically dissimilar, psychotherapies of short-term duration may be divided into two types: (1) *anxiety-provoking* or dynamic; and (2) *anxiety-suppressive* or supportive.

ANXIETY-PROVOKING PSYCHOTHERAPY

Similar in theory to psychoanalytic or dynamic psychotherapy and offered to individuals who have some strengths of character, this kind of treatment emphasizes that a certain degree of anxiety is necessary during the interview because it motivates the reluctant patient to understand the nature of his emotional conflicts, to recognize the reactions that he utilizes to deal with them, and to enable him to have a corrective emotional experience. Anxiety generated during the interview may be used as a tool in assisting the patient to change his maladaptive behavior and to attain a state of improved emotional functioning.

Anxiety-provoking psychotherapy is goal oriented and in most cases can be: (1) *short-term therapy* (18), which I define in this paper as lasting anywhere from two months to one year, with an average of four months; or (2) *crisis intervention* (21), defined as lasting up to two months. These time intervals are not arbitrary and are mentioned simply as guidelines. Only rarely may they be extended over longer periods of time. Psychoanalysis is, of course, anxiety-provoking psychotherapy of long-term duration.

Short-term Anxiety-provoking
Psychotherapy

This type of psychotherapy is offered to patients selected according to the following criteria (20): (1) the patient must be of above average intelligence, as demonstrated by work or educational achievement; (2) he must have had at least one meaningful relationship with another person during his lifetime; (3) he must be flexible and able to interact with the evaluating psychiatrist by expressing some affect during the interview; (4) he must have a specific chief complaint; and (5) he must be motivated to work hard during his treatment and have fairly realistic expectations of what can be achieved.

It may appear that patients who fulfill our criteria for short-term anxiety-provoking psychotherapy are so healthy that they do not require any treatment at all. Quick value judgments about the triviality of the patient's difficulties should be avoided, however, and emphasis should be placed upon how serious the emotional disorder is and how the patient who is suffering from it can function before and after treatment (20). Before the patient is accepted for psychotherapy, his motivation for treatment must be further assessed in a final goal-setting interview (23). This is crucial prognostically.

Important as selection criteria may be, it is realized that to assess some of the points that have been outlined is not easy. Sometimes one discovers the seriousness of certain narcissistic, masochistic, dependent, or acting-out tendencies only after psychotherapy has begun.

Case 1. We saw a 35-year-old married banker who complained of anxiety when his boss talked with him about the prospects of his becoming a vice-president. He said he had been contented with his job and did not want any more responsibility. This characteristic dated back to his relationship with his father, whom he had always tried to please, and had continued subsequently with people in authority.

He liked to view himself as a "good boy," and mentioned that as an adolescent he had had syphilophobia without ever having had sexual intercourse. He remembered that his mother had reassured him about this but cautioned him not to talk to his father about it. He was fairly happy in his marriage but was always uneasy about sexual relations, which he tried to avoid whenever possible. This seemingly passive streak was considered ominous, but because he fulfilled our criteria and seemed to be functioning reasonably well, he was accepted for treatment.

In his second interview he announced that another man had been made the vice-president of the bank, and he claimed that his anxiety had disappeared. From then on he talked in his interviews only about pleasant memories, such as "basking in the sun during his vacation." His passivity had been underestimated during the evaluation and as soon as his anxiety disappeared his motivation to understand himself vanished. He developed no understanding of himself; therefore his therapy proved to be ineffective.

Requirements and technique (18, 20, 22)

The interviews are face-to-face, once a week, lasting for about 45 minutes. The therapist encourages the establishment of rapport with the patient and tries early to create a therapeutic alliance. He utilizes the patient's positive transference feelings explicitly as the main therapeutic tool. His specific goal is to concentrate on a circumscribed area of unresolved emotional conflicts underlying the patient's symptoms. He actively bypasses character traits such as masochism, excessive passivity, and dependence which give rise to therapeutic complications.

The therapist takes advantage of the fairly lengthy time lag in the appearance of the transference neurosis in relatively healthy patients in order to perform his therapeutic task. Thus he avoids its development. His emphasis is on problem solving so that such techniques as have been learned by the patient can be utilized effectively by him in the future after therapy has been terminated. The treatment ends early, when the patient starts giving hints that the goals of therapy have been achieved, or warnings that he wants to prolong therapy.

Follow-up

This is a summary of the patients' statements about the results of treatment (18, 20). They usually point to only moderate symptomatic relief. Their original expectations of the results of psychotherapy have become more modest and realistic (16). They describe psychotherapy as "a new learning experience," "unique," "rare," or "unusual." The level of their self-esteem seems to have been raised. They show that a limited dynamic change has occurred with the substitution of a new defense mechanism for an old one. There is evidence of problem solving and acquisition of new adaptive patterns. Those who show these changes rarely return for further treatment.

Crisis Intervention (21)

An emotional crisis (17) is defined as an "intensification of a painful state which has the potential of becoming a turning-point for better or for worse." It usually follows a particularly stressful event which induces some individuals, who are otherwise emotionally healthy, to seek immediate assistance. Three factors are required to estimate properly the intensity of the emotional crisis: (1) the history of the hazardous situation which led to its development; (2) a precipitating event which produced the sudden intensification of anxiety; and (3) a series of unsuccessful attempts to cope with this anxiety. With these factors in mind, the criteria for selection of patients are similar to those used for short-term anxiety-provoking psychotherapy.

Requirements and technique

Emotional crisis intervention focuses specifically on the resolution of the emotional crisis, using anxiety-provoking techniques. It emphasizes: (1) the quick establishment of rapport and transformation of the therapeutic work into a learning experience; (2) the utilization of the patient's positive transference, but not, however, as explicitly as in short-term anxiety-provoking psychotherapy due to the shorter time interval; (3) the active review and understanding by the patient of the steps that have led to the development of the crisis itself; (4) the challenging and minimizing by the psychiatrist of action taken on the part of the patient which the doctor considers to be antitherapeutic and which may lead to difficulties in the future; (5) the learning by the patient to anticipate situations that are likely to produce unpleasant emotions. He does this by comparing his present problems with potentially similar experiences likely to occur in the future and thus prepares himself to meet future trouble by these problem-solving rehearsals. The therapeutic intervention is terminated after a few appointments.

Follow-up

The patients usually overcome the emotional crisis that brought them to the clinic. Some feel that they are better equipped to deal with future difficulties, having achieved a better level of emotional functioning than that which existed prior to the onset of their difficulties. They are able to anticipate. They claim to have been taught to solve problems.

The differences in technique between these two kinds of anxiety-provoking psychotherapy are a matter of degree. In short-term psychotherapy the patient's transference is utilized systematically to achieve a limited dynamic change. This is an ambitious goal. In crisis intervention the therapist encounters his patient before his emotional conflicts crystallize into a psychiatric symptom and helps the patient learn to anticipate and solve future problems. The goal here is on prevention.

In sum, anxiety-provoking psychotherapy is both a therapeutic and a learning experience for the patient.

ANXIETY-SUPPRESSIVE PSYCHOTHERAPY

This kind of psychotherapy, offered to severely disturbed patients, aims to decrease or eliminate anxiety by use of supportive techniques such as reassurance or environmental manipulation, with or without drugs. It may be: (1) *brief* therapy, lasting anywhere from two months to one year; or (2) *crisis support,* lasting up to two months. It may also be of long-term duration, such as anaclitic therapy (19).

Brief Anxiety-Suppressive Psychotherapy

Patients with character defects who give a history of recent and rapid decompensation from a precarious level of emotional functioning, and who complain of lifelong psychological difficulties and poor interpersonal relationships, are selected according to the following criteria: (1) ability to maintain a job; (2) a strong appeal for help; (3) recognition that these symptoms are psychological in origin; and (4) willingness to cooperate in psychotherapy.

Requirements and technique

The therapist sees the patient in face-to-face interviews once, twice, or even three times a week lasting anywhere from a few minutes to an hour. He tries to convince the patient that he is eager to help and allows him to talk freely without interruption. He "lends himself" to the patient by taking over some of his decision-making functions. He helps him to understand the ways in which he handled his feelings when faced with hazardous situations. He predicts the patient's future behavior on the basis of his past performances and thus prepares him to avoid future difficulties. He uses appropriate medication when necessary. The following example illustrates these points.

Case 2. A 24-year-old man who had been an overt homosexual since the age of 16 entered the Psychiatry Clinic complaining of panic, inability to work, and thoughts of killing himself as a way out of his misery. These symptoms had appeared as soon as his homosexual partner, with whom he had been living, left him following an argument. He had a history of lifelong emotional difficulties and had been admitted to mental hospitals on two occasions because of suicidal attempts. Both of his parents had died in an automobile accident when he was two years old, and he had been brought up by relatives.

He was an intelligent high school graduate who had a fairly steady work pattern and seemed to be eager for help. In twice-a-week psychotherapy an attempt was made to relieve the acute distress over the loss of his boyfriend. His reaction pattern to previous losses was reviewed. He was complimented for seeking help in the clinic rather than resorting to suicide. The prospect of future troubles was discussed in detail. After a while, he started to feel better and returned to work. He was able to talk about his angry feelings at having been abandoned and soon established a new homosexual relationship. In four months he was symptom free.

Follow-up

Although we have not studied the follow-up findings of this group as extensively, there seems to be: marked symptomatic relief, some evidence of ability to avoid situations that give rise to the difficulty, a tendency to view the clinic rather than the therapist as the supportive agent, no evidence of dynamic change, and a tendency to return to the hospital at times of future difficulties.

Crisis Support

Patients similar to those selected for brief anxiety-suppressive psychotherapy and facing an acute crisis are offered crisis support. Lasting up to two months, this therapy attempts to eliminate as quickly as possible the factors that are responsible for the patient's decompensation and to help him overcome the acutely traumatic situation in which he finds himself. The emphasis here is also on using anxiety-suppressive techniques. Drugs are given freely. The patient is seen frequently for short intervals, depending on his needs. The follow-up findings are similar to those obtained in brief anxiety-suppressive psychotherapy.

DISCUSSION

It should be evident that these two different kinds of psychotherapy, anxiety-provoking and anxiety-suppressive, should not be compared to each other since they are neither technically similar nor offered to the same type of patient population. On the other hand, every effort should be made to validate separately the results of each kind by research studies.

In the last four years we have set up a research project to appraise the results of short-term anxiety-provoking psychotherapy. More recently we selected 40 patients according to the criteria already set forth. We designated alternately 20 as experimental and 20 as control patients, subdivided them into age groups of 17 to 21 and 22 to 40, and matched them according to age and sex. Ten are males and 30 females.

All are seen by two independent evaluators and are given an MMPI test. The control patients wait for approximately the same time that it takes their counterparts to be treated. After the end of therapy of each experimental patient, both he and his control counterpart are again seen by the same evaluators and given the MMPI once more. The control patients are then taken into treatment. Every effort is being made to follow up these patients every six months for at least two years.

Since this work is ongoing, the findings will not be presented formally at this time. It can be stated, however, that although the difficulties of such a research project are many, it appears that our original impressions of the results of short-term anxiety-provoking psychotherapy are being substantiated by this more systematic approach.

SUMMARY

In this paper two technically different kinds of short-term psychotherapy have been presented. The *anxiety-provoking* type is similar in theory to psychoanalytic therapy and focuses on the resolution of emotional conflicts that underlie the patients' symptoms. It is offered to patients with well-circumscribed neurotic symptoms, selected according to specific criteria. Depending on its length of time, it is subdivided into: (1) *short-term* therapy, which emphasizes problem solving and usually achieves a limited dynamic change; and (2) *crisis intervention*, which helps the patient to overcome an emotional crisis quickly.

Anxiety-suppressive psychotherapy is offered to a selected group of seriously disturbed patients who have recently decompensated and produces symptomatic relief by use of all sorts of supportive techniques. Depending on its length of time it is also subdivided into((1) *brief* therapy; and (2) *crisis support*. In follow-up, the patients seem to benefit in different ways from these two kinds of short-term psychotherapeutic techniques.

REFERENCES

1. Alexander, F. Principles and techniques of briefer psychotherapeutic procedures. In M. S. Wortis, M. Herman, and C. Hare (Eds.), *Psychiatric treatment*. Baltimore: Williams & Wilkins, 1953.
2. Alexander, F. The dynamics of psychotherapy in the light of learning theory. *Amer. J. Psychiat.*, 1963, **120**, 440-449.
3. Alexander, F., and French, T. *Psychoanalytic therapy*. New York: Ronald Press, 1946.
4. Bellak, L. *Emergency psychotherapy and brief psychotherapy*. New York: Grune & Stratton, 1965.
5. Gillman, R. D. Brief psychotherapy: A psychoanalytic view. *Amer. J. Psychiat.*, 1965, **122**, 601-611.
6. Hollender, M. H. Selection of patients for definitive forms of psychotherapy. *Arch. Gen. Psychiat.*, 1964, **10**, 361-370.
7. Knight, R. P. Evaluation of the results of psychoanalytic therapy. *Amer. J. Psychiat.*, 1941, **98**, 434-439.
8. Knight, R. P. A critique of the present status of psychotherapies. *Bull. N.Y. Acad. Med.*, 1949, **25**, 100-115.
9. Knight, R. P. *An evaluation of psychotherapeutic techniques, psychoanalytic psychiatry and psychology*. New York: International Universities Press, 1954.
10. Malan, D. H. On assessing the results of psychotherapy. *Brit. J. Med. Psychol.*, 1959, **32**, 86-105.
11. Malan, D. H. *A study of brief psychotherapy*. Springfield, Ill.: Charles C. Thomas, 1963.
12. Malan, D. H.: personal communications.

13. Masserman, J. H. (Ed.), *Current psychiatric therapies*. Vols. **1-6**. New York: Grune & Stratton, 1961-1965.

14. McGuire, M. T. The process of short-term insight psychotherapy. *J. Nerv. Ment. Dis.*, 1965, **141**, 83-95.

15. McGuire, M. T. The process of short-term insight psychotherapy. II. Content expectations and structure. *J. Nerv. Ment. Dis.*, 1965, **141**, 219-230.

16. Sifneos, P. E. Phobic patient with dyspnea: Short-term psychotherapy. *Amer. Practitioner*, 1958, **9**, 947-952.

17. Sifneos, P. E. A concept of emotional crisis. *Ment. Hyg.*, 1960, **44**, 169-179.

18. Sifneos, P. E. Dynamic psychotherapy in a psychiatry clinic. In J. H. Masserman (Ed.), *Current psychiatric therapies*, Vol. 1. New York: Grune & Stratton, 1961, pp. 168-175.

19. Sifneos, P. E. *Ascent from chaos: A psychosomatic case study*. Cambridge, Mass.: Harvard University Press, 1964.

20. Sifneos, P. E. Seven years' experience with short-term dynamic psychotherapy. In *Sixth International Congress of Psychotherapy, London, 1964: Selected lectures*. New York: S. Karger, 1965, pp. 127-135.

21. Sifneos, P. E. Crisis psychotherapy. In J. H. Masserman (Ed.), Current psychiatric therapies, Vol. 6. New York: Grune & Stratton, 1966, pp. 125-128.

22. Sifneos, P. E. Psychoanalytically oriented short-term dynamic or anxiety-provoking psychotherapy for mild obsessional neuroses. *Psychiat. Quart.*, 1966, **40**, 271-282.

23. Sifneos, P. E. The motivational process: A selection and prognostic criterion for psychotherapy of short duration. Paper presented at the Fourth World Congress of Psychiatry, Madrid, Spain, September 1966.

23. Stone, L. Psychoanalysis and brief psychotherapy. *Psychoanal. Quart.*, 1951, **20**, 215-236.

25. Wolberg, L. R. *Short-term psychotherapy*. New York: Grune & Stratton, 1965.

Chapter 7

A Concept of Ego-Oriented Psychotherapy

Mary A. Sarvis, M.D., Sally Dewees, M.S.,
and Ruth F. Johnson, M.S.S.

This paper reports our efforts to formulate a concept of flexible, relatively time-limited, ego-directed psychotherapy. Although, in the settings in which we have developed this concept, philosophical and expedient motives—for example, responsibility to a large, relatively fixed patient population with equal rights to service—have been important, we do not feel that this type of ego-oriented psychotherapy is a method of desperation, but rather one of choice for a wide range of patients.

Much of the increasing interest among members of the psychological disciplines—psychiatrists, psychiatric social workers, and psychologists—has been in terms of differentiating goal-limited psychotherapy from psychoanalysis, trying to separate dynamic from supportive goals, and trying to clarify ways in which treatment might be shortened without significant loss of therapeutic effectiveness. Our own initial interest in this problem was stimulated by job situations which forced us to differentiate treatment goals because of the wide range of motivation and need demonstrated by different patients.

We worked, separately or together, with military personnel in transit, in a public school guidance department, on a research unit in brief psychotherapy, in the psychiatric clinic of a student health department, and on the psychiatric service of a prepaid health plan. In all of these agencies, some kind of service was felt to be obligatory and intake could not easily be limited or closed. We were impressed by the large number of patients who could make use of a psychotherapeutic transaction when it was offered promptly and without predetermined criteria for motivation or readiness.

Reprinted from *Psychiatry*, 1958, **22**, 277-287, by special permission of The William Alanson White Psychiatric Foundation, Inc., and the authors. Copyright 1958, The William Alanson White Psychiatric Foundation. Dr. Sarvis was a member of the Department of Psychiatry, Cowell Hospital, Berkeley, California. Mrs. Dewees is a staff member of the Student Health Service, Department of Psychiatry, Cowell Hospital, University of California, Berkeley. Miss Johnson recently retired as Chief Social Worker at Cowell Hospital.

THEORETICAL FRAMEWORK

The philosophical attitude underlying our concept of therapy is that of *process*. We feel that, throughout life, a person is involved in a continuing process of adaptive or maladaptive integrations and that, at various times, psychotherapeutic intervention may be useful to him. Actually, of course, the concept of the adaptive-maladaptive process is inherent even in the most intensive treatment. Freud, in *Analysis Terminable and Interminable*, refers to the impossibility of analyzing latent conflicts, and in many papers discusses the need for further analysis in the face of new life situations or new dynamic stresses, emphasizing how much the stable outcome of analysis may depend on the future life circumstances of the patient (2). In fact, the lifelong process of adaptive-maladaptive integration seems self-evident and is widely subscribed to in theory. Yet, in practice, this conceptual model is not widely followed. On the contrary, psychological disturbances are often treated like infectious diseases, in which the suitable approach is to make the diagnosis—in the manner of identifying the organism—hopefully to apply some specific and definitive therapy, and to discharge the patient, with luck, as cured, in the sense of free of disease. Both administrative arrangements and tacit attitudes of therapists operate to maintain an 'infectious disease' model of psychotherapy.

Granted the concept of process and the fact that all therapy is limited to some degree at a given time in its exploration of personality, how can the differences of level, goal, and intensity of therapy further be conceptualized? We believe that a useful distinction can be made between psychoanalysis—and intensive, analytically oriented psychotherapy—with their *relatively* unlimited goals, and the *limited therapies*, one form of which is described in this paper.

In psychoanalysis, the goal is the sytematic elaboration, understanding, and interpretation of the patient's total psychic structure, insofar as this is possible. This is achieved by the induction and systematic working through of a *regressive transference neurosis* by the use of, or in conjunction with, techniques which result in a focus on irrational, repressed, warded-off unconscious processes. These techniques are free association, frequent visits, relative anonymity and invisibility of the analyst, and so on. The eventual aim, whatever parameters (or deviations from the interpretive method) are introduced, is resolution of conflicts by interpretation alone—that is, the analysis of all parameters.

Intensive, analytically oriented psychotherapy has a similar, although perhaps more limited goal—limited either in the extensiveness of characterological exploration or by the introduction of some unanalyzed parameters. In some situations, the frequency of interviews is less than in classical analysis, and within this limitation the patient's motivation and tolerance for anxiety do not permit essentially analytic goals. In other situations, the intensity and duration of treatment are similar to classical analysis, but the nature of the patient's problems demands modifications of analytic technique. But in terms of our discussion here, both analysis and intensive, analytically oriented psychotherapy will be considered relatively unlimited or nonfocused therapies.

Despite the fact that the most important criteria for these relatively unlimited therapies are dynamic—for example, in terms of the induction of a regressive transference neurosis—rather than mechanical, in terms, for instance, of frequency of visits, the mechanics of the treatment situation do exert a limiting factor at the extremes. Thus, a patient seen once a month cannot be analyzed. Empirical evidence suggests that, to make the dynamic goals of analysis possible, many or most patients must be seen four or more times a week, some patients three times a week, and a few, perhaps, twice weekly—although here it seems more likely that analytical goals are modified. Psychotherapy once a week seems to exclude psychoanalytic goals in the sense described. Obviously this does not mean that once-a-week psychotherapy precludes *insight* as a goal; however, the mechanical situation does not permit the systematic neurosis. The therapy has become *limited* with respect to systematic character analysis. If the treatment goals of once-a-week psychotherapy are not conceptualized in their own right, a sort of attenuated or diluted analysis may be attempted, leading to chaotic regressive transferences without the technical situation which would permit the constructive utilization and working-through of these regressive manifestations.

Perhaps the goals of limited psychotherapy have not been adequately conceptualized because it has seemed less respectable than psychoanalysis; if this is the case, it seems unhealthy for both. Another source of confusion may lie in the lack of distinction between, first, utilizing psychoanalytic insight or knowledge in therapy, and, second, operating in a technically psychoanalytic way in all treatment situations. The former, we believe, is the basic framework for all kinds and levels of therapy, whether the primary goals are dynamic insight, support, consolidation of identification, systematic character analysis, or any other. If anything, the therapist attempting limited psychotherapy needs to have a greater fund of psychoanalytic knowledge rather than less, particularly if he strives for dynamic insight as a therapeutic goal. However, this is not to be confused with treating all patients as if they were in psychoanalysis, regardless of the goal or mechanical limitations of treatment.

There have been various ways in which the range or goal of limited therapy has been conceptualized. Rogers and his followers limit the range of what the therapist does by concentrating largely on reflecting back and clarifying what the patient has said (5). Pre-set time limits have been used to focus psychotherapeutic transactions, with or without the philosophical concept which Rank emphasized when he advocated setting a termination date at the outset of treatment (4). Felix Deutsch, in sector analysis, used free asssociation around the dynamically pertinent aspects of the material elicited in the initial interviews (1).

MAIN CHARACTERISTICS OF EGO-ORIENTED PSYCHOTHERAPY

Our concept of ego-oriented psychotherapy begins with the assumption that a patient requests psychotherapeutic help at some point of disruption of his adaptive-maladaptive integration. This disruption is not necessarily an external crisis or a dramatic precipitating event, yet *something*—usually, but not always, traumatic—has occurred in the life of a patient which leads him to request technical assistance at a given time. We believe that many patients, if seen promptly, can be helped to achieve an adaptive integration out of the disruptive experience with the kind of psychotherapy being described. The crucial question to be kept in mind is what brought the patient to the therapist *at this time*. Obviously this question becomes meaningless if the patient is not seen promptly. The administrative situation should also permit maximum flexibility in handling so that the frequency of visits may be daily for a time, weekly, monthly, or whatever seems useful to patient and therapist. It must be possible for the patient to return as readily as he originally came.

Ego-directed psychotherapy has two further important characteristics. First, both patient and therapist know that it is time-limited. Second, the therapist tries actively to empathize with, conceptualize, and interpret the patient's material—particularly preconscious trends; the current therapeutic interaction; and the evidence of transference, in terms of ongoing integrative adaptations rather than toward regressiveness. For instance, transference distortions which are irrelevant to the current problem are corrected realistically; they are not allowed to proliferate in a regressive direction. Within these two general principles, time-limitation and ego-direction, the course of a given therapeutic transaction is determined dynamically and not externally: there are no predetermined time limits, the therapist does not restrict his attention to current material or to a certain range of operations with the patient, such as reflecting, he is not engaged primarily in supportive or 'repressive' maneuvers, and so on.

Perhaps we should emphasize that this concept of therapy does not mean that the therapist focuses on or sets a treatment goal arbitrarily in terms of his independent estimate of the patient's psychopathology. The focusing in a given psychotherapeutic transaction is a *process* arising out of the interchange between patient and therapist. It is patient-determined in that it depends on data given by the patient—that is, what is usable or accessible to the patient, and, hence, to the therapist, at a given time. It is therapist-determined in that the therapist is responsible for trying actively to perceive preconscious trends in the patient and to begin focusing them with the patient in an ego-directed fashion, from the earliest moments of treatment. The therapist's reactions or focusing must be at the level of tentativeness which suits the concrete data, but he is trying from the beginning to react to, or clarify, the preconscious trends which appear in the data. It follows that the initial interview is not sharply differentiated from later psychotherapeutic transactions.

In our opinion, the initial interview should be essentially a therapeutic experience for the patient rather than primarily a diagnostic or administrative task. The therapist should be free to listen, without preconceptions, to what the patient has to say about himself and his reasons for seeking treatment at a particular time. Excursions into past history or anything else before the patient has had an opportunity to discuss current conflicts make little sense to the patient and often encourage magical fantasies of the cure to be expected. As the genetic roots become pertinent to the task at hand, they will begin to unfold in a meaningful way. We believe that usually the patient must first find acceptance of how the current problem feels to him, or be helped to work through whatever critical resistances are keeping him from communicating these feelings. This follows from the importance we place upon considering with a patient in active terms his reason for coming to the therapist at a particular time, beginning with him at the point of his current 'crisis,' be this internal or external, acute or cumulative in nature. A therapist's philosophical convictions—and consequent attitudes in treatment—in this regard are critical in determining the initial direction of therapy and its subsequent course. Whether or not the patient is to be transferred to another therapist for further treatment, our feeling is that ego-oriented, adaptive integration is promoted and unnecessary regressive situations are averted, if the initial interviewer is free to proceed in this dynamically oriented way.

Perhaps we should explain that when we describe ego-directed therapy as focusing forward in terms of adaptive integrations, 'adaptive' does not mean 'adjusted,' in the sense of conformity to external expectations. Rather we refer to an ego-adaptive or an integrative synthesis of past, present, and future in terms of the patient's long-term goals, which should include—but not be circumscribed by—external pressures upon him.

Perhaps we should also emphasize again that this concept does not mean arbitrary restriction of the data or of the therapeutic transaction to the current precipitating situation. It means that the therapist, first, listens to the patient's account of his life and his current situation, and, second, observes, responds to, and interprets the interpersonal transaction in therapy and the manifestions of transference, with his attention focused on *utilizing* this material in terms of the present adaptive possibilities. Interactions and interpretations are designed explicitly to avoid *unnecessary*—in the sense of extraneous to the current goal—regressive transference situations. The therapist makes an active effort to listen for a *pattern* in the patient's life—which is preconscious—to empathize with its *emotional* meaning to the patient, and then to utilize this emotionally meaningful pattern in an ego-directed way. He begins tentatively to direct or redirect the transaction, or to focus with the patient on the relevant data, as soon as the emotional pattern makes imaginative—not intellectual—sense to him, rather than to wait for it to be crystallized out in the unfocused productions of the patient.

CASE ILLUSTRATIONS

Some case fragments may help to clarify the concepts and approaches in this type of ego-oriented therapy.

Case 1: A 19-year-old college student felt that he should be making better grades, and was referred by the college doctor, who believed that emotional problems might be keeping him from doing so. The patient did not seem overtly anxious or depressed; his manner was naive, compliant, and singularly undefensive. In the first interview, the therapist felt that the patient's evaluation of his general situation was realistic and responded accordingly. At the end of the interview, the therapist suggested another session, but without raising the question of continuing therapy. The patient's realistic assessment was confirmed in the second interview, when he came in saying, "You know, I've been thinking and I've decided maybe I'm not doing so badly after all. Let's face it! Some people are just smarter than other people and, in order to make decent grades, I have to spend more time studying than most of my friends."

In the first interview, the patient had talked about his parents and his sister, with whom he had close, warm relationships, and of life on their farm. Gradually he expressed his loneliness on the huge campus, in the competitive college atmosphere, which stood out in confusing and disturbing contrast to his sheltered background. In the second interview, he said that he felt somehow better able to handle these things after having had a chance to "yak" about himself and to find out that he wasn't so odd after all. Diffidently, he added that maybe some of his fraternity brothers had the same feelings or, at least, might understand his having them.

The therapist, while suggesting that he come back at any time, felt that it would be a mistake to encourage him to continue in therapy at that time. The patient had his share of personality distortions; indeed, he had come in because of his lack of confidence in his own judgment, his overcompliance with benign authority, and the lack he felt of any nurturant person in a busy and impersonal college atmosphere. The therapist felt that if he had been encouraged to assume the "identity of a patient," he would have settled down happily to a long period of therapy, with a lifelong pattern of compulsive compliance emerging as the primary transference resistance to be worked through. He might, in the future, decide that such an extended period of therapy was necessary, but his emergent conflicts at this time did not seem to warrant it. Meanwhile, he had apparently been able to shift from a defensive impasse to a productive direction in which he could take autonomous responsibility in his search for a personal identity. He had made productive use of a brief therapeutic encounter in which he found acceptance of what had seemed to be unacceptable feelings and gained renewed confidence in his ability to pursue his own aims in his own way; at the same time he dared share more of himself with the people of importance in his current life situation.

From a technical point of view, it will be seen that both the patient's conscious motivation and his characterological structure would have made it easy for him to comply with a prescription of long-term or intensive treatment. Yet, in the first interview, the therapist's impression that the patient's presentation of his situation was relatively undistorted and realistic permitted the patient to work through a *preconscious* attitude—the explicit recognition that his loneliness and unsureness of his own values in the new situation had made him anxious and that this anxiety had been transferred on to questions about his intellectual functioning, where his own estimation had previously been realistic. He then submissively complied with the doctor's referral for psychiatric evaluation of his "learning problem." Therapy was terminated on the basis of this insight. In terms of our previous discussion of how focusing is done, it will be seen in this case that the patient set the goal by his preconscious ability to integrate, and the therapist collaborated in this goal by facilitating integration rather than by responding to the conscious compliance or to the unconscious ramifications of the characterological attitude.

Case 2: A patient came in complaining of interpersonal difficulties, particularly his inability to form durable, emotionally meaningful relations with women. These difficulties were related in large part to his counterphobic attitudes and his need to tailor his relations with women to suit. Over the course of two years, he was seen in four separate psychotherapeutic transactions for a total of thirty sessions. The primary focus in therapy was on the meaning of his counterphobic attitudes, their history, and their influence on his current life. During each treatment period, the patient would, after a few therapy sessions, form a new relationship with a woman and wish to leave treatment (counterphobically) to see how it would work out.

In spite of the resistance and acting out implicit in this, the therapist felt that the patient was gaining increasing insight into the emotional meaning of his counterphobic attitude. Each successive relationship he involved himself in during treatment seemed to be one in which he could be a little more intimate and realistic. Finally, in the fourth period in therapy, when he again talked of interrupting, the therapist pointed out the counterphobic mechanisms operating in therapy itself, suggested that these could be discussed rather than acted on, and proposed that the patient continue in treatment for a time with the goal of clarifying them. This was done, and both the defensive and the integrative meanings of previous interruptions could be utilized therapeutically.*

In this case, flexible handling enabled the patient periodically to utilize therapeutic understanding, while, at other times, he tried to work through his problem in his actual relationships. This represented acting out in terms of his characterological defense; at the same time, he also made progress in modifying this defense or "working through" his problem.

Case 3: To the question on the face sheet, "What brought you to the clinic at this time?" one patient answered, "Compulsive masturbation." This man was a rather rigid, externalizing young business executive, who said that his symptom had gone on for many years and that he had sought psychiatric help because an Air Force physician had recommended it. He minimixed difficulties in his marriage or current life and presented the symptom in an isolated way. It seemed that he would need very long-term, intensive treatment, for which he was not at all motivated. However, in the initial interview, when he was asked to tell about his background, he described a situation which made his symptom emotionally meaningful to the therapist. His parents were divorced when he was very young; he and his mother lived with the maternal grandparents. The grandfather was a weak, ineffectual figure in the household, the grandmother was domineering, and the mother combined to a striking degree an officially repressive attitude toward the adolescent sexual interests of the patient with almost overt seductiveness and interest in his sexual development and experiences.

In this context, the therapist could say, "It doesn't seem surprising that you have mixed feelings about women." It will be seen that this comment, first, tried to shift the patient's attention from his symptoms to his as yet undisclosed difficulties with his wife, and, second, utilized the emotional pattern of a genetic (adolescent) situation to focus on the meaning of a current relationship. The patient responded by discussing

---

* The patient has continued to come in intermittently to date.

his dissatisfactions in the marriage, his interpersonal sexual problems, and the exacerbation in his symptom which had occurred on an Air Force base where there was much inducement to transient relations with sexually stimulating women. This situation had led him to talk of his problems with the Air Force physician.

In view of the patient's ambivalence about psychological help, it was suggested only that he come in again to talk things over further; later four sessions were suggested. Near the end of the fourth interview, he said that he felt he needed to come in once more because he had come to realize that he was prejudiced against women; he had become aware that although he was very tolerant of the masturbation in his own case, he would be extremely upset if he discovered that his wife were doing such a thing. These prejudiced attitudes were explored in the fifth interview, and the patient terminated with the explicit goal of trying to understand and work through more satisfactory emotional relations with his wife. It is interesting to note that, by the end of therapy, he also reported much less tension and improved function on the job, although difficulties in that situation had not been much discussed; he had only mentioned peripherally that he was tense with male authorities.

This case illustrates the avoidance of a regressive transference situation and the utilization of genetic experiences—when the therapist can get the feeling of the emotional pattern or meaning to the patient—in terms of the ongoing adaptive process. If, in the intial interview, the patient had denied any historic difficulties in the same way that he minimized his problems with his wife, then an ego-oriented therapeutic transaction would not have been possible. Perhaps it should be emphasized that the therapist had to be quite active in questioning the patient for exact, concrete details of his genetic experiences and relationships, before the emotional meaning became clear. The patient was not an introspective person and tended to give a terse account of the external circumstances. The therapist found these suggestive and encouraged concrete, detailed exploration until the emotional pattern was clarified. Yet, as suggested above, if this emotionally meaningful material had been massively defended against or deeply unconscious, the patient could not have produced the relevant data in the early interviews, however much the therapist encouraged him.

Case 4: An overtly passive, dependent young man came in because of feelings of depression, hopelessness, and lack of direction, which had existed for as long as he could remember. As the therapist listened to what he had to say and observed the way in which he presented himself, certain chronic depressive attitudes and regressive expectations became clear. It seemed that if the patient were allowed to proceed without focusing, he would utilize many therapeutic hours ruminating about his hard lot in life and his feelings of ineffectuality in coping with it. The therapist felt not only that this would be to little purpose but that it would actively serve the negative interests of the patient's resistance to change and would work against his assuming the responsibility of which he was so afraid.

In addition, it seemed that a passive attitude on the therapist's part would reinforce the patient's demand for transference gratification and increase his unrealistic expectations with regard to the results of therapy. If one does not intervene in such a case, the implication to the patient is that the therapist accepts his presentation of himself as the whole of his reality, approves of his regarding things in this light, and eventually will fulfill his demand for an omnipotent, all-giving parent who accepts his helplessness and his need on unconditional terms. In short, with this particular patient, it was felt that nonintervention would have the direct result of stimulating regressive tendencies, developing unnecessary, distorted transference attitudes, and thereby militating against the understanding and mastery that the patient might achieve if therapy could be reoriented and maintained on the ego level.

The therapist pointed out to the patient that he talked about himself and his circumstances as though he felt no hope, and asked if this was really how it felt to him. Such an attitude had been so chronic and totalistic to the patient that the doubt implied by this question was a new idea to him. With even this small distance established from the taken-for-granted nature of his life-view, the direction of therapy shifted. The patient gradually began to think of himself as a *person* with problems, not just as a hopeless problem. The therapist tried actively to mobilize whatever latent forces existed within the patient for responding as an active agent in his own behalf, rather than reinforcing his image of himself as a passive victim, thus justifying his failures and at the same time wrecking any chance of the success he wanted so much. As it happened, this man was seen in circumstances which precluded intensive therapy or analysis involving the systematic working through of regressive transference phenomena. However, if these limitations had not existed, the therapist still would have felt that briefer, ego-directed therapy was the treatment of choice for this patient at this time.

Case 5: A very anxious man was referred by his internist because of anxiety symptoms which had persisted acutely for over six months. He had lost his business, at least partly because of his symptoms, was scarcely able to work, even at such tasks as painting his house, and often was totally incapacitated by his symptoms. The initial sessions were focused on clarifying and helping the patient to accept the fact that he was extremely upset and angry with his doctor about the psychiatric referral, which, to him, meant that he was crazy. At first, this seemed to the therapist to be the probable therapeutic goal.

However, as the onset of symptoms was explored in detail in an effort to discover the emotional meaning of the disruption in the patient's adaptive balance, new dynamic factors became clear. This patient was a chronically dependent, passive, somewhat anxious man. Six months previously his brother-in-law had suffered a sudden coronary occlusion while on a motoring trip. Within two weeks, the patient had symptoms of heart disease. He had gone to the doctors and been studied for this; when the results were negative and he was told, essentially, that it was "in his head," he developed the acute anxiety symptoms described. The coincidence in timing was not originally noted by the patient or by the doctors and was elicited only by detailed exploration of what was going on around the time of onset of the acute disruption of function. Many other things were also going on which obscured this particular event, which, when reported quite incidentally, suddenly enabled the therapist to begin to make emotional sense of the situation.

As the patient talked further of his past experiences and relationships, he again mentioned only incidentally—but with marked terseness and embarrassment—that a maternal uncle had died in a psychiatric hospital after a long illness due to central nervous system disease. It should be emphasized that this was brought out in a context of many other events and that the patient did not recognize its relevance. However, to the therapist, the emotional meaning it must have had to the patient, when he was told that he did not have heart disease, suddenly became intelligible and could be interpreted to the patient. It became clear that the primary time when he had felt "crazy" was not at the point of psychiatric referral, but when he was told that his somatically vivid cardiac symptoms were "just in his head."

The avoidance of regressive transference was calculated in this case because the patient pressed quite massively for an extremely dependent relationship. He was the only son of an overprotective mother, had married late, and had many open passive, dependent attitudes. These dependency needs kept him in treatment despite his fear that psychotherapeutic exploration would prove he was crazy. In this case, such attitudes in the transference were managed rather than interpreted; they were explicitly explored and interpreted in connection with his wife.

The patient was seen a total of 24 times, with the last several contacts being spaced to give him support during the period when he was achieving an adaptive reintegration—learning to function despite some symptoms, opening another business, and so on. One further technical maneuver might be mentioned; after the principal dynamic pattern had been understood and the patient had lost his most severe symptoms, but when his regressive and dependent urges were still tempting, he wished to take a trip to see his sister, which meant essentially indulging in a period of regression, dependency, and lack of responsibility. The therapist felt that the actual *preconscious* trend at this time was integrative—although the conscious pressure from the patient was regressive. The dynamic meaning of the visit was discussed, but the trip was not opposed by the therapist. The patient discovered for himself that such a situation was somewhat unsatisfying, despite the indulgence of regressive needs. He developed an impetus, which had been lacking before, to take arms against his troubles and consciously to recognize the emotional values of realistic function on an adult level, despite some symptoms. When he was seen by chance two years after the termination of treatment, it appeared that he was continuing to function effectively.

Case 6: An extremely anxious and poignant young man came in saying that he was "seeing too many coincidences." He was frightened by the fact that he found himself reading a pattern or design into things which he recognized were probably coincidental. The therapist felt that this patient was clearly on the verge of an eruptive paranoid schizophrenic episode. The precipitating circumstances were a recent automobile trip across the country with three other men, with whom the patient became progressively more panicky, and the fact that, within a week, he was due to leave his rooming house and move into the much more intimate atmosphere of a fraternity.

It seemed clear that latent homosexual factors precipitated the acute symptoms. Problems of intimacy with men and the feared sexual implications of such closeness were discussed in terms of concrete material brought out by the patient, largely about his college experiences. His acute anxiety abated, he was able to enroll when college began, shortly thereafter, and he stabilized well for a time, continuing his studies. However, he eventually did develop gross paranoid schizophrenic symptoms and had to be hospitalized. The young man's capacity to evoke sympathy and his overtrustfulness in the therapist, while they had enabled early improvement to be made, also implied impossible expectations and the eventual paranoid developments. Presumably his relations with other people outside the therapeutic situation had run a similar course. Thus here is an instance of a situation in which this form of psychotherapy did not prove adequate.

Of course, selecting out the crucial dynamic material gives an illusory clarity to these cases. The point to be emphasized is that the dynamically important data were *not* clearly perceived by the patient; they were usually presented in a texture of other experiences and feelings without special emphasis or insight. Experiences which the patient already recognizes as crucial may need to be understood in relation to other events or worked through in therapy, but they do not require such an active effort at empathy or perception of the emotional pattern on the part of the therapist. In the case of material which the patient presents without recognizing its significance, but in such fashion that the therapist can see an emotionally meaningful pattern, we assume that the emotional meaning is preconscious or accessible in a brief therapeutic interaction. However, you will note that the therapist actively listens for such a pattern and discusses it with the patient as he becomes aware of it, *at the level of tentativeness* which suits the data. This does not mean theorizing or forming an intellectual judgment about the meaning of data; intellectualization with patients does not result in useful dynamic insights. To carry dynamic impact, this approach must be tied very closely to concrete data and subjective cues from the patient; the therapist tries to *sort out* or imagine or formulate these data as soon as possible with respect to their preconscious emotional meanings or patterns in the life of the patient.

It will be seen that this concept of therapy presupposes that much working through and therapeutic consolidation may occur outside therapy, during a planned interruption or a termination based on the understanding that the patient may return as needed for further clarification of the problem, or with new problems which have come up. Interruption and termination become overlapping concepts, differing largely in how the therapist views the future probabilities and thereby phrases the definiteness of return to the patient. Ideally, interruptions in therapy should develop intrinsically from the dynamics of treatment, and not arbitrarily. If the therapist is alert to the possibility, he will see, in many therapeutic transactions, a progression from exploration of the problem, through understanding of its dynamic meaning, to a spontaneous peak of significant insight or shift in direction on the part of the patient, which suggests that he could make constructive use of a period of consolidation, experimentation, or working through on his own, outside of therapy. Such "integrative crests" are not devoid of defensive features—as in the case of the counterphobic patient described earlier—but they differ from "flights into health" in being substantially based upon significant dynamic insight.

DURATION OF TREATMENT

If a clinic tries to function with the concept of ego-oriented psychotherapy, how will this be reflected in the duration of treatment transactions for the total patient group? Table 1 shows the distribution of patients in terms of frequency of visits during one calendar year in a student health clinic. It should be clear, by this time, that the patients seen for briefer periods were not "rejects" for therapy; within the limitations of therapist fallibility and inertia in the administrative machinery, the length of a given therapeutic transaction was considered to be either optimal or useful at the time for the patient.

TABLE 1

Duration of Therapeutic Contact with Patients in a Student
Health Clinic in 1955*

	Number of Visits					
	1	2-4	5-10	11-24	25 & over	Total
No. of Patients	83	269	258	185	29	824
Per cent of Patients	10.1	32.6	31.3	22.5	3.5	100

* Department of Psychological Medicine, Cowell Memorial Hospital, University of California (Saxton Pope, M.D., Director). The total includes patients who had last visited the clinic in the calendar year 1955 and had, at the time of the tabulation (1957), not returned.

SELECTION OF PATIENTS

The types of patients with whom this approach may be useful cannot be described in standard psychopathological categories. It is not limited to certain diagnostic groups, to patients with given external or internal crises precipitating referral, or to patients who would not be motivated in the usual sense of conventional psychiatric treatment. The cases discussed above included (1) a situational problem in a compliant character, (2) a compulsive character, (3) a counterphobic character, (4) a depressive character, (5) an anxiety state with somatization, and (6) an eruptive schizophrenic panic. All other diagnostic categories could have been illustrated. The usefulness of time-limited, ego-oriented psychotherapy depends on whether the adaptive-maladaptive integrations or emotional patterns of the patient's life can be perceived and made use of in connection with the forces that brought him to the clinic at a given time and can be dynamically focused in relation to ongoing development and readaptation. In our present state of conceptualization, there are no objective criteria for whether or not ego-oriented therapy would be helpful in a given situation. Tentative interpretations of an ego-oriented kind, in the initial phases of treatment, seem to be the most reliable guide.

When, on the other hand, a regressive transference situation is *necessary* for a useful therapeutic transaction, the goal of brief therapy would be to work this out with the patient—still, however, trying to focus preconscious trends in an ego-oriented way—and to help him plan emotionally and practically for this intensive level of treatment. Many patients obviously could benefit from either level; the patient's goal and expediency—often financial—become the criteria.

Again, this approach to treatment does not disclaim the fact that there are treatment transactions in which the primary goal is and should be different. Many patients need long-term, sustained, but not intensive relationships. For instance, social workers in community agencies are well aware of the very regressive, dependent, chaotic patients who need to be supportively maintained over an indefinite period of time. We would suggest, from our experience with ego-oriented psychotherapy, that conceptualization of treatment goals early, tentatively, and flexibly, in delicate interaction with the data and emotional patterning as they develop, might enable the therapist in many kinds of therapeutic situations to minimize unnecessary regression and to space or time therapeutic transactions more usefully and economically.

ADMINISTRATIVE FACILITATION

Certain administrative structures implement this concept of psychotherapy. First, the open intake has been mentioned. This means that a clinic must reserve enough therapist time for initial evaluations and brief contacts so that a patient can be seen within a week or two of application or reapplication; otherwise the question, "What brings you to the clinic at this time?" loses its meaning. In the prepaid health plan clinic,* both limited and relatively unlimited therapy, including some analysis, were done. The therapist's philosophical convictions about ego-oriented psychotherapy clearly became the determining factor in whether this approach was utilized in appropriate cases. However, as a rough administrative yardstick, it seemed that a therapist who was interested in ego-oriented psychotherapy could safeguard enough time for it if he reserved about one-half of his patient treatment time for initial evaluation and ego-oriented psychotherapy. This psychiatric clinic saw a large number of patients briefly, however, as a part of planning for their total program of medical care. Another type of psychiatric clinic might find that this proportion of time needed to be amended.

Second, outgo must equal intake. Ideally, as has been said, termination of a therapeutic transaction should arise naturally out of the dynamics of the transaction, within the general knowledge on both sides that there *is* a limitation in time. Practically, interruptions or terminations must sometimes be entered into for expedient reasons of case load; like friction in a machine, these expedient transactions are probably inevitable, but the clinic should work toward minimizing them.

Third, this concept of brief therapy works most easily in a clinic which does not segregate intake function—that is, where all senior or experienced therapists do initial interviewing. Such a departure from custom may require additional training for psychiatrists and psychologists, and it may necessitate some encouragement of social workers to take more responsibility for acting on their data in the intake interview than they have taken historically. Nonsegregated intake with little or no transfer of patients—except for particular psychodynamic or practical reason—seems optimal for the facilitation of ego-oriented psychotherapy. However, this is not crucial; the essential administrative concept is that the initial interviewer have authority to operate and make disposition in psychodynamic terms as perceived in the initial contacts with the patient, rather than be bound to wait for a dispositional decision elsewhere†

* Permanente Psychiatric Clinic, Kaiser Foundation Hospital, Harvey D. Powelson, M.D., Director.

† The destructive possibilities of the intake without dispositional authority are vividly expressed in the third interview cited by Gill et al. (3). A sensitive initial interview with a schizophrenic patient which leads her beautifully into a therapeutic relationship, is suddenly disrupted at the end, because the therapist has to withdraw from the patient. "The therapist can say little more than he does because he does not know what possibilities there are for treating her at her institution or what the next step would be . . ." (p. 409). (The account goes on to elaborate the therapist's inability to continue dynamically with the patient.)

The advantage of such an arrangement is that focusing in a therapeutic direction can begin as soon as it seems to be dynamically suitable and does not wait for a decision made in an intake conference and assignment to a therapist. We feel that this is extremely helpful in ego-oriented psychotherapy. It seems that the more data given by the patient in the interests of a "history" or in an informational context, the greater the patient's expectations may be of having these problems eradicated in terms of the "infectious disease" model of therapy. Focusing by the therapist at the optimal *dynamic* points is an important aid to brief therapy.

Fourth, the administrative structure being recommended would result in the intake or evaluation conference usually being concerned less with disposition and more with dynamic considerations, medico-legal responsibilities, and so on. Acceptance or rejection of patients would seldom be a problem, since the question being asked is: "What is a useful therapeutic transaction for this person at this time?"

In the conventional clinic structure, despite the valuable work done with accepted treatment cases, there are several questions raised by these concepts of ego-oriented psychotherapy: Should clinics expand their concepts to meet the needs of a broader motivational range of patients? Should they try to embark on therapeutically oriented transactions with such patients in connection with what they would find useful at the time of application? Is treatment in some cases artificially prolonged by standard clinic procedures?

So far as the last of these questions is concerned, we believe that some standard clinic practices do artificially prolong treatment. Among such practices are the primarily information-oriented intake, dispositional intake conference, and transfer of cases, which we have already mentioned. Further, a waiting list, particularly one set up before the initial interview, seems likely to prolong treatment; patients often expect to be treated at least as long as they have waited. We feel that such a waiting list may also select hostile, dependent patients and aggravate in them these very problems. Patients who wait for a considerable length of time and then are rejected or referred have not been handled therapeutically. In addition, intake, when it is a segregated function, has the disadvantages already described. Furthermore, it seems that therapists who are insulated from the pressure of applications and the need for formulating treatment goals may

---

Our question would be, if the initial interviewer cannot proceed as dynamically indicated, whether he should utilize his skill to induce the patient to enter a therapeutically oriented transaction of this kind, in view of the serious disruption and disappointment clearly implied by the patient's responses at the end of the interview.

tend to develop stagnant case loads, in which regressive transferences may proliferate without the technical possibility of using them to therapeutic advantage.

REFERENCES

1. Deutsch, Felix. *Applied psychoanalysis.* New York: Grune & Stratton, 1949.
2. Freud, Sigmund. Analysis: Terminable and interminable. In *Collected papers,* Vol. 5. London: Hogarth Press, 1950, pp. 316 357.
3. Gill, Merton, Newman, Richard, & Redlich, Frederick C. *The initial interview in psychiatric practice.* New York: International University Press, Inc., 1954, pp. 106-409.
4. Philips, E. Lakin, & Johnston, Margaret S. H. Theoretical and clinical aspects of short-term parent-child psychotherapy. *Psychiatry,* 1954, **17,** 267-275.
5. Rogers, Carl R. *Client-centered therapy.* Boston: Houghton Mifflin, 1951.

Chapter 8

Time-Limited Brief Psychotherapy

Jacob Swartz, M.D.

In a previous paper (1) the inception of a program of time-limited psychotherapy was described and discussed. This program was instituted in 1962 and consisted of assigning to each psychiatric resident a number of patients who were designated as time-limited cases and whose treatment was to consist of no more than one hour of psychotherapy per week for 12 weeks. These 12 hours of psychotherapy could be arranged in any way that would best suit the clinical situation and the residents were encouraged to be flexible both in terms of the duration of each interview and the spacing of the interviews. Thus, a patient who was seen for thirty minutes per week could be seen for 24 weeks as could a patient who was seen for an hour every other week. A review of the foci and goals of treatment reveals that the treatment goals for the patient tended to cluster around certain major areas. These were the management of crises, assistance with maturational transitions, reestablishment of previous modes of function, and maintenance of patient equilibrium.

The most difficult, challenging, and yet most important decision that is made in time-limited therapy is the one which revolves around what area the allotted period of therapy time is to be spent. In our procedure, this decision is made when the patient is first discussed by the therapist with any member of the senior staff, and it is this member of the faculty who, because of his experience and knowledge, is usually called upon to suggest the area of focus to the therapist. Once the focus is established every effort is made to stay within the chosen area because the limited period of time has to be spent in as effective and concentrated a manner as is possible. Clearly if the focus proves to be an unsuitable one, it can be changed during the course of treatment during which time the therapist is discussing the case with his time-limited therapy supervisor.

The most common focus that is chosen revolves around the

Reprinted from *Seminars in Psychiatry*, 1969, **1**, 380-388, by permission of the publisher and the author. Copyright 1969, Grune and Stratton. Dr. Swartz is Professor of Psychiatry at Boston University School of Medicine.

precipitating stress: that is, the reason that the patient gives, or the reasons that we surmise the patient has, for having come for treatment at a particular time. Some common reasons have already been enumerated. At the same time, it should be pointed out that in many instances more than one focus of attention for therapy is possible, and in such instances the likelihood is that we choose the one that has been the cause of the most recent distress. Having chosen a focus, it is not discarded lightly.

Some clinical instances of the ways in which a focus is chosen and the reasoning that goes into it will be described in an attempt to give examples rather than in an attempt to provide an exhaustive or all-inclusive listing. It is hoped that in this way the principles rather than the minutiae or variations will be clear. The groupings that will be suggested or presented are not necessarily presented in order of frequency but as clinical illustrations.

There are a group of patients presenting with anxiety, depression, or phobic symptomatology in whom the symptoms themselves are not necessarily focused upon. In the more traditional psychotherapeutic or psychoanalytic situation, the symptoms and their associations would be observed and connected, the nature and sequence of the defenses would be observed and dealt with and, so long as some movement took place, the patient would proceed pretty much at his own pace. This is clearly not the case in time-limited brief psychotherapy. In this modality of treatment the therapist, on the basis of his knowledge and understanding of the development of human personality, of conflict, of instinct, of defenses, actively delimits the area in which the therapeutic work will be done. This has been decided upon by our understanding of the dynamics involved rather than by following the pace of the patient's associations over a considerable period of time. As will be seen in the following case, the symptoms themselves are not necessarily the focus of attention.

Case 1: A 33-year-old separated female, the mother of a 12-year-old daughter, presented herself for psychiatric treatment because of a severe anxiety attack that had taken place on the previous Sunday when she was at church with her parents, her brother and her daughter. She remembered yelling. It seemed to her as though her voice was reverberating in an echo chamber, and she was afraid she was going to lose her mind.

The first attack of this kind had occurred six months before, again on a Sunday evening shortly after she, her boy friend and her daughter had to flee from a small fire in her apartment building.

Fourteen years previously she had married a man primarily because she was afraid she was pregnant, although it was not at all clear to her or to her husband that intercourse had taken place. She had had an exceedingly strict upbringing, no education on sexual matters and so even though she was 19 years old, consciously at least, the basic facts of reproduction were a mystery to her. It turned out that she was not pregnant but she did become pregnant shortly before her husband left on a two-year tour of military service. When he returned, the marriage deteriorated. He was not gainfully employed, and he was interested neither in her nor the child. They separated, but the separation had not culminated in divorce, at one level for religious reasons, and at another level because the patient had some vague and undefined concerns about what would happen to her husband if she left him permanently. Shortly after the separation, she met a man who she believed was divorced, only to find out later that he was separated and was being about as active in getting a divorce as she was. He was in the Navy and she began to see him regularly on weekends. The boyfriend began to live in her apartment on weekends and since she lived close to her mother, her mother very quickly became aware of the nature of the relationship and criticized the patient severely for this "immoral" alliance. Although her mother's steady harassment made her feel very badly, she also managed in one way or another to call her mother's attention to the fact that this relationship continued. Her mother's vigil extended also to what amounted to a Sunday morning ritual to make sure that the patient went to church with her parents.

Her family history was that of being born into a family in which she was the middle of three siblings. As she described it, life seemed altogether grim, hard, and built upon injunctions and commandments. Her mother was the more domineering of her parents, nagging and badgering her husband as well as other members of the family. The patient saw her father as the weaker but the more affectionate of her parents.

The specific reason for the anxiety attacks on this particular Sunday was revealed in a later interview in which it turned out that this particular Sunday was three days before and the closest Sunday to her wedding anniversary.

She was sitting in church with her parents and thoughts about her husband and the forbidden relationship with her boyfriend came into her mind. She did not feel right about being in church. Her daughter was sitting beside her and she began to think how she had to set an example for her daughter.

It is clear that selection of a focus of therapy in this case presented us with a few choices. There were the symptoms themselves: those of anxiety occurring in a specific setting and clearly relating to forbidden sexual as well as aggressive wishes. The symptoms developed in church in a setting in which the patient did not feel free to confess because she was living with another man despite the fact that she was not divorced and in any case in a situation of which the church would disapprove. The aggressive side of the conflict had to do with her feelings about her mother who criticized and demanded attendance at church. There was the entire matter of the relationship to her daughter who was approaching adolescence and who was, by virtue of living with her mother, witness to the fact that a man came to the apartment each weekend who was neither her father nor the patient's husband. This was a particular source of conflict to the patient because she was raised as a "very good girl" and it was her intention to bring her daughter up in the same way.

Another possibility for a focus had to do with the nature of the patient's relationship to her mother, and it was finally in this area that we decided to work. It was felt that, whatever else was going on, the patient's relationship to her mother was a central one and was composed of a number of conflicting and troublesome elements. On the one hand, the patient was dependent upon her mother, lived near her, responded to her insistence that she go to church, and responded with shame and guilt concerning mother's attacks upon her about the relationship with her boyfriend. On the other hand, she invited a good deal of this behavior by living so physically close to her mother and in one way or another seeing to it that her mother was kept apprised of all these forbidden activities. It was felt that the development of anxiety symptoms in church represented not only the patient's relationship to the church as a religious body but contained very markedly within it the relationship to her mother who was seen as a harsh, implacable, and demanding superego. It was believed also that in some way her ambivalent relationship to her husband was connected to the ambivalent relationship to her mother, and although she did not and could not live with her husband because of his attitude toward the pregnancy and his failure to support the family, she nevertheless did not wish to take the final step of a permanent separation from him because she was concerned about what might happen to him. This, too, resembled her relationship to her mother; living near her mother and being subject to the barrage of criticism and hostility was unpleasant for her. Yet she could not bring herself to break away from it either. It was felt that if she could be helped to see herself as somewhat more independent of her mother that she would also be helped with her excessively strict relationship to her own daughter.

We see here that we decided to focus neither on the symptoms nor upon their symbolic meaning but upon the issue of independence from her mother and to focus on its conscious and preconscious aspects rather than upon its extensive unconscious ramifications.

Another general principle in deciding upon a focus in time-limited psychotherapy is that the preferred focus is upon some potentially progressive rather than upon some potentially regressive area. To put it in another way, the present or past accomplishments, successes or interests are selectively called to the patient's attention, even in a setting in which the patient behaves or feels as though he is inadequate, or without strengths.

Case 2: A 19-year-old college student was referred for an emergency evaluation because of abdominal pain, anorexia, crying, hopelessness, and suicidal ideas. His symptomatology and complaints were known to the director of his dormitory, to the counseling and guidance department, and there was such concern about him that prior to the emergency evaluation one of his instructors took the patient home for the weekend. One of his sisters or his mother was in daily communication with either the patient or various college personnel. He had just returned to school for the second year after a first term during which he was periodically depressed, quite openly stating that the depression was precipitated by the fact that his mother had left him at school. He wondered whether he ought to go home and said that the only thing he would like to do would be to stay in bed, to be fed, and to watch television. Part of the way in which the patient and his family attempted to deal with his difficulties was that his mother encouraged him to call home every night. Even the telephone calls setting up an appointment were made for him by the director of his dormitory because it was felt that the patient was unable to do it himself.

The patient was born into a family in which he was the youngest of three children and the only boy. His mother was described as having high blood pressure and numerous allergies related, according to the father, to family arguments. On one occasion the mother had an allergy attack, could not breathe, and the patient performed mouth-to-mouth breathing on her while the father stood by unperturbed. It was our further impression that the patient knew altogether too much (having learned it from his mother) about the sexual life of his parents. His early years were marked by a number of illnesses which did not sound particularly serious but which caused him to be viewed as a sickly boy. Academically he did exceedingly well in junior high school, and even though he participated in some minor delinquent activities his grades and school performance remained very high. In high school his excellent academic performance continued, he worked at a job during the evening, played on the football team and was elected co-captain.

It is important to emphasize that the patient's behavior was wildly regressive. He drew classmates, roommates and faculty members into his difficulties. He cried in class. He discussed personal problems with strangers and altogether demanded that the environment take care of him immediately, yet he still suffered and insisted he could not go on.

With our knowledge of his excellent high school record and his athletic and social skills, a specific therapeutic attitude and approach were decided upon. The focus of therapy was to review with him repeatedly how it came to be that a young man with his record, with his accomplishments in the past, a young man who had demonstrated that he could do well, felt now that he could not make it and was actually making an incredible nuisance of himself. The patient's response was to deprecate all his past achievements and in addition to begin to describe additional problems like compulsive symptomatology, the amount of time he spent watching shockingly advertised movies and other apparently alarming activities. His descriptions of further symptoms were tactfully disregarded except to observe that when he described his symptomatology or deprecated his abilities, he was intent on portraying himself as too incompetent to manage. In therapy he continued to insist on how much he suffered, how much he could not do his school work, how his compulsions and voyeuristic tastes and tendencies were indicative of serious pathology. Nevertheless, these were not explored with him but he improved in a number of his courses, came to feel that some of the crisis decisions that he felt that he had to make on the spot were not so urgent and he found it less necessary to seek solace and advice from anyone who would listen. By the time termination of therapy was in order, he was continuing on in school and was doing quite well.

Case 3: Another kind of therapeutic involvement was recommended in the instance of a depressed 21-year-old female student. She stated that her life had been smooth and orderly until her father died about a year and a half prior to her appearance at the clinic. He was a professional person and had had coronary artery disease for many years. The patient began to realize that he was not well in high school and shortly after she began her second year in college she had a premonition that she might not see her father again, went home for a weekend on a Friday, and the next day her father collapsed at his office and died. She considered him a brilliant and loving father who was clearly the head of the household and with whom she shared many interests until she was 12 or 13 years old when he had to curtail activity because of his illness. At the time of her father's death, the patient felt that the responsibilities for the immediate funeral arrangements and the making of decisions that resulted from his death evolved upon her despite the fact that she had an older brother and a mother. She thought her brother was unavailable because he had recently married and was busy with his studies at medical school. Her mother was very depressed and, as the patient saw it, disorganized. The patient took care of these matters, grieved actively for her father, but then broke up with her first serious boyfriend shortly after the death. Although her father had left the family well provided for, the patient felt under considerable financial pressure with the patient feeling that she could not ask her mother for any money at all.

Using the fact that she did not feel there was enough money for her living expenses and her personal needs as an external justification, the patient gradually retired from social activities. At the time that she was seen she was living alone in a miserable apartment, living on an allowance that was hardly enough for her to buy adequate food let alone any minor amenities. In contrast to this description of how she had been living, she described her mother as having recovered from her father's death and leading a very active life including extensive travel.

Because her family was comfortable financially, the patient felt that her childhood was different from that of the other children in her neighborhood. She felt further that because of ethnic and religious differences in the neighborhood that it was not possible for her to make very many friends. Despite her isolation and loneliness she held class offices and was quite popular at school.

It was clear to us that the patient's current symptomatology and behavior revolved around her feelings about her father's death and the role that she had to play in the events immediately following. All of this was, of course, unconscious and was related to her relationship to her father. Our task was to suggest a focus for time-limited psychotherapy that would help her to move away from the path of self-deprivation, depression, and hidden anger that she had chosen.

We understood further that there was an admixture within her of masochistic character traits with an actively punishing and depriving super-ego. We decided in turn to be active with her in suggesting that she might be angry and that one of the manifestations of her anger was to deprive herself materially while insisting upon maintaining the fantasy that her mother neither wished to nor could provide her with college expenses or the most simple amenities. She was to be encouraged to test reality by really finding out if in fact, some time ago, all the funeral arrangements had been left to her by her older brother and her mother and more recently what the situation was in regard to how she was supposed to live.

We decided through our focus to ally ourselves actively against the masochistic character traits and against the punishing super-ego which was seen as emanating from those around her. This was done by actively encouraging her to get more money to live on, to make herself personally more attractive and not to assume, by her silence during her contacts with them, that her family wanted her to live in an atmosphere that was devoid of emotional as well as reasonable material comfort. This focus worked remarkably well and the patient was able to talk over some long-standing grievances with her mother after the second interview.

It is neither possible nor necessary to catalog every possibility on how we delineate a focus. For instance, two additional examples can be briefly mentioned. Even in the instance of the so-called sociopathic or asocial character, we have attempted time-limited psychotherapy. We are not under the misconception that this seriously or permanently affects the behavior but we have worked with such patients in the area of reality testing. In this instance, this means a review with the patient concerning his awareness of the consequences of his actions. We have felt that some purpose could be served if consequences of action could be reviewed with such a patient in a nonpunitive setting. We did not think that it would radically alter anything but at least it would diminish the possibility that the patient would be able to tell himself that he had no awareness of cause and effect. In still another instance, the focus that is chosen is that of the relationship of a mother to her children, focusing specifically on the children's growth, struggles, and conflicts. Such a focus sometimes permits a patient to discuss her own struggles through the identification with the children, particularly when the patient finds it difficult to have little or no perspective on some difficulties in her own current life that bear a remarkable resemblance to what is going on with the children.

Discussion of and careful agreement about a focus is a central issue in time-limited psychotherapy. This is not to imply in any way that as the material develops there is only one possible focus. The fact of the matter is that there are two, three, or four paths that might well be chosen. We try to choose the one that is most acute, or is most characteristic of the patient's way of handling himself, or the one that we think will provide the most therapeutic leverage. The more important point is to choose a focus that is reasonably consistent with the history, the current illness and therapeutic goal and to stay with it. This is often not easy, nor does it mean that one has to feel that he is absolutely right about the chosen path. It does mean there there is the recognition that there is a limited period of time to accomplish a realistic and modest therapeutic task.

Although time-limited psychotherapy represents an attempt to apply a complex body of theory, knowledge, and practice to the expressed and actual needs of large numbers of people for at least some help with emotional problems of varying severity, it is not a method of treatment which, because of its brevity, is for the less trained, the less skilled and the less knowledgeable. As a matter of fact, in many ways the tasks involved in time-limited psychotherapy require more knowledge, more sensitivity and are more demanding than the tasks involved in the more traditional and longer psychotherapeutic endeavors. It may be that time-limited psychotherapy is even more difficult for more experienced therapists because such a therapist often sees more facets and more roots of the problems involved, and has to check his wish to investigate them as well as the natural bent to try to approach them psychotherapeutically. Be that as it may, some general guidelines have emerged from our experience in doing time-limited psychotherapy and from supervising those who do it.

Perhaps the first issue that arises has to do with the very way in which the plan of treatment is understood by the therapist and presented to the patient. One of the manifestations of the discouragement which the therapist may feel about the forthcoming venture has to do with how the time-limited venture is discussed with the patient. It would seem to go without saying this would be the first item discussed: that the therapist would make it clear to the patient (and to himself) that there are a specific number of hours that would be utilized in a particular way and that at the end of that period of time treatment would stop. It has been our experience that for one reason or another therapists have sometimes not mentioned this fact until half way through the therapy and then, on some occasions, only after persistent reminders. Sometimes this is because the therapist is discouraged by the magnitude of the task; at other times it is because the therapist finds it difficult to adopt modest and reasonable goals and to leave it at that. A corollary to this hedging and avoidance of discussion of the length of therapy has to do with the setting of the fee. This too is an important issue and it is important to observe that the therapists tend to set fees that are considerably below what many of the patients can reasonably afford to pay. Again, this may well be related to the devalued notions about therapy in general but perhaps about this particular mode of therapy specifically.

Having navigated the shoals of informing the patient of the length of time involved and having set a reasonable fee, the therapy is already in motion. The therapist is then confronted with the fact that he has a time limit as well as the patient, and this time limit means that exceedingly close scrutiny of the material is in order. This close scrutiny has as its purpose a review of the focus that was suggested when the patient was first assigned for treatment, and a determination on the part of the therapist that the therapy stay within that focus unless there is a very good reason for changing it. It is difficult to work within a narrow range but the task cannot be successfully fulfilled if the field becomes obscure. It is certainly clear that more than one focus is possible in any given case, because the conflicts, defenses, symptoms, character structure, and decompensating situations are multi-determined. It is hoped that the one that is chosen is more workable, or more characteristic of the patient's difficulties, but in any event the focus that is decided upon is adhered to unless there is unmistakable evidence that the initial hypothesis was inaccurate. This is often difficult to do because in therapy the therapist is sometimes confronted by a patient with alarming symptomatology. As the process moves along there may be minimal improvement and discouragement on the part of the patient at the prospect of accomplishing anything in so short a period of time. Again, one has to be aware of the fact that the therapist himself may also be clouding the issues because of his own feelings about the complexity of the task.

A second important principle for the therapist is that he must develop the capacity to exclude material, interesting though the material may be, but to exclude it if it is not pertinent to the focus of the treatment. In some ways, this is harder for a more experienced therapist because of his more extensive awareness of the significance and meaning of symptomatology, character structure, and the relationships between them. On some occasions this means that specific obsessional symptomatology, for instance, is not dwelt upon because the focus of treatment has to do with the fact that the obsessional symptomatology has been exacerbated in a setting in which the individual is attempting to live independently of his parents for the first time in his life though he is a man in his early thirties. In another instance it might be quite apparent to the therapist that an important underlying issue is related to a continuing oedipal attachment to the mother but it is also clear that such a focus means long-term treatment. In this instance the focus of treatment remains one in which the patient's daily insistence that he cannot deal with simple everyday tasks remains the focus while the deeper meaning of his attachment to the mother is not investigated. It is a challenge for the therapist to discipline himself to stay within the original focus of therapy.

The amount of therapist activity is an important consideration in time-limited psychotherapy. One kind has already been stated when we indicated that the therapist has to develop the capacity to exclude certain kinds of material. The converse is also true; if an issue is clear and if it is in the chosen focus of treatment, it is not only indicated but mandatory that the therapist introduce it even if the patient has not himself introduced the issue directly. There are many areas in which the therapist has to be more active, and again this begins with the initial interview. Being more active does not necessarily mean that the therapist talks more but it certainly does mean that he has to be more directive within the therapeutic context. This neither means nor implies that the therapist takes over running the patient's life for him or that advice-giving is particularly more pronounced with time-limited psychotherapy than in other kinds of psychotherapy, but it does mean that the therapist introduces issues if it is pertinent to do so and is more active in seeing to it that the focus is maintained.

The very fact that this is a time-limited contact introduces the issue of termination immediately and it is an issue which has to be closely watched. It is an important issue both for the therapist and the patient in that it keeps clear to both of them that there is a lot of work to be done. Discussion of termination is certainly an area in which the therapist must be active. Very often central and lively issues revolving around the patient's initial contact with the clinic become connected with the management of termination. Termination is a crucial issue even though the contact is a brief one. Recrudescence of symptomatology, regression, disappointment concerning fantasied expectations all come to the fore exactly as one sees in long-term psychotherapy or in psychoanalysis except that the pace is accelerated.

Questions naturally arise about the selection of patients for time-limited psychotherapy. In fact the criteria for selection were and are not remarkably different from the selection of patients for any psychotherapeutic modality that is to take place in the setting of an outpatient clinic. Given limitations of personnel, space, and time we have always directed our attention toward patients whom we felt we could help over relatively short periods of time. Thus our facility did not usually undertake treatment of problems of drug or alcohol addiction, of seriously disturbed impulsive behavior, of patients who had been treated in many facilities for what would turn out to be a ceaseless quest for narcissistic supplies. In short, if a patient was eligible for treatment in our clinic, he was eligible for time-limited treatment. This was how we began and this is how, with relatively minor variation, we have continued. However, we feel we have learned from our involvements and so we can say that specific diagnostic categories are not nearly as important as whether or not we can delineate a focus of therapy. Accordingly, for time-limited psychotherapy we assign patients with long-standing characterologic difficulty, not in an attempt to change character structure but certainly, if such is the case, to restore a certain previously better mode of function. By using the criterion "Is there a focus?", we cut across diagnostic lines and address ourselves to the situation at hand recognizing its conscious and unconscious roots in the history of the patient's development and in the history of his object relationships.

We hope that we have succeeded in conveying the view that time-limited psychotherapy is not a modality of treatment used by the less skilled and intended for the less challenging or interesting patient. It is a modality devised for the purpose of delivering at least some care to many who might otherwise have none. The therapy is brief but clinical judgment, knowledge and skill are in no way neglected.

REFERENCE

1. Swartz, J. The outpatient clinic. In B. Bandler (Ed.), *International Psychiatry Clinics*, Vol. III. Boston: Little, Brown, 1966.

Chapter 9

Precipitating Stress:

An Approach to Brief Therapy

M. Robert Harris, M.D., Betty L. Kalis, Ph.D. and
Edith H. Freeman, Ph.D.

Techniques of psychotherapy differ in dimensions of time, orientation, approach, and other variables. In this paper we describe some techniques involved in one model of brief psychotherapy. Its goal is a resolution of the stress precipitating the request for help through exploration of the conflict derivative involved in that stress.

This model of psychotherapy developed out of a three-year investigation of the disruption of functioning leading to the application for psychiatric help, a disruption we termed precipitating stress. An earlier report (6) described the procedure of data collection and presented a definition of stress. We saw, within 24 hours of their request, 43 unselected applicants to the outpatient department of a neuropsychiatric institute. The exploration of precipitating stress in the interviews helped to establish a new adaptive balance, usually within seven sessions.* Efforts were made to conceptualize this process and extend the

Reprinted from *American Journal of Psychotherapy*, 1963, 17, 465-471, by permission of the publisher and the authors. Dr. Harris is Chief, Clinical Services, Langley Porter Neuropsychiatric Institute and Associate Clinical Professor, Department of Psychiatry, University of California School of Medicine, San Francisco. Dr. Kalis is Associate Clinical Professor of Medical Psychology, University of California School of Medicine, San Francisco. Dr. Freeman is Project Psychologist, Pediatrics Comprehensive Care Program, Mount Zion Hospital and Medical Center, San Francisco.

* One of the criteria for terminating an interview series was some resolution of the presenting crisis. Although the level of the new adaptation varied widely from case to case, 38 of the 43 patients (88%) were seen for seven or fewer interviews. (Mean = 5:09, Range = 1-13.) An important focus in all interviews was the exploration of motivation for continued treatment. Thirteen of the patients (30%) continued in long-term treatment; and one (2%) was in need of hospitalization at the time of application. Three patients (7%) returned for a second brief series of contacts within several months.

approach simultaneously to many other patients in our outpatient department.

A number of symposia and papers on the subject of brief psychotherapy vary in emphasis. In general they agree that psychotherapy differs from psychoanalysis in its goals. Whereas psychoanalysis aims at the induction and full resolution of a transference neurosis, psychotherapy, as Gitelson (5) has pointed out, "will bring the reaction (transference neurosis) to an end at any point of stability."

In the therapy described here, clarification and resolution of precipitating stress is the *only* goal. All our interventions and focusing have this aim. Our thesis is that all patients apply for help at a time when something has occurred to disrupt their previous level of adaptation. This thesis is a logical extension of the homeostatic view of human functioning which underlies current psychodynamic theory. In this view, the ego is a constant mediator between demands from within and without, facilitating adjustment and readjustment to the environment. During this ongoing process certain stresses periodically disrupt the level of adaptation and require a reorganization of psychic resources. The request for help, then, is regarded as a response to such stress, and the therapeutic aim is to facilitate resolution of the crisis and establish a new adaptive balance.

Fenichel (2) points out that "there are precipitating factors for psychoneuroses or for non-neurotic acute upset states which can be compared with traumata. A person may have evolved from old infantile conflicts into a state of relative equilibrium between repressed and repressing forces. An external alteration may mean a disturbance of this equilibrium, and thus make a hitherto attained adjustment more difficult." The anxiety indicates the re-emergence of conflict which recapitulates early traumatic states, and a new equilibrium must be sought. The "external alteration" becomes important in this context only in its role of evoking internal distress. In our definition, stress is the interaction of events with the conflict derivatives they engender or reflect.

Thus, simply identifying and isolating the factors that precipitate the request for help is only a beginning step. Our model of therapy has as its goal the working through and resolution of the conflict derivatives involved in the stressful disruption. Our hypothesis is that such exploration and working through facilitate the establishment of a new adaptive balance.

Gill (4) has suggested one theoretical rationale for such an occurrence: "Both Gitelson and Reider speak of the fate of these [derivative conflicts] in psychotherapy, though Gitelson emphasizes that they are partly solved, and Reider that they are partly unsolved. The implication is that there exists a basic conflict and that without resolution of the basic conflict no real solution of a derivative conflict can be made. This may be true, but I would like to hold open the question that even though the basic conflict is unsolved, and under sufficient stress can once again reactivate the derivative conflicts, the derivative conflicts develop a relative degree of autonomy and exist in a form which allows a relatively firm resolution."

We consider that relative resolution is possible even of those derivatives that are still intimately tied to core conflicts as well as those which have developed autonomy. If personality functioning is thought of as organized and interrelated, then any change at any level necessarily alters the structure as a whole. Indeed, long-term psychotherapy is frequently described as working through a succession of derivatives. There is no "sudden breakthrough" but rather a systematic investigation of many facets of the patient's difficulties.

Menninger (7) states that "the ego always does *more* than attempt to manage the immediate emergency. In spite of resistance implicit in the semi-stablized emergency adjustment, the ego perennially endeavors to return to its original normal adjustment level."

We have found that restoration of equilibrium is facilitated by understanding the precipitating stress—stress that is not conscious at the point of application. While the events evoking conflict are remembered by the patient, they may not be reported, at least immediately, and are often not specifically connected with the subjective distress. To establish such connections is the primary task of the therapeutic transaction. Asked why he comes now, the patient cites long-standing difficulties, vaguely refers to the build-up of tension, or offers other rationalized explanations. It seems that if he could really answer the question, he would be better able to cope with his distress and achieve a new psychic equilibrium. To promote such coping and readaptation, then, is the goal of this treatment. The nature of the re-adaptation will vary with many factors, including, among others, the previous level of psychic equilibrium, the severity of the disruption, the availability of coping mechanisms and environmental supports, and the speed and appropriateness of intervention.

The most apparent difference between this type of brief treatment and more traditional forms of psychotherapy is in the systematic focusing on the current situation, with historical material utilized only as it arises spontaneously and relates directly to the current problems. Attention is focused on the present situation not because it is intrinsically important, but because in this way we learn about the current conflict derivatives involved in the stress. As Fenichel (2) has pointed out, "conflicts arise when new experiences occur that are connected with what had previously been repressed. Then there is a tendency on the part of the repressed to use the new events as an opportunity for an outlet; it tends to displace its energies to it, to turn the new event into a 'derivative.' " Elsewhere (3) he states that "we must work not only at the point of actual instinctual conflicts, but at the point of the *most important* current instinctual conflicts. It is the point of the most important conflicts *at the moment.*"

Two examples will indicate more precisely the nature of our approach. Precipitating stress is rarely conscious when a patient applies for treatment as the following case illustrates. The patient came to her first interview in an obviously anxious state but described recent experiences that were not too different from some she had handled alone in the past. With the constant focus on the meaning and implications of her current situation, the significance of these recent experiences emerged.

A thirty-year-old housewife sought psychiatric treatment three days after a quarrel with her husband in which he had beaten and bruised her. For the first time in one of these frequent quarrels, the patient's twelve-year-old daughter had participated and asserted that she would protect her mother with physical force. When the husband threatened to retaliate against the daughter, the patient took all the children and went to her father. She told mutual friends where she was so that her husband could reach her, but he did not do so. These events were reminiscent of a quarrel the patient at age twelve had with her mother in which she was physically aggressive.

This marriage, like her previous one, was extremely stormy, and violent quarrels were common. It developed in the interviews that this particular quarrel had a special quality in that the sequence of events duplicated for the patient some aspects of a traumatic adolescent experience. At that time she left her home and went to stay with her father, and the mother did not get in touch with her or ask her to return.

She began the first interview by saying it was her husband's idea that she needed treatment, and lashed out at him for his physical brutality and lack of understanding. The therapist interrupted to ask how she herself could be helped. The patient briefly mentioned her husband's idea that she was still bothered by her alienation from her mother; but she soon returned to berating him.

In the second visit, she was remarkably calmer, had temporarily returned to her husband, and now described some of her earlier troubles with her mother. In response to the therapist's focus, she detailed the situation that led to her leaving home at the age of twelve. She described quite poignantly her disappointment in her mother. She then moved to her feelings of hurt with her husband, and the therapist tied in the hurt at her husband not looking for her with the feelings she had as an adolescent when she ran away and her mother had not tried to find her. The patient agreed, and in the next two interviews developed more fully her feeling that she had always been alone, with no one to care for and protect her, neither husband, father, nor mother. Her tone in contrast to her frenetic activity at the time of the first interview suggested that she was better able to cope with the situation. The patient indicated that she could handle her situation now, even though she was separated again, and probably permanently, from her husband. The contacts were ended at the fourth visit, with the expectation that she would be seen in the medical student training program for a short series of interviews.

The treatment process with the preceding patient involved a gradual sifting and sharpening activity by the therapist which led to their mutual recognition and understanding of the basis of the patient's current distress. The emphasis was always on the subjective meaning of events, that is, the conflictual feelings that the stressful events engendered. This patient's identification with her adolescent daughter apparently reactivated her own conflict around loss, leading her to re-enact earlier behavior and to experience the same feelings of desolation she had felt before.

In the six interviews with the second patient, the circumstances producing the personal crisis and his subsequent request for psychiatric help gradually emerged. This understanding appeared to effect the re-establishment of an adaptability in some ways more flexible than before the disruption.

A thirty-five-year-old man requested help for vague complaints of irritability and tension. He remarked almost incidentally in the first interview that he and his wife had separated and that he had made a major career change some six months earlier. His application at this late date, however, did not seem to result directly from disruption around the separation or the job change. In the first and second interviews he was rigidly self-contained, developing the theme that to his wife and business associates he always seemed to be cast in the role of "fall guy."

In the third interview he began to express some disappointment at the impending divorce and for the first time mentioned his "homosexual" problem, namely, his feeling that he was not sufficiently masculine and his wife's accusations that he was more interested in his men friends than in her. Their separation had come about through his bringing into the home a male friend who had just arrived in the city; his wife saw the friendship as a sexual affair and left. He denied any sexual involvement, saying that he had had homosexual experiences only rarely in the past during his wife's absences and now wanted very much to become more "masculine," that is, more interested in women.

Encouragement of free expression in that interview led him to consider his current situation more specifically in the next visit. He had recently become aware of violently aggressive thoughts which frightened him. He then disclosed that four weeks before the application he had moved into an apartment with a homosexual woman friend and another man. His roommates drank a good deal and became abusive and belligerent, and his aggressive fantasies were directed toward them. In the fifth interview, he revealed that not only were both roommates homosexual, but they brought their partners home with them and taunted him that he, too, was homosexual. He could not help wondering whether they were right. The therapist pointed out that they were in a sense thrusting homosexuality on him and that realistically this was an upsetting situation. At this point, both therapist and patient understood that these circumstances made him afraid of losing control over his impulses and, therefore, impelled him to treatment. There was a good deal of discussion of his new-found absorption in fantasy, the release and elation he experienced after describing his feelings in the interviews, and the fear of losing control if he allowed himself to experience too much emotionally. The therapist thereupon reassured him about the difference between thought and action, and also pointed out that his habitual use of so much control might make him more apprehensive than necessary. The therapeutic intent was to alter the defensive structure so that he could permit himself freer expression.

He came to the sixth and last interview with plans to leave his present living situation; there was a possibility of reconciliation with his wife but he was unsure whether this was what he wanted.

The stresses leading these two patients to apply for help occurred at different times in relation to their applications and emerged differently in the course of therapy. The length of time between stress and application and the duration of the therapeutic search for stress cannot be conceptualized in chronological terms, because they depend upon the therapeutic process. The time varies according to the individual patient, his circumstances, his defenses and resistances, on the one hand, and according to the therapist and his skill, training, and experience in these particular techniques on the other.

In the time relationship between the precipitating stress and the request for help several variables need to be considered. For a patient who has maintained a constantly precarious and shifting kind of adjustment, the precipitating stress may have developed within hours of the call for help. For another kind of patient for whom stability is more dependable and for whom long-standing adaptations are the rule, weeks of struggle may ensue before the anxiety resulting from the disruption eventuates in the call for help. The common factor in both instances is the necessity for identifying from the interview material the previous level of adaptation and the point of its disruption. To do this successfully, one must see the patients promptly, while such material is still accessible. The patients in this study were seen within 24 hours of their call, but work by Dewees et al. (1) suggests a possible outer limit for the initial interview of two weeks after the request.

The process of resolving the disrupted state varies among other factors with the complications of the derivative conflict, the adequacy of the patient's coping mechanisms, his capacity for insight. Working through a derivative conflict will enable many patients to maintain a stable equilibrium without further help.

Others can achieve only a tenuous balance that is constantly endangered by the eruption of fresh derivatives.

Our work with this approach, however, suggests that this type of focused treatment is appropriate for all patients applying to a psychiatric clinic. Since an important aspect of the focus includes the exploration of attitudes and expectations toward treatment, one result is that patients are helped not only in achieving a new adaptive balance but also in clarifying their motivation for further treatment. Motivation for treatment of long-standing difficulties may in fact be increased by the experience of a successful brief therapeutic transaction.

REFERENCES

1. Dewees, R. F., Johnson, R. F., Sarvis, M. A., & Pope, S. T. An open service in a university psychiatric clinic. *Ment. Hyg.*, 1961, **45**, 57.

2. Fenichel, O. *The psychoanalytic theory of neurosis.* New York: W. W. Norton, 1945.

3. Fenichel, O. *Problems of psychoanalytic technique.* Albany: Psychoanalytic Quarterly, Inc., 1941.

4. Gill, M. Psychoanalysis and exploratory psychotherapy. *J. Am. Psychoanal. Ass.*, 1954, **2**, 793.

5. Gitelson, M. Psychoanalysis and dynamic psychiatry. *Arch. Neur. Psychiat.*, 1951, **66**, 287.

6. Kalis, B. L., Harris, M. R., Prestwood, A. R., & Freeman, E. H. Precipitating stress as a focus in psychotherapy. *Arch. Gen. Psychiat.*, 1961, **5**, 219.

7. Menninger, K. Psychological aspects of the organism under stress. *J. Am. Psychoanal. Ass.*, 1954, **2**, 305.

Chapter 10

The State of Crisis:

Some Theoretical Considerations

Lydia Rapoport, M.S.S.

Social workers have always been confronted with clients who seek help because of singular or multiple problems and who are suffering from the ill effects of stress. Clients come because they are in "need," have a "problem," are under "stress," or are in a "crisis." All these familiar terms are used interchangeably, or, at best, are used descriptively and not in a sufficiently precise conceptual manner. How we conceptualize the problem and the state of being which propels people to seek help will influence the methods and techniques we develop and the way in which we deploy community and professional resources.

This paper seeks to explore the theoretical underpinnings of the concept of the state of crisis and to examine some of the distinctive ideas that characterize it. It is hoped that such a characterization may help the practitioner to differentiate the theoretical notions about crisis from more familiar but loosely used concepts—such as "problem," "need," and "stress"—found so prominently in social work thought.

THE NATURE OF THE STATE CRISIS

The term "crisis," generally used in a rather loose and indeterminate way, covers a variety of meaning. In lay language, a crisis is usually equated with disaster, an environmental event which poses an external threat. Erikson and others talk of developmental crises which are induced by the special tasks required by each new developmental phase in the sequence of psychosocial maturation (5). Moreover, the terms "crisis" and "stress" are often used interchangeably. The term "stress" itself is

Reprinted from *Social Service Review*, 1962, **36**, 211-217, by permission of the publisher and the author. The author is Professor of Social Welfare, School of Social Welfare, University of California, Berkeley.

used to denote three different sets of phenomena: (1) stress is equated with the stressful event or situation; (2) it is used to refer to the state of the individual who responds to the stressful event, and thus we talk of the client who responds with feelings or symptoms of stress; (3) more often, stress refers to the relation of the stressful stimulus, the individual's reaction to it, and the events to which it leads.

In addition, it has been noted that the concept of stress tends to carry with it a purely negative connotation: Stress is a burden or load under which a person survives or cracks. Thus, stress is assumed to have pathogenic potential. In contrast, a state of crisis is conceived to have a growth-promoting potential. W. I. Thomas, the social theorist, saw crisis as a catalyst that disturbs old habits, evokes new responses, and becomes a major factor in charting new developments (12). Thus conceived, a crisis is a call to new action; the challenge it provokes may bring forth new coping mechanisms which serve to strengthen the individual's adaptive capacity and thereby, in general, to raise his level of mental health.

The concept of crisis as formulated by its chief theoreticians, Dr. Erich Lindemann and Dr. Gerald Caplan (8), refers to the state of the reacting individual who finds himself in a hazardous situation. Not all individuals, faced by the same hazardous events, will be in a state of crisis. On the other hand, there are certain common hazardous events, such as loss by death and its sequel of grief and bereavement, which will induce a state of crisis of lesser or greater intensity, or of lesser or greater duration, in nearly all individuals. This fact, incidentally, has important implications for programs of primary preventions.

A state of crisis is not an illness. Dr. James Tyhurst, a Canadian social psychiatrist, states that what we call illness is also an opportunity for growth, however severe the impasse may appear. He writes: "Too often, with its emphasis upon symptomatic treatment, present-day psychiatry denies the patient this opportunity . . . to benefit from his troubles by dint of personal growth and development in relation to the problem" (11). The person, however, may be suffering from chronic or temporary symptomatology or pathological patterns of behavior when he goes into a state of crisis. These two conditions have to be conceived of and evaluated separately. For example, in response to a hazardous event—the death of a loved person—an individual will react with depression, which is found to be a part of the normal process of mourning (1). This type of depression has to be differentiated from a clinical syndrome in which a patient presents a pathological degree of depression as the main symptom. In the latter instance, it is more nearly correct to speak of a depressive illness, whether it takes the form of melancholia or of an agitated depression. The depressive illness may or may not be the reaction to the hazardous event.

Crisis in its simplest terms is defined as "an upset in a steady state" (14). This definition rests on the postulate that an individual strives to maintain for himself a state of equilibrium through a constant series of adaptive maneuvers and characteristic problem-solving activities through which basic need-fulfilment takes place. Throughout a life span, many situations occur which lead to sudden discontinuities by which the homeostatic state is disturbed and which result in a state of disequilibrium. In response to many such situations, the individual may possess adequate adaptive or re-equilibrating mechanisms. However, in a state of crisis, by definition, it is postulated that the habitual problem-solving activities are not adequate and do not lead rapidly to the previously achieved balanced state.

The hazardous event itself requires a solution which is new in relation to the individual's previous life experience. Many individuals are able to develop new solutions by means of the normal range of problem-solving mechanisms stemming from their general life experience and maturation, and are thereby able to deal adequately with the hazardous event. Others are unable to respond with appropriate solutions, and the hazardous event and its sequelae continue to be a source of stress.

The hazardous event creates for the individual a problem in his current life situation. The problem can be conceived of as a threat, a loss, or a challenge. The threat may be to fundamental, instinctual needs or to the person's sense of integrity. The loss may be actual or may be experienced as a state of acute deprivation. For each of these states, there is a major characteristic mode in which the ego tends to respond. A threat to need and integrity is met with anxiety. Loss or deprivation is met with depression. If the problem is viewed as a challenge, it is more likely to be met with a mobilization of energy and purposive problem-solving activities.

Since the hazardous event, although posing a problem in the current life situation, may contain a threat to instinctual needs, it is therefore likely to be linked with old threats to instinctual needs and to trigger off and reactivate unresolved or partially resolved unconscious conflicts. The previous failure may act as an additional burden in the present crisis (3, pp. 8-9). It has been observed by various investigators that during a crisis memories of old problems which are linked symbolically to the present are stimulated and may emerge into consciousness spontaneously or can be uncovered and dealt with by relatively brief therapeutic intervention (10). However, with or without therapeutic intervention, the energy needed to maintain repression of the earlier unsolved problem may now become available to solve the current problem in a more appropriately mature manner. The crisis with its mobilization of energy operates as a "second chance" in correcting earlier faulty problem-solving.

The above discussion indicates that there are three sets of interrelated factors that can produce a state of crisis: (1) a hazardous event which poses some threat; (2) a threat to instinctual need which is symbolically linked to earlier threats that resulted in vulnerability or conflict; (3) an inability to respond with adequate coping mechanisms (9).

THE CHARACTERISTICS OF THE STATE OF CRISIS

Certain characteristics of the state of crisis may be delineated. The first important characteristic is the view that the crisis is self-limiting in a temporal sense. It does not continue indefinitely. Dr. Caplan maintains that the actual period of the crisis tends to last from one to six weeks. Some solution is sought for the state of upset to restore a sense of equilibrium. The solution itself may lead to the prior level of equilibrium. It may lead to a more adequate or higher level of functioning or to a lower level of functioning and a lower level of mental health.

The second feature of the state of crisis is that there are certain typical phases which characterize the period of upset. One could talk of a beginning, middle, and end.* Dr. Tyhurst, referring to crisis in the nature of more major disasters, identifies the period of impact, period of recoil, and the post-traumatic period (11, p. 150). Dr. Caplan describes the phases and the processes of development in the following way: In the initial phase, there is a rise in tension in response to the initial impact of stress. During this period habitual problem-solving mechanisms are called forth. If the first effort fails, there will be an increase in the level of tension with an increase in feeling upset and ineffective. This state may then call forth "emergency problem-solving mechanisms" (4). Three things are likely to happen: (1) the problem may actually be solved; (2) there may be a redefinition of the problem in order to achieve need-satisfaction; (3) the problem may be avoided through need-resignation and the relinquishment of goals. If the problem cannot be solved in

* It might be noted that social workers are familiar with individuals and families who live in a chronic state of crisis. Here one might say that being in a crisis state is part of their life style because of a general inadequacy in social functioning. Crises for such individuals do not have a beginning, middle, and end, but flow into each other and are compounded and circular. It is clear that the concepts of crisis and its management discussed above do not apply to individuals and families who are beset by multiple problems, chronic and continual states of heightened tension and disorganization. Here one is dealing with a different order of phenomena, which is not adequately explained by crisis theory as defined in this statement.

any of these ways, a state of more major disorganization may ensue.

Various investigators have studied the phases of the state of crisis more systematically in relation to specific hazardous events. For example, Dr. John Bowlby and James Robertson, of the Tavistock Clinic, have studied the separation trauma experienced by young children entering a hospital. Three distinct phases have been isolated—protest, despair, and detachment (2). In the phase of protest, the young child maintains the hope that the mother will return and protests his condition vigorously and loudly with much crying and overt distress. In the phase of despair, there is increasing hopelessness. The predominant affect is depression, as part of grief and mourning. There is increasingly withdrawn behavior and inactivity. The third stage is detachment, which Bowlby formerly called "denial." It is a quiet period in which the young child seems to be making an "adaptation"; indeed, it is often mistaken for contentment, rather than seen as the result of resignation. In this phase defenses are developed, such as denial of the longing for the mother and detachment in relation to nurturing adults. The child at best forms shallow attachments, becomes increasingly self-centered, and becomes attached to material objects.

Dr. Erich Lindemann has observed another example of the phases of the state of crisis and the coping mechanisms linked with it in acute grief following bereavement (7). In studies made after the disaster of the Coconut Grove fire in Boston, Dr. Lindemann noted that the duration of the grief reaction seemed to be dependent on the success with which a person did his "grief work." A normal course of grief reaction begins when the bereaved (1) starts to emancipate himself from the bondage to the deceased, (2) makes a readjustment in the environment in which the deceased is missing, (3) forms new relationships or patterns of interaction that bring rewards and satisfactions.

A third example of phases of crisis that have been identified comes from studies of families in crisis as a result of the event of the birth of a premature infant. These studies, still in progress, are being made by Dr. Caplan and his team of research workers at the Family Guidance Center in Boston. From the work of one of the team members, David Kaplan (6), four phases have been isolated which are linked with the psychological tasks that need to be achieved in order for the crisis to be resolved in a healthy way. First, the mother must prepare herself psychologically for a possible loss—stillbirth or postnatal loss—through the process of anticipatory grief work. Second, the mother needs to acknowledge to herself some feelings of maternal failure and guilt in her inability to deliver a normal, full-term baby. Third, when it is clear that the baby will survive, there needs to be a resumption of the process of relating to the baby. Fourth, the mother must be able to recognize the special needs and requirements of a premature infant.

In addition to isolating temporal and phasic aspects of the state of crisis, various investigators have described other characteristics of the upset state. As previously mentioned, there is a rise in tension which may push toward a peak. There is also a general feeling of helplessness. In part, this may be a state of cognitive confusion wherein the individual literally does not know how to think of his problem, how to evaluate reality, and how to formulate and evaluate the outcome of the crisis and possibilities for problem-solving. In extreme states, there may also be perceptual confusion such as in the temporal or spatial sense.

Some disorganization and lack of effective functioning may ensue. Disorganized behavior may take the form of activity which is related to attempts to discharge inner tension, rather than to solving the problem in the external situation. It should be noted that the feelings of tension that arise are in themselves a problem with which the individual seeks to deal. The rise in tension may be experienced as anxiety; it may be converted into somatic symptoms; or it may be denied by means of repression.

Various characteristic coping patterns have also been described. Certain patterns of coping while in crisis are essentially maladaptive. For example, an individual may deal with the hazardous event and his feelings about it with magical thinking or with excessive fantasy; he may respond with regressive forms of behavior, with somatization, or, in extreme situations, with withdrawal from reality.

Other types of coping patterns are essentially adaptive in nature. For example, the activity of the individual or family may be task-oriented. The problem may be broken down into component parts and efforts made to solve each aspect of it. The "mental work" may be directed to correct the cognitive perception, which means predicting and anticipating outcome through cognitive restructuring. The mental work may also entail "rehearsal for reality"—preparation for the anticipated activity or affect. The individual or family may actively seek out new models for identification and for the development of new interpersonal skills as part of problem-solving, particularly in crises of role transition. In general, the patterns of responses for an individual or family necessary for healthy crisis resolution may be described as follows: (1) correct cognitive perception of the situation, which is furthered by seeking new knowledge and by keeping the problem in consciousness; (2) management of affect through awareness of feelings and appropriate verbalization leading towards tension discharge and mastery; (3) development of patterns of seeking and using help with actual tasks and feelings by using interpersonal and institutional resources (3).

IMPLICATIONS FOR PRACTICE

Problem-solving during a state of crisis is facilitated by various conditions. The above formulation of patterns of response necessary for healthy crisis resolution also contains guides for intervention. For example, if need for cognitive grasp and restructuring is crucial as a first step in problem-solving, then the first task of the professional caretaker or social worker is to clarify the problem that leads to the call for help. Factors leading to the disruption of functioning are often preconscious and unintegrated. Identifying and isolating these factors to arrive at a formulation of the problem and hence to facilitate cognitive restructuring and integration, in and of itself, may be enough, in many instances, to promote a return to the previously achieved balanced state. In the precipitating stress studies of Dr. Kalis, previously referred to, the conclusion has emerged that the individual is not fully aware of the precipitating stress and its consequences and that prompt therapeutic focusing on the precipitating stress, with clarification of relevant circumstances and conflicts, facilitates restoration of emotional equilibrium.

Second, for the expression and management of feelings, there needs to be an explicit acceptance by the helping person of the disordered affect, irrational attitudes, or negative responses, but this needs to be placed in a rational context by understanding and clarifying the natural history of such reactions.

The third point is the availability and use of interpersonal and institutional resources. It has been noted that a major upset in a system—be this in an individual, family, or community group—tends to arouse supporting features and to mobilize energy for reaching out by others in the social network. This is dramatically demonstrated in times of actual disaster. Thus, the individual or group can draw comfort, support, and need-satisfaction from the network of human relationships. Formal institutions and agencies, caretakers in the community, and social processes developed in the culture—such as rites of passage—all serve to offer support, to restore equilibrium, and to ease role transition. In this connection, Dr. Tyhurst offers a provocative opinion. He states that some people in turmoil come to the attention of the social institution called "psychiatry," where they are usually defined as "ill," largely as a matter of social convention. He states further that "turning to the psychiatrist may represent an impoverishment of resources in the relevant social environment as much as an indication of the type of severity of disorder (11, p. 164).

The major observation, worthy of note because of its implications for social work practice, is the fact that the person or family in crisis becomes more susceptible to the influence of "significant others" in the environment. Moreover, the degree of activity of the helping person does not have to be high. A little help, rationally directed and purposefully focused at a strategic time, is more effective than more extensive help given at a period of less emotional accessibility. In addition, the helping person needs to view himself as intervening in a social system—as part of a network of relationships—and not as a single resource. These considerations raise important issues for the activities of all helping professions, not only for social work. There is a need to develop programs and skills that are geared to making help rapidly available at times and places where a state of crisis may develop. Only then can preventive or corrective intervention be maximally effective.

CONCLUSION

Crisis theory, as conceptualized by Lindemann, Caplan, and other mental health workers, is particularly compatible with general social work theory. The crisis-theory framework is applicable to the individual, to the family, and to the group. It makes use of ego psychology as well as newer social science concepts now being incorporated into social work theory, such as role, role-transition states, and social network. It offers the additional advantage of more sharply defining and characterizing a state which occurs frequently in the life cycle of the individual or family and during which the helping professions and caretakers are likely to have access to people and are likely to be active. The theoretical formulations give greater precision and clarity to the nature of the operative conditions, processes, and hence possible techniques which might be developed for intervention.

REFERENCES

1. Bowlby, J., M. D. Grief and mourning in fancy and early childhood. *Psychoanalytic Study of the Child*, 1960, **15**, 11-12.
2. Bowlby, J., M. D. Separation anxiety. *International Journal of Psychoanalysis*, 1960, **41**, 89-113.
3. Caplan, G., M. D. Patterns of response to the crisis of prematurity: A preliminary approach. Unpublished paper.

4. Caplan, G., M. D. Formulated in seminars at the Harvard School of Public Health, 1959-60.
5. Erickson, E. Growth and crisis of the 'healthy personality.' *Personality in nature, society, and culture.* Clyde Kluckholn, Henry A. Murray, and David M. Schneider (Eds.), 2d ed., rev. and enl.; New York: Alfred A. Knopf, 1953, Chap. xii.
6. Kaplan, D. M. & Mason, F., M. D. Maternal reaction to premature birth viewed as an acute emotional disorder. *American Journal of Orthopsychiatry*, 1960, **30**, 539-52.
7. Lindemann, E., M. D. Symptomatology and management of acute grief. *American Journal of Psychiatry*, 1944, **101**, 141-48.
8. Lindemann, E., M. D., & Caplan, G., M. D. A conceptual framework for preventive psychiatry. Unpublished paper.
9. Parad, H. J. & Caplan, G., M. D. A framework for studying families in crisis, *Social Work*, 1960, **5.**
10. Sarvis, M. A., M. D., Dewees, S. & Johnson, R. A concept of ego-oriented psychotherapy. *Psychiatry*, 1959, **20**, 277-87; and B. L. Kalis et al. Precipitating stress as a focus in psychotherapy. *Archives of General Psychiatry*, 1961, **5,** 219-26.
11. Tyhurst, J. S., M. D., The role of transition states—including disasters—in mental illness. *Symposium on Preventive and Social Psychiatry.* Washington, D.C.: Walter Reed Army Institute of Research, 1957, p. 164.
12. Volkhart, E. (Ed.), *Social behavior and personality contributions of W. I. Thomas to theory and social research.* New York: Social Science Research Council, 1951, pp. 12-14.

II. Brief Therapy in the Context of Community Mental Health

Growing concern with the immediate needs of the poor, who have until the last few years felt alienated from and excluded by the mental health establishment, has led to experiments with new approaches, geared to providing readily accessible emergency assistance. Walk-in clinics offer crisis-oriented and other forms of immediate intervention without the dissuading formality of elaborate intake procedures and their concomitant delays.

Jacobson, Wilner, Morley, Schneider, Strickler, and Sommer outline a walk-in program that is limited entirely to crisis intervention with a maximum of six visits. Impressive numbers of patients can be seen with minimal wait, and there are no admission criteria which would create barriers for "poor-risk" patients. Treatment goals are clearly limited by the crisis framework, and one-third of the patients seen are subsequently referred for further therapy. The authors provide a detailed description of their crisis intervention methodology, emphasizing focus on the immediate problem and the means of resolving it.

Normand, Fensterheim, and Schrenzel describe a walk-in clinic designed for a similar low socioeconomic population, but with a somewhat different emphasis in technique. Impressed by the fact that noxious environmental forces frequently trigger disturbed behavior in patients in this social stratum, the authors often choose to direct their interventions at elements in the environment, when this is considered the most effective leverage point. In order neither to overemphasize nor to overlook intrapsychic factors, the authors suggest that two different formulations be elaborated for each patient. Developing both dynamic and action formulations multiplies therapeutic options. The therapist can provide meaningful treatment that is congruent with patients' expectations.

Hansell gives a broad public health perspective. Concerned with the total care-giving system, he believes that mental health professionals have a responsibility to provide assistance to all who require it in the community they serve. Treatment priorities must be established accordingly, since therapists do not have the freedom to "export" patients whom they might not ordinarily be interested in treating. Meeting the totality of needs of a catchment area necessitates reformulation of the objectives of psychotherapy. Hansell emphasizes what he regards as a central component: the therapist's communication of hopeful expectancy that the patient has the capacity to change, in an effort to rekindle an active search for independent functioning. Too often, by labeling patients as mentally ill, society reinforces a sense of helplessness which generates what Mechanic calls "illness behavior" (1). Hansell stresses that dependent needs cannot be perpetuated in prolonged treatment relationships, which would quickly clog the care-giving system. Hansell's provocative paper introduces a larger dimension and a sweeping challenge to the mental health professions.

REFERENCE

1. Mechanic, D. Therapeutic Intervention: Issues in the care of the mentally ill. *American Journal of Orthopsychiatry*, 1967, **37**, 703-718.

Chapter 11

The Scope and Practice of an Early-Access Brief Treatment Psychiatric Center

G. F. Jacobson, M.D., D. M. Wilner, Ph.D.,
W. E. Morley, Ph.D., S. Schneider, Ph.D.,
M. Strickler, M.S.W., and G. J. Sommer, Ph.D.

Walk-in psychiatric outpatient centers are sufficiently new in this decade to arouse questions regarding their *modus operandi,* the premises under which they operate and the impact they are likely to have. Does the populace really make use of such facilities? Are the persons who come to such clinics genuinely in need of psychiatric help? What skills are really needed in such a setting? Do short term contacts really help? Answers to these questions will help to decide whether walk-in centers are elements in a passing parade of false starts or important components of the network of psychiatric services of the future.

This paper describes the scope and practice of one such walk-in clinic, the Benjamin Rush Center, offering, for adults, service without undue delay, on a treatment schedule that almost invariably does not exceed six visits, has no financial restrictions, and is non-hospital-based.* Treatment emphasis is on the nature of the current problem or crisis rather than on long-standing pathology.

The Center now in its third year of operation is a division of the Los Angeles Psychiatric Service, a non-profit community outpatient clinic that has been in existence since 1942. The

Reprinted from *American Journal of Psychiatry,* 1965, 121, 1176-1182, by permission of the publisher and the authors. Copyright 1965, the American Psychiatric Association. Dr. Jacobson is Executive Director, Los Angeles Psychiatric Service. Dr. Wilner is with the School of Public Health. U.C.L.A. Dr. Morley is Deputy Director, Los Angeles Psychiatric Service. Dr. Schneider is with the Psychology Section, National Institute of Mental Health. Dr. Strickler is Deputy Director, Los Angeles Psychiatric Service. Dr. Sommer is Clinical Psychologist, Los Angeles Psychiatric Service.

* This program is supported in part by a grant of National Mental Health Act Funds by the State of California Dept. of Mental Hygiene.

parent service offers intermediate and longer term individual and group treatment. Training programs for residents and medical students in psychiatry, as well as for psychologists and social workers, are affiliated both with the Benjamin Rush Center and the parent service.

The basic objectives of walk-in psychiatric clinics like the Rush Center are common to all health professions, that is, the optimal use of professional manpower to cope effectively with illness. In all illness, the steps to treatment would seem to include two irreducible elements, self-perception on the part of the person that he needs assessment and treatment, and the existence and availability of culturally familiar and desired agents of treatment.

In the mental health professions—and particularly in the outpatient field—the matter is complicated by the acute shortage of skilled manpower, and by the fact that much of this manpower in community clinics is devoted to intermediate and longer-term treatment, thereby limiting the total number of patients who can be treated. In addition, most present-day clinics cannot meet frequent patient demands for help without delay. Finally, some patients may look for a different kind of help than is typically offered in present psychiatric clinics, such as help with a current life situation. In short, for some persons, outpatient psychiatric help is either altogether unavailable, or existing facilities may appear undesirable and even beyond familiar comprehension.

Walk-in centers would offer increased treatment opportunities for these persons who, while suffering from psychological disorders, might ordinarily have great difficulty in engaging with existing psychiatric outlets or might refuse to do so altogether. Within this frame of reference, walk-in clinics would supplement and not substitute for other kinds of outpatient clinics; the conjunction of the Benjamin Rush Center within the parent service is illustrative of this approach.

From the foregoing framework of theory and strategy and guiding the Benjamin Rush Center from its inception were a number of ideals or intentions regarding its basic operations. Five will be singled out at this time for special mention.

(1). The first was the policy of providing service either at the time it is first requested, or as close to this time as available staff permits, and virtually always within a week. The scarcity of immediate psychiatric service for anyone unable to pay for private treatment is well known.

Early intervention provides the occasion and the instrumentality for preventive psychiatric treatment in much the same way that acute physical disease is served by medical care brought to bear soon after the physical disease is disclosed.

(2). Second, the clinic would offer brief treatment up to six visits. If such treatment is to be effective, one cannot attempt to do in abbreviated form what is elsewhere done over a longer period of time.* Rather, the service offered must be appropriate and specific to the time allotted.

Since the latter was our purpose, a specialized approach is used which is based on the generally accepted premise that psychiatric exacerbations, however deeply or superficially rooted in experience, have immediate precipitating events, and that one can fruitfully work with these in a limited period of time,† and, in fact, cannot logically work with them for extended periods. Crisis theory, as developed by Gerald Caplan (1) and others has a major bearing on this issue, and will be discussed more fully later. Caplan suggests that a crisis is resolved for better or worse in four-six weeks, a period usually coinciding with Rush Center treatment arrangements.

These considerations provided a theoretical framework for a specific time-limited approach. The plan was *not* to replace longer-term treatment when indicated, especially for cases with well-established characterological or other pathology. From the beginning, the program provided for the possibility of referrals for further work *after* the contractual treatment effort dealing with the current crisis and *not* before. It was expected that even if further treatment might prove indicated, substantial gain might have been achieved by the crisis intervention. And it was also expected that a substantial number of patients would not be referred for further treatment.

(3). The third intent was the policy of admitting patients for treatment without exclusions of any sort except for those in treatment elsewhere. The intention was to offer treatment opportunity to all persons, including inevitably those seen as "bad risks" in traditional settings, and thus to avoid contributing to the inadvertent "conspiracy" to withhold treatment opportunity from a significant number of persons in need of it. The Rush Center was to serve a wide range of psychiatric cases, particularly including: (i) some persons who for socio-cultural

---

* Even so, it is of interest that in psychiatric clinics the nation over, 4 was the median number of visits by patients, many of whom received only diagnostic service, according to a survey conducted in 1959 of outpatient psychiatric clinics in the United States (6). The authors of the survey suggest that not all these are cases of missed psychiatric opportunity, but some are included who considered their problem sufficiently alleviated. Perhaps these patients wanted brief contact and attempted to use the diagnostic procedures as treatment, however limited or inadequate they may have been for that purpose.

† Harris, Kalis, and Freeman (4, 5) have developed a related concept in a somewhat different setting at the Langley Porter Institute.

reasons are generally outsiders to the network of psychiatric treatment facilities, older persons, persons in lower economic status, and racial minorities. Issues here are those that relate to potential patients themselves, e.g., unfamiliarity with the discourse of psychiatry; as well as those that relate to the potential therapist, e.g., discomfort with persons seeking help who are unfamiliar with psychiatric language and concepts. (ii) Younger persons and those better off economically who for psychological reasons do not perceive that the problems troubling them arise in the self and thus abjure ordinary psychiatric solutions.*

Two further goals are more instrumental and designed to implement the first three:

(4). The fourth intention was to seek to make widely known, in the entire metropolitan area, the existence of the services of the Center. The mass media were in fact employed, using descriptive language designed to overcome some of the barriers just mentioned—socio-cultural and personal—that inhibit some individuals from obtaining psychiatric help.

(5). Finally, the fifth intention was to provide administrative procedures of such flexibility as to insure special handling of particular cases with urgency, when necessary. This was insured by appointment of a professionally mature intake officer, sufficiently experienced to make judgments about immediacy of need; cases in need of *immediate* attention were to be seen at once.

THE FIRST NINETEEN MONTHS
OF OPERATION

So much for ideals and intentions. It is possible now to see how well they match up to the reality of day-to-day clinic operation during approximately the first year and one-half of the Rush Center's existence. Certain numerical data will be consulted that derive from systematic procedures to monitor the characteristics of the new service that were established when the Center first opened its doors. The information was obtained from three primary sources: (i) intake forms filled out by the patient during the brief waiting time before the first clinical session; (ii)

---

* The terms "treatment," "therapy," "psychiatrist," "patients" are rarely used at the Rush Center. Instead the nouns used are "consultant" (for "therapist") and "consultee" (for "patient"). This usage is in line with the desire to provide appeal for persons who in the Center's view are in need of professional psychiatric assistance, but who do not consider themselves in such need. On the other hand, no attempt is made to conceal the psychiatric auspices of the service.

therapist forms filled out by the therapist during the first and subsequent sessions (and of course useful in diagnostic and treatment contexts); and (iii) final summaries of cases and routine records.*

In the first nineteen months of operation, 776 patients were seen. This represents a pace of about 500 per year, perhaps twice the number of patients seen with staff of similar size and composition in more traditional clinics.

In the first month of the clinic's operation approximately 100 patients sought access to the Rush Center, a pace of about 1,200 patients per year. This substantial response to the Center's offerings and mode of operation was clearly related to the high visibility given the Center in the newspapers, radio, and television in the period prior to the Center's opening. To have continued at this pace would have meant violating the first intention mentioned above regarding the early access feature of the Center. As a consequence, the publicity about the Center was attenuated so that there could result a balance between service capacity and demand.† In other words, while conscious effort is made at present to modulate the visibility of the Rush Center, the vast majority of persons presenting themselves for treatment *obtain it* within a day to a week of requesting it.

One of the substantive intents of the Rush Center was to provide treatment opportunity for persons ordinarily not favored as theapeutic good bets and who may, in traditional settings, not even make more than casual effort, easily aborted, to obtain treatment. Our evidence indicates that several categories of ordinarily under-represented treatment populations did in fact tend more to seek treatment at the Rush Center, particularly in the first six months of clinic operation. In the first six months (January 1st to June 30th of 1962), 39.0% of patients were 45 years of age or over. In two subsequent six-month periods, the corresponding figures were 29.5% and 25.5% respectively. In the first six months, 18.5% had less than high school education; for subsequent six-month periods, the figures were 11.9% and 8.4%. The first six months, it will be recalled, was the period during which the effects of vigorous publicity regarding the Center's

---

* The data were tabulated and analyzed at the UCLA Health Sciences Computing Facility using the IBM 7094 Computer. Valuable assistance was received in the continuous analysis of Rush Center data from staff of the Division of Biostatistics, UCLA School of Public Health. Mrs. Mae Ziskin, former staff psychologist, Los Angeles Psychiatric Service, also rendered valuable assistance in data compilation and processing.

† It might be said in passing that after a period of stable operation at the 500 a year level, plans for increased staff are now being developed that will permit treatment of approximately 1,000 patients a year.

offerings were still felt, and before reduction of visibility obtaining efforts.*

In the entire nineteen-month period, 45% of the Rush Center patients were men. This is higher than the proportion of men found among California outpatient clinics as a whole. This may in part be related to the clinic's evening hours; it represents another aspect of the Center's pattern of providing service to under-represented groups.

Are the persons who come to the Rush Center in need of psychiatric help? The answer is apparently clearly yes. The diagnostic impressions of patients by therapists treating them are given in Table 1.

About 60% of the patients—divided equally—showed psychoneurotic and personality disorders, with approximately one-sixth of the patients showing transient situational disorders. Almost one-fifth of the patients were psychotic. It might be noted that this distribution of diagnostic categories is comparable to national and California data (8-10, 12). Only the "transient situational" category is higher at the Benjamin Rush Center.

Are acute upsurges in fact the events that precipitate the effort to seek assistance at the Center? For approximately three-quarters of the patients on whom data are available in the seven-month period January 1-July 31, 1963, 15.1% had mainly acute problems and 63.1% had chronic problems with acute problems superimposed. Thus 78.2% of patients showed some acute component of the condition; and for 73.3% a recent precipitating event preceded the patient's appearance at the Rush Center.

The contract of treatment at the Rush Center cannot usually exceed six visits, and it was expected that many would need less than the maximum opportunity. Table 2 shows that in the first year and one half, in fact, 43.3% of patients saw the therapist four or more times, and about one-quarter of patients saw the therapist only once.

Do all patients receive treatment at the Rush Center? No, but the majority do: 84.8% of patients have received treatment, irrespective of the number of visits. It is one of the tasks of the therapist during the first visit to make a treatment plan and to attempt to implement it. Even patients who have only one visit are under certain circumstances considered treated. Therapeutic intent is present from the start in a conscious and systematic way,

---

* The relationship between age and education on the one hand and source of referral on the other, distinguishing between self-referral (including that derived from publicity) and professional referral, is discussed in detail in another paper (11). It has turned out that the professional referral network of the Los Angeles metropolitan area has begun to refer patients to the Rush Center in significant numbers.

TABLE 1
Diagnostic Impressions of Rush Center Patients
(January, 1962-July, 1963)

	Per Cent
Transient situational disorders	16.5
Personality disorders	28.2
Psychoneurotic disorders	31.6
Psychotic disorders	18.7
Others, including mental deficiency, brain disorders, etc.	5.0
Total in sample	(n=776)
Per cents based on	(n=721)

TABLE 2
Number of Visits by Rush Center Patients
(January, 1962-July, 1963)

Number of Visits	Per Cent	
More than 6	1.8	
6	21.3	43.3
5	9.1	
4	11.1	
3	14.0	
2	16.5	
1	26.1	
Total in sample	(n=776)	
Per cents based on	(n=735)	

with no formal separation of treatment and diagnosis, and each hour is considered as if it may be the last treatment opportunity.

Were patients considered in need of no further treatment after their visits to the Rush Center or were they referred for subsequent psychotherapeutic attention? Our data regarding patient disposition show great similarity to figures of disposition from more traditional outpatient clinics in California. About one-third were referred for further therapeutic work; about one-third of the patients withdrew; about one-quarter were terminated without referral.

Whatever the disposition, it is our view that crisis-centered therapy has had advantage for the patient. For the person referred elsewhere, the urgency of the patient's problem, though not necessarily his motivation to continue treatment, is commonly diminished as a result of his experience in the Rush Center, so that the patient can now tolerate better the nearly universal delays in obtaining longer-term clinic help.

There is an even larger issue involved, namely the potentially preventive effect of crisis-centered early treatment. It is our feeling that this kind of treatment program may substantially modify the patient's pathology with which future treatment will have to deal.

For persons who receive no further treatment, the issue of benefit received is of major import. If there is substantial benefit, it is evident that a walk-in clinic can provide a significant saving of professional manpower.

The full answer on this crucial matter depends on plans that are shortly to be under way for a long-term systematic assessment Center. For the present, we must rely on our evidence regarding therapists' judgments on condition of patient upon termination of treatment; approximately two-thirds of patients were considered treated and improved as a consequence of their experience at the Rush Center.

THE TREATMENT PROCESS

We turn now to a brief discussion of selected psychotherapeutic techniques employed at the Benjamin Rush Center. Just as clinic format and intake policies differ from those in longer-term facilities, so the approach of the therapist to the Rush Center patients is significantly different from that in other settings. From the start, the focus of treatment is on the patient's failure to cope in the here-and-now problem rather than on any long-standing pathology.

Many of the patients whom we see are in a state of crisis instigated by a variety of possible causes: a death or other loss of significant person, family break-up, or by still other often precipitous changes in the person's life situation. As Caplan defines it (1), "A crisis is provoked when a person faces an obstacle to important life goals that is, for a time, insurmountable through the utilization of customary methods of problem-solving. A period of disorganization ensues, a period of upset, during which many different abortive attempts at solution are made. Eventually some kind of adaptation is achieved, which may or may not be in the best interests of that person and his fellows."

Crisis is therefore a function both of the event itself and the previous life history and coping ability of the person experiencing the crisis. As Caplan further suggests, crisis represents adaptive opportunity as well as danger to the person. It is danger because previous coping now fails; it is an opportunity because this very failure opens the way to new learning. A post-crisis level of adaptation may therefore be more effective, less effective, or as effective, as a pre-crisis level.

The minimum therapeutic goal at the Rush Center is to restore the patient's functioning to the level which existed prior to a recent decompensation; the maximum goal is for improvement in functioning. To this end, different forms of treatment are used as needed, including individual interviews, family group interviews, and adjunctive pharmacotherapy.

Since time is at a premium, a therapeutic climate is generated that commands the concentrated attention of both therapist and patient. A goal-oriented sense of commitment develops that stands in sharp contrast to the more modest pace of more traditional treatment modes. It will be recalled that diagnostic assessment is not firmly separated from treatment. Whenever he can, the therapist accomplishes the following during the first hour: He screens the patient for possible hospitalization, he makes a working diagnosis, tentatively formulates his treatment plan, and begins the therapeutic intervention.

As has been mentioned earlier, three-quarters of Rush Center patients appear to be in acute phases of some life crisis. Sometimes this crisis may be clearly evident, as in the case of a recent marital breakup; or, after careful investigation by the therapist, it may emerge from amid a welter of long-standing complaints.

What then is the methodology appropriate to these patients in crisis? The following is an outline of the steps involved which we have found useful for training purposes:

(1). Actively explore the current situation in order to identify the precipitating event in the instances where it is not obvious. Ask: What is the most recent threat, challenge, or loss that has caused present disequilibrium? What is new in the patient's on-going situation? When did he begin to feel worse or become acutely upset? Who is the significant person or persons involved in the crisis? What is the *immediate* problem, as differentiated from the *basic* problem?

(2) Listen for mention of situations in the person's past even symbolically analogous to the current predicament. Ask about similar problems encountered earlier in life or in more recent times. What is the impasse brought about by the new element? Why can the patient not handle the present problem by previously used mechanisms, e.g., repression, denial, withdrawal, projection? Formulate *in your own mind* the dynamics of the current situation as thoroughly as you can, regardless of how much of your understanding is communicated to the patient.

(3). Now state the patient's problem *to him* concisely and in language he can understand. In terms of the psychodynamic surface-depth continuum, remain sufficiently close to the surface so that the formulation can be assimilated in the available time.* Remember: "Factors leading to the disruption of functioning are often preconscious and un-integrated: Identifying and isolating these factors. . .to facilitate cognitive. . .integration in and of itself, can promote a return to the previously achieved balanced state" (7). In addition to the cognitive aspects, assist the patient in getting in touch with current feelings which he has warded off.

(4). If this last intervention has been successful, the patient will now show a tangible increase in ability to deal with the problem, and a corresponding decrease in anxiety. Lend appropriate support to the patient's new efforts at solving his now defined problem. Explore alternative ways of handling the problem, and ways of viewing it in a different light. Take a relatively passive role *for the first time* in order to allow the patient to gain self-confidence in his restored problem-solving capacities. Review with the patient his accomplishments in dealing with the current crisis.

(5). Do *not* get involved in prolonged discussions of chronic problems at any time; or there is the risk of furthering regression which is anathema to the crisis approach and can produce sticky dependency problems at termination.

(6). Be prepared to find that in many instances the patient does not desire or require further professional help after equilibrium is restored. For this group, brief, walk-in type of help represents the treatment of choice. For others, consider referral for further treatment, looking for evidence of need in the form of long-standing problems together with clear-cut motivation and realistic goals to be pursued in further treatment, as well as availability of mental health resources in the community. Whenever feasible, refer for private psychiatric treatment. In all events, leave all discussion of possible referral for more help to the last one or two sessions. If referral is discussed earlier, there is a risk of procrastination because of the knowledge that more treatment is planned in the future.†

As this outline suggests, this treatment method presupposes the development of specialized skills based on an understanding of crisis. As M. Donald Coleman (2) and others as well as we have observed, such an approach requires an orientation distinct from other settings, such as that of our parent clinic. Definite morale problems followed the introduction of these new methods for us.

---

* Glover's (3) concept of "inexact interpretations" is relevant in this connection.

† As already mentioned, about one-third of the cases are referred for further treatment.

The problems gradually diminished as staff acquired skills appropriate to a brief-treatment, ready access clinic.

SUMMARY AND CONCLUSIONS

The Benjamin Rush Center was organized as a walk-in clinic to provide brief (up to six visits) and ready-access treatment, with emphasis on resolution of acute crises with the goal of restoration of functioning.

In the first nineteen months of operation, 776 patients were seen, at about the rate of 500 a year, perhaps twice the number that could have been served with similar staff in clinics offering more customary service.

Research monitoring of Rush Center operations revealed the following: (i) service was provided for a wide range of cases, including patients ordinarily less well represented in traditional treatment settings: older persons; the less well-educated; and; men; (ii) Rush Center patients are genuinely in need of psychiatric assistance, the distribution of diagnostic impressions being comparable to national and California clinic data; (iii) some acute personal crisis, accompanied by identifiable precipitating events, was found in three-fourths of the patients; (iv) more than 40% of patients saw a therapist four or more times; (v) whatever the number of visits, 85% of patients received treatment from the very first session, a number being referred for further psychotherapeutic attention.

The basic theoretic premise is that personal crisis, often precipitated by a death or other loss, results in a significant deficit in psychological functioning; and that preventive and therapeutic opportunities exist—that might otherwise be lost—if the patient is seen soon after the crisis occurs. At the Rush Center, the therapist gets to work at once, in the very first session attempting to establish a working diagnosis, setting a treatment plan where possible, and beginning the treatment. A variety of treatment modes are employed including adjunctive pharmacotherapy. Emphasis is on clarification and definition of the precipitating event, restoring the patient's problem-solving capacity, and putting him in touch with warded off feelings. These techniques require the development of new skills. Two-thirds of patients are viewed by therapists as having improved as a consequence of Rush Center treatment.

REFERENCES

1. Caplan, Gerald. An approach to community mental health. New York: Grune & Stratton, 1961.

2. Coleman, M. Donald. *Ment. Hosp.*, May 1960.
3. Glover, Edward. *Int. J. Psychoanal.*, 1931, **12**, 397.
4. Harris, M. Robert, Kalis, Betty L., and Freeman, Edith H. *Am. J. Psychother.*, 1963, **17**, 465.
5. Kalis, Betty L., *et al. Arch. Gen. Psychiat.*, 1961, **5**, 219.
6. Norman, Vivian B., Rosen, Beatrice M., and Bahn, Anita K. *Ment. Hyg.*, 1962, **46**, 321.
7. Rapoport, Lydia. *Soc. Service Rev.*, June 1962, **36**.
8. State of California Dept. of Mental Hygiene. California State Mental Hygiene Clinics, Outpatient Psychiatric Clinics, State Hospital Aftercare Facilities Statistical Report Year Ending June 30, 1962.
9. State of California Dept. of Mental Hygiene. State Local Mental Health Services Annual Report Fiscal Year Ending June 30, 1962.
10. State of California Dept. of Mental Hygiene. Non-State Aided Community Outpatient Psychiatric Clinics Fiscal Year Ending June 30, 1962.
11. Strickler, M., Bassin, E. G., Malbin, V., and Jacobson, M. D. The community-based walk-in center: A new resource for groups under-represented in outpatient treatment facilities. *Am. J. Public Health*, 1965, **55**, 377-384.
12. U.S. Dept. of Health, Education, and Welfare. Outpatient Psychiatric Clinics Special Statistical Report 1961.

Chapter 12

A Systematic Approach to Brief Therapy for Patients from a Low Socioeconomic Community

William C. Normand, M.D., Herbert Fensterheim, Ph.D., and Susan Schrenzel, M.S.S.W.

A major task for the professions concerned with mental health is to provide more adequate services for the poor. One approach to this task has been the establishment of new kinds of clinical centers, such as walk-in clinics, reported by Bellak (1964), Coleman and Zwerling (1959), Jacobson and associates (1965), Normand and colleagues (1963), and Peck, Kaplan, and Roman (1966). However, the danger exists that such centers will tend to follow traditional patterns of treatment, rather than to develop the new and more flexible approaches that are needed (Albee, 1965).

Since its inception in January 1962, the Walk-In Clinic of the New York Medical College—Metropolitan Hospital Center has been concerned with these problems. The clinic serves mainly a low socioeconomic population and has been attempting to develop new approaches to meet the clinical problems posed.

Clinical experience in this setting has led to a reformulation of goals of treatment. The clinic undertakes to provide immediate professional intervention in a problem situation in which, to greater or lesser degree, psychological disturbance is involved. The goal is not to "cure," but to ameliorate symptoms and to re-establish the previous, more effective state of equilibrium or, hopefully, to achieve an improved equilibrium state. The intervention is limited to six visits, but referral for various forms of extended care is available.

The term "problem situation" is purposely nonspecific to

Reprinted from *Community Mental Health Journal*, 1967, **6f**, 349-354, by permission of the publisher and the authors. Dr. Normand is Associate Professor of Psychiatry and Director, Psychiatric Outpatient Service, New York Medical College—Metropolitan Hospital. Dr. Fensterheim is Assistant Professor of Psychiatry, and Miss Schrenzel is Assistant Instructor of Psychiatry, New York Medical College—Metropolitan Hospital.

indicate that the clinic is not limited to meeting crisis situations. Included among problem situations is psychologically disturbed behavior which is primarily a consequence of the nonoptimal nature of the environment in which most of our patients live. To produce disturbed behavior, of course, the environmental stresses must interact with the particular personality, and treatment dealing primarily with the personality organization is included. Nonetheless, the most effective therapeutic approach frequently involves changing the environment rather than changing the person.

In this perspective, the concept of "intervention" takes on a broad meaning. The immediate, short-term intervention may involve primarily one of the various forms of brief psychotherapy, as described by Bellak and Small (1965), Coleman (1960), Rosenbaum (1964), and Wolberg (1965). However, it may also focus on environmental intervention. A wide range of such interventions is available: vocational rehabilitation, job finding, intervention with community agencies, to name only a few. These environmental interventions may be used alone, used as adjuncts to psychotherapy, or used as the major intervention modality with psychotherapy being adjunctive.

Thus, there are many different modes of intervention available to serve as the core of the treatment plan. Indeed, the number of possible modes of intervention is so great that it becomes a problem to decide which method of intervention would be optimal in a given case. The present paper is addressed to this specific issue: to increase the effectiveness of a walk-in clinic by providing a means for the systematic selection of the most appropriate intervention technique. To achieve this end, the authors have been experimenting clinically with a modification of the diagnostic process that would allow for such systematic selection.

THE DIAGNOSTIC MODEL

The model being presented has evolved out of experience in treating patients of low socioeconomic class, and it was formulated with the intent of avoiding two of the more obvious potential hazards of brief therapy. The first hazard is the reliance on an exclusively "common-sense" approach that ignores the knowledge of personality dynamics developed over the past half-century. Overemphasis on personality dynamics, on the other hand, leads to the second hazard (more common in psychiatric clinics at present), which consists of leaving out of account the hard realities with which the poor are burdened. This tends to restrict the interventions to traditional forms of psychotherapy, brief or long term, and the potential power of other types of intervention is lost.

To avoid both hazards, and to aid in selecting the optimal intervention technique, the diagnostic model that has been developed makes use of two different kinds of formulations for each patient. One is a dynamic formulation, which stresses the characteristics of the patient, of the environment, and of the interaction between them. The second is an action formulation, a working hypothesis, which is primarily concerned with treatment strategy rather than with the characteristics of the disturbed behavior.

DYNAMIC FORMULATION

The dynamic formulation is similar to that customarily made in a psychiatric clinic. It attempts to achieve an integrated survey of the current psychopathology and of the strengths and weaknesses of ego functions and of the current environment, including supportive as well as pathogenic features.

The formulation emphasizes the symptomatic picture and minimizes the genetic aspects. The emphasis on symptoms is mainly for the purpose of determining and describing target symptoms so that the goals of intervention may be concretely and specifically delineated. For the same reason, a description of the equilibrium state that existed just prior to the current disturbance is needed. Often, it is not essential that the current problem be thoroughly understood in relation to past events. However, though often minimized, genetic aspects are not ignored. Sufficient history is taken to provide at least tentative conceptualization of the genesis of the current dynamics.

Perhaps the major change introduced in this dynamic formulation, a change more of degree than of kind, concerns the emphasis on the patient's current environment and life situation. Although the extent of this emphasis varies from case to case, a rule of thumb is that equal attention is paid to environmental aspects and to intrapsychic forces. This is necessary, not only because of the possible role of a nonoptimal environment in the precipitation of disturbed behavior, but because an understanding of the specifics of the life situation may be important in determining the appropriate intervention technique.

To help achieve the integrated survey of intrapsychic and environmental variables, the initial interviews were jointly conducted by a psychiatrist-social worker team. Despite the overlap in the concepts used by the two team members, it was found that the interaction of the perspectives of the two mental health professions did serve to bring about a more comprehensive formulation that maximizes the chance of ferreting out an avenue of approach to brief therapy. If a collaborative approach is to be used, the joint interview is an economical procedure. It eliminates the need for a second interview with the other professional and avoids redundancy in data gathering; and it shortens the time required for consultation between the two professionals without sacrificing the closeness of the collaborative effort.

ACTION FORMULATION

The action formulation, or working hypothesis, is derived from the dynamic formulation. The action formulation is intended to be an explicit blueprint for action, as suggested by Ewen Cameron (1953), and it describes the general strategy that is to govern the therapeutic interventions. It is basically a working hypothesis, stated in deliberately oversimplified terms, which attempts to relate intrapsychic and/or environmental aspects to the disturbed behavior (target symptoms) that is the major concern.

The working hypothesis is action oriented. No claim can be made that it is either complete or completely accurate. It is based on the dynamic formulation, which itself is limited. However, it is not intended to be such a completely accurate statement; it is intended to lead to planned and integrated action. If this action is effective, i.e., if it relieves the target symptoms and restores an equilibrium state, the treatment goals are accomplished. If the action is not effective, there is the option of formulating a new working hypothesis, which leads to a different set of planned and integrated interventions. Thus, the therapeutic strategy may be deliberately and systematically changed.

The main point to note is that, although it is framed in terms of the patient and his life situation, the working hypothesis is not primarily about the patient. It is the dynamic hypothesis that attempts to explain the patient. The working hypothesis is about the therapeutic plan and the strategy and tactics to be used.

An aid to action, the working hypothesis is formulated in terms of one of four "levels": situational variables, ego functions, emotional conflicts, and character structure. While it is evident that all four levels are significant in every patient, it must be remembered that the working hypothesis is not primarily about the patient. The purpose of this conceptual tool is to indicate where the major, although not necessarily the exclusive, intervention will take place. It indicates the core of the therapeutic tactics, for each level "connects" with a different kind of intervention.

The terms that designate the levels are used in their common meanings and do not need elaboration except perhaps in the case of "ego functions." With reference to the action hypothesis, the term refers to tactics that involve support, modification, or strengthening of specific ego functions, including both autonomous functions and mechanisms of defense. An example is given below in which a defense mechanism was restored to effective functioning. Another example involves counseling a profoundly homosexual young Negro woman to obtain training with which she could get a desired job. This played a part in relieving the depression with which she had presented herself and contributed to a better adaptation in her generally troubled life setting. Ego defects based on organic disorders often are formulated at this level. These various types of ego disorders are treated by generally similar tactics, which involve various means of improving particular ego functions or recognition and acceptance of ego defects. Frequently, adjunctive interventions in the environment help to achieve or reinforce the desired changes.

Selection of the other levels also tends to lead to specific types of intervention. A formulation at the "environment level" leads to environmental modification. In one case the core of the intervention was to find a new apartment for the patient. In another case, the husband was called in, and attempts were made to modify his behavior in order to relieve a stress on the primary patient.

A formulation in terms of "emotional conflicts" tends to lead to verbal psychotherapy, often brief insight therapy, as the major intervention. For example, a 48-year-old grocery clerk of Italian background presented with "attacks" of pain in his arms, accompanied by moderate anxiety. The initial interview indicated that the pain resulted from muscle tension and was a conversion symptom. It was determined partly by his attempt to struggle against his identification with his mother, who had "the shakes" due to Parkinsonism, and partly by his need to control his rage at his sister and brother-in-law with whom his mother (to whom he was pathologically attached) was residing. The patient was made aware of these concepts, and he stopped treatment after five visits, symptomatically much improved.

A "character disorder" formulation often serves to limit action in the Walk-In Clinic and may lead to the use of chemotherapy for symptom amelioration as the primary mode of intervention or to immediate referral for long-term treatment, analytic or supportive, or to referral to a social agency for long-term casework. In these cases, it has been found that service can sometimes be rendered to other members of the patient's family in helping them to cope with the problems that arise from the patient's disturbance.

It must be noted that action is not limited to the single indicated level. However, when action is taken at another level, this is supplementary or ancillary to the main core of action at the level indicated by the hypothesis. In this way the integrated nature of a whole series of actions is maintained and coordinated.

In the conceptual model presented, a series of interventions are at the disposal of the therapist to help reach the goal of relieving target symptoms and restoring a state of equilibrium. A modification of the diagnostic process allows for a systematic choice of the intervention technique to be used and for the integration of different interventions. The model may be clarified, and its strengths and weaknesses more specifically illustrated, by considering its use in a particular case. The case chosen is not the most dramatic nor the most successful in the authors' series, but it is typical of the severe social and psychological pathology with which the clinic deals and of the setting up and achieving of limited goals.

CASE ILLUSTRATION

The patient was a 31-year-old Negro woman, separated from her husband, with one child. She was very anxious and tense and was afraid that she was going crazy. These symptoms were precipitated when the guidance counselor at her child's school told her that her child was disturbed, that the disturbance was because the mother spent so little time with the child, and that for the sake of the child she must stop working. This meant that she had to apply for Welfare. The symptoms appeared during her last day of work and rapidly exacerbated.

The history revealed that she was the oldest of nine children and was brought up in the South. When she was twelve, her mother moved to the North leaving her to care for the family with little help from the father. Five years later the patient herself moved North, worked hard for long hours, and eventually brought up four of her siblings and put them through school. She had married at the age of 19 and one year prior to her present disturbance had separated from her husband because he had been drinking excessively for some time and she had become "fed up." During the marriage, there had been an incident where she had been in jail for several days for stabbing her husband. Just prior to the current disturbance, she had been employed as a laundry worker and had to travel an hour each way to work. She would leave home at seven in the morning and return home at seven in the evening, while her six-year-old son was left to cope for himself. During the evening, she would speak to friends on the telephone, an activity she would have to give up when she went on Welfare. The clinical evidence, including brief evaluation by a psychologist, indicated that she had a basically psychotic personality and was presently decompensating.

The dynamic formulation stressed her unresolved dependency needs, feelings of deprivation, and the resulting rage and guilt, her intense fear of loss of control of her aggressive impulses, and the consequent danger to herself or her son. These, combined with difficulties in sexual identification, made the role of woman and mother intolerable. Her work and the telephone partially removed her from this role and at the same time helped her to maintain the image of being good. Ego strengths and environmental support were not very adequate

The need to work in order to maintain her compensation and the need to be good served as the basis for the action formulation. What was implied by the school authorities was that she would be a "bad" mother if she did not stop working. This is what made her give up her job. Possibly she felt guilty about even wanting to work. It was the equation that work equals being bad that made it impossible for her to use this much-needed defensive technique and that set off the decompensation.

The formulation was made at the level of ego functions, and counseling became the major intervention technique. The aim of the counseling was to reassure her that she wasn't bad because she wanted to work and that she could be "good" if she worked part time (for contact with the school guidance counselor did indeed indicate that her child had severe problems). Ancillary action was taken at the environmental level through intervention with other agencies, but this was still based on the core concept of breaking down the equation that work equals bad. An employment agency was contacted to help her find a job. The social worker made this contact rather than having the patient make it, for the intent was to demonstrate in action what had been said in words: that it was all right to work. The school counselor was contacted and the patient's need to work was explained. This served to remove the reinforcement of the work-bad equation.

In the second interview a few days later, she was compensated and did not want to return for further treatment. The ego defense was restored and the former equilibrium re-established. An attempt at a follow-up contact was made several months later, but the patient had moved and direct communication could not be established. However, it was learned from the school counselor that the patient had sent the child to live with her mother, who could spend more time with him, and that she herself had returned to full-time work. The fate of the child could not be followed up in this case although this is obviously important from the viewpoint of prevention (an important aspect of the walk-in clinic, but beyond the scope of this paper).

DISCUSSION

Although in this instance the target symptoms were ameliorated and the previous equilibrium (somewhat changed) was restored, it does not mean that the working hypothesis was verified. It appears that the therapeutic intervention did restore a previously effective ego defense, but it is difficult to be certain what made the treatment effective. However, the working hypothesis did contribute an organized focus of activity. The contacts with outside agencies were coordinated with the goals of the counseling sessions. There was even a basis provided for deciding whether the patient or the social worker should contact the employment agency.

Implicit in the model that has been presented are concepts of limited goals and of a treatment approach that does not follow the psychoanalytic treatment model (though psychoanalytic theory is used in formulations) but that is comparable to the way in which people use a family doctor. Treatment is geared to the presenting problem, and often is not definitive. The patient feels better and stops coming. The illness may recur and the patient can return for additional therapy; or exacerbations in the course of a chronic disorder can be dealt with as they occur. This is consistent with the desires and expectations of most of our patients. In the case presented, the patient terminated before the therapists were ready to stop, a common event in the Walk-In Clinic.

This frame of reference makes it easier for the therapist to help the patient. One of the strengths of the model is its influence on the therapist. Often a therapist dealing with poor people feels overwhelmed, particularly when hit with the real problems of living under deprived circumstances. Depression, a common symptom in this clinic, may serve as an example. Typically, the depression stems from the ego's awareness of inability to cope (Bibring, 1953). Low socioeconomic status contributes essentially to this depressive process. In the developmental phases deprivation fosters ego weaknesses, and the forces with which the adult ego cannot cope are frequently in themselves overwhelming. Thus the psychodynamic forces are intimately associated with the environmental circumstances and the therapist himself may see no way to deal with the problems. Hence, the therapist himself begins to feel frustrated and helpless in facing what appears a limitless sea of irremediable misery and may detach himself from his patients or continually set goals that cannot possibly be achieved. What the diagnostic model does is to structure the clinical situation for the therapist. It sets limits that permit him to direct his action meaningfully to what is possible and feasible.

A difficulty arises from the fact that therapists are usually analytically trained and oriented. Many years have been spent in sensitizing themselves to the expressions of emotional conflict and character structure. Person-environment interactions tend to be interpreted in a way that illuminates intrapsychic processes, and working hypotheses tend to be formulated at the "emotional conflict" level and psychotherapy chosen as the optimal treatment method. The model presents two barriers to this stereotyped approach. The fact that other levels must be considered with each working hypothesis tends to bring about a more flexible approach; and the fact that the social worker is present for the purpose of stressing the environmental-social perspective, whether or not the social worker himself has been trained in psychotherapy or psychoanalysis, also leads toward a greater flexibility.

A possible weakness of the model lies in the absence of explicit guiding principles for the selection of the level to use in the action formulation. However, the problem situations are variegated and complex and specific principles might restrict the flexibility of action. The careful evaluation by the joint psychiatrist-social worker interview of the strengths and weaknesses of both ego and environment does facilitate finding a course of action that is possible in the circumstances.

Although a diagnostic model has been presented, reference has also been made to the limited-goal, professional-intervention type of brief therapy that it serves to coordinate and guide. Both the diagnostic and the treatment methods are part of the emerging pattern of new kinds of engagements that are developing between mental health professionals and the poor they are now attempting to serve. The treatment techniques in themselves are not new. What is new is the attempt to facilitate their systematic and flexible use as an aid to providing high-quality mental health services to the poor.

REFERENCES

Albee, G. No magic here. *Contemp. Psychol.*, 1965, 10, 497-498.

Bellak, L. *Handbook of community psychiatry and community mental health.* New York; Grune & Stratton, 1964.

Bellak, L., & Small, L. *Emergency psychotherapy and brief psychotherapy.* New York: Grune & Stratton, 1965.

Bibring, E. The mechanism of depression. In Phyllis Greenacre (Ed.), *Affective disorders.* New York: International Universities Press, 1953.

Cameron, E. A theory of diagnosis. In H. Hoch and J. Zubin (Eds.), *Current problems in psychiatric diagnosis.* New York: Grune & Stratton, 1953.

Coleman, M. D. Emergency psychotherapy. In J. Masserman (Ed.), *Progress in psychotherapy*, Vol. V. New York: Grune & Stratton, 1960.

Coleman, M. D., & Zwerling, I. The psychiatric emergency clinic—a flexible way of meeting community mental health needs. *Amer. J. Psychiat.*, 1959, 115, 980-984.

Jacobson, G., Wilner, D. Morley, W., Schneider, S., Strickler, M., & Sommer, G. The scope and practice of an early-access brief treatment psychiatric center. *Amer. J. Psychiat.*, 1965, 121, 1176-1182.

Normand, W., Fensterheim, H., Tannenbaum, G., & Sager, C. The acceptance of the psychiatric walk-in clinic in a highly deprived community. *Amer. J. Psychiat.*, 1963, 120, 533-539.

Peck, H., Kaplan, S., & Roman, M. Prevention, treatment, and social action: a strategy of intervention in a disadvantaged urban area. *Amer. J. Orthopsychiat.*, 1966, 36, 57-59.

Rosenbaum, C. P. Events of early therapy and brief therapy. *Arch. Gen. Psychiat.*, 1964, 10, 506-512.

Wolberg, L. The technic of short-term psychotherapy. In L. Wolberg (Ed.), *Short-term psychotherapy*. New York: Grune & Stratton, 1965.

Chapter 13

Casualty Management Method

An Aspect of Mental Health Technology In Transition

Norris Hansell, M.D., M.S.Hyg.

No man is an island, entire of itself; every man is a piece of
the continent, a part of the main; if a clod be washed away
by the sea, Europe is the less, as well as if a promontory
were, as well as if a manor of thy friends or of thine own
were; any man's death diminishes me, because I am involved
in mankind; and therefore never send to know for whom
the bell tolls; it tolls for thee.

—John Donne, 1624

ENTRY INTO A NEW HISTORICAL PHASE

The mental health professional technology has been in rapid
change in the 20th century, and in the last ten years can be
regarded as entering a new phase: deployment to a whole society.
Mental health treatment effectiveness has been in slow
development since the beginning of civilization with the gradual
development of a definition of illness, a classification of kinds of
illnesses, of particular persons within the society designated as
special caregivers, and of special institutions and a care
technology.

An important movement occurred when Philippe Pinel, in
1792, struck the chains from the mentally ill and marked a
redefinition of the problem from one of punishment,
containment, and exorcism to one nurturing a concern for the
potentiality for renewal of function of the troubled person
involved. Then, in 1792, William Tuke established the Retreat at
York, an institution with a more precisely designed in-care

Reprinted from *Archives of General Psychiatry*, 1968, **19**, 281-289, by permission of the publisher and the author. Dr. Hansell is Assistant Professor of
Psychiatry, Northwestern University Medical School, Chicago, Illinois.

159

method. He elaborated a philosophy which emphasized participation in a particular social value system, a method which became known as the moral treatment. The method was exported to the new world by Thomas Kirkbride in 1841 at the Department for the Insane of the Pennsylvania Hospital in Philadelphia (9). Then Dorothea Dix, in 1843, placed the treatment of the mentally ill on a publicly funded vehicle, often a state vehicle, and firmly established the principle that the management of the mentally ill would be given a substantial priority in the use of public funds.

John F. Kennedy and the 88th Congress, in the Federal Community Mental Health Act of 1963 (8, 15, 16) established more fully *a non-institutional focus*. The act notes the role of the expectations of the community, of the family, and of the care-giving professions in the efficacy of treatment (15, 16). Also emphasized in the Message to Congress of Feb. 5 1963 (8) and in the Regulations for the Act (16) are the pertinence of the beliefs of the consumer in the design of services, and of a community or territorial focus in planning.

Following on this evolution in mental health method, the psychiatrist and the technology professionally centering around him have moved from dyadic settings to group settings: family systems, agency systems, bureaucratic systems, and community systems. The psychiatrist has been asked to enter roles as service administrator, planning agent, change agent, consultant to several kinds of casualty management professions, and to many public service facilities. The psychiatrist is asked to be therapist, teacher, decision counselor, and social leader.

The information that mental health professionals need in order to do their work has grown from the physical examination, history, mental status, social review, and psychometrics to include epidemiology, demography, numerical descriptions of casualty flow rates, and data on facility utilization, service distribution, and service effectiveness.

The way the psychiatrist examines his own training and skills and the effectiveness of his professional operations, is moving from a method centering around the individual case to a method centering within a territorial or community frame of reference.

Psychiatrists are working with healthy groups to promote health and reduce risk of illness, as in the Peace Corps and Job Corps. Psychiatrists are working with others to deliver health and social competence services to the poor and to populations which have not utilized mental health service effectively even though they show substantial rates of disability. Psychiatrists are developing programs directed to healthy populations, for instance, school children, and demonstrating an increased rate of role success and decreased rate of sickness-disability development in the population(7).

Psychiatrists are developing catchment area casualty management programs emphasizing more effective management of established casualties and reduction of residual disability. Each of these professional growth areas involves an evolving new technology. The growth edge of the art looks a little different in each place.

This paper looks at five areas on that growth edge of the art concerned with a more effective management of established casualties. It is an incomplete and parochial view. It should be balanced with the view from other positions on the edge.

GROWTH

1. A Territorial Description of Professional Responsibility

Professional-patient relationships for years have been an interpersonal matter between the psychiatrist and patient. The relationship has been monitored by professional peer supervision, formalized and informal, and by the patient's own appraisal of the satisfactoriness of his treatment and the availability of selection in a free market. Now the "I-thou" contract is evolving increasingly into an agency-community contract or into a group-territory contract. A territory is often the closest approach that can be made to defining a collectivity, a community, as the responsibility perimeter of the service agent. The agency becomes a system with discrete perimeters in territory, mission, funds, service, staff, and skills. It develops an internal structure and organizes to refine and alter the mission, policies, and activities. The whole structure relates to and is glued to a territory.

Early demonstrations of the territorial method, for instance, the Saskatchewan Plan (10), have shown that there are clear advantages to defining casualty management problems in territorial terms, advantages which result in dramatic increases in the effectiveness of care and in the precision of the use of resources. A usual territorial plan is that a single administrative group has responsibility for in-care, out-care, home care, and after-care, for patients within that territory, as well as for public relations, inter-agency negotiations, and risk group definition in triage settings.

The staff group gradually gains competence in the several modes and settings of care. It seems centrally important that the administrative unit have a solid corridor of responsibility within which it can operate but from which it cannot export its treatment failures to another auspices. As long as the option is available to export treatment failures from its own professional scrutiny, the unit does not become competent to manage them. Conversely, the requirement to become competent to manage all casualties of the several degrees of severity maximizes the likelihood and rate of the development of such skill. When a patient does have to be transferred from a high velocity treatment facility, it is best if he stays within the administrative scrutiny of the same organization so as to minimize the likelihood of his moving out of the sunlight of professional and community concern.

A fully engaged territorial casualty management agency declines both the option to export its failures and the option to allow a waiting list. Most of the troubles that are part of mental illness solidify and rigidify with time. The heat of crisis usually is the best time to enter a situation. A waiting list separates an agency from its clients at the moment it can be most effective and tends to separate the agency from those difficult cases which would mature staff competence most efficiently.

Innovation flourishes in an agency or system attached to a territory with an unequivocal and specific risk group commitment. Skill in home care, out-care, and noninstitutional management develops. Store-fronts soon develop for making triage decisions and for linking a person in trouble to the members of his ordinary social network. The necessary professional reading habits and skill development occur almost automatically after the attachment is made unequivocally by the agency.

An agency which develops a definition of its mission with clarity and specificity may find itself in professional conflict with some of its own members, with other agencies, and with members of the consumers and public in its environment. There is no way to avoid this conflict besides a strategy with lack of definition. A strategy with lack of definition may avoid conflict but also precludes the highest levels of effectiveness. A community sometimes will make quiet or even noisy protest in the beginning, but as the strategy develops effectiveness and its feasibility and value become demonstrated, the conflict melts. During the period before the heavy conflict melts and matures, it is important that the mental health professionals indicate their deep concern for the central values of that community. The community will give permission for change-agents to tamper with some methods of casualty management which have fallen into limited effectiveness *if* the community sees evidence that the agency can be trusted. If the staff "wears a white handkerchief" and behaves in a conventional manner in ways which do not directly affect professional care, then the community will tolerate the ways in which professional operaations may be new or offensive. Wearing the white handkerchief gives permission for major tampering with cherished but ineffective patterns of care-giving.

The community respects an agency that defines its objectives in a language which the community understands and endorses. The agency must give up talking about "treatment" and "therapy," terms which professionalize and close such a dialogue. The agency can open the discussion by talking about "managing trouble" so as to help a person remain or become an effective citizen, an effective family member, and a person with minimal or usual levels of distress. The definition of the agency's product within a framework of role performance in the ordinary community, rather than within an intrapsychic frame, generates community participation and respect. If the definition of the product involves troubled people moving from a care-need state to a noncare-need state, the community will not require that the goal be completely achieved in all cases. Rather, it will ask that the objectives be specified and remain as continuing objectives in each individual situation.

2. Clustering the Staff around the Mission

In the process of starting an agency or giving an agency a new mission, the psychiatrist will need to convert an assembly of people into a structured and effective system. The professional operations used to convert an assembly of persons into an effective mental health service organization include skills often not a part of residency training programs in past times but which are increasingly built into such training.

The psychiatrist, in a territorially linked, no export option treatment facility, is called upon to teach and interpret the mission to those who will be engaged in it with him. If he shrinks from the role of the rhetorical description of the mission to the staff and the various publics, he may not be the leader of the enterprise; he may be a reluctant technical implementer of operations he may not fully endorse. The psychiatric leader of a group with a territorial charge is called upon to refine the mission and describe a pattern of operations which has a reasonable chance of being effective. He needs to develop a language for describing and containing this mission and its rationale. He identifies the principle issues and conflict around these issues, and he interprets the whole to boards, staffs, and various publics. Especially pertinent in involving the citizen and consumers are *terms* precisely describing the risk groups, or types of casualties, which the agency will assume as its domain.

The staff of the agency should be regularly convened; in the convened setting, the leader and the staff must describe and refine the mission, record it, and discuss it in detail. Periodic announcement of changes which have occurred can be made and interpreted on an evolutionary continuum of "how far we have come" and "where we are headed." Periodic announcements are enhanced in agency-building value if associated with ceremonies and visual signs that this cluster of people is engaged in the process of becoming a unit and is addressing itself to a unitary mission. The staff meetings should occur with regularity and frequency. Meetings have greatly increased staff clustering value if the deliberations are recorded, distributed, and further discussed after the convened group has disbursed.

It is important that during the development process no scapegoating of any staff persons be allowed. It will be found that, at particular times in the development of an agency, particular people's productivity will appear low or may, in fact, be low or trivial with respect to the mission. The agency must not scapegoat these persons; usually their personal trouble can be found to be system-linked. In a longer view of the professional team's growth, *the distribution of apparent low productivity is randomly distributed in the system.* It falls somewhere in the system at any point in time. If the leader draws a perimeter around the group and forbids, by his own behavior and example, the scapegoating of the members, *his expectation that everyone has the capacity to develop the competence to deliver his part of the mission will be lived out by the members.* Also, when the scapegoating of staff is disallowed, the scapegoating of patients by staff and its lessor derivative, the stereotyping or placing of low expectations on certain patients will be aborted.

The professional team addressed to a territorial mission at the edge of the art usually finds its training is incomplete for the task. Its current level of skills would prescribe a mission much less effective and much less valuable than one they can otherwise envision. The psychiatrist administrator must make it clear that he understands the current lack of full competence for the more valuable mission but expects a gradual skill development. Such an evolutionary process is associated with significant and special opportunity valued by staff members who wish to grow. As the mission becomes more rationalized, in operations as well as plans, it becomes more understandable and more linked to the current level of staff skills.

3.   The Power of System Expectance

The most important ingredient in treatment is the expectation of the observer. Mental health professionals must notice beauty, truth, lovableness in patients if they be present only in trace quantities. One must be selectively inattentive to kicking, biting, suspiciousness and to assaultive, sucking, clinging behavior. At the same time, one must manage assaultive, clinging suspiciousness so that the troubled person does not harm himself or staff or further extrude himself from the ordinary social scene. Staff belief and attitudes must show that their true attention lies in the possibility of affection, of important social service, of self-esteem, and of community esteem that lie within the patient.

In fact it may be said that in a moment of crisis a person is mainly aware of his own pain and anguish. He does not have an idea of who he is or where he is going. His identity is quite fluid, nonspecific, unelaborated, or deteriorated. At these times, the expectation of the observer is critical in what kind of persisting identity will be developed. Stereotypes about the chronic patient, the old patient, the repeating patient, the schizophrenic patient, and the retarded person, which lie within many citizens and many mental health professionals must be contained and aborted: they are importantly self-fulfilling prophecies.

For staff, for patients, for families, and for the whole community, the same assumptions are made: that attitudes are fluid and multivalent; that negative attitudes can soften; that sterotypes can fade. Assume that people want help in learning to want and expect what is better. And for all this movement, expectance is the most powerful tool.

Albert Glass had demonstrated and effectively documented the tremendous power of the method of expectancy, originally in military settings (3). The expectation that the person will get over this crisis and will go on to renewed periods of growth and productivity is a principal ingredient in care (6). Drugs, relief from responsibility, temporary comfort, counseling, insight, and understanding, are also important. The necessary, and almost sufficient ingredient, is the power of the expectation of the social system, family, and mental health professionals.

Wallace (19-22), Tyhurst (18), and Sargant (17) have reviewed the clinical aspects of humans in crisis, or transition states, and have mentioned a range of types of transition states. There is usually a short attention span, distractability, emotional lability, rumination over a small range of details, lack of clear attitudes, lack of awareness of a life strategy, and aborted decision-making.

The clinical properties of the transition states are both the special management problem and the special opportunity within crises for people in trouble. It is most important that the individual's life space be stabilized with minimal risk of exit from on-going responsibilities and minimal movement into dependent or passive life strategies. Equally important is the attempt to minimize stereotyping effect and automatic social consequences that follow from the conclusory labels, "schizophrenic" or "psychotic." A diagnostic process is necessary for professional growth and for precision in treatment, but it should be circumscribed and detached from a general conclusory labeling system which unlinks the professions from an effort to restore competence and which unlinks the family and society from an effort to manage the person's trouble in position in society.

Mental health skills associated with decision counseling are turning out to be particularly relevant to the management of persons in crisis so as to maximize the positive aspects of transition states. In decision counseling, the therapist, in interaction with the troubled person, focuses attention on cognitive transactions. (1) The patient and therapist determine and describe the limits of the trouble: the parts of the life space that are troubled; those that are not troubled. They inventory the extent of damage difficulty. (2) They, together, inventory the options open for change and for action. (3) They develop a decision model for selecting from among the options. (4) The patient is then asked to go through the decision model and make a decision. (5) Together they establish a commitment to action. The results are monitored to determine how effective the response has been. Maybe they will have to go through it again because it has not worked.

The counseling method emphasizes the individuality of the person's own response to trouble. At the same time, another person is going through the trouble with him: He does not become unlinked from society. It minimizes the necessity of labels and conclusory judgment about what will happen. It maximizes the opportunity and options open to the person in the midst of the flexibility of crisis. Becoming a particular kind of person after crisis is simply the result of a decision to become that kind of a person. The decision is simply the result of a demand to become that kind of a person placed upon the individual in trouble by the observer. The demand to become is simply the result of the joint awareness of the possibilities and the excitement and activism generated by an inventory and hopeful expectancy. The counseling method minimizes the likelihood of converting a crisis casualty into a chronic casualty.

Another method, using the heat of crisis to good advantage in mental health work, is the Ludwig-Benson resocializing method. The state and county mental hospitals of the United States in 1968 contain several hundred thousand people as semipermanent residents who have a physiologic status compatible with an outpatient location or with residence in a noninstitutional setting. Many of these patients are not interested in going outside. They often do not have families interested in them. The Ludwig-Benson resocializing method (12, 13) takes individuals who have been substantially desocialized by chronic care in a large institution and activates them within a smaller individualizing setting. The small interpersonal group setting raises new excitement about entering the outside world and reactivates social and interpersonal skills which have become dormant. The Ludwig-Benson resocializing method places patients in charge of each other's predicament and makes specified and reasonable demands for conventional behavior. Patients are placed in charge of rating each other against a specified code and of taking care of one another in such a way that they will all return to the community as soon as possible. It is a method on the edge of the art and is driven by a high expectance of return to substantially full competence in the majority of patients. The staff communicates this expectance to patients who then develop the competence to return to the community. The method of expectations, central to the Ludwig-Benson method, is combined with the development of job skills, halfway houses, sheltered workshops, and the whole array of modes of partial care.

4. A Package of Responses for a Package of Troubles

Many patients who come into mental health treatment facilities, especially ones in the public sector dealing with substantially ill casualties, are persons in anguish, in chaos, with deteriorated social skills, loss of family connections, and loss of job skills. They have generally caused a circle of friends to give up on them and extrude them from relationships in their part of the community. They have begun to be labeled in one way or another and are traveling the path of alienation and export to a special containment or management enclosure. The ordinary patient with substantial social disability arrives with a *package of difficulties,* including lack of job skills, membership in a fracturing family group, lack of a place to live, diffused identity, and lack of life strategy. The mental health service response must develop a way of helping with each of the aspects of this package of troubles. Each part of the trouble increases the risk of institutionalization and of return to institutionalization after discharge. Each one not handled contributes to the further development of the social breakdown syndrome (4).

The *placement* of the setting where a solution to a crisis develops plays a major role in the relevance of that solution. Solutions developed in institutions prepare a person well for continuing institutional life. Solutions developed in position in society are more pertinent to living within society. The quality of treatment can be measured by the number of feet of distance it is located separate from the person's ordinary space of life. There is no magic in hospitalization except for the briefest possible time. Removal, if necessary, must be local, brief, and coordinated for maintenance of family, role, and friendship linkages.

The community of Geel (2) has demonstrated that substantial degrees of disability can be managed in outpatient and home care status and that this pattern is not only more effective and less costly but perhaps more permanently effective than any kind of institutionalization. Pasamanick et al. (14), in Louisville, recently demonstrated the tremendous effectiveness of home care for very substantial degrees of mental illness, including clearly developed schizophrenia.

Some mental health professionals are devoted to attempts to create small and special utopias or therapeutic environments, a tradition well represented by Thomas Kirkbride in 1856; "It is desirable that the pleasure grounds and gardens should be securely enclosed to protect the patients from the gaze and impertinent curiosity of visitors and from the excitement occasioned by their presence on the grounds (9). Professionals now are turning to the more challenging but more pertinent task of developing an in-care milieu which promotes linkages with the patient's ordinary social life space and which promotes skills and competence that will keep a person linked to his ordinary environment (5, 23). It is becoming clear that the direct professional ministrations of mental health staff are helpful but not sufficient. The most helpful ministrations have to do with linking a person to his family, to his ordinary life space, to pertinent social skills, to a place to live, and to sources of social and personal esteem. For these linking objectives, *setting* of care, the *persons* who are made a part of the care-giving process, and their *expectations* are the main features of effective operations.

The mental health expediters at the H. Douglas Singer Zone Center in Rockford, Illinois, have developed a terminology of the method of making social links (5). Most of the patients that the expediters deal with at the Singer Zone Center are substantially or partially alienated from their families and communities; technical maneuvers which do not establish effective links to the community and to family membership do not maintain the person in ordinary social life in a noninstitutional setting. Expediters distinguish four grades of link: (1) *an informational link:* information is given to the patient about emergency service, addresses, job information, and agency services; (2) *monitored contact:* the expediter follows the patient and sees that he arrives at a certain place or makes a contact which begins a critical link; (3) *monitored effectiveness:* the patient is followed for a substantial period of time, the link is altered or recemented with trouble-shooting to determine that it remains strong and effective; (4) *community embrace and family embrace:* the linking process is carried a step further toward attitudinal change: a person who was formerly felt to be dangerous, offensive, or unwanted, is found attractive, interesting, and belonging.

5. Object Relations, Care-Giving, and Casualty Management

Diminished social competence in mental health casualties is associated with a need for help, an increased dependence on the care giver, and an increased risk of institutionalization (23). Mental health service operations addressed to patients at maximum risk of institutionalization can be considered a service pipeline through which people-in-trouble move and become temporarily related to helpful persons and programs. The key element of a pipeline model is that mental health professionals have to become skilled in the development of transitional social object relationships. Otherwise, the pipeline becomes clogged with persons with a continuing need for help. The clog becomes a waiting list and promotes bureaucratic and professional deterioration into comfortable but irrelevant habits. *A mental health skill on the edge of the art in 1968 is that of developing, for staff and for patients, transitional object relations and facilitating linkages between persons in trouble and social objects which have a permanent place in the patient's ordinary social life space.*

Staff must become familiar with the fact that they will become quickly important and related to patients. They must signal the patient early, and understand clearly themselves, the transitional and temporary nature of the relationship. When this is not understood by both parties, a marked deterioration often occurs when the staff begin to talk about discharging a patient or about sending him on to day care or halfway house care. The patient's behavior may signal in this way his doubt that he can make it on his own. Also, he may be signaling his attachment to people who have been helpful to him and his wish not separate from them.

Separating from an institution or a helpful care-giving agent is a process not unlike loss of a love object, or mourning. Bowlby (1) and Lindemann (11) have discussed the clinical management of separations. A valuable relationship has been established which may be especially meaningful for a person who may have very few love objects or who has diminished ability to establish new love objects and new social object relationships.

Mourning counseling operations are especially relevant to the consideration of the method of rapid development of social object relationships which are transitional. The goal is to help the patient move to more permanent relationships in his real environment.

Regularly and systematically the therapist has to start and guide the mourning counseling process. The first phase is an inventorying of the events and functional meaning of the relationship which has developed: a cataloguing, naming, and attaching of importance to the parts of the relationship. In the second phase, the patient and mental health professional identify replacements in the real environment. For each one of these replacements, they identify a satisfactoriness and equivalence to what has been achieved in the in-care or professional setting. For the third step, they seek a commitment to move into this replacement strategy. The expectation of the therapist is that the patient will identify and establish replacements of elements of the relationship which have been helpful. After the commitment to action, review and evaluation are carried through.

By these means, mental health professionals clearly establish expectations for an independent and competent life style for the patient. Professionals signal they are not going to be a continuing part of the patient's world: The patient can make it on his own. This expectation, exemplified in the experience of decision counseling, is a principal ingredient in the patient's becoming competent to replace the help he has gotten in an in-care setting. The mourning process frequently includes helping the patient set up friendship networks, job opportunities, access to job skills and a place to live; conceptualizing it as a mourning process makes clear that there is a separation occurring in a relationship which has been helpful but which is transitional.

Agencies and staff who are not willing to face the pain of clear and distinct separations only displace that pain on to patients who cannot, therefore, make the separations and who, therefore, become dependent. These troubled people become attached to staff, clog up the system and unlink it from its territorial mission.

SUMMARY

Five skills at the edge of the art in 1968:

(1) *A group of mental health professions is deployed against a territorial description of its responsibility.* It has no option to decline any members of the risk group for which it has accepted responsibility, and it declines the option to export its difficult patients to another administrative auspices or to a place outside its own professional scrutiny.

(2). *A group of mental health professionals becomes clustered into a unified body which can describe its objectives, design its operations, and systematically deploy and evaluate them within a corridor of responsibility* and accountability to patients, to professional peers, and to all citizens who have a call on the group's skills.

(3) *The expectation of the observer is the principal ingredient in care.* Even for the most severely troubled psychiatric casualty, expectation is the most powerful instrument. Persons in crisis and persons in great turmoil have lost their idea of who they are and where they are going; if there is any idea, it lies in a concerned person who explores a vision of what could be, and who sees esteem, beauty, and citizenship as real potentialities for this human being even if they are present only in trace quantities at this moment.

(4) *Management in position is best.* There is no special magic in in-care or in hospitalization except for the briefest possible time. Treatment in situ is the most effective, most reasonable, and generally least costly method. The quality of treatment can be measured by the number of feet of distance it is located from the person's ordinary space of life. If removal is necessary, it must be brief, local, and coordinated for maintenance of the family, role, and friendship linkages. This requires the expediting of getting a job, a residence, job skills, and maintaining or establishing small group support systems. This anti-extrusion strategy requires full attention to a whole package of responses *in order for flow rates to be maintained.*

(5). *Mental health professionals must learn the skills of linking and of supplying transitional social objects.* Care-giving professionals must not, as a tool of their trade, establish permanent or semipermanent relationships with patients. This temporary solution to the patient's difficulty very soon fills up the treatment system with patients who need a continuing relationship with the care-giving persons in order to maintain effective life. The professional must address himself to the more difficult but more useful task of establishing permanent personal and object relationships for the troubled person by using persons who are part of the patient's environment. This is called linking technology and is a mental health skill on the edge of the art in 1968.

Mental health technology has never been more relevant and has never been in a state of more rapid change. Professionals who have developed a style of stopping their training at the time they graduate from a formal period of training carry grave personal and professional risks during this period of rapid change. A society takes the service mandate away from a profession that shrinks from the interface with change.

REFERENCES

1. Bowlby, J. Separation anxiety. *Int. J. Psychonal.*, 1960, 41, 1-25.
2. Dumont, M.P., & Aldrich, C.K. Family care after a thousand years—a crisis in the tradition of St. Dymphna. *Amer. J. Psychiat.*, 1962, 119, 116-121.

3. Glass, A. J. Principles of combat psychiatry. *Milit. Med.*, 1955, **117**, 27-33.

4. Gruenberg, E.M. The social breakdown syndrome—some origins. *Amer. J. Psychiat.*, 1967, **123**, 1481-1489.

5. Hansell, N. Wodarczyk, M. & Visotsky, H. M. The mental health expediter. *Arch. Gen. Psychiat.*, 1968, **18**, 392-399.

6. Hausman, W., & Rioch, D. McK. Military psychiatry: A prototype of social and preventive psychiatry in the United States. *Arch. Gen. Psychiat.*, 1967, **16**, 727-739.

7. Kellam, S. & Schiff, S. A four year followup on the Woodlawn Mental Health Program for first graders. Read before the Annual Meeting of the American Orthopsychiatric Association, Chicago, March 20-22, 1968.

8. Kennedy, J. F. *The message to Congress of February 5, 1963.* Washington, D.C., 88th Congress, HR Document No. 58, 1963.

9. Kirkbride, T.S. Construction, organization, and general arrangements of hospitals for the insane, originally published: Philadelphia: J. B. Lippincott Company, 1856. Reprinted in *Ment. Hosp.*, 1955, **6**, 14-20.

10. Lafave, H.G., et al: The Weyburn experience: Reducing intake as a factor in phasing out a large mental hospital. *Compr. Psychiat.*, 1967, **8**, 239-248.

11. Lindemann, E. Symptomatology and management of acute grief. *Amer. J. Psychiat.*, 1944, **101**, 141-148.

12. Ludwig, A.M. & Farelly, F. The code of chronicity. *Arch. Gen. Psychiat.*, 1966, **15**, 562-568.

13. Ludwig, A.M. & Farrelly, F. The weapons of insanity. *Amer. J. Psychotherapy*, 1967, **21**, 737-749.

14. Pasamanick, B. et al. *Schizophrenics in the community: An experimental study in the prevention of hospitalization.* New York: Appleton-Century-Crofts, 1967.

15. Public Law 88-164, Washington, D.C., 88th Congress, S. 1576, Oct. 31, 1963.

16. *Regulations for Community mental health centers act of 1963.* Title II, Federal Register, Washington, D.C., May 6, 1964, pp. 5951-5956.

17. Sargant, W. *Battle for the mind.* Garden City, N.Y.: Doubleday & Co., 1957.

18. Tyhurst, J.S. The role of transition states, including disasters, in mental illness. In *Symposium on social and preventive psychiatry, Walter Reed Army Institute of Research.* Washington, D.C., 1957, 149-172.

19. Wallace, A.F.C. The biocultural theory of schizophrenia. *Int. Rev. Med.*, 1960, **173**, 700-714.

20. Wallace, A.F.C. Mazeway disintegration: The individual's perception of socio-cultural disorganization. *Hum. Org.*, 1957, **16**, 23-27.

21. Wallace, A.F.C. Mazeway resynthesis: A biocultural theory of religious inspiration. *Trans New York Acad. Sci.*, 1956, **18**, (Ser 2), 626-638.

22. Wallace, A.F.C. Stress and rapid personality changes. *Int. Rec. Med. Gen. Pract. Clin.*, 1956, **169**, 761-774.

23. White, R.B. The concept of competence. *Psychol. Rev.*, 1959, **66**, 297-333.

III. Techniques and Programs for Specific Patient Populations

Brief therapeutic strategies based on more specialized clinical experience are valuable in increasing understanding of patients of illness and in developing appropriate treatment programs. The articles in this section provide some illustrations of useful approaches for target populations.

Blaine examines the treatment of college students in a paper antedating most of the others in the book. Interestingly, even at a time when many therapists considered short-term therapy unsuitable for most adult patients, college students were regarded as more accessible and resilient. Blaine illustrates how students respond openly and actively to brief therapy. In recent years, university health programs have taken increasing cognizance of the need and the opportunity to make brief psychotherapy an integral part of their responsibilities. The college years are a period fraught with turmoil and crises, and early intervention has vital preventive potential in averting premature drop-outs and other impulsive decisions, and in assisting students during transient work blocks, identity crises, or confusional states precipitated by experimentation with drugs.

Browne describes a technique of behavior modification which he employs in a general medical practice. Assertive therapy stresses the practice of more self-affirming behaviors by passive, submissive patients, and the clarification of attitudes toward self and others. Of additional interest is Browne's use of adjunctive techniques such as tape recordings to reiterate and underscore key issues, and to show patients what their timidity sounds like. Self-analysis between sessions is encouraged. Hypnosis and auto-hypnosis are also employed. The major emphasis is on changing behavior.

Within mental health clinics, treatment services for children are often the most inadequate component. Indirect techniques such as play therapy tend to be time-consuming and inefficient. Practical, direct techniques for children are sorely needed. Weinberger feels that the few brief approaches for children which have been tried are for the most part merely a truncation of long-term methods and that they basically retain traditional objectives. He questions traditional preoccupations with extended exploration and working through of genetic and unconscious elements as a uniform model of therapy.

173

Weinberger argues for an approach which explicitly delineates areas of unacceptable behavior, rather than attempting to teach the child and his parents the new language of psychoanalysis. He seeks specific behavior change both by confrontation with the child and by modification of the reinforcing family system which often unwittingly perpetuates the very behavior it deplores.

Recently, the effectiveness of time-limited psychotherapy with children has been documented in a carefully designed, controlled study done by Rosenthal and Levine (1) (not reprinted in this volume). These authors showed that brief therapy results were comparable to those with a control group who were treated for five to seven times as long. Examining the children who had failed to respond to brief therapy, the authors were able to abstract some relative counterindications, such as the chronicity and severity of symptoms, severe parental discord or psychopathology, and family distintegration. They commented upon the irony of the fact that it is just these families who tend to be treated briefly in clinics, while relatively healthier families are chosen as better candidates for long-term therapy. Rosenthal and Levine stress that there are other factors which are at least as important in determining the outcome of brief therapy. In successful brief-treatment cases, the therapist establishes a "brief therapy set" for which the patient and family are asked to share responsibility. Thus there is an expectation of improvement within a given period on the part of both the family and the therapist. Hopefully, additional studies such as these will be forthcoming to document the effectiveness of brief procedures, and to further define their critical elements.

Psychiatric reactions to physical illness, particularly when it is life-threatening, are extremely common, and all physicians should be equipped to deal with them. Stein, Murdaugh, and MacLeod describe a clinic setting for patients with more complex reactions, for which they felt that psychiatric skills were required. Patients were seen for a maximum of six interviews of variable length. In treating reactions to physical illness, the authors emphasize the need to deal with denial mechanisms, feelings of violation of the sense of wholeness, and misconceptions about the actual nature of the illness.

Rada, Daniels, and Draper describe the use of brief contact sessions in a setting which additionally provides a socialization experience and creates an *esprit* among the staff which is quite in contrast to the average after-care clinic. This is an excellent demonstration of how short-contact therapy can be utilized flexibly in developing an economical but effective therapeutic program for patients with chronic illnesses.

Gerber's program for bereaved individuals is of particular interest because it is a pilot attempt at primary prevention, offering unsolicited assistance to bereaved families. It has had a striking rate of acceptance in the community. This crisis oriented approach, based on Lindemann's classic formulations, provides concrete support in helping bereaved individuals to find new roles and develop practical future plans. Research is proposed to study the extent to which such a program will prevent subsequent maladjustment.

REFERENCE

1. Rosenthal, A. J. & Levine, S. V. Brief psychotherapy with children: A preliminary report. *American Journal of Psychiatry*, 1970, **127**, 646-651.

Chapter 14

Short-Term Psychotherapy with College Students

Graham B. Blaine, Jr., M.D.

Short-term psychotherapy is particularly effective with patients in the college age group. Although it can be a useful method with adults and children, treatment at these ages usually must be long term.

Child psychiatrists utilize a type of therapy that involves the therapist to a greater degree than the patient. Because of the language barrier, communication must be through the symbolism of play and the direct expression of emotion instead of the more easily understood symbolism of speech. It takes a long time to understand fully what the child is trying to get across and even longer to establish a method by which the therapist can get ideas back to the patient. The problems of communication, then, tend to make therapy with children a long-drawn-out process.

Adults have firmly set patterns of behaving and thinking. Even though their behavior causes them distress and they come to the therapist for help in changing these patterns, the unconscious forces that make them behave in this neurotic and disliked pattern are well established and deeply set. It takes much time spent in therapy hours and the living through of many life experiences to effect a change in behavior for many of them. Here, unlike the child, the patient himself does the lion's share of the work of therapy, being expected not only to contribute significant material but also, for the most part, to make his own interpretations. If the therapist plays too active a part in adult therapy, he may stimulate resistances that cannot be overcome. Most adults cannot learn by being told what to do; they have to teach themselves by putting together isolated bits of material they bring into therapy and adding up individual episodes in their

Reprinted from *The New England Journal of Medicine*, 1957, **256**, 208-211, by permission of the publisher and the author. Dr. Blaine is Chief, Psychiatric Service, Harvard University Health Services.

everyday lives to make a meaningful conclusion—meaningful not simply in the intellectual realm of ordinary logic but in the emotional insight that can bring about changes in behavior and relief of symptoms. All this bringing together of masses of information, correlating it, living through experiences and learning by them takes a long time and constant attention. Certainly, it is not surprising that therapy relying on this approach takes years. With patients of college age, verbal communication is possible—even easy and neurotic patterns are not yet too firmly set. Short-term dynamic therapy can therefore be attempted. It need not be exclusively supportive therapy but can often be interpretive and on a deep level. Psychoanalytic theory forms the core of the treatment, but the technics are modified to some degree.

TECHNICS EMPLOYED IN SHORT-TERM THERAPY

The armamentarium of the short-term therapist includes a variety of effective weapons. Among them are the following:

Environmental Manipulation

The first weapon, that of environmental manipulation, is self-explanatory. It involves maneuvers such as a change of school and manipulating parents into treatment—that is, finding the true source of neurosis in a family constellation and helping to eliminate it rather than doing therapy with the individual who presents himself first and who may not be ill at all.

Giving Information

The second device, giving information, seems simple. Perhaps some think that it is not the psychiatrist's job to be a teacher, but education often turns out to be therapeutic. Sometimes, misinformation or misconceptions on the part of the patient are responsible for serious neurotic symptoms, which may appear at first glance to be far more complicated and to have deeper sources.

A college sophomore came to me because he was shy about going out with girls. He knew that he was sufficiently attractive and was able to talk intelligently, but he never seemed able to take a girl out more than once. He had feelings of anxiety when he thought of calling up a girl a second time. In the course of working with him, I found out, quite surprisingly, that he was under the misapprehension that his erection was different from everybody else's because it was vertical and not horizontal. He thought this would prevent him from having intercourse. This misconception was contributing greatly to his anxiety. Once it was relieved, simply by supplying the correct physiologic information, he began to be less afraid of girls and better able to carry out a long-term relation.

Getting out Information or Emotion

Another simple technic is obtaining information or the expression of emotion. This has been described as ventilative treatment or catharsis. Knight (1) uses the term "expressive" therapy. The recollection of a childhood memory or the expression, in the therapeutic hour, of hitherto unexpressed emotion against a parent or some other person who has been a source of resentment for years can be dramatically alleviating at times. One must be careful, when using this type of therapy, not to get into difficulties with a patient whose conception of psychotherapy is that it is a search for a key incident in his life, which, when remembered and revealed, will immediately cure his whole complicated neurosis. Many people, from their reading about psychiatry, have this idea. Sometimes, patients seem to want to talk about nothing except their childhood. They become very frustrated and upset when they are unable to dredge up "forgotten memories" during an interview. It often turns out that this is because they think that they are supposed to search for a recollection of the time they got kicked by a horse or stumbled into their parents' bedroom. Usually, this kind of ruminating is a waste of time. There are occasions, however, when the recollection of some unremembered event will be a real turning point in treatment, as in the following case.

A college junior who was in therapy with me for several months came to treatment because he had been having crying spells, when talking to his instructors, for no reason he could think of. This happened also with colleagues and contemporaries, and particularly when he was out with his fiancee. He was at a loss to explain this, and we worked for several months at trying to understand what the source of this distress could be. It seemed clear to me that he felt very unworthy and guilty and that, at times, he was overcome with these feelings of guilt and began to cry. But this explanation on my part did not seem to change his behavior. He continued to feel tense, and once at 3 A.M. he called me on the telephone to say that he had to see me right away. He had just seen his fiancee and had an argument with her about how far he should be allowed to go in their petting. She told him that she thought she wanted to break the engagement. He said that he had become so upset after leaving her that he had pulled his car over to the side of the road, started to scream as loud as he could, and then begun beating the steering wheel with his fists. This behavior had frightened him so much that he thought he ought to talk to someone right away about it. I went to see him, and toward the end of the interview, he said "I've suddenly thought of something that happened when I was ten years old and I don't know why I think of it now." He went on to describe some sex play that had taken place with his younger sister. This was something that he had never been able to recollect in any interviews before. His anxiety was immediately alleviated, and he felt perfectly able to return to his room and go to sleep.

This interview proved to be a real turning point in therapy. From then on this patient was really able to believe in and to understand the irrational feelings of worthlessness and guilt that had to do with his symptoms, and it was not long afterward that he was able to discontinue therapy because he was no longer troubled by crying spells. This experience differs from insight because, in this case, at the time of recall, the incident was not connected in the patient's mind with his symptoms. All he did was bring this incident up and talk about it. I gave some reassurance, which immediately gave him relief and was therapeutically effective without the necessity of having the correlation between the incident and the symptom pointed out or understood.

Transference

The fourth factor, transference, is a word that has come to have many meanings. The original, classic definition of transference referred to emotional feelings transferred from parental figures to the therapist. These irrational, positive or negative feelings were the only ones included in the definition. Recently, the term has been broadened in common usage, referring more generally to the total relation between the patient and the therapist, and it is in this sense that I am using it here.

There are two principal ways in which transference can be therapeutic in short-term psychotherapy. One is through the building up of trust in patients who have come to distrust the world at large because of various experiences that they may have had in childhood with unrealiable, rejecting parents. A clinical relation with a therapist may be a way to re-establish trust in the world at large, in that the patient knows that the therapist is a doctor and therefore interested and anxious to help. Because of this he can often begin then to trust. If the doctor remains a solid person who is predictable and nonpunitive, trust can be increased and transferred later from the therapist to other people in the patient's outside environment.

Another effective use of transference is replacement. By that I mean that the therapist actually plays an active part in the patient's life, replacing a father figure, a parental figure who has died or one who has no adequate role in the life of the patient. Replacement can be dangerous and has to be done carefully. Several things can result in a negative way from this kind of part playing. One of these is overdependence. The patient may become so demanding that the doctor has to set up limits. The patient may interpret this as a rejection, and the illness may be perpetuated instead of treated. Also, the assumption of a role by the therapist is sometimes more frightening than relieving to the patient. The patient may be fearful of people who offer advice or represent authority figures. If the therapist behaves in a directive manner, the patient may become resentful and believe that he has to terminate treatment.

There is another pitfall in this type of therapy if a part of the illness is the acting out of rebellion. The therapist can get a certain enjoyment out of listening to the equivalent of "Till Eulenspiegel's Merry Pranks." It is often hard not to chuckle when a boy describes throwing a cherry bomb down the toilet at school and all the furor that it caused, or stretching a wire across the doorstep to trip up his father as he comes in from work. Of course, if the therapist chuckles and asks for more details about these pranks, he plays into them. He does just what the parents do by getting interested and excited about bad behavior and ends up by encouraging more acting out.

Transference in the classic sense sometimes plays a part in the treatment program, but usually in short-term therapy the actual transference of childhood resentments against a parent is seldom experienced. Even when this does occur and it is obvious to the therapist, it is seldom possible to make the patient aware of what is happening. An interpretation of this sort usually cannot be accepted until after many months of therapy. It often works out, however, that the patient reacts to the therapist in a manner similar to that in which he reacts to his teachers or his colleagues—rejecting help when it is offered, for instance, or suspecting the motives behind an expressed interest in his welfare. This irrational behavior within the interview situation can often be interpreted with profit and is another valuable use of transference.

Insight

Insight is a very effective therapeutic tool and can be more help in the deep-seated types of illness than any of the other factors discussed so far. Insight is an exceedingly difficult thing to bring about, however, because there is a stubborn barrier between emotion and intellect in everyone, and, quite often, this barrier is reinforced by the intellectual values stressed in a college environment. For insight to be effective, it must penetrate that barrier and reach the patient on a feeling level.

A boy seen this year at the University Health Service represents an interesting example; he was helped to understand his problem on an emotional level by a dream.

He was an undergraduate who was disturbed because he was unable to establish a close relation with a girl. He seemed to pick out girls who he knew were going to reject him. He would go out with them, take their abuse for a while, and finally be completely rejected and thrown over. In fact, he would stimulate the rejection himself. He could see this happening, was upset by it, and was afraid that it would keep him from getting married. We talked for a number of interviews about this and discovered that his mother had been a very seductive person herself. She had been extremely resentful of all his girls, and had warned him against women. She told him that they were deceiving and out to trap him. This contributed to his feeling that the only kind of girl who was safe was a girl who would throw him over. The girl with whom he could succeed was dangerous because she was bound to hurt him. He understood all this intellectually. He was a psychology student who had a good deal of knowledge of psychiatry and was pleased by all these intellectualisms that we were tossing around, but there was no change in his symptom.

One day he came in and reported a dream that he thought was important. He had dreamt that he was at a nightclub, sitting at a table with his mother. They were eating peas and carrots, and across at another table was a beautiful chorus girl, who kept looking at the patient and beckoning to him. He felt panicky and unhappy and was unable to go over to her. This dream seemed to be a confirmation of what we had talked about. The patient understood this but he said, "There's something important about those peas and carrots. I don't know what they mean but they stood out awfully clear. I think we ought to find out what they mean." So we talked for the rest of the hour about peas and carrots. We discussed the significance of the color green and the color orange. We talked about the fact that carrots were long and thin and that peas were round, but nothing seemed to have much meaning for him.

When he came in for his next interview a week later, he said, "You know, something happened. I suddenly realized what those peas and carrots meant. Every time before I went out with a girl, my mother would say to me, mind your p's and q's. Suddenly, when I remembered that, I felt as though what we've been talking about all these weeks had meaning for me in a different way."

Actually it did have new significance for him. The intellectual insights we had discussed for so many weeks had penetrated to an emotional level as a direct result of this dream. His symptoms did improve and he now has a warm relationship with a college girl who is accepting and appreciative. Here, intellectual insight gave way to emotional insight after a dream, and symptoms were relieved through the attainment of this insight on a feeling level.

Reality Testing

Reality testing, at first glance, seems to be therapy in reverse. It is especially utilized in what Knight calls "suppressive therapy," and is effective in patients who are delusional, have ideas of reference, and have not been entirely relieved of their symptoms by other kinds of therapy such as psychoanalysis, shock treatment, or prolonged hospitalization. They still function reasonably well, except in limited areas, where they are definitely out of touch with reality. They have a sort of encapsulated psychosis. Sometimes, it is transient and best not treated by deep probing. In fact, sometimes, attempts to interpret the symbolic significance of their "crazy" thoughts upsets these persons more than it helps them. They respond more satisfactorily to the therapist as a reality tester. They come to talk about these delusions and ideas of reference and to check with the therapist about them. They often say, "Is this crazy, or isn't it?" They are able to talk as frankly about it as that, often gaining enough reassurance to maintain their adjustment at home or in jobs because of this help in suppressing symptoms.

A senior in college who came to the clinic because of intermittent depression revealed in the course of treatment that he had a plan for reorganizing the economics of the world by having the population live on rafts, leaving the land for cultivation. He had worked this out to the minutest detail, with what he termed "cost analysis." He had invented many new words and was convinced that this was the Great Plan. His behavior, otherwise, was perfectly appropriate. He had many friends, went skiing, played tennis, did well academically but still he had this delusion, which he told to only a few people who were very close to him.

With a boy like this, by being a reality tester, who helps him understand how farfetched his reasoning is but who, at the same time, admits that the patient needs to reason this way at the moment, a therapist can help keep this kind of thinking out of other parts of the patient's life. Often, after he gains competence in other areas and a greater confidence in himself, such a patient can abandon his weird fantasy completely.

CONCLUSION

The college student presents a very different picture, characterwise, from either the child or the adult. He is at a stage of development that is both remarkably vulnerable and remarkably treatable. He is flexible, impressionable, elastic and resilient, but also brittle when hit too hard. He often bends into bizarre forms but still is malleable enough to return to a conventional appearance with gentle and patient handling. He can be stretched too far, however, and snap. At any rate, he is usually in a mood to talk—to discuss values, ethics, motivations, life, death, suicide, and so forth. He is often anxious for guidance—direct advice, too—from someone who, he believes, is bringing order out of his own chaos, not superimposing direction on him or trying to get him to conform to a family pattern. In other words, the adolescent wants help toward self-expression—toward being himself—not molding by someone who had preconceived ideas about how young men should behave. If therapy is offered in this spirit, the adolescent responds in a most gratifying manner. He accepts interpretations with interest and curiosity without resenting them and without being frightened by them. His behavior, his productiveness, and his degree of happiness often change markedly in a short period.

Psychotherapy, more than any other specialized treatment, depends for its effectiveness on intuition and other unmeasurable quantities—it is truly an example of the art of medicine rather than the science. One cannot measure rapport, interpretations, and transference in ounces or grams, nor can one measure improvement in terms of fall in temperature and pulse rate or sterile blood cultures, but one can have a conceptual framework within which to operate; it seems to me essential that with each patient the therapist know what he is doing in terms of such a framework, and that he have at least a sketchily outlined plan of procedure for the course of therapy as well as to use later as a check to establish progress or lack of it. I have tried to outline such a framework and to describe the various weapons the therapist doing short-term psychotherapy has in his armamentarium and how they can be used with considerable effectiveness in helping college students cope with their special kinds of problems.

REFERENCE

1. Knight, R. P. Evaluation of psychotherapeutic techniques. *Bulletin of the Menninger Clinic*, 1952, **16**, 113-124.

Chapter 15

Short Psychotherapy with Passive Patients

S. E. Browne, M.D.

The most pressing problem in general practice today is the provision of adequate psychotherapy for psychogenic illness, which is responsible for 30% of all consultations (College of General Practitioners, 1958) and only a small proportion of which can be treated by trained psychiatrists. This paper describes a form of brief psychotherapy directed towards modifying neurotic character traits and securing freer expression of personality assets in the passive compliant type of personality which was found in 71% of all patients specially interviewed in late 1959 and 1960 in a working-class Belfast practice.

THE PASSIVE PERSONALITY

The personality pattern was basically similar in each case: the typical patient was timid, shy, passive and lacking in self-confidence. He was too anxiety-ridden to risk friction or rebuffs in personal relationships, so was submissive and ingratiating in order to gain approval, allowing himself to be imposed on or offended without protest; he was an habitual "yes-man" who was unable to assert his own views, wishes, and feelings. Though often above average in ability and industriousness, he was driven to disparage himself and feel inferior, and was often only at ease with friends or people of lower social grades. In addition, the patient was usually over-conscientious and perfectionistic at work or household duties.

Passivity originates as a (rather ineffective) defense against the anxiety engendered by faulty parental attitudes such as over-protectiveness or authoritarian aloofness. Horney (1945, 1950) has shown how in an unhealthy environment the child may become submissive and affection-seeking, or hostile and

Reprinted from *British Journal of Psychiatry*, 1964, **110**, 233-239, by permission of the publisher and the author. Dr. Browne is in General Practice in Dartford, Kent, England.

aggressive, or may withdraw into isolation; these solutions alternate in conflict with each other before one becomes rigidly compulsive. In the passive child, conflicting aggressive drives are deeply repressed, but are constantly reinforced by resentment of inadequate parental affection and acceptance.

The dependent child tends to grow up feeling divided and lacking in confidence because compulsive submissiveness prevents free assertion and awareness of his own natural wishes and feelings and of his aggressive hostility. The resulting self alienation by blocking the development of self-acceptance and a feeling of identity, perpetuates anxiety and defensive compliance in all later relationships.

The submissive person attempts to compensate for his weakness and anxiety by actualizing an idealized image of himself. The anxious child tries to be more truthful, punctual, hard-working, or successful at school than any of his peers; adults, while unceasingly striving to attain an unrealistic degree of perfection in work or in gaining social approval by their generosity, helpfulness and humility, usually feel their efforts to be hopelessly inadequate. The frequent attacks of self-contempt, depression and increased anxiety caused by the unrealistic demands of their idealized selves were discussed during therapy.

SELECTION AND SYMPTOMS

In late 1959 and 1960 a total of fifty-six patients were seen by appointment because of failure to respond to such measures as drug therapy or brief discussion of problems; forty of these were of the predominantly submissive character-type. Twenty-three patients from this group at interview expressed a desire to have therapy, and twenty-one were selected for treatment and follow-up over a period of two years, two patients being excluded because of severely limited intelligence. The remaining seventeen were mainly of low mental status with no motivation for psychotherapy. This article does not include a description of the therapy of the sixteen patients with other types of personality disorder.

Eighteen patients in the group studied were of working-class and three of middle-class origin. Thirteen presented with somatic complaints such as peptic ulcer, asthma, eczema and dysmenorrhoea, and six with chronic anxiety. Two patients had each been treated twice in mental hospitals without improvement, one being a case of borderline schizophrenia and the other of hysteria in a schizoid personality. The average duration of symptoms was 9.7 years; the youngest patient was twelve and the oldest forty-seven.

TREATMENT TECHNIQUE

Treatment was directed towards a greater degree of self-realization by substituting self-assertive and self-accepting attitudes for submissive and self-rejecting ones, and some degree of basic change in this respect was considered essential for long-term improvement. Kent Oral (Kent, 1923) Tests were used to help in deciding the treatment schedule. Of the twenty-one patients, four were of superior intelligence, five were average, and twelve less than average.

With seventeen patients who were not excessively anxious, treatment was of necessity highly directive and brief because of pressure of routine work. To offset this difficulty, most interviews after February, 1960 were tape-recorded and patients were encouraged to listen to play-backs and to make notes of significant points. The average number of long sessions (1-1½ hours) was 2.2, of brief sessions (15-25 minutes) in surgery was 3.6, and of tape play-backs 1.8.

Speed in treatment was made possible by a number of factors. The character structure was basically similar in each case. The use of tape-recordings avoided time-consuming recapitulation and increased considerably the therapeutic potential and emotional impact of each interview. Patients gained insight into their timidity by listening to their hesitant manner of speaking. Progress was also facilitated by the pre-existing rapport available to the general practitioner and the opportunity at surgery visits of giving added support and encouragement, and of renewing contact with the few patients who had shown resistance to continuing treatment. An important factor in securing lasting improvement was the capacity of patients to do a great deal of self-analysis between sessions and for a long period after termination of treatment; progress was usually gradual and often more marked after than during therapy. The need for further treatment was assessed after a period of self-analysis had followed each session.

Hypnosis was used with eleven patients on an average of 6.7 occasions. With patients who showed resistance by persistently discussing somatic symptoms such as headaches, these were removed and then recalled by its use in order to indicate their psychogenic origin. At the end of most sessions the patient was hypnotized and given suggestions that his confidence, spontaneity, assertiveness and ability to relax would increase *pari passu* with improvement in his symptoms. All patients achieved a useful depth of trance and improved as subjects with practice. Post-hypnotic suggestions of this kind helped to make treatment goals more meaningful, increased motivation and belief in the possibility of change, and strengthened the therapeutic relationship without undue stimulation of dependence. Auto-hypnosis was found useful in aborting acute attacks of asthma, peptic ulcer pain, colitis, and other symptoms and for daily auto-suggestion.

A further factor in shortening treatment was the focusing of attention on the interaction of the patient with persons in his environment, rather than on fostering and interpreting dependency phenomena in the therapeutic relationship, although sometimes unduly submissive behaviour during a session was commented on. Emphasis was laid from the start on the need for change through active efforts by the patient, thus preventing the development of expectations of magical help from the therapist. Advice was given in general terms, leaving the patient to use his own initiative in deciding the timing of assertive moves; it was suggested that initially he should practise these with acquaintances or social inferiors rather than with more intimidating figures such as strangers, employers, or foremen. Consequently, while an attitude of acceptance, approval and sympathetic interest helped to improve the patient's self-esteem and self-acceptance, no undue dependence nor reluctance to discontinue treatment was noted.

With four other schizoid patients, self-rejection was too great to allow early instigation of assertive responses. These patients were markedly passive and anxious and had a very limited range of personal relationships because of their greater tendency to withdraw into isolation. With this group, emphasis was placed primarily on increasing self-acceptance, so decreasing anxiety to a level where they could become more assertive and self-directing. One patient, a borderline schizophrenic, had 84 interviews, two others each had 26, and a university student had 4 sessions (subsequently played back).

As early as possible in treatment, the presence of submissive attitudes was detected by discussing the patient's passive reactions when imposed on by friends or neighbors, given bad service by tradesmen or waiters, or abused by strangers. Lack of self-acceptance was expressed by such symptoms as discomfort at social functions, or a feeling of not being "as good as" or respected by other people.

While some patients had considerable insight into their own submissiveness, full awareness of its compulsive nature and consequences was sought by discussing the following outline of the psychodynamics, presented with an emphasis appropriate to the individual patient.

The passive patient attempts to gain the approval and regard of everyone he meets, even when he is being imposed on or abused. He devotes his energies to doing favours for others instead of looking after his own interests, and is always pleasant and polite in the expectation that others will reciprocate. This technique works to some extent with other passive people, but fails completely when he meets the aggressive, exploiting personality type. The more polite, helpful and self-effacing he is, the greater the disdain with which he is treated, and the more he is imposed on. His expectations of friendship are disappointed and he becomes a "doormat." He resents this treatment bitterly, but his need to be friendly and his fear of retailiation prevent awareness or expression of his rage. He is helped to become aware of how his pride in being popular and well-thought of is hurt, what little self-esteem he has often being submerged in acute self-contempt, and how unconscious resentment builds up until it erupts on the slightest of pretexts with inoffensive people. This happens usually in the family circle, where he feels safe from attack and is often chronically irritable; when he expresses his rage with people outside the home, he is anxious and frightened of possible repercussions. These outbursts also act as a very necessary safety-valve for the active externalization of his temporarily acute self-hate. The patient's repressed rage and his hate and rage against himself may produce a wide range of somatic symptoms such as headache, tiredness, asthmatic attacks, and exacerbation of peptic ulcer pain and colitis. He is asked during treatment to attempt to connect any sudden increase in symptoms with incidents when unconsciously his resentment of others' attitudes or actions may have been repressed or his pride in winning others' approval may have been hurt.

The passive patient is, therefore, constantly balanced on a razor-edge; he is driven to seek approval, but destined to be rebuffed and exploited. His self-esteem is precarious and ever vulnerable, being at the mercy of everyone he meets.

The patient must get as deep an appreciation as possible of these factors operating in his life, and come to see the futility of submissiveness as a solution of his problem. It is essential for him to learn to be less sensitive to and less concerned about other people's attitudes and opinions, and to develop more self-interest instead of compulsively helping others. He is taught to restrict his need for friendship to people whom he really respects and likes.

It is important that he should realize how his preoccupation with approval leads him mistakenly to imagine that inadvertent aloofness or inattention is a deliberate snub. Many patients admitted to considerable anxiety after passing acquaintances who failed to see and acknowledge them. This undue sensitivity is due to underlying self-contempt which, in being passively externalized to others, makes relationships precarious, and in patients like the borderline schizophrenic in this series can produce ideas of reference.

Instead, the patient should learn to assert his own feelings and wishes more freely and to express firmly his resentment if imposed on or offended; he must not interpret this advice as an invitation to ride roughshod over his own family or submissive friends, in whose interests, as well as the patient's, a clear distinction requires to be made between assertion and hostile aggression as opposites. Assertion is spontaneous, healthy, flexible and constructive; it is based on strength and acceptance. Cameron (1950) has stated that man has a basic need to control his environment; healthy assertiveness affords him a greater measure of control over himself and other people. Aggression, on the other hand, is rigidly inflexible, compulsive and destructive; it is a neurotic trait developed to compensate for weakness, self-rejection and fear of others. Therapy should aim at helping the patient to be firm on issues which really matter, rather than aggressively develop "a chip on his shoulder."

It is also important for him to see that he can only acquire true self-esteem by respecting himself instead of seeking approval from others. While confidence and assertiveness can grow in the passive patient with self-acceptance and a new and warm appreciation of his assets, they are stillborn as long as deep and pervasive self-contempt prevents him from feeling good about any achievement, however meritorious. The result is a permanent "cold war" and paralysing dichotomy between the discriminating "I" and the despised "me," a split which can only be healed by self-acceptance.

It is surprising how obstinately the more anxious passive patient can resist becoming aware of assets such as his skill and diligence at work, and his genuine kindness and consideration, and in general taking a more balanced view of himself. It seemed helpful to the more intelligent patients to use the analogy that, just as in the completeness of nature the full day consists of day and night, the light and the dark, the seasons of the cold and the warm, the dry and the wet, so human nature is inevitably compounded of positive as well as negative qualities and can never be altogether worthless. With continued emphasis on his definite assets, the patient can begin to feel some pride in himself and his total self-disapproval can slowly disappear.

It was also found valuable to encourage the patient to accept his shortcomings as facts and not as faults for which he must blame himself. Imperfection is to be seen as a basic condition of existence with which he must learn to live in a spirit of acceptance rather than of crippling antagonism to self.

To assist the patient in achieving the difficult transition from profound self-contempt to self-acceptance the presence of potential inner resources was indicated by the use of post-hypnotic suggestions that he would feel more assertive, confident, energetic, spontaneous in conversation, and at ease socially than ever before. Although short-lived, the novel feeling of integration, spontaneity, and confidence demonstrated how self-acceptance could help him to assert and realize himself, and free him from the constant need to prove and improve himself. As Wenkart (1955) states, "acceptance is life-affirming and a premise of inner growth."

All improved patients in becoming assertive spontaneously developed more self-accepting attitudes and confidence, but the more timid were slower in learning to assert and required help in improving their self-concept both before and after doing so. While with all patients attention was focused mainly on the present, discussion of obvious childhood genetic factors in their passivity helped to deepen insight and relieve guilt.

RESULTS

The average period between termination of treatment and follow-up was two years. At follow-up all patients were seen at least twice and opinions were obtained from relatives to insure accurate evaluation of progress. Patients were classed as much, considerably, or not improved. Inclusion in the first category required symptom cure together with marked change in self-awareness, self-acceptance, and assertiveness. Self-acceptance was described in statements such as "I feel as good as anyone else," "I respect myself and am not now easily hurt," and "other people respect me more." Increases in self-assurance, spontaneity, available energies, and freer expression of feelings were noted. Improved domestic or marital (including sexual) and social relationships and the adoption of a more healthily relaxed attitude to work and leisure instead of compulsive habits of perfectionism and "always being on the go" were regarded as important evidence of progress. In improved patients, absence from work through illness was greatly diminished.

The considerably improved category was composed of those whose symptoms had been markedly but not completely relieved and who reported a similar or less definite degree of change in personal attitudes.

Nine patients were considered much better, seven considerably improved, and five unimproved. Of the latter, the borderline schizophrenic relapsed twice; the one other schizoid patient rated unimproved achieved considerable insight and complete relief from a peptic ulcer and colitis without becoming more self-accepting or assertive and a third patient reported some change in this respect without permanent relief of his prurigo. Among symptoms completely relieved were—severe asthma, peptic ulcer, frigidity, dysmenorrhoea, stammering, and eczema.

Evidence of effectiveness of treatment was strengthened by interviews with relatives who often spoke of "a great change" in the patients and by the fact that seven patients were exposed to major stress in the follow-up period without deterioration.

No significant long-term difference was noted in the improvement rate in this small series between patients treated with and without hypnosis, but with it progress was quicker and in three patients improvement seemed mainly due to its use.

DISCUSSION

The preponderance of submissive patients in this series might be partly attributed to local cultural factors such as the rather later survival of authoritarian parental attitudes, or to the selective effect of the therapist's personality on the composition of his practice; however, similar findings have been reported in a number of studies. Miles, Barrabee and Finesinger (1951) noted that among 62 cases of anxiety neurosis almost all the males were passive and most of the females shy and timid. Portnoy (1959) stated that, whatever the surface picture in anxiety states, the underlying pattern most frequently found was that of self-effacement and passivity. Alexander (1950) placed dependency needs in a central position in patients with psychosomatic disorders. With regard to prognosis in passive patients, Ross (1923) found treatment much easier and more successful than with authoritarian narcissistic patients.

A significant aspect of self-assertiveness as a primary goal in psychotherapy is that the assertive patient experiences anxiety mainly as a challenge and a positive and healthy force leading to a more constructive self-affirmation; while still passive and self-effacing his anxiety is qualitatively and quantitatively very different and is a sick, negative and paralysing influence on his growth. Summoning "the courage to be" and to assert "I am" leads to a new "awareness of being" in which inner resources are liberated and conflicts are more easily surmounted. One patient in this series began to assert himself with a bullying uncle and other people after one interview (six play-backs) in which he complained of life-long timidity, inferiority feelings, anxiety and stammering. At follow-up he was free from stammering, self-confident, felt as good as and respected by other people, and his marital and social relationships were much improved. A boy of twelve with a history of severe somatic symptoms for ten years recovered completely after asserting himself with a bully.

Self-assertion is thus an intensely meaningful experience for the passive patient and can often produce a degree of change which is usually regarded as being attainable only after lengthy psychotherapy. Martin (1952) has pointed out that the extent and

awareness of total involvement in inner conflict is some measure
of the degree of insight and re-integration achieved by the patient
in analysis, and that re-experiencing painful conflicts rather than
unpleasant memories is the vital factor in recovery. He illustrated this conclusion by reference to psychotherapies throughout the ages and, in particular, to the work of Alexander and
French (1948), and Shorvon and Sargant (1947). Successful
analysis of the passive patient requires that he should become
fully aware of his hostility, which he repressed because of anxiety and fear of annihilation during his infantile or childhood
conflicts.

   When first venturing to assert themselves the patients in this
series were sufficiently self-accepting to become involved in re-
experiencing conflict between dependency and aggression and
solving it by releasing their repressed hostility. In so doing,
without any frightening repercussions, their childhood terror
was relieved and they became more integrated, confident, self-
accepting and less hostile with each assertive move; recovery
occurred without awareness of the presence of conflict in all life
situations. This process of experiencing conflict, expressing and
thus integrating repressed aggression and so becoming freely
assertive and self-directing is found in play-therapy, abreactive
techniques, L.S.D. and analytic treatment of the passive patient
as well as in group therapy. However, the "acting out" of
aggression outside the consulting room is unfortunately not
utilized and is indeed discouraged in orthodox treatment. Where
marked involvement in conflict occurred during assertion,
patients experienced anxiety symptoms such as rapid or deep
breathing, trembling and stomach tension, but afterwards felt
much more confident and their anxiety was greatly relieved. Just
as some patients required further help in improving their self-
concept before becoming freely assertive, others (seen in a later
series) who had before treatment developed a degree of
assertiveness ranging from occasional outbursts under extreme
provocation to firm resistance against being imposed on, but who
in most cases experienced anxiety afterwards, were helped to free
themselves from inferiority feelings and so enabled to become
more genuinely confident and assertive. Other untreated passive
patients in the practice improved greatly in self-esteem and
confidence after becoming fully assertive spontaneously; in two
cases sudden marked change occurred after inner conflict had
erupted in epileptic convulsions. In adolescents, newly-acquired
friendships occasionally led to self-acceptance and subsequent
normal assertiveness; this spontaneous process of recovery is
similar to that occurring in therapy where even a brief experience
of acceptance sometimes leads to patients "feeling different" and
gaining sufficient self-respect to become assertive later.

In becoming more assertive and self-accepting and so gaining an increased sense of inner certainty and identity, patients progressed from their infantile despair at feeling unlovable and unloved and withdrawal from genuine relatedness to being confident of and reciprocating the love and respect of others. The compulsive search for a meaningful substitute for love and completeness through approval-seeking submissiveness, admiration won by actualizing the idealized image, fantasies, sexual aberrations or alcohol became unnecessary. For example, a girl who had fantasies of an ideal mate and was very uncertain of her feelings towards her boyfriend became engaged shortly after terminating treatment; a married woman with frigidity resumed a normal and satisfying sex-life and relinquished her perfectionistic drives.

Many critics have suggested that approximately two-thirds of both treated and untreated psychoneurotic patients recover, and Eysenck (1960) has stated that 90 per cent of neurotics recover spontaneously in a period of five years. In this series the patients had been having medical treatment for symptoms for an average period of 9.7 years and had a history of personality problems since childhood. It is probable that they represented a more "chronic" type of patient and that the improvement rate of 76 per cent can be accepted as significant proof of the value of the form of psychotherapy used.

Primary emphasis on self-assertion in psychotherapy has been described by Cameron, Salter, Wolpe and Stevenson. Cameron (1951) encouraged passive patients to become assertive with other people and finally with a "key figure" (usually a parent) in their environment. Wolpe (1958) has derived from modern learning theory a technique of instigating assertive responses to diminish patients' anxiety by a process of reciprocal inhibition in a comparatively short number of sessions. He states that many psychoanalysts indirectly influence patients towards assertive behaviour without being aware of its central curative role. Salter's (1949) approach has its origin in Pavlovian theory; he considers people to be either assertive or inhibitory, the latter being treated by "excitation" of their real feelings. Stevenson (1959) finds that treatment by active instigation of assertive behaviour is as effective as, and much shorter than, psychoanalytic therapy. Stevenson and Wolpe (1960) have also described the long-term cure of sexual deviations by encouraging self-assertiveness.

It seems valid to conclude that the form of therapy described is both feasible and valuable in general practice except with very anxious and schizoid patients, with whom treatment is long and often unrewarding. The improvement in general health and attendance at work noted in this series points to the importance for the national economy of developing a health service in which the family doctor has the time and training to deal adequately with psychogenic illness.

SUMMARY

An account is given of an active and brief form of psychotherapy in general practice with 21 patients of the passive personality type, which was found in 71 per cent of all patients interviewed.

Treatment was directed towards increasing self-assertiveness and self-acceptance which were regarded as basic aspects of a unitary process of recovery through greater self-realization. It involved the use of hypnotic techniques and the play-back of tape-recorded interviews; reassurance, clarification, and interpretation of the patient's attitudes to himself and others and active persuasion and suggestion were the main elements in therapy.

Sixteen patients were considered on follow-up two years later to be much or considerably improved. It is suggested that this method of psychotherapy is simple and effective enough to be of value to general practitioners, as well as in psychiatric practice.

REFERENCES

Alexander, F. *Psychosomatic medicine. Its principles and applications.* New York, 1950.

Alexander, F., & French, T. *Fundamentals of psychoanalysis.* New York, 1948.

Cameron, D. E. *General psychotherapy. Dynamics and procedures.* New York, 1950.

Cameron, D. E. The conversion of passivity into normal self-assertion. *Amer. J. Psychiat.*, 1951, 108, 98-102.

College of General Practitioners Working Party Report. Psychological medicine in general practice. *Brit. Med. J.*, 1958, ii, 585-590.

Eysenck, H. J. *Handbook of abnormal psychology.* London, 1966, pp. 697-725.

Horney, K. *Our inner conflicts.* New York, 1945.

Horney, K. *Neurosis and human growth.* New York, 1950.

Kent, G. H. F. *Appl. Psychol.*, 1923, 7, 246-257.

Martin, A. R. The dynamics of insight. *Amer. J. Psychoanal.*, 1952, 12, 24-38.

Miles, H. W. H., Barrabee, M. S., & Finesinger, J. E. Evaluation of psychotherapy. *Psychosomat. Med.*, 1951, 13, 83-105.

Portnoy, I. The anxiety states. In *American Handbook of Psychiatry.* New York, 1959.

Ross, T. A. *The common neuroses.* London, 1923. (Republished 1945).

Salter, A. *Conditioned reflex therapy.* New York, 1949.

Shorvon, H. J., & Sargant, W. Excitatory abreaction. *J. Ment. Sci.*, 1947, 93, 47-56.

Stevenson, I. Direct instigation of behavioural changes in psychotherapy. *Arch. Gen. Psychiat.*, 1959, 1, 99-107.

Stevenson, I., & Wolpe, J. Recovery from sexual deviations through overcoming non-sexual neurotic responses. *Amer. J. Psychiat.*, 1960, 116, 737-742.

Wenkart, A. Self-acceptance. *Amer. J. Psychoanal.*, 1955, 15, 135-143.

Wolpe, J. *Psychotherapy by reciprocal inhibition.* California: Stanford University Press, 1958.

Chapter 16

Brief Therapy with Children
and Their Parents

Gerald Weinberger, Ph.D.

Traditional psychotherapy with children has generally rested upon basic psychoanalytic notions that the child's problems are symptomatic of underlying and unresolved conflicts, usually unconscious, which can only be removed through an understanding and resolution of these conflicts. To this end, the child is encouraged to express these conflicts via symbolic play which is then interpreted by the therapist. In this theoretical framework, the parents play a relatively minor part in resolving the child's problems because the problems (even overt parent-child conflict) are seen as expressions of internal conflicts which have to be "exorcised" (although traditional child therapy often includes the treatment of parents for their own personal or marital difficulties which are presumed to be displaced onto the child and responsible for his "problem"). Thus most child treatment, no matter what the techniques used, occurs within the framework of an "illness" model in which the underlying "disease" is treated. At the same time, most child treatment is conceptualized as a long-term process due to such factors as resistance, the intricacies of intrapsychic processes and their expression, and the need to develop a relationship of trust and closeness with the child.

Brief psychotherapy with children, when attempted, has usually not been what it purports to be. Rather, it is either an elongated diagnostic evaluation in which the child is *prepared* for therapy, or it becomes a compression of the long-term process into a shorter period of time, or else it is crisis-oriented, designed to deal with an acute episode in the life of a child, and is *then* followed up by long-term therapy. However, brief therapy, to be efficient and effective, is a treatment method with its own

Dr. Weinberger is Chief Psychologist, Children's Psychiatric Center, Eatontown, New Jersey and Clinical Associate, Teachers College, Columbia University, New York.

techniques, based upon an entirely different rationale about the helping process and about what problems are considered to be.

Brief, time-limited therapy with children arises first out of a set of hard facts which have been conveniently ignored for years, although all child therapists, especially those working in clinics and other community facilities, have always been aware of them; namely, that national statistics indicate that most cases are seen for only an average of four to six interviews, which does not permit the leisurely development of a relationship in order to "get at" underlying conflicts. Children are in therapy by the grace of their parents and leave therapy because their parents are either satisfied (if there is rapid dissolution of the overt problem for which they sought help) or dissatisfied (because they have been ignored, because the child resists, or because most parents are unprepared for and unaccepting of jargonistic formulations and the need for lengthy treatment to handle underlying problems which seem to them to have little or nothing to do with why they sought help).

What is being suggested is that the prevailing model for the treatment of all children is one that is appropriate and relevant for at best 5-10% of those children sent for help (and often those who are verbal, bright, and well-to-do) and yet it has been imposed upon all children, including those whose problems are relatively minor or are expressed in conflicts with other people or other systems (such as the schools, the main source of referrals of children for therapy). When these children are not helped, the theory has not generally been questioned, but rather its proponents use it to explain away failure and try, at best, only to modify it. Brief therapy is based upon an entirely different set of perceptions utilizing a "health" model which sees clients as basically coping and adaptive but experiencing problems which may be caused by ignorance, inappropriate expectations, social surroundings, or other factors which do not implicate the parents as malevolent and pathogenically motivated.

The vast majority of children are seen not privately but in community child guidance clinics, hospitals, and medical centers. They are sent because their *behavior* is disturbing someone directly or because someone decides (e. g., a teacher or a Juvenile Court judge) that their behavior is disturbed according to the experience or expectations of the referring person. Parents vary greatly in the extent to which they are concerned about their child, the extent to which they feel pressured by others to seek help, the extent to which they blame and are angry with their child, the extent to which they hold themselves responsible for their child's "problems," the extent to which they view his behavior as "disturbed," and the extent to which they are prepared to involve themselves in understanding and changing the child's behavior. With such a great number of variables affecting the application for help, it becomes crucial for the therapist to ascertain as quickly as possible what the parents see as the problem, how they conceptualize the problem (e.g., unsympathetic teacher, hereditary taint, marital problems, etc.), and what they expect of the child's therapist in "fixing up" (or straightening out) the child. A contract must be drawn with the parents, one as explicit as possible, in which both sides are clear as to what is expected of each other and what can be done by each. This contract, which most often initially focuses on eliminating undesired behavior (as seen by the parents) and less often means promoting desired behavior (e. g., good grades, socially acceptable activities), can more or less involve the parents depending upon their willingness and the therapist's evaluation of the necessity of their participation. In all cases, this contract involves selecting out certain current behaviors which are troublesome, and endeavoring to effect change, in a delimited sense, and in a short period of time (at the author's clinic the time limit, set before the parents are ever seen, is a maximum of 6 weeks and 12 sessions for all family members seen, inclusive).

Turning from the parents to the child, one begins with the assumption that the child may not have the faintest idea what kind of place he is in, to whom he is speaking, and for what purpose. Parents are notoriously anxious and vague about telling their children where they are going and why. Often the child is told half-truths, or half-lies; when he is told fully, the message is that he has behaved badly and will see somebody who will change him in line with the desires of the parents or another agency (thus implicitly aligning the therapist with the child's adversaries). Of even more importance is the fact that the child may not agree at all with the parents' perception of the problem; he may feel he has none and others are over-reacting or distorting, or he may be concerned about a totally different problem than are the adults. In more traditional and time-unlimited treatment, the child is often presumed to be unaware of his "real" problem and thus there may never be a contract explicitly drawn and agreed upon. Even where there is a setting of the contract, this proceeds at a leisurely pace while the therapist attempts subtly to get the child to state his problems. In brief therapy, setting the contract and delimiting the problem is the first, immediate, and overt focus of treatment, whereby the cooperation of the child in solving *his* problem (the way he sees it) is enlisted.

A crucial concept in brief treatment with any age client is *confrontation:* the therapist's direct and overt attempt to focus the conscious attention of the child (client) on his behavior as perceived by others and/or experienced by the therapist in his relationship with the client. Often the child will disavow any knowledge of why he has been brought for help or will evade the issue because of anxiety or because he wishes to find out what the therapist knows. The therapist must then explore whether the child inquired as to why he was being brought to this place, and what the parents told him. He will also determine if the child agrees with the parents' concern, and if not, whether he has disagreed openly with the parents (and if so, what happened). If the child still claims ignorance, he is confronted with the presenting complaints of the parents and any other referring agency (e. g., "The school has told your parents you fight all the time"). Thus, the starting point, on a directly verbal level, is to confront the child with his problem as seen by others, and to begin to deal with his reaction to this.

From this starting point with the child, the therapist operates as if the child is able, on his own developmental level, to verbally discuss his problems in an open manner with the therapist. Free play is considered both time consuming and irrelevant, since the focus is not upon the symbolic expression of internal conflicts but on the child's active discussion of his current behavior which may be bothering someone else and perhaps the child. The child is asked to describe behaviorally what happens (as for example, in his being rejected by peers) and alternative modes of behaving are suggested by the therapist, often connected by him to related self-attitudes of the child which are responsible for his behavior (e. g., "You like to be the best, but when you brag about it other kids don't like you"). Generally the source of these attitudes (e.g., as emanating from the parents) is ignored, for the focus is on those self-attitudes which lead to self-defeating behaviors according to the child's own stated interests and goals. To this extent, play can be used in two carefully delimited ways: certain activities can be suggested which will bring out more fully and clearly those behavioral characteristics or attitudes which need changing (e. g., playing checkers so that the child's difficulty in accepting realistic limitations on his competence will be expressed when he loses; throwing darts so that an inhibited and constricted child can directly see that he, and his world, can survive his being more aggressive); and play as a means of reducing tension and making a child more comfortable so that he will be able to discuss his problems without becoming so threatened that he must either evade or ignore the therapist's comments.

In brief therapy, the therapist must openly, directly, rapidly, and frequently confront the child with how he appears to the therapist, and how he affects other people in those areas selected for change; or where certain of the child's attitudes either block change or serve to maintain self-defeating behaviors. The child's relationship to the therapist, and the display within this relationship of certain attitudes and behaviors which have proven troublesome to the child, provide one of the main arenas if not the exclusive one for this focused confrontation. Initially, the way the child handles the probing of how he sees his problem provides the therapist with direct diagnostic information about the child. Using his own feelings about the impact of the child upon him, the therapist can relate this direct experiencing of the child to the child's problems with others and with his feelings about himself. These impressions are fed directly and rapidly back to the child who must then deal, often for the first time, with an adult who clarifies his attitudes and points out for him how he behaves, but who does not necessarily react to him as significant others have (e. g., with anger, confusion, weeping, etc.) On the basis of the child's reactions, and his altered behavior, the therapist will also modify his comments, alter the intensity of the confrontation, and raise or lower his expectations about what the child can do.

As the child is being actively encouraged to cope with and master his problems as he sees them, the brief therapist can work concurrently and highly effectively with the parents. As in the usual model for private practitioners, in which one therapist sees the entire family (but which curiously has been ignored in clinics, where the "team" reigns supreme, and its efficacy remains unchallenged and unproven), brief therapy works best with one therapist responsible for the entire family. Parents are most eager to learn of the therapist's impressions of their child, and the therapist is in a more advantageous position to influence them if he is acting upon direct experiential knowledge of the child rather than on what someone else tells him (a therapist telling parents that the child's therapist sees him as provocative may bring questions about the therapist's judgment and competence; a therapist telling the parents that he himself, in his contacts with the child, sees him as a "little monster" and that he sympathizes with what the parents have to deal with, is seen by the parents as an understanding ally who knows what it's like to have to deal with such a child).

Working with the parents is similar to working with the child; namely, one directs one's attention to the current behavior or problems with which the parents are concerned, and their attitudes and expectations which sustain these behaviors or can alter them. The therapist's first job is to identify and delimit the area(s) of concern to the parents, and then, through active probing, to select out the crucial area on which to work with the parents. This area can be viewed as the key in a log-jam (remove one and the whole thing breaks up) or it can be an area which, when successfully handled, can most clearly illustrate to the parents their unrealistic expectations of and attitudes about the child and thus most easily help the parents to learn principles of child management which can be generalized to other areas of behavior (e. g., setting firm limits, breaking up power struggles, over-reasoning to no avail). Once the selected area is decided upon (e. g., "she needs to be nagged constantly to do anything") the therapist must insist upon a precise and detailed behavioral description of the problem (e. g., what do the parents mean when they complain that their daughter is "sloppy," or their son's grades are "bad"?). Too often therapists have accepted vague and affectively laden descriptions of the child's behavior and have not asked the parents to concretely and behaviorally describe what exactly the child, and they, are actually doing. This, unfortunately, prevents any evaluation of whether it is more the child's behavior which is of concern, or whether it is the parents' expectations which are inappropriate and need modification. For example, when parents complain about their child's under-achievement, one needs to ascertain what achievement level they feel the child can reach, and then mesh this with an objective evaluation of the child's intellectual capabilities; another example might involve family arguments about how late an adolescent wishes to stay out on a date. Here again a knowledge of the child's age, maturity, realiability, as well as local norms for adolescents all contribute to the therapist's reaction to the relative appropriateness of the demands of both parents and teen-agers.

Once the therapist has obtained as accurate a picture as possible of the child's behavior, he needs to focus on what the parents have been doing to handle and resolve the problem. Again he must insist on their being precise and concrete in describing their efforts. Too often when parents say they "have tried everything and nothing works," the traditionally oriented therapist has focused on parental feelings; the brief therapist has neither the time nor the inclination to do so. He may lightly touch on their frustration and sense of failure, but he will query the parents as to what exactly they did and how the child reacted to their efforts. As the therapist obtains an ever more detailed and richer picture of the current state of the parent-child relationship, he begins to do two things. First, he confronts the parents openly and directly with a clarifying view (thought of as an initial working hypothesis subject to constant modification and refinement) of the problem which helps to conceptualize for the parents central issues underlying the problem they are having with their child, or he is having with others. The major work here is to illuminate parental attitudes about themselves and their child and to underscore parental expectations of and goals for their child in the particular area of concern. The therapist tries to relate these attitudes and expectations (often conscious ones, but occasionally the parents are not aware of certain premises which underlie their behaviors) to how they perceive and react to their child. Since these attitudes have led to self-defeating behaviors by the parent (e. g., he won't do his homework unless I sit over him because he is irresponsible and it is my job to see that his work gets done), pointing out fallacies and distortions in parental attitudes leads to suggesting different ways of viewing and evaluating both parental roles and expectations (e. g., how is he to develop responsibility if you sit over his homework every night?).

Secondly, the therapist begins as rapidly as possible to suggest different ways to view the behavior and different ways of handling it so that a mutually inappropriate and maladaptive relationship is ended and a different, and more satisfying one for both parties is substituted, if only in one small area (e. g., coming in on time after a date, getting up in the morning, putting dirty clothes in the laundry). The therapist not only must be precise as to what he feels the parents need to do, but it is also very helpful to anticipate for the parents (based on the therapist's knowledge of the particular child and children in general) what the child may do in response to the parents' new ways of relating to him. If the parent is capable of grasping new ideas and principles rapidly, the therapist may need to do little actual suggesting of alternative behaviors; however, in some cases such as in disorganized families or with helpless and overwhelmed parents, the therapist may have to do virtually all the programming and tell the parents exactly what should be done. While this means for the moment the therapist has assumed full responsibility for making decisions for the family, his eventual goal is *always* to increase parental confidence in their ability to reassume their role as the responsible authorities and decision-makers in the family.

Subsequent weeks in brief therapy are devoted first to carefully following up on what the parents are doing and how the child is reacting, and then modifying (or even discarding) the plan of action on the basis of what the child does or the therapist's ever-growing knowledge of the parents' capabilities or both. Secondly, the therapist may seek to enlarge the area of the changed parent-child relationship or seek to modify different areas of the child's relationships with others. Thirdly, to solidify and stablize the new behavior, the therapist continually feeds back to the parents his thoughts as to which of their attitudes about children and themselves as parents and spouses contributed to the old ineffective struggles, misperceptions, misunderstandings, and unhappiness. A major part in this working through is to help the parents not only recognize and accept their own and their child's limitations, but to set more realistic goals for themselves as parents, and their child as a child with a unique life style of his own which must be understood, respected, and not enmeshed in their own needs and problems.

It should also be pointed out that, concurrent with alterations in parental perceptions and behavior, the therapist may be asking the child if he sees his parents as behaving differently, and, if so, how he feels about this. With children from the ages of roughly seven to eleven, this joint process works best, as a general rule, if the parents and child are seen separately (although an occasional family session may be most helpful in clarifying issues and impcctations of different family members). With children younger than seven, it is suggested that the main focus of work be with the parents. Changes in their handling of the child often lead to rapid changes by the child who has not yet sufficiently internalized and solidified those attitudes which will enable him, as he gets older, to act more independently of adults. With children over eleven, and especially with adolescents, the process of modifying family relationships seems to work best in family sessions in which the therapist can confront all members, at the same time, with what is going on and with what needs to be changed.

CASE ILLUSTRATIONS

The following case excerpts are chosen as examples of the brief therapeutic approach with children and/or parents of different ages and with different problems:

A. Susan B., age 4

Susan, the only child of the B.'s, was brought because of her intense and frequent temper tantrums. Mrs. B., age 24 had been in analysis for several years but had been told that her problems with her daughter could not be handled in her own therapy but would best be treated at a child guidance clinic. When first seen, Mrs. B. was quite depressed and overwhelmed by Susan's behavior; she felt helpless at stopping the tantrums and saw them as proof that she was an inadequate mother. At the same time, marital problems were emerging: Mr. B., a very warm and concerned father, was beginning to resent coming home to find a depressed and upset wife, and he began to feel angry at her inability to handle Susan. Mrs. B., in turn, resented both his lack of sympathy for her plight and his lack of actual assistance.

Traditional psychotherapy would most likely have focused on two areas: the marital strain, which would probably have been related to "unconscious" conflicts, and Mrs. B.'s depression, which in her own therapy was seen as related to her feelings toward her own mother. In the brief therapy contact, Susan was seen only once: She was a most vigorous and powerful young lady with a mind very much her own, who liked, and was succeeding in getting her own way. The main focus in therapy was on Mrs. B. She was informed that she was, despite her fears, generally doing a good job with Susan but that she had been overly sensitive to the implication of very normal behavior, temper tantrums. Mrs. B. was quite surprised (as are many young parents with their first born) to learn that most children have temper tantrums, and receptive to the idea that they had continued because she had over-reacted to them, and then, by appeasing Susan to stop the tantrums, had reinforced the very behavior she was trying to eliminate.

By the end of the first meeting with Mrs. B., the above formulation had been presented, and a program ending the tantrums developed. This program amounted essentially to ignoring the tantrums, and, if necessary, putting Susan in her room until they ceased; Mrs. B. was also warned that for a brief while, as Susan tried to intimidate her mother, the tantrums might increase in intensity. Mrs. B. was determined to try and, with a plan of action, no longer felt so impotent. One week later, the B.'s came together, beaming about the cessation of the tantrums. Mrs. B.'s depression had lifted, the marital tension had eased considerably, and Mrs. B. expressed feelings of accomplishment and mastery. Her evaluation of her ability as a mother was much higher, her husband was delighted, and Mrs. B. was enjoying Susan's company for the first time in months. The B.'s were seen for several more sessions to reinforce the new attitudes and behavior. There was no relapse, and follow-up three years later indicated all was going well.

B. Howard R., age 10

Howard, the oldest of three children, had been brought to the clinic at age nine because of both diurnal and nocturnal enuresis, poor grades, and no friends. He and his parents were seen for six weeks and terminated after the elimination of enuresis, enrollment in peer activities after school, and a planned transfer to another school and away from a rigid and unsympathetic teacher. One year later, his parents called again and asked to return. There had been no recurrence of the enuresis and Howard's grades were improved, but his parents were now concerned at his lack of friends and his frequent quarrels with his mother. Mrs. R. was furious both at Howard and at his father for Mr. R.'s lack of support for her and his lack of interest in his son.

Howard was seen as an immature boy who had developed few social skills and was thus teased and rejected by peers. His solution to this was to generally withdraw and to either stay in the house after school or play with much younger children; in both cases, he could feel adequate and in control. The fights with the mother were seen as secondary to a general lack of confidence which had been reinforced by the R.'s failure to demand more age-appropriate behavior of Howard and the father's failure to provide a visible model by which Howard could develop some means of coping with the ordinary give-and-take relationships with his peers. Treatment with Howard focused on his peer relationships, on how Howard felt about his rejection, why he thought his peers rejected him, and what he had done about this situation. New coping behaviors were suggested by which Howard could deal with some particular tormentors, which involved fighting back, a response which had been previously inhibited because Howard had felt he could not succeed and his parents would disapprove and punish him. Ways of approaching peers and of making friends were also suggested and practiced in therapy.

Of crucial importance in working with this family was effecting change in the R.'s relationship with their son so that they could encourage and support his spending more time with his peers (so that he would have to deal with them) and discourage his well-developed avoidant behavior. It was also considered necessary to reduce Mrs. R.'s over-involvement with her son, which was unwittingly maintaining his immature behavior, and to consistently increase Mr. R.'s involvement with Howard. The initial step was to confront the R.'s with an assessment of the problem, and capitalizing on Mrs. R.'s stated and felt desire to see less of her son, to help her get him out of the house. Confirming the validity of her anger at his staying home, Mrs. R. was told to firmly insist that Howard go out after school whenever the weather was nice and not be permitted to return until supper. (Mrs. R. asked in amazement, "You mean it is really alright to insist that your son go outside?") The therapist anticipated with the R.'s how Howard would try to get back in the house by exploiting his mother's guilt and sympathy for his lonely and sad wandering, and they were instructed to stand firm. Within days, after realizing his mother would not give in, Howard began to play with some neighborhood children who had approached him (previously he would either have not been outside at all or would have fled inside at the first overture). To reinforce Howard's increased time with peers the R.'s were again directed to enroll him in structured after-school recreational activities. Finally, focus was placed on re-engaging Mr. R. with the family and with his son, and, to Mrs. R.'s surprise, he was more than willing. Exploration revealed he had resented his wife's demands and her taking over some of his functions, but had, as Howard, withdrawn rather than deal directly with his feelings. Confronting both parents with how they were relating to each other opened up communication for the first time and led to rapid change.

This case was seen for six weeks and closed. Monthly follow-ups have indicated that the changes during brief therapy have been maintained, consolidated, and further developed. Howard will never be a socially gregarious boy, but he now has a few friends, withdraws much less frequently, and fights considerably less with his mother. Simply removing him from the premises meant less time spent with mother which meant less mutual irritation which meant that when Howard was at home Mrs. R. was in a much better mood and able and willing to relate more warmly to her son.

C. Roger M., age 16

Roger was referred because of chronic under-achievement in high school, where despite measured superior intelligence, his grades were generally C's and D's (although at times he would get an A when interested in a certain subject). The M.'s were very worried because they wanted Roger to go to college but were afraid his poor grades would prevent him from doing so.

The parents were concerned, protective, overly involved and controlling individuals who were also very confused about Roger and the expectations that they should have for him. They had always stepped in and taken charge of Roger when difficulties arose, yet he was never held responsible or accountable for what happened. For example, the M.'s, and Roger, blamed much of his poor achievement upon the school; they claimed that the teachers were inadequate and that Roger had been subjected to humiliating experiences. Their confusion about Roger lay in the fact that, despite what they tried to do for him, he continued on in the same way in school; however, and significantly, in all other areas he seemed to be adjusting quite well; he had friends, played in a band, and worked responsibly at a part-time job. When seen at the clinic, Roger was very pleasant and cooperative, in a somewhat passive fashion, as if waiting for the therapist to lead the way. At the same time, Roger actively portrayed himself as the victim of circumstances and therefore not responsible for his behavior. His one complaint was that his parents were too involved with him and should grant him more independence; he was fairly satisfied with his grades and fully expected to go on to college in business administration.

It was readily apparent that parents and son were caught in a tightly drawn power struggle in which everyone was losing and quite unnecessarily so in view of Roger's many strengths. His complacency about school, however, only added fuel to the M.'s concern and anger at his doing so poorly. Therefore, the main therapeutic focus was to alter family relationships so that Roger would be free to take on the responsibility for his actions, and, if the parents could cease responding to his maneuvers, end the struggle. The M.'s were confronted repeatedly with the fact that as long as Roger could shift responsibility for his actions onto others, with his parents' consent and involvement, he would continue to do poorly in school. It was also emphasized that in some ways Roger was immature and that for him to grow the M.'s had to loosen their hold on him. Unfortunately, it became apparent that this was going to be quite difficult for the M.'s to do, especially since they required proof of responsibility before giving indepdencence. At Roger's insistence, a trial attempt was made; the M.'s were to set no rules or conditions upon Roger's homework or study habits, nor were they to nag or criticize his plans. Roger felt he would be able to do his work better under these conditions and the M.'s, with considerable misgivings, agreed. The trial lasted only a week because Roger immediately, according to the M.'s, stopped doing any homework or studying; Mr. M. finally couldn't stand it any longer and resumed control over Roger's behavior.

After this rapid failure, which had clearly resulted from the M.'s over-anxious reaction to the predictable testing by Roger of their promise to keep their hands off, the situation changed dramatically. For the first time, the M.'s accepted the notion that they were over-involved (and that Roger was able to seduce them into this behavior which then justified not having to work). It also became clear that Mrs. M., a trained psychologist who had never worked, not only read too much meaning into Roger's everyday behavior, but that she did not have enough to do at home to keep her occupied. Mrs. M. eagerly accepted the idea of working (and quickly began seeking employment, which she has kept for over a year since the end of brief therapy) but all the M.'s, including Roger (who had also accepted the idea that his parents' susceptibility to his maneuvers was not really gaining him greater freedom), felt that their relationships were too deeply engrained to change unless they could dramatically snap the cycle and get, temporarily, some distance from each other. Working together, and making joint decisions, a private school nearby was found for Roger where he could live but still see the M.'s frequently. It was emphasized to the M.'s that they had to make a commitment for at least one school year and to try their best to avoid interfering with Roger or falling prey to his minor complaints. At this point, brief therapy ended with the M.'s pleased at this solution to their problem which they all saw as appropriate to their greater understanding of their relationship with Roger.

No further treatment has been necessary in over a year. Faced with the loss of his "out," his parents, Roger drew upon his always evident resources to improve his grades at the private school. When at home the M.'s were more comfortable in giving him more freedom and letting him, when it was appropriate, face the consequences of his own behaviors. Clearly, more traditional therapy could have focused on the marital relationship, the oedipal triangle resulting in the learning block, and Roger's own conflicts about masculinity. Instead, by focusing upon the verbalized goals desired by both parents and son, that of his gaining more independence and responsibility, the therapist was able to point out to all how they were working against their goals. By clarifying the nature of their interlocking struggle, they were freed to develop more effective ways of reaching their goals, which also meant recognizing and accepting their own limitations (and without ever analyzing why).

D. Roberta L., age 16

Roberta and her parents were seen in a 90 minute family session one week after they had applied to the clinic. Two days before application, Roberta had been returned by the police after a five day runaway and the kettle was still boiling at home. The police had left the decision to file charges up to the parents who had as yet not made up their minds; they were asking for help in calming down the household and in deciding what to do with Roberta. In the initial phone call, Mrs. L. indicated that the runaway was the culmination of six months of a deteriorating relationship between Roberta and her parents (much fighting and defiance) which focused on parental disapproval of her boyfriend (twenty years old, living alone, with a police record) and her "hippie" friends. Recently there had been instances of Roberta lying and sneaking out late at night to meet her friends; she had also had intercourse with her boyfriend. Prior to these tumultuous six months Roberta, an only child, had been considered a model child, very independent, neat, and self-sufficient.

Roberta turned out to be a very verbal, exceptionally honest and articulate, and bright, interpersonally sensitive girl. Her father looked tough but was a quiet and interested participant. He spoke very softly, supported at times both Roberta and her mother, and functioned, when needed, as the detached reality tester of the family. Mrs. L. was an attractive foreign-born bleached blond who was both very verbal and very anxious. At times she was redundant and her thinking seemed rigid as she returned repeatedly to issues which had seemingly been resolved (one of Roberta's complaints, confirmed by her father, was that her mother constantly brought up the past). Mrs. L. was the most hurt member of the family and had interpreted Roberta's runaway as both a personal rejection and as evidence of her own failure as a mother.

The session was a most active but surprisingly low-keyed one. All three talked to each other and at no time did anyone really get angry, with Roberta especially working hard to clearly express herself. She was currently under good self-control; she felt her runaway had been reasonably unpleasant (she had eaten nothing for the last three days) and she was obviously glad to be back, although initially unwilling to concede this. She had no intention of leaving again and so the focus of the session was on why things had deteriorated at home and why she "disliked" her mother (she had modified this word from "hate") especially when compared to her father, whom Roberta liked and felt close to. Roberta was also very expressive about her feeling that her intrusive mother needed to keep Roberta tied closely to her because Roberta was all she had. Mrs. L. cannot have more children and Roberta wished she could have so that there would have been less focus upon her. Mrs. L. constantly compared Roberta's defiance toward her with Mrs. L.'s obedience to her own parents. Roberta agreed she was not as compliant but resented being grilled by her mother, and she also pointed out that while she enjoyed doing things with her parents (as she had frequently up to age fourteen) she preferred to be with her friends.

The therapist, seconded by the father, stressed repeatedly to Mrs. L. that she had done a good job with Roberta, who had many qualities other parents would be delighted with, and it was also pointed out that Roberta was not even challenging the L.'s around limits the way many teen-agers did (Roberta felt she was given sufficient freedom and that parental rules were reasonable ones). Mrs. L. kept returning to the issue of trust which was countered by stressing that this was in the past, and that one reason for the family upset was that she had tried too hard with Roberta and now she must hold back and wait for her daughter to come to her instead of the reverse. Roberta helped here by agreeing that she had a temper and could provoke, but convincingly said that she wanted home to be different, and that she wished to stay and graduaté from high school. She even, without a fuss, accepted her parents' decision that she could not see her boyfriend for one year while he worked and saved money to convince the L.'s that he was reformed and a suitable mate for Roberta.

By the end of the session, it seemed that the crisis was over, and that Roberta's intense acting-out, culminated by the runaway, had been a signal that change was desperately needed within the family. As such the session succeeded in greatly opening up and facilitating communication between mother and child and thus clarifying for both the source of the tension between them. As the session ended, the L.'s felt they understood the problem much better now. Mrs. L. did not feel as angry at Roberta and as sorry for herself, and they all felt that they could handle the situation by themselves without further assistance from the therapist. Fourteen months later a follow-up indicated that all was well and no further treatment has been necessary.

DISCUSSION

Brief therapy, to be effective, must focus on current behavior. It is the contention of this paper (partially based on five years, and about 3,000 cases at the author's clinic) that this approach is sufficient for approximately 50% of all children coming to a general community clinic. For another 20% of the cases, psychotherapy is not a relevant tool, either because different services are needed (e. g., perceptual training, vocational rehabilitation, special classes, residential placement, etc.) or because of a total lack of cooperation. For approximately 30% of the children, more extensive therapy is needed than can be fit into the initial brief period of time allotted for treatment. These families include those with multiple deeply engrained problems, who are resistant to changing self-defeating behaviors, and those whose cooperation is not enlisted as fully as it was in the case examples. (It is, however, suggested that utilization of a problem-focused, pragmatic, and time-limited approach makes more sense to clients than does the often vaguer and less structured long-term, intra-psychic approach. At the author's clinic, over a period of five years, the withdrawal rate has been less than 10%.) For these children, parents, and families needing further help, many of the techniques and the general emphasis upon the client's healthy coping abilities are maintained. However, focus on more traditionally explored areas, such as parental conflict and its effect on the child (or the parents' inability to effectively be parents), feelings, and the etiology of attitudes, become more relevant and productive.

The brief therapist (and the case examples do not provide sufficient illustrations) must also work actively and extensively with not only the referring agency but also with significant others who can affect the child's behavior. This occurs not only during the brief therapy period (e. g., helping a school redesign for a troublesome adolescent a class schedule more compatible with his skills and interests) but often during the follow-up periods when the therapist and agency may contact each other. Thus, change occurs not only within the child and his family, but also within the community, and all three serve, at best, to reinforce each other instead of fighting with each other as at the time of referral.

The case examples, selected for their range in age and problems, may sound too pat in their successful resolution. It is more typical of cases seen in brief therapy that they finish with many loose ends left dangling. The goal is not to have all the problems wrapped up neatly, but to make a beginning; to give the clients techniques and understandings with which to work, and the experience of behavioral change before they go out on their own. To successfully do brief therapy, the therapist must have confidence in the ability of the client to maintain and continue change, to further grow and develop; this confidence can only exist if we cease to view clients as "sick."

To summarize, brief treatment with children, adolescents, and their parents focuses on current and explicit behavior, with the therapist actively seeking to modify family relationships in such a way as to further generate new and more satisfying ways for the family members to live with each other. The therapist may suggest ways for parents and children to get what they want from each other; he may reduce anxiety by altering or making more realistic mutual expectations about what the child and the parent are capable of doing; and he may educate, give advice, and make suggestions as to what should be done. Little or no attention is paid to such traditionally scrutinized areas as the parents' sexual life or their relationships with their own parents; even the marital relationship is ignored unless conflict within it prevents the parents from carrying out effective plans of action. In this view, which capitalizes upon the active coping potentialities of both child and parent, the child is not viewed as a woeful and passive recipient and carrier of parental misdoings and conflicts. Rather, he is seen as an actively engaged individual, capable of responsibility for his own actions, who has become ensnared in an unsatisfying relationship with his family, other institutions, his peers, or between his own actions and his stated goals and desires (e. g., expecting to go to college despite getting failing grades; driving without a license while on probation, yet ostensibly not wishing to go to a reformatory). To effectively do brief therapy, it is crucial that one accept the notion that changes first in overt behavior can then lead to changes in understanding, attitude, self-concept, and self-esteem. These in turn lead to further behavioral changes in an ever-growing and widening spiral. This view is almost antithetical to the more traditional psychoanalytic focus on "elegant insight" which is presumed to be not only necessary but a prerequisite to generate and maintain new behavior by resolving unconscious conflicts originating in the past. Too often our "whys" are mere hypothetical speculations; it is not unusual for clinicians to never really know why a child has acted in a certain way, and most parents are not really interested in the "whys." They are interested in the present problem that they are seeking help for because they have been unsuccessful in handling it; clinicians do know how to effect changes in overt behavior and attitudes, and these changes are not merely "symptom removal" but significant and maintained changes which generate, in both parents and child, enhanced feelings of competence, growth, and mastery over their own lives.

Chapter 17

Brief Psychotherapy of Psychiatric Reactions to Physical Illness

Edward H. Stein, M.D., Jessica Murdaugh, ACSW,
and John A. MacLeod, M.D.

In recent years increasing attention has been directed toward the development of techniques of short-term psychotherapy (1, 9, 21, 22, 29, 31-33, 37, 41, 42). During the course of work in a short-term psychotherapy clinic, we have noted a number of cases in which the psychiatric disability seemed to be an outgrowth of some organic medical illness or physical trauma. This paper will report on techniques applicable to the brief treatment of psychiatric reactions to physical illness. Attention will be focused upon a case example of a man who developed an incapacitating anxiety reaction following a myocardial infarction and several episodes of cardiac arrest.

The renewed interest in brief treatment methods is in part a response to the ever-increasing numbers of patients requiring psychiatric treatment and the limited number of trained personnel available (4, 5). Other stimuli to the development of brief treatment have been social and financial pressures. There is an increasing trend toward insurance coverage for outpatient psychiatric treatment, yet financial considerations often limit such coverage to relatively few visits, with an emphasis upon early detection and intervention (24). Tompkins has pointed out that insurance introduces "the expectation of shorter periods of treatment" and has highlighted the profession's responsibility to further elaborate treatment techniques for short-term therapy (35).

However, the indications for short-term therapy do not stem merely from the unavailability of longer-term treatment. It is

Reprinted from *American Journal of Psychiatry*, 1969, **125**, 1040-1047, by permission of the publisher and the authors. Copyright 1969, the American Psychiatric Association. Dr. Stein is on the faculty of the University of Chicago School of Medicine. Mrs. Murdaugh is social work consultant, Visiting Nurses Association of the Cincinnati Area. Dr. MacLeod is Associate Professor of Psychiatry, University of Cincinnati College of Medicine, Cincinnati, Ohio.

increasingly recognized that there are many instances in which short-term therapy is the treatment of choice (13, 21, 41, 42). There seems to be a real place in the psychotherapeutic armamentarium for a self-respecting short-term psychotherapy aimed at the achievement of *limited yet significant* goals.

Frequently patients may not desire long-term reconstructive psychotherapy or would not benefit from such endeavors. Wolberg has stressed the deleterious effects that long-term treatment may have in certain patients, notably patients with marked dependency needs who have been functioning tenuously at a marginal level of independence and who may regress with long-term treatment into refractory positions of dependency, and patients with fragile ego structures who may develop disruptive transference reactions or may disintegrate following probing efforts to release repressed material in long-term treatment (40, 41). The concept of "emotional crisis" is highly useful in brief treatment work (30, 33), and a brief course of treatment centering around a focal crisis may frequently set into motion a process of growth by enabling the individual to utilize the healthy elements in his personality.

Much attention has rightly been given to the identification of the types of patients that are treated most appropriately by short-term psychotherapy (21, 22). One category of patient that has often responded quite favorable, in our experience, consists of those who have succumbed psychiatrically to the aftereffects of physical illness, trauma, or surgery. In the past, attention has focused largely on training the nonpsychiatric practitioner to deal with the emotional problems of general medical and surgical patients (6, 17). While this general approach is of extreme importance, it has been our impression that frequently the psychiatric reactions that develop following illness are sufficiently complex to require the training and skill of the psychiatrist for optimum treatment. Additional participation by psychiatrists is needed in this interface between medicine and psychiatry, and new techniques should be developed and applied (36).

The clinical setting in which our experience has been accumulated is an early-access brief treatment subdivision of a large community-supported outpatient psychotherapy clinic, Central Psychiatric Clinic, which is affiliated with the department of psychiatry at the University of Cincinnati. The brief treatment project has been described previously by MacLeod and Tinnin (20). Patients are accepted from referral sources within a few days after the initial application and are seen for up to six sessions, each lasting from 15 to 50 minutes. Visits are paced to patient needs but usually average one visit per week.

The emphasis is upon accepting patients who have acute and

relatively severe problems of recent onset, often in response to a "focal precipitating event." Psychological testing and collaborative casework therapy are available and frequently used. Traditional criteria for suitability for insight-oriented therapy, such as psychological-mindedness, are not emphasized in the selection of cases. Treatment goals are purposely kept limited—restoration to a previous level of psychological functioning and social adaptation, as well as relief of symptoms.

Gottschalk and his co-workers have conducted research studies on the therapeutic outcome of patients treated in this emergency brief psychotherapy clinic division (15). Their results have confirmed that a symptomatic and functional improvement occurs in a majority of patients treated, and this improvement tends to last through their period of observation. In their paper, they also discussed criteria for patients most likely to benefit from short-term treatment, as well as therapist factors and their relation to treatment outcome.

To illustrate many of the principles involved in treating patients with emotional reactions to physical illness, we shall present the following case report of a patient recently treated in this short-term treatment clinic.

Case Report

The patient is a 50-year-old married man who applied for treatment because of extreme nervousness and inability to work, which developed subsequent to a heart attack. He was a foreman at a metal-working factory, and his history indicated that he had always been an extremely hard worker with almost no absenteeism. About a year and a half prior to our contact with him, he had developed angina pectoris. His angina progressed and he developed EKG changes revealing coronary insufficiency. His internist felt that a myocardial infarction was impending and advised him to take a few months off from work. However, the patient could not be prevailed upon to slow down from his routine of working 11-hour shifts.

Four months prior to our contact with him, he developed severe chest pain which awakened him from sleep, and he was taken to a local hospital's emergency room. His physician met him there and discussed with the patient's wife how to broach the news of the coronary to the patient, anticipating that there would be an adverse reaction. When his physician finally went over to the patient and told him that "he wouldn't be able to work for several hours," the patient suddenly stopped breathing and turned blue. A diagnosis of cardiac arrest was confirmed by EKG, which revealed ventricular fibrillation.

He was treated promptly and definitively for cardiac arrest, with full cardiac resuscitative measures. Soon after effective cardiorespiratory action was restored, he suffered another arrest and again cardiac action was restored. He was kept on the pacemaker for four days. When he regained consciousness, he was unable to see for one and one-half days, apparently due to cortical blindness from cerebral anoxia. He also had amnesia for three days, as well as loss of the senses of smell and taste, presumably also on the basis of cortical anoxia.

His subsequent medical course was uncomplicated, and he made an excellent recovery. However, his reactions to the acute illness and hospitalization were noteworthy. He was restless and "angry that this had happened to him." He was upset by the intravenous cutdown and the oxygen tent and once ripped off the pacemaker. He was found out of bed against orders, walking around in his room, and was described as "very uncooperative." One day he refused breakfast, was very upset, and said he "didn't want anyone to feed him and didn't want to stay in bed." He insisted on leaving the hospital after 31 days and continued his convalescence at home for two and one-half months.

One month before our first clinic contact with him, he persuaded his internist to let him return to work. He returned to his job at the metal-working factory, but found that he was anxious, scared, and nervous. He felt inadequate, had no confidence in himself, and wanted to run away from work. While at work he broke down and cried in the nurse's office several times and had to leave work. He experienced restlessness and difficulty in sleeping, and cried frequently at home.

Whereas before his infarction he had worked daily, despite anginal pain, he was unable to return to work at this time and no longer wanted to do so. His wife and daughters were supporting the family and making most of the decisions. Whereas before he had always been hyperindependent, his wife now described him as "looking like a whipped puppy." This was his state when he was referred for psychiatric treatment and was admitted to the Special Services Project for early-access short-term psychotherapy.

At the initial diagnostic evaluation, the clinical impression was acute anxiety and depression, with a question of organic brain syndrome secondary to the period of cortical anoxia. In line with our general policy of contacting the referring physician for information, we contacted his internist and consulted and reviewed the hospital chart from his hospitalization for the coronary. Also in accordance with the project policy of frequently involving significant family members, a casework appointment was set up with his wife. Formal mental status examination revealed deficits in immediate recall and in ability to concentrate. The patient was encouraged to consider returning to work so that we might work with the anxiety feelings we anticipated would occur.

Since it was suspected that the patient had misconceptions and anatomic distortions about the myocardial infarction process and the subsequent healing process, an early effort was made to explore his understanding of these processes. He was very reluctant to share his thoughts about this, insisting that he was no doctor. With much effort and strong encouragement on the therapist's part, the patient "opened up" and indicated that he understood that the heart is a muscle and that it "tears like a piece of paper" during a heart attack and then "heals with a scar." In describing the heart attack itself, he said: "I died twice, turned blue, and my veins collapsed, and they had to cut into my veins to get them up." He was puzzled by the disappearance of angina since the heart attack, and his understanding of this was that in a heart attack "the strain tears the heart valves, and they are now healing and may heal still better."

When asked why he felt his memory and brain were not working right (these were major concerns of the patient), he replied that each part of the heart has an artery coming off it and he guessed his heart attack had occurred at the opening of the "artery to the brain." Thus he presumed that the ensuing "healing by scarring" must have occluded this artery, resulting in insufficient blood supply to the brain. At this point, the therapist drew a rough sketch of the heart to ensure that he fully understood the patient's conception of his heart and the circulation to his brain (see Figure 1).

The therapist then proceeded to correct the distortions involved. He explained that there is a single common outflow artery, not any one artery to the brain that arises directly from the myocardial wall. A great deal of time was spent on correcting the patient's cognitive grasp of the events of his myocardial infarction and the circulation to the brain. Because of the memory deficit revealed in the mental status examination and the suspicion of organic brain damage, psychological testing had been carried out. These results indicated no evidence of organic deficit but considerable impairment due to marked anxiety. The therapist shared with the patient the finding that anxiety, not organic damage, seemed to be causing his memory troubles, and this was reassuring to him.

During concurrent casework interviews with the patient's wife, it was learned that her mother had suffered from a heart ailment. Some of her childhood fears about her mother's illness were being reactivated by her husband's heart attack, resulting in her being overprotective and infantilizing toward him. As a result of casework therapy, she was able to allow him to assume more responsibility around the house.

In later sessions with the patient, attention was directed to his fears that working would damage his heart. Direct reassurance was given that he could work to the limits allowed by his internist, who at this time felt he was physically quite able to return to work. Medical facts were reiterated, and famous people who had coronaries and returned to useful work were cited as examples in an effort to promote identification. By the sixth and final session, the patient reported that he had returned to work for half days, with some symptoms of faintness and dizziness. He was now sleeping without difficulty. He was encouraged to follow through on his return to work, and he left saying that it was "now time for him to get in the driver's seat and see if he couldn't make it through."

Follow-up interviews with the patient's internist, one year after termination of the six-session course of brief treatment, indicated that the patient had rapidly returned to regular work as a laborer at the same company, working a 50-hour week of active physical work. His wife reported that his nerves were "now better than before the heart attack."

At a two-year follow-up, it was learned that the patient had continued working regularly, but had recently been hospitalized by his internist for diagnostic studies because of increasing angina. At this time the patient

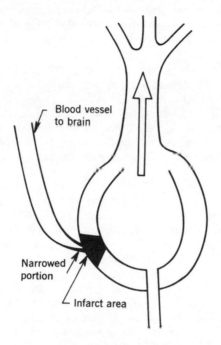

Figure 1.   Patient's conception of circulation.

could accept the doctor's recommendation to seek lighter work (in contrast to his response earlier) and was cooperating with company officials in finding such work. Psychiatrically, the internist judged that the patient was doing remarkably well.

TECHNIQUES FOR BRIEF TREATMENT OF REACTIONS TO PHYSICAL ILLNESS

It seems appropriate to review some of the principles we have found to be of particular value in the brief treatment of these psychiatric reactions to physical illness. Many of the general techniques that have been employed in short-term psychotherapy, and described elsewhere, are utilized: keeping treatment goals limited, with an aim of symptom relief or restoration to a previous level of functioning; early institution of treatment as soon after symptoms appear as possible; a focus upon the precipitating stress; and flexibility about frequency of visits (7, 9, 21, 29, 41, 42).

Early formulation of the clinical material is essential in brief treatment (20). Theoretical guidelines assist in organizing the clinical material and greatly facilitate early formulation. Some of the themes we have found useful as guidelines are the following: (1) focus on *denial* as the primary defense; (2) attention to the *narcissistic injury* which is so frequently created by the illness or trauma; and (3) emphasis upon the patient's *cognitive* understanding of the illness, with a particular search for *cognitive blocks* which must be detected and dealt with. Familiarity with these recurring themes has assisted early formulation and enhanced our ability to initiate treatment quickly and effectively. These principles will be considered in some detail.

1. Denial

Denial is one of the most prevalent defenses utilized by patients in response to blows to self-esteem or bodily injury. Although much has been written on the definition of denial (34, 39), we shall use denial here to refer to an unconscious ego defense against "danger" or "pain," which operates in the service of avoiding narcissistic injury. Denial is often the primary defense with which we deal in the treatment of emotional reactions to illness and trauma (12, 27). Treatment success generally hinges on how effectively we are able to develop techniques for working through denial with a given patient, relying heavily all the while upon the therapeutic alliance.

Lindemann has likened denial to the pupillary action of the eye (19). Just as the iris constricts when necessary to avoid overstimulation of the retina by too much light, so the ego defense of denial serves to protect the ego from overstimulation by excessive input stimuli. While denial may serve an important protective purpose, an ever-present danger is that denial mechanisms may be maintained long after the need for them has passed, thus preventing accurate reality assessment.

Analytic observations have traditionally focused primarily on the inner struggle between the instincts and the ego, and less emphasis has been placed upon denial as a primary pathogenic mechanism (14). Lindemann's paper highlighting grief and its denial is well known, and Rado has described the relationship of denial to the development of traumatic neuroses (18, 25).

Rosen, in a study of patients who manifested pathological psychiatric responses following acute surgical removal of body parts, noted in the patients' life histories a pattern of dealing with threatening situations by a characteristic combination of denial and active mastery (28). He links these two character traits by noting that in the young child it is largely the ability to deny the possibility of bodily injury that enables the child to attempt active mastery. This combination of character traits in many ways fits the coronary character (38). Certainly, in the case we have presented, active denial of body danger was closely linked with a character style of active mastery through work and physical activity.

Denial was a prominent defense in this patient, as witnessed by his inability to acknowledge the angina he was experiencing prior to the attack or to take time off from work when his doctor felt an infarction was impending. It is interesting that it was when this denial was punctured by the doctor's toned-down statement that the patient "wouldn't be able to work for a few hours," that ventricular fibrillation ensued. "Sudden death" has been reported under similar circumstances (11, 43). The onset of the acute infarction, with the undeniable physical restrictions and medical measures, appears to have broken down the patient's "denying mechanisms" too abruptly, and with it went the "active mastery" style that had served him so well previously. With this gone he became physically incapacitated and was no longer able to "carry on" in work as he had done so stalwartly before.

Thus a major task in therapy was to rework the occurrence of the acute infarction, in a gradated fashion, with frequent countering of the exaggerated pessimism and unwarranted hopelessness which prevailed after his denial mechanisms had been broken down even though good medical recovery had occurred. The therapist was serving in a role similar to the protecting parent who makes painful and threatening reality less intolerable to the child, thus enabling the child to accept and face reality, with its hazards, rather than having to deny and "shut out." In this way, a more adaptive adjustment was achieved.

The dangers of excessive reliance upon ego defenses of denial in attempting to exclude painful external realities have been recognized, for the adult is always subject to "assault from without" (14). Reality occurrences, like the coronary in this case, impinge and force an abrupt change of life. The ego then finds itself once more confronted with the same threats it has learned to deal with only by denial—hence the vulnerability of patients with this character defense pattern. The task of the psychiatrist in such problems is to sensitively "titrate" denial with reality, with heavy reliance upon the therapeutic alliance—to help the patient accept the reality of the illness or disability without at any time "overwhelming" the ego in the process. It is the overstimulation and excessive intensity of experience which constitute the trauma and which must be avoided (16). The therapeutic aim is to present reality in a gradated way, over an

adequate period of time, so that the ego may deal integratively
with the reality that must be accepted. Thus economic considerations of dosage and timing are of primary importance in
dealing therapeutically with denial, and the success of treatment depends largely upon these variables.

2. Narcissistic Injury

A central focus in our work has been on reactions to the
narcissistic injury which surgery, trauma, and illness frequently
produce. Patients often react to loss of a body part or organ,
whether by surgery or by trauma, as a blow to their concept of
physical integrity or "wholeness." Causal relationships between
the narcissistic injury and the psychiatric symptoms are often
obvious to the therapist, but are, with astonishing frequency,
quite "unconnected" in the patient's mind. Direct discussion of
these connections and relationships with patients is often
beneficial.

When denial does not serve to avert narcissistic injury,
symptom formation or clinical decompensation frequently
occurs. Bibring emphasized the role such narcissistic blows serve
in the production of depression (10). We have found narcissistic
injury to be equally important in the production of
incapacitating anxiety reactions (as in the case example cited),
psychotic reactions, and a variety of other psychiatric syndromes.
Often affective responses such as anger, rage, and hostility result
from narcissistic injuries. Although it may be prominent, this
intrinsic anger is often quite unrecognized by the patient.

The patient who has suffered mutilating surgery or
debilitating illness is really angry "at what has happened to
him." However, displacements of these angry feelings often
occur, with no awareness that the anger is really intrinsic,
stemming from the narcissistic blow itself. The usual lack of any
appropriate external object for these angry feelings only
compounds the difficulties the patient has in dealing with these
feelings. Bringing this intrinsic anger over narcissistic injury to
the patient's attention and identifying displacements of anger are
highly important therapeutic activities.

Negative counterfeelings are easily aroused in physicians and
family members by the patient's displacing his angry feelings
onto them, as frequently occurs. When such angry feelings are
displaced onto the surgeon, for instance, alienation in the doctor-
patient dyad frequently occurs, and the patient thereby deprives
himself of the very source of support he needs the most, namely,
his physician (23, 26). Similarly, displacement of "intrinsic anger
at a narcissistic injury" onto family members or other important

objects can introduce alienation in important family relationships, only worsening the patient's plight. Frequently, identifying with the patient the intrinsic nature of the angry feelings and pointing out displacements helps to diminish alienation in these important relationships, thus making continuing support from them available to the patient.

3. Cognitive Blocks

A technique we have found of particular importance in working with these psychiatric syndromes that occur as sequelae to physical illness is a careful search for medical misconceptions and anatomic distortions the patient may have about the illness. We have been most impressed with the frequency with which some *cognitive misconception* exists concerning some important facet of the illness (8, 9). These misconceptions are not easy to elicit. The patient is generally all too content to demur on the grounds that he is not a doctor or does not have the necessary knowledge of medicine to answer inquiries. But the central importance of one's own body and one's own health is such that there are bound to be some cognitive efforts at understanding the illness, and it is these cognitive gropings that we find so often to be incorrect, distorted, and incomplete.

In the example cited, it took forceful and persistent efforts on the part of the therapist to get the patient to overcome his shame enough to share his notions about his illness. Yet they turned out to be of crucial importance. With a cognitive block, such as his belief that there was an "artery to the brain" arising directly from the heart at the point of his myocardial infarction, which had become occluded by the scarring, it is difficult to envision how any amount of dynamic interpretation or working through would have led to alleviation of the anxiety stemming from his conviction that his brain had sustained irreversible damage.

Arieti has emphasized the importance of cognition in psychotherapy (2, 3). Many important emotional responses are intimately related to cognitive processes, and cognitive processes themselves often create clinically important emotional reactions. Our own observations reinforce the importance of these concepts. Particularly when cognitive distortions and misunderstandings reach proportions where they constitute a cognitive block, it is necessary to deal directly with these. While at times cognitive misconceptions may arise merely from lack of exposure to proper information, often despite the availability of such information, anxiety and dynamic conflict have interfered with proper integration of that information. Although a dynamic basis often exists for the fantasies and cognitive distortions, we generally do not explore or deal with these "roots" of the misperceptions in short-term treatment but concentrate, rather, at the cognitive level. In working toward *cognitive mastery*, the important steps include, first, the gradual working through of denial, with heavy reliance on the therapeutic alliance, and second, gradual presentation of reality after the fantasies and cognitive distortions have been explored and clarified. The resulting improved cognitive perception of reality permits a more stress-free adaptation to be achieved.

REFERENCES

1. Alexander, F. The dynamics of psychotherapy in the light of learning theory, *Amer. J. Psychiat.*, 1963, 120, 440-449.
2. Arieti, S. Studies of thought processes in contemporary psychiatry. *Amer. J. Psychiat.*, 1963, 120, 58-64.
3. Arieti, S. Conceptual and cognitive psychiatry. *Amer. J. Psychiat.*, 1965, 122, 361-366.
4. Avnet, H. H. *Psychiatric insurance: Financing short-term ambulatory treatment.* New York: Group Health Insurance, Inc., 1962.
5. Avnet, H. H. Short term treatment under auspices of a medical insurance plan. *Amer. J. Psychiat.*, 1965, 122, 147-151.
6. Balint, M. *The doctor, his patient and the illness.* New York: International Universities Press, 1957.
7. Bellak, L. Psychology of physical illness. In L. Bellak, (Ed.), *Psychiatry applied to medicine, surgery, and the specialties.* New York: Grune & Stratton, 1952.
8. Bellak, L., & Haselkorn, F. Psychological aspects of cardiac illness and rehabilitation. *Social Casework*, 1956, 37, 483-489.
9. Bellak, L., & Small, L. *Emergency Psychotherapy and brief psychotherapy.* New York: Grune & Stratton, 1965.
10. Bibring, E. The mechanism of depression. In P. Greenacre (Ed.) *Affective disorders: psychoanalytic contribution to their study.* New York: International Universities Press, 1953.
11. Burch, G. E., & DePasquale, N. P. Methods for studying the influence of higher central nervous centers on the peripheral circulation of intact man. *Amer. Heart J.*, 1965, 70, 411-422.
12. Druss, R. G., & Kornfeld, D. S. The survivors of cardiac arrest. *J.A.M.A.*, 1968, 201, 291-296.
13. Frank, J. D. The dynamics of the psychotherapeutic relationship: Determinants and effects of the therapist's influence. *Psychiatry*, 1959, 22, 17-39.
14. Freud, A. *The ego and the mechanisms of defense.* New York: International Universities Press, 1964.
15. Gottschalk, L. A., Mayerson, P., & Gottlieb, A. A. Prediction and evaluation of outcome in an emergency brief psychotherapy clinic. *J. Nerv. Ment. Dis.*, 1967, 144, 77-96.
16. Kohut, H., & Seitz, P. F. D. Concepts and theories of psycho-analysis. In J. Wepman and R. Heine, (Eds), *Concepts of personality.* Chicago: Aldine Publishing Co., 1963.

17. Levine, M. *Psychotherapy in medical practice.* New York: Macmillan Co., 1942.
18. Lindemann, E., Symptomatology and management of acute grief. *Amer. J. Psychiat.*, 1944, **101**, 141-148.
19. Lindemann, E. The psychiatrist in the community. Harvard Mental Health Training Film, Boston, 1965.
20. MacLeod, J. A., & Tinnin, L. W. Special service project. *Arch. Gen. Psychiat.*, 1966, **25**, 190-197.
21. Malan, D. H. *A study of brief psychotherapy.* Philadelphia: Tavistock Publications (J. B. Lippincott), 1963.
22. McGuire, M. T. The process of short-term insight psychotherapy. *J. Nerv. Ment. Dis.*, 1965, **141**, 83-94, 219-230.
23. Meyer, E. Psychiatric consultations with patients on medical and surgical wards. Patterns and processes. *Psychiatry*, 1961, **24**, 197-220.
24. Myers, E. S. Major psychiatric benefits start for UAW members. *Psychiatric News*, September 1966, p. 1.
25. Rado, S. Pathodynamics and treatment and traumatic war neurosis (traumatophobia). *Psychosom. Med.*, 1942, **4**, 362-368.
26. Reiser, M. F. Emotional aspects of cardiac disease. *Amer. J. Psychiat.*, 1951, **107**, 781-785.
27. Rosen, J. L., & Bibring, G. L. Psychological reactions of hospitalized male patients to a heart attack. *Psychosom. Med.*, 1966, **28**, 808-821.
28. Rosen, V. H. The role of denial in acute postoperative affective reactions following removal of body parts. *Psychosom. Med.*, 1950, **12**, 356-361.
29. Semrad, E. V., Binstock, W. A., & White, B. Brief psychotherapy. *Amer. J. Psychother.*, 1966, **20**, 576-599.
30. Sifneos, P. E. A concept of "emotional crisis." *Ment Hyg.*, 1960, **44**, 169-179.
31. Sifneos, P. E. Dynamic psychotherapy in a psychiatric clinic. In J. H. Masserman, (Ed.) *Current Psychiatric Therapies.* Vol. 1. New York: Grune & Stratton, 1961.
32. Sifneos, P. E. Seven years' experience with short-term dynamic psychotherapy. In *Sixth International Congress of Psychotherapy, London, 1964: Selected Lectures.* New York: S. Karger, 1965, pp. 127-135.
33. Sifneos, P. E. Crisis Psychotherapy. In J. H. Masserman, (Ed.), *Current Psychiatric Therapies.* Vol. 6. New York: Grune & Stratton, 1966.
34. Sperling, S. J. On denial and the essential nature of defense. *Int. J. Psychoanal.*, 1958, **24**, 1-14.
35. Tompkins, H. J. Health insurance and psychiatric therapy. *Amer. J. Psychiat.*, 1963, **120**, 345-349.
36. Tompkins, H. J. The future of psychiatry. In J. H. Masserman (Ed.), *Current Psychiatric Therapies.* Vol. 6. New York: Grune & Stratton, 1966.
37. Tompkins, H. J. Short-term therapy of the neuroses. In G. L. Usdin (Ed.), *Psychoneurosis and Schizophrenia.* Philadelphia: J. B. Lippincott, 1966.
38. van Heijningen, H. K., & Treuniet, N. Psychodynamic factors in acute myocardial infarction. *Int. J. Psychoanal.*, 1966, **47**, 370-374.
39. Weinstein, E. A., & Kahn, R. L. Denial of illness: Symbolic and physiological aspects. Springfield, Ill.: Charles C Thomas, 1955.
40. Wolberg, L. R. Methodology in short-term therapy. *Amer. J. Psychiat.*, 1965, **122**, 135-140.

41. Wolberg, L. R. The technic of short-term psychotherapy. In L. R. Wolberg, (Ed), *Short-term psychotherapy*. New York: Grune & Stratton, 1965.
42. Wolberg, L. R. Perspectives in short-term therapy. In J. H. Masserman, (Ed.), *Current Psychiatric Therapies*. Vol. 6. New York: Grune & Stratton, 1966.
43. Wolf, S. Sudden death and the oxygen-conserving reflex. *Amer. Heart J.*, 1966, **71**, 840-841.

Chapter 18

An Outpatient Setting for Treating Chronically Ill Psychiatric Patients

Richard T. Rada, M.D., Robert S. Daniels, M.D., and Edgar Draper, M.D.

Community Mental Health programing has recently become a major focus of psychiatric attention. Following the publication of *Action for Mental Health* (8) and the passage of the Community Mental Health Centers Act of 1963, considerable interest has developed for establishing new community mental health clinics and centers. As a result, a number of emergency psychiatric services, crisis-oriented psychiatric clinics, and combined crisis-oriented and mental health consultation services have been reported (1, 7, 9, 10, 16).

Recently, however, Kraft and associates (11) have pointed to the relative neglect of the chronically ill psychiatric patient in community mental health planning. With improved and more effective use of psychopharmacologic agents (4), briefer hospitalization, improved therapeutic intervention, and increased number of psychiatric units in general hospitals, more patients are being maintained for longer periods of time in the community. New models of treatment for the chronically ill are needed.

The purpose of this paper is to present an eight-year experiment with an outpatient clinic designed for the treatment of the chronically ill, the type of therapy administered, and aspects of the training of mental health professionals in this clinic.

Reprinted from the *American Journal of Psychiatry*, 1969, **126**, 789-795, by permission of the publisher and the authors. Copyright 1969, the American Psychiatric Association. Dr. Rada was with the University of Chicago and is now Chief, Department of Neuropsychiatry, Sandia Base Army Hospital, Albuquerque, New Mexico. Dr. Daniels is Associate Dean, Social and Community Medicine, Division of the Biological Sciences, University of Chicago. Dr. Draper is Professor, Department of Psychiatry, University of Michigan, Ann Arbor.

THE CLINIC SETTING

The Thursday Afternoon Clinic (TAC) at the University of Chicago Hospitals and Clinics (a private teaching general hospital) was initiated in 1960 to meet the needs of a group of chronically ill psychiatric patients poorly served by other resources. This group of patients could neither profit from nor tolerate customary individual psychotherapy, and they characteristically had greatest difficulty with issues of separation, closeness, and trust. Nevertheless, they were in intermittent or constant need of a permanent helping resource. The TAC was designed to foster trust and an "institutional alliance" (2) through which personal closeness and distance are maintained at a level optimal for the patient's adaptation.

The clinic was organized along the lines of a medical clinic; it is similar to a clinic described by MacLeod and Middleman (13), which one of us (E.D.) helped to establish. The TAC meets every Thursday except on national holidays for a two-and-one-half-hour period. Patients are seen in their order of arrival. On the average, 30 patients are scheduled weekly, and approximately 75 per cent attend. The standard clinic fee is $8 although lower fees may be charged when indicated. Seventy-five per cent of the patients pay the full fee. The TAC is staffed by three to five psychiatric residents; sophomore, junior, and senior medical students (on elective); a social worker; a receptionist; and two attending staff psychiatrists, one of whom is available during the clinic period for consultation, supervision, or patient interaction.

During the TAC's first year of operation, patients were seated with other patients being seen in the psychiatry outpatient department. Social interaction in this setting was limited, distant, and awkward. Subsequently, a conference room was designed as a separate waiting room for TAC patients, an arrangement that has proven successful and has been continued. Chairs are placed along three walls, and a table decorated with plants, utensils, and a coffee urn is placed along the fourth wall.

Upon his arrival at the clinic, the patient is greeted by the receptionist, who escorts him to the waiting area. The staff joins the patient and his family members in the waiting room where light refreshments are served (15). The staff fosters patient-to-patient, patient-to-staff, and staff-to-staff interaction. These interactions are usually social in nature. The waiting room experience has been particularly useful for patients who need help and practice in basic social skills. Patients are not seen individually during the first one-half hour of the clinic.

After the waiting experience, staff members begin to interview patients individually. Marital couples and families are also seen when indicated. Interviews last 15 to 25 minutes, during which an attempt is made to: (1) ascertain the patient's current life situation; (2) discover current intrapsychic and interpersonal problems; (3) assess the psychotherapeutic intervention indicated; (4) try these techniques out, observing responses carefully to see whether or not they are effective; (5) attend to the patient's medical situation when indicated (e. g., check blood pressure, do hemogram and urinalysis; (6) evaluate the patient's current medication status and modify his prescription as necessary; and (7) make an effective closure, with instructions for intervening activity and a return visit. Following the individual interview, the patient may return to the waiting area for more coffee and socialization.

During the eight years of the TAC's operation, more than 600 patients have been treated, of whom approximately 150 are currently active (arbitrarily defined as a minimum of two visits per year). Frequency of visits is highly individualized, ranging from weekly to once every six months. A patient may decide (preferably with his therapist) to become inactive in the TAC, but his case is never officially closed. After dropping out, a patient may reappear during a time of stress and reinvolve himself without impediments to his readmission. Patients seen less than weekly know they may visit the clinic sooner than their scheduled appointments if the need arises. The staff meets for 30 to 45 minutes at the end of the clinic to discuss problem patients, techniques of therapy, and new referrals. The TAC staff considers new patients only after careful diagnostic evaluation and necessary initial therapeutic management have been completed by the referring source (e.g., inpatient, outpatient, or consultation section). The referring psychiatrist and the TAC staff then discuss the suitability of the patient for the clinic. This procedure eliminates inappropriate and inadequately prepared patients.

Four members of the staff are permanent personnel of the clinic; these include the two attending staff psychiatrists, the social worker, and the receptionist. The attending psychiatrists, both of whom are psychoanalytically trained, actively participate in the waiting area experience. They serve as administrative supervisors of the clinic, and this participation provides them an opportunity for continued direct contact with the patients as well as the opportunity, often through casual conversation (14), to keep informed of the patient's current problems and life situation. The attending psychiatrists do not see patients individually (except in cases of emergency) but remain readily available throughout the clinic period for the unique advantage of on-the-spot supervision and consultation. Finally, the attending psychiatrist conducts the staff group meeting at the end of the clinic.

The social worker is the only permanent member who regularly sees patients on an individual basis. The receptionist, an interested but professionally untrained young woman, acts as hostess for the clinic. Her presence provides continuity for both patients and staff. Her participation during the waiting area experience is particularly valuable because it reduces patient anxiety and promotes social interaction.

Residents rotate through the TAC during their first and second years of residency while serving three-to six-month block rotations on the consultation, inpatient, and outpatient sections. During his inpatient rotation the resident is required to see only those patients he directly refers to the clinic. Residents therefore usually spend 15 months of their residency in the TAC and may elect to participate further during their third year. On arrival in the clinic, residents are assigned patients for whom they are responsible until the end of their rotation. The patient sees the same therapist for three months to a year and is aware that he will be transferred to another therapist from time to time.

THE PATIENT POPULATION

Statistical data were obtained on 100 randomly selected active patients of the TAC (see table 1). The average age was 48 years, with a range of 22 to 74 years. There were 72 women and 28 men. The group consisted of 78 white and 22 Negro patients. Religious affiliation was as follows: 42 Roman Catholics, 39 Protestants, 13 Jews, and six other. Marital status showed 68 married, 17 single, seven widowed, seven divorced, and one separated. Eighty-two per cent of the men were gainfully employed and only eight per cent of the total group were unemployed. Seventy-five per cent of the patients were living with their secondary family (spouse and/or children), 16 per cent lived with their primary family (mother and/or father), and 9 per cent lived alone. The socioeconomic status of the patients was considered typical of the University of Chicago Clinic population.

Evaluation of psychiatric diagnosis showed that 53 per cent of the patients were psychotic. The relatively high percentage of psychoneurotic disorders (see Table 1) does not indicate less psychopathology, as the majority of these patients have severe characterologic problems. Severe hypochondriasis, psychophysiologic disorder, and borderline states were included in the diagnosis of personality disorder. Half of the patients were referred to the TAC by the medical, surgical, and obstetric services in the hospital through the psychiatric consultation service. The others were referred by the psychiatric outpatient

TABLE 1

Statistical Data on Age, Sex, and Psychiatric Diagnosis on 100
Randomly Selected TAC Patients

Category	Per cent	Number
Age		
20-30		3
30-40		23
40-50		30
50-60		25
60 +		19
Sex		
Male		28
Female		72
Psychiatric diagnosis		
Psychotic disorders	53	
Schizophrenia		31
Paranoid state		4
Involutional depression		11
Psychotic depression		6
Manic-depressive psychosis		1
Psychoneurotic disorders	36	
Depressive type		29
Other		7
Personality disorders	10	10
Chronic brain syndromes	1	1

and inpatient sections. Three-fifths of the patients were on
medication; approximately half were on antidepressants and half
on ataractics.

TAC patients are comparable in regard to age, sex, and
psychiatric diagnosis with a group of patients seen in a similar
type of clinic at a city hospital (13). An important difference is
that the majority of TAC patients are in the middle rather than
the lower class.

ADAPTIVE PSYCHOTHERAPY

Psychotherapeutic treatment of the chronically ill
psychiatric patient has too often taken the form of "hand-
holding," a "pat on the back," or "tender loving care." "The
main thing is to be supportive" all too readily becomes a cliche
behind which lies imprecise diagnosis and stereotyped or
disinterested management. In treatment of the chronic
psychiatric patient efficacious psychotherapeutic techniques
cannot be administered in a nonspecific, general manner.

"Adaptive psychotherapy" (2, 3) is the term applied to the
psychotherapeutic technique that: (1) fosters the adaptation, not

the adjustment, of the patient, (2) addresses itself to the patient's specific disabling problem and maladaptation, and (3) springs ideally from ego-syntonic and adaptive derivatives within the therapist. The term "adaptive psychotherapy" was taken from Hartman's concept of adaptation (6). Patient adaptation ideally implies lack of disturbance in productivity, ability to enjoy life, and mental equilibrium. Adaptation is differentiated from adjustment insofar as adjustment implies passive submission to the goals of society, whereas adaptation implies active collaboration on and attempts to change societal goals. Progressive adaptation alters society for the better and implies intrapsychic growth. Regressive adaptation is tolerated or accepted by society but implies intrapsychic arrest or movement toward the infantile self.

In adaptive psychotherapy attention is focused on specific maladaptations; major intrapsychic alterations of character are not a goal of treatment. With infantile and schizoid personality disorders, those aspects of the behavioral repertoire that defend the patient against overt psychosis and keep him in an acceptable role in society are strengthened and rewarded. No attempt is made to change the basic character disorder and its defenses.

In certain cases regressive adaptation is considered a goal of treatment. When progressive adaptation (ego growth and development) is considered temporarily or permanently impossible, transference cures and flights into health are encouraged. In this regard, primitive and infantile transferences are accepted and supported when they positively contribute to the patient's ties to the institution or enable him to accept the therapist's interventions. Another goal of adaptive psychotherapy is reality education emphasizing sharpening objectivity, reduction of omnipotent fears, and correction of referential distortion when it is disabling.

Adaptive psychotherapy in this setting is characterized by: (1) patient contact over an extended, sometimes indefinite, period of time; (2) contacts generally less than 25 minutes and less frequent than weekly; (3) the frequent use of drugs; (4) goals that are varied but not aimed primarily at insight, transference exploration, or interpretation; and (5) techniques that include support, suppression (12), an institutional alliance, advice, environmental manipulation, attention to life happenings, and promotion of reality testing.

Certain aspects of the technique need amplification. The concept of the institutional alliance is a modification of the working alliance originally introduced by Greenson (5) and is used instead of the more common term "institutional transference." The working alliance includes: (1) the positive transferences, (2) the real situation between patient and therapist,

(3) the participation of rational, nonconflictual ego function, (4) a split between the observing and experiencing ego, and (5) an alliance between the therapist and patient established for the therapeutic benefit of the patient.

In adaptive psychotherapy in this setting an attempt is made to establish an analogous alliance between the patient and the clinic or institution. The institutional alliance can then be fairly easily transmitted from therapist to therapist. Secondly, in psychoanalytic treatment interpretations are intended to be complete and correct; in adaptive therapy interpretations are usually incomplete and are directed to the specific disabling conflict. In addition, the therapist's intervention is judged on the basis of the patient's subsequent adaptation, not on the basis of the correctness of the dynamic interpretation.

Finally, adaptive psychotherapy emphasizes the use of the natural personality and adaptive derivatives of the therapist as an ally to the patient's adaptive possibilities. Educators frequently give support to the notion that the resident in training should develop his own personal strengths and attributes and incorporate them in his therapeutic armamentarium. Adaptive psychotherapy understands that certain personality traits of the therapist may be useful in helping patients toward a more efficacious adaptation. Ideally the adaptive psychotherapist is aware of his natural and syntonic characteristics and how they may be useful for the patient's adaptive purposes.

A case vignette will illustrate the concept of the institutional alliance, specific but incomplete interpretation, and use of the natural and ego-syntonic resources of the therapist.

Case 1

A 42-year-old married, devout Roman Catholic Negro woman was brought to the emergency room by her husband one evening. The woman was a long-standing TAC patient, subject to episodes of psychotic depression and occasional paranoid states. Her characterologic diagnosis was schizoid personality. For the previous several months the patient had been adapting well and therefore one week earlier had decided on her own to discontinue her medication (trifluoperazine and imipramine hydrochloride). As in many past episodes, the patient's cessation of medication was soon followed by exacerbation of psychotic symptoms and firm, frequently paranoid, refusal to again take her medicine. On this occasion she had been compulsively reading her Bible for more than 18 hours, muttering to herself that she had killed someone, and occasionally breaking out in sobs and tears.

The patient was seen by the resident on call, whom she recognized from previous contact in the TAC. He determined that the acute episode was precipitated by an altercation with her rebellious late-adolescent daughter, who aroused her mother's deep separation anxiety and anger when she threatened to leave home. The patient openly stated her delusion that she had committed the terrible sin of killing her daughter. The resident, a doctor with previous theologic and ministerial training, knew from his earlier TAC contacts with this patient the importance in her life of religious rituals. He therefore informed her that she had not killed her daughter but had instead committed the sin of breaking her agreement with the clinic by stopping her medication without consulting her therapist. The resident, however, as a representative of the clinic said he would forgive her this sin provided she again began taking her medication. As penance she was expected to resume her usual household duties, care for her family, and return to the TAC the following Thursday.

Two days later the patient returned to the TAC accompanied by her husband. She had taken her medication and resumed her household duties, and both she and her husband were in good spirits. Over the course of the next few weeks the basic issues between the patient and her daughter were discussed with her therapist.

Staff Attitudes

Residents in training (and even staff members) frequently dislike or avoid clinics designed for the treatment of the chronically ill psychiatric patient. Among the reasons for this attitude is the tendency to depreciate the techniques of treatment and the patients themselves. In many programs, the psychoanalytic model of technique and goals is held in highest esteem. Characterologic change induced over long periods of time is often construed as the only significant therapeutic gain. Chronically ill patients are often felt to be, at best, nonpsychologically minded and, at worst, "crocks" and "incurables."

Once the therapist begins participation in the TAC certain anxieties continue to promote his dislike for the clinic and its patients. The waiting room experience is a particularly stressful situation. Socialization in the waiting area requires the removal of the usual blank-screen role of the therapist and raises issues about revealing himself and the difficulty of being therapeutic in a nonstructured setting. Individual sessions with the patient are also stressful because the brief 15-to 25-minute contact requires a marked change of pace from the 50-minute hour. Many find it difficult to make an accurate dynamic diagnosis and also intervene in an adaptive manner within the shorter period of time.

Several aspects of the TAC have been instituted in a direct attempt to offset and change these negative attitudes. Faculty interest and support of the clinic has been demonstrated by the actively involved eight-year participation of two psychoanalytically trained psychiatrists. Their continued interest in transference cures, symptom relief, and "flights into health" has lent weight to the importance of these issues in the care of psychiatric patients. In adaptive psychotherapy, effective intervention requires the therapist's precise dynamic understanding. Training in this clinic therefore emphasizes the importance of dynamic understanding and de-emphasizes the importance of the psychological-mindedness of the patient.

Several aspects of the waiting experience help to diminish anxiety. Cookies and coffee, first instituted as a symbolic support for patients, have come to be equally appreciated by the staff. The hostess-receptionist has been an important social support for staff, especially residents just beginning their rotation through the clinic. The receptionist's lack of professional training may contribute to her relative ease in a social setting viewed as uncomfortable by most staff.

DISCUSSION

The Thursday Afternoon Clinic has provided unique advantages for patients and staff. Patients have been pleased with the flexibility of scheduling appointments, the attention given to minor medical needs, and the socialization aspects of the waiting area experience. Trainees appreciate the wide variety of personality types seen in the TAC, the increasingly rare opportunity to follow the natural history of chronic psychiatric patients during three years, and the opportunity for on-the-spot supervision and consultation from respected teachers.

The TAC was established in a private general hospital, supported by patient fees and populated by primarily middle-class patients. Although the fee structure was flexible, most patients paid a standard $8 fee. The fee was frequently considered an important element in the psychotherapeutic interaction. Requests for fee reduction by patients frequently reflected their current psychodynamics. For example, at various times it was a request to be regarded as special, it was an expression of dissatisfaction about how much gratification was given, and it was an attempt to obtain limits from the therapist on insatiable demands. Maintaining the fee frequently undercut guilt and shame and promoted a sense of value and worthwhileness. Therapists who requested fee reductions for their patients were sometimes expressing questions about this type of therapy or their capacity to administer the treatment effectively. Careful attention to the fee frequently resulted in important psychotherapeutic transactions.

From a recent questionnaire sent to past residents it was

learned that three residents had started similar clinics in other places and that many residents found principles of adaptive psychotherapy useful in their private or institutional practices. For eight years the TAC has been serving the general needs of the population of the University of Chicago Hospitals and Clinics. The applicability of this type of clinic for the community mental health planning for a specific catchment area is clear. The treatment of the chronically ill need not be considered dull or second-rate; it need not be a financial burden to either the doctor or the patient.

The structure of the TAC offers an opportunity for planned experimentation in treatment technique and training programs. Until recently, training has focused primarily on psychiatric residents and medical students. Future planning includes the addition of nurses, occupational or recreational therapists, psychiatric aides, psychologists, and volunteers. Staff members are currently exploring the applicability of principles of adaptive psychotherapy to modes of treatment other than the dyadic —e.g., small groups emphasizing socialization or activity experience.

REFERENCES

1. Caplan, G. Types of mental health consultation. *Amer. J. Orthopsychiat.*, 1963, **33**; 470-481.
2. Daniels, R., Draper, E., & Rada, R. Training in the adaptive psychotherapies. *Compr. Psychiat.*, 1968, **9**, 383-391.
3. Draper, E., Daniels, R., & Rada, R. Adaptive psychotherapy: An approach toward greater precision in the treatment of the chronically disturbed. *Compr. Psychiat.*, 1968, **9**, 372-382.
4. Engelhardt, D., Rosen, B., Freedman, N., & Margolis, R. Phenothiazines in prevention of psychiatric hospitalization. *Arch. Gen. Psychiat.*, 1967, **16**, 98-101.
5. Greenson, R. The working alliance and the transference neurosis. *Psychoanal. Quart.*, 1962, **34**, 155-182.
6. Hartmann, H. *Ego psychology and the problem of adaptation*. New York: International Universities Press, 1958.
7. Jacobson, G. F., Wilner, D. M., Morley, W. E., Schneider, S., Strickler, M., & Sommer, G. J. The scope and practice of an early-access brief treatment psychiatric center, *Amer. J. Psychiat.*, 1965, **121**, 1176-1182.
8. Joint Commission on Mental Illness and Health. *Action for Mental Health*. New York: Basic Books, 1961.
9. Karp, H. N., & Karls, J. M. Combining crisis therapy and mental health consultation. *Arch. Gen. Psychiat.*, 1966, **14**, 536-542.
10. Koegler, R., & Brill, N. *Treatment of psychiatric outpatients*. New York: Appleton-Century-Crofts, 1967.
11. Kraft, A., Binner, P., & Dickey, B. The community mental health program and the longer-stay patient. *Arch. Gen. Psychiat.*, 1967, **16**, 64-70.

12. Levine, M. Principles of Psychiatric Treatment. In F. Alexander, and H. Ross, (Eds.), *Dynamic Psychiatry*. Chicago: The University of Chicago Press, 1952.
13. MacLeod, J., & Middleman, F. Wednesday afternoon clinic: A supportive care clinic. *Arch. Gen. Psychiat.*, 1962, **6**, 56-65.
14. Mazzanti, V., & Bessell, H. Communication through the latent language. *Amer. J. Psychother.* 1956, **10**, 250-260.
15. Rada, R., Draper, E., & Daniels, R. A therapeutic waiting area experience for patients with chronic psychiatric illness. *Compr. Psychiat.*, 1964, **5**, 191-199.
16. Wilder, J. F., & Coleman, M. D. The walk-in psychiatric clinic, some observations and follow-up. *Int. J. Soc. Psychiat.*, 1963, **9**, 192-199.

Chapter 19

Bereavement and the Acceptance
of Professional Service

Irwin Gerber, Ph.D.

Bereavement, "the emotional state, behavior, and conduct of the survivors immediately following the experience of separation by death from a person who fulfilled dependency needs, especially needs related to emotional interaction" (Volkart and Michael, 1957), is a universal occurrence which has generated a new surge of scientific interest and investigation. Observant clinicians have been repeatedly struck by a relationship between the death of a close one and subsequent morbidity and maladjustment. Regardless of the prevailing public attitude toward death, which is a combination of evasion, euphemism, and stoical acceptance (Fulton, 1965; Gorer, 1965), there are strong indications that bereavement is associated with various medical, psychological, and social problems (Baler and Golde, 1964; Cobb et. al., 1939; Grinberg, 1964; Lindemann, 1945; Marris, 1958; Parkes, 1964; Shoor and Speed, 1963). A more dramatic association with bereavement is the probability of early death of the survivors themselves (Kraus and Lilienfeld, 1959; Ress and Lutkins, 1967; Young et al., 1963).

These various bereaved reactions are, as is true for all illness, community problems requiring the attention of preventive and rehabilitative intervention. Nevertheless, bereavement and its related morbidity and maladjustment have only recently been recognized as a social condition in need of professional support and assistance (Caplan, 1964; Duhl and Leopold, 1966; Eliot, 1930; Silverman, 1967). For the survivor, bereavement is a deeply private matter associated with highly emotional overtones. The prevalent attitude of denying that the loss of a close one produces major maladjustments supports the intimate nature of

Reprinted from *Community Mental Health Journal*, 1969, **5**, 487-495, by permission of the publisher and the author. Dr. Gerber is head, Social Research Unit, Department of Social Medicine, Montefiore Hospital and Medical Center, Bronx, New York.

bereavement. However, from a public health point of view the privacy of bereavement is not a very strong argument for denying the need for professional intervention because, as systematic observations have indicated, the death of a family member does in fact affect the normal functioning of survivors. Another significant reason why professional intervention is needed is that the customary lay support and assistance supplied by close family members or friends does not appear to be very effective in preventing or reducing morbidity and maladjustment (Maddison and Walker, 1967).

Although these considerations necessitate some thought as to what type of program could be most effectively offered to bereaved individuals, one major question at the present time is how to secure the survivor(s) acceptance of a professional service. The reference here is to an unsolicited offer of professional assistance. This is a critical question because in order for such a service to be successful it must first overcome the bereaved individual's feelings of privacy and the denial that critical problems do exist. Since practitioners do not have stable guidelines for offering this type of service, it would seem to be of value to discuss such factors. Such a discussion is all the more important because our concern is with a relatively new type of prophylactic program, touching a comparatively atypical group.

Recently, a five-month pilot study was completed at the Montefiore Hospital Medical Group (for a description of this HIP group see Silver et al., 1957). It explored whether recently bereaved families would accept an offer of unsolicited professional assistance. The service was administered by a psychiatric social worker under the supervision of staff psychiatrists. The pilot program, which was supported by Montefiore Hospital and Medical Center, was in preparation for a large-scale demonstration and evaluation of "brief psychotherapy" to bereaved families. In the pilot program, consideration was given only to deaths due to cancer and cardiovascular diseases, which represent 85% of all deaths at the HIP group. The major stimulus for the preliminary investigation was that no adequate data were available to guide the researchers as to whether bereaved family members would accept an offer of unsolicited help. The only available information was an overall impression, from those colleagues who were consulted, which indicated that a 50% rate of acceptance should be accepted, and welcomed. The results of the pilot program were well above this estimate—90% (18 out of 20 family units) of the families who were approached accepted the service.

The unexpectedly high rate of acceptance was considered sufficiently significant in itself to warrant this paper, but of equal importance the acceptance rate stimulated considerable thought about what factors predisposed bereaved families to accept the unsolicited service. In an attempt to interpret the high rate of acceptance, the ensuing discussions will focus on certain characteristics of bereavement which bring about a crisis situation, and the legitimate need by bereaved individuals for support and assistance from a professional practitioner (a psychiatric social worker) who is not normally approached for individual and family problems. Furthermore, based on the interpretive scheme, several areas for research will be presented. At this point, it seems appropriate to clearly emphasize that the discussion will be more conjectural than empirically verified. The presentation is based on a limited amount of data which could be ascertained from the five-month pilot study, the author's observations, and informal conversations with the psychiatric social worker, and on information derived from the literature on bereavement. Nevertheless, it is hoped that the presentation will be of significant interest and value for clinicians and researchers interested in bereavement and its associated problems, as well as for those concerned with the general question of why individuals accept or reject a new professional service.

BRIEF OUTLINE OF THE SERVICE

The orientation of "brief psychotherapy" was based upon the consideration that the course of the normal grief reaction involves the full recognition and conscious experience of object loss, the emancipation from strong emotional bondage to the deceased, readjustment to the environment in which the deceased is missing, and forming new relationships and patterns of behavior. Consistent with the foregoing, the tactical methods of therapy (only five of the nine methods will be presented) were restricted to:

(1) Permitting and guiding the patient to put into words and express the affects involved in: (a) the pain, sorrow, and finality of bereavement; (b) a review of the relationship to the deceased; and (c) feelings of guilt toward the deceased.

(2) Acting as a primer and/or programer of some of the activities of the patient and organizing among available, suitable friends or relatives a flexible, modest scheme for the same purpose.

(3) Assisting the patient in dealing with reality situations, care of children, and legal problems.

(4) Mediating referrals to family doctors for prescriptions of psychic energizers, if necessary for excessive depression and insomnia.

(5) The offer of assistance in making future plans.

During the treatment sessions, family members were led to talk about the deceased person, and their relationship with him (her). Survivors were encouraged to examine and eventually accept their feelings of rejection, desertion, and anger at having to suffer such a loss while the "whole world went on as usual." In practice, the service was mainly emotionally supportive in nature, with the addition of professional assistance in areas of employment, offspring's school problems, and family financial problems. It should be noted that after the first home visit, the majority of survivors traveled to the psychiatric social worker's office at the medical group. The willingness on the part of family members to see the social worker at her office, as opposed to meetings at the home, highlights the need which the individual had for the professional service.

METHODS OF PROCEDURE

Sampling of bereaved families, who were HIP subscribers, was completed for a ten-week period. When the Medical Group's administrative office was notified of a death which was within the diagnostic category of either cancer or cardiovascular diseases, the research office was alerted. Approximately three days after actual death, the family physician sent a personal letter of condolence to the "key family member," e.g., the surviving spouse or, if none, the oldest surviving offspring.

Five days after the physician's letter, and eight days after the death, the family doctor was asked to contact the key family member for the purpose of introducing the service and, of course, to elicit a statement of acceptance. The research office contacted the physician to inquire about the key family member's response to the offer of assistance. Regardless of whether the response was of acceptance, rejection, or one of hesitation the social worker proceeded to make her first contact. The content of this first social work contact was basically the following: The social worker identified herself as a colleague of the family physician upon whose suggestion she was calling; she then offered her condolences and attempted to arrange an appointment to visit the surviving family members at their home. When asked what kind of help she could give, the social worker explained that HIP physicians were aware of the way in which pain weighs on people and they thought that talking to a person who is not a close friend or relative might help.

ACCEPTANCE OF A NEW SERVICE

In the analysis of the acceptance of a new service, Freidson

(1959, 1961) has presented a heuristic scheme based on the perceived needs (the "lay demand system") of potential clients of various services. In his discussion of the general rejection of the social work service, which was part of a health team composed of a family physician and public health nurse, Freidson compares the place of various health practitioners within the need systems of patients. For the purpose of resolving a problem, the affected person will first turn to those practitioners who handle problems which the lay individual defines as normal everyday occurrences. In most cases, these practitioners have been approached for previous health and social problems, and therefore their service is for events which are considered typical. A practitioner, as well as a lay source of assistance, who is not part of this customary means of problem-solving will stand a good chance of being rejected by the lay individual. The social work service was rejected because it was considered isolated from everyday events, i.e., a service primarily of an office nature, and therefore seen as a specialty service.

An additional factor in the layman's decision to turn to one source of assistance as opposed to another is the dimension of "attraction to normality." Lay individuals have a tendency to initially define their health and social problems as normal conditions which have been equally observed for other individuals. This attraction is made legitimate by choosing a supportive resource who is a customary source of assistance. If the individual accepts the assistance of a person who is not an immediately available and customary resource, then the attraction to normality is redefined and the problem becomes a crisis. The condition is considered a crisis when there is an awareness that normal sources of assistance are not able, or will not be able, to adequately relieve the problem. In reference to the social work service, Freidson (1959) indicated that the social worker was seen as a practitioner who would be approached only after customary techniques had failed and the problem became serious. The strong implication here is that a practitioner who is not a customary source of assistance will only be approached, or service accepted, when the condition is defined as a crisis.

BEREAVEMENT AS A CRISIS SITUATION

The interpretation of the high rate of acceptance of the psychiatric social work service is based on the notion that bereavement contains many unique characteristics which produce a crisis situation and therefore predispose recently bereaved individuals to accept an offer of professional assistance, in particular, a source of assistance which is not customary.

(1) Bereavement is a period of crisis because "there is an imbalance between the difficulty and importance of the problem and the resources immediately available to deal with it" (Caplan, 1964). A major factor in considering a stressful condition as a crisis is when customary techniques and means of assistance are inadequate, i.e., have failed, and are perceived as inadequate in meeting the problem. When one rejects customary resources, e.g., close friends and relatives, because of inadequate support and assistance, and seeks help from individuals who are not normally approached for problems, the situation becomes a crisis. Furthermore, the slower the resolution of the problem, the faster the condition will be defined as a crisis (Bloom, 1963).

(2) A significant factor about bereavement is that it is a social situation that is not commonplace in one's lifetime. Most individuals have little contact with death (Stub, 1966), and because of the prevailing nuclear family orientation within our society few of us have many opportunities to be legitimately bereaved. This means that bereavement is a stressful situation for which we have little past experience (Caplan, 1964). Because of this lack of exposure, we are unaware of the type of problems presented by the loss of a close person and the most appropriate sources of support and assistance. The result of this unstructured situation is a behavior pattern which seeks out those individuals who have in the past offered assistance for nonbereaved problems.

(3) Besides the individual's lack of experience with playing the bereaved role, modern society, as opposed to anthropologically studied social systems, does not offer the bereaved person socially sanctioned and ritualistic means of support. Modern society reserves ritualistic bereaved behavior for the death of a select few individuals. Recent examples of this would be the ceremonial burial and national mourning for John Kennedy and Winston Churchill. Because bereavement and its support are not ritualized in our society, survivors seek out and are surrounded by close relatives and friends who are, in most cases, part of the small group of individuals who are defined as legitimately bereaved (Sudnow, 1967, pp. 153-168). These individuals constitute the customary or normal sources of assistance because they have in the past been consulted for nonbereavement problems. However, these customary sources offer only shortlived support which is totally ineffective in resolving the problems associated with the death of a close person. This ineffective support takes the form of a set of stoical statements which is assumed to be the most beneficial type of support. To "be strong," "hold your chin up," and "start making a new life" are certainly presented in good faith, but they offer little concrete assistance to the bereaved individual (Maddison, 1967). Furthermore, within a month or sooner after death, close friends and relatives usually revert to

their normal lives, leaving the bereaved individual by himself to handle the situation (Silverman, 1967). For survivors, new roles (occupational and familial) are required, emotional and medical problems have to be resolved, family affairs must be put in order, and a complete reorientation of future family plans must be considered. It is at this point that the survivor is urgently in need of concrete support.

(4) An important consideration for defining bereavement as a crisis situation is the individuals perception of the inadequacy of lay customary support. Recent discussions of this point have indicated that within the first three months of bereavement survivors do perceive that customary sources of support are, or have been, inadequate (Cadden, 1964; Caplan, 1964; Maddison, 1967). At this juncture, bereavement takes on the definition of a crisis. As the survivor's difficulties increase, there is a greater need to seek or accept assistance from individuals who are not customary sources. It can be assumed that a large percentage of bereaved persons do reach the point when customary support is perceived as inadequate and bereavement becomes defined as a crisis. This definition, and the dynamics leading to it, predispose recently bereaved individuals to accept an offer of unsolicited help from a practitioner who is not a normal, customary source for assistance.

(5) A potential obstacle to the seeking or accepting of assistance from other than customary resources is the individual's desire or need to continue maintaining his "attraction to normality." For whatever reasons, the bereaved person finds it more satisfying and rewarding to continue with the customary support or to "go it alone," rather than to seek other avenues for assistance. One possible explanation for this behavior, aside from the obvious one that in fact customary support is adequate, is that the individual's self-concept as a stoical person gains legitimacy by rejecting outside sources of assistance. The most difficult challenge for the offer of professional assistance to recently bereaved individuals lies within this attraction to normality group.

The relationship between the acceptance of the social work service and the conditions which bring about a definition of bereavement as a crisis situation gains some credence when we turn our attention to those survivors in the bereaved family pilot study who initially rejected the offer of assistance. Originally, four family units refused the service. However, approximately four months after the rejection, two of these families contacted the social worker for assistance. The reason given for their belated acceptance was that the survivor found that family members and close friends were not able to give the needed assistance, and the emotional problems which the bereaved individual thought could be handled were still present.

The remaining two family units did not attempt to contact the social worker. Of these two units, one survivor refused the service because, "he felt that he could handle his problems without assistance." The surviving spouse in the second family offered the same reason, and further informed the social worker that she herself was a practicing psychiatric social worker. It could be conjectured that the two survivors who contacted the social worker initially had a stronger attraction to normality than did the majority of bereaved individuals. However, as time passed the problems associated with bereavement increased, imposing an awareness that lay support was in fact inadequate for the survivor's needs. With this awareness the survivor rejected the definition of bereavement as a normal condition, i.e., a state which could be resolved with the assistance of lay support and accepted the situation as a crisis, i.e., in need of other than customary support.

Further support for the previous discussions is based on the responses to a follow-up questionnaire mailed to those survivors who accepted the bereaved service. The questionnaire probed how helpful the service was, what were its good and bad points, and how the service could be improved. Only 2 of the 26 survivors within the 18 families who accepted the service indicated that the service was not very helpful. Of the 24 respondents who thought the service was "very helpful" or "helpful," ten reported that the service was beneficial because it was good to talk to someone who "was not a relative or friend." Eight indicated that because they had a chance to talk to "a professional" their anxieties were reduced. The remaining six respondents thought the service was helpful for various reasons, such as, it gave them a chance to "get out of the house," "to meet new people," or it offered a chance "to stop thinking so much about the past."

From this limited data it appears that for those bereaved individuals who accepted the service and thought it was helpful, the majority (18 out of 24) gave as their reason for liking the service the fact that the social worker was a source of assistance who was a professional, and not a relative or friend. This observation seems to support, to some degree, the previous discussions of the dynamics of bereavement which create a crisis situation in need of other than customary support.

AREAS FOR RESEARCH

A paper such as the present one is certainly limited in the necessary hard data from which one can generalize. Nevertheless, a significant product, whether intended or not, of such a paper is its heuristic ability to discover and suggest various areas for future research. One major question in the study of bereavement is at what point during bereavement professional intervention will be most effective. Basically, one could approach this problem by investigating whether survivors who receive professional assistance at the point of bereavement have less morbidity and maladjustment than those who receive assistance at a later time. If it appears that earlier intervention is the most effective, then an important question to be empirically investigated is at what early point after the death survivors will accept an offer of professional assistance. The bereaved family pilot study has indicated that survivors will accept unsolicited professional assistance within the first two weeks of bereavement.

A final area for possible research, although the list could certainly be expanded, is the documentation of various characteristics of survivors which influence the bereaved individual's acceptance of an offer of professional assistance. For those practitioners who are interested in this specific area of preventive intervention, knowledge of such characteristics will greatly assist in the actual offering of the service. The present paper has suggested that one characteristic which may influence the individual is the degree to which he derives satisfaction from an "attraction to normality." The more the individual considers his condition normal, the greater the chance he will refuse professional intervention.

REFERENCES

Baler, L. A., & Golde, P. J. Conjugal bereavement: a strategic area of research in preventive psychiatry. Vol. 2. Boston: Laboratory of Community Psychiatry, 1964.

Bloom, B. L. Definitional aspects of the crisis concept. *Journal of Consulting Psychology*, 1963, 27, 498-502.

Cadden, V. Crisis in the family. In G. Caplan, (Ed.), *Principles of preventive psychiatry*. New York: Basic Books, 1964, p. 39.

Caplan, G. *Principles of preventive psychiatry*. New York: Basic Books, 1964.

Cobb, S. Bauer, W., & Whiting, I. Environmental factors in rheumatoid arthritis. *Journal of the American Medical Assn.*, 139, 113, 668-670.

Duhl, L. J. & Leopold, R. L. Mental illness. In H. Becker, (Ed.), *Social problems: A modern approach*. New York: John Wiley, 1966, pp. 277-316.

Eliot, T. D. The adjustive behavior of bereaved families. A new field for research. *Social Forces*, 1930, 8, 543-549.

Freidson, E. Specialties without roots: The utilization of a new service. *Human Organizations*, 1959, 18, 112-116.

Friedson, E. *Patients' views of medical practice*. New York: Russell Sage Foundation, 1961.

Fulton, R. (Ed.) *Death and anxiety*. New York: John Wiley, 1965.

Gorer, G. *Death, grief, and mourning*. New York: Doubleday, 1965.

Grinberg, L. Two kinds of guilt—their relations with normal and pathological aspects of mourning. *International Journal of Psychoanalysis*, 1964, 45, 366-372.

Kraus, A. S., & Lilienfeld, A. M. Some epidemiological aspects of the high mortality rate in the young widowed group. *Journal of Chronic Diseases*, 1959, 10, 207-217.

Lindemann, E. Psychiatric problems in conservative treatment of ulcerative colitis. *Archives of Neurology and Psychiatry*, 1945, 53, 322-324.

Maddison, D., & Walker, W. L. Factors affecting the outcome of conjugal bereavement. *British Journal of Psychiatry*, 1967, 113, 1057-1067.

Marris, P. *Widows and their families*. London: Routledge & Kegan Paul, 1958.

Parks, C. M. Effects of bereavement on physical and mental health—a study of the medical records of widows. *British Medical Journal*, 1964, 2, 274-279.

Rees, W. D., & Lutkins, S. G. Mortality of bereavement. *British Medical Journal*, 1967, 4, 13-16.

Shoor, M., & Speed, M. H. Death, delinquency, and the mourning process. *Psychiatry Quarterly*, 1963, 37, 540-558.

Silver, G. A., Cherkasky, M., and Axelrod, J. An experience in group practice, Montefiore Hospital Medical Group 1948-1956. *New England of Journal of Medicine*, 1957, 256, 785-791.

Silverman, P. R. Services to the widowed: first steps in a program of preventive intervention, *Community Mental Health Journal*, 1967, 3, 37-44.

Stub, H. R. Family structure and the social consequences of death. In J. R. Folta, and E. S. Deck, (Eds.), *A sociological framework for patient care*. New York: John Wiley, 1966, pp. 191-200.

Sudnow, D. *Passing on*. New Jersey: Prentice-Hall, 1967.

Volkart, E. H., & Michael, S. T. Bereavement and mental health. In A. H. Leighton, J. A. Clausen & R. N. Wilson, (Eds.), *Exploration in social psychiatry*, New York: Basic Books, 1957, p. 282.

Young, M., Benjamin, B., & Wallis, C. The mortality of widowers. *Lancet*, 1963, 454-456.

IV. Innovative Group, Family, and Hospital Approaches

Many of the techniques of brief therapy can be translated into strategies for group and family psychotherapy, though experimentation with these methods so far has received relatively little attention. Until recently, short-term group techniques had been used mostly as a practical intake method. Sadock, Newman, and Normand describe a format for an open-ended group which patients attend for a maximum of ten sessions. The setting is a walk-in clinic serving a deprived population, earlier described in this volume in the paper by Normand, Fensterheim, and Schrenzel. This time-limited group is concerned with problem-solving, and goals are defined in terms which are realistic in the time available. The authors have found that peer support is especially beneficial to socially deprived patients who feel that a barrier exists between them and a therapist of a different social class.

Donner and Gamson describe time-limited groups made up of families. Family therapists generally attempt to shift the focus from the scapegoated individual to the family system. Multiple family groups enable families to observe some of the pathological components of each other's family systems, sharing their difficulties and successes for their mutual benefit. Donner and Gamson have found that this modality is particularly suited to the treatment of adolescents caught in the crossfire of conflicting value systems of family and peer group.

Pittman, DeYoung, Flomenhaft, Kaplan, and Langsley have developed a technique of crisis family therapy that is an effective means of preventing potentially regressive psychiatric hospitalization, in a demonstration project with major implications for psychiatric practice. This family treatment unit has shown that patients randomly selected for family crisis therapy as an alternative to hospitalization fare a good deal better than patients who are hospitalized, as measured by subsequent role performance and the incidence and duration of rehospitalization (1, 2). In the tradition of family therapy, family crisis intervention immediately shifts the focus from the family member who has been labeled as the patient to the total family unit and its efforts to avoid responsibility. The presupposition is that the whole family is in a crisis state to which all are reacting.

Treatment emphasizes the analysis of family role assignments and the introduction of new rules and roles.

There is little evidence that long-term hospitalization produces proportionate therapeutic benefits, and its hazards, such as reinforcing the sick role, are becoming a matter of increasing professional concern. In an effort to show that effective hospitalization need not be a lengthy process, Weisman, Feirstein, and Thomas have developed a three-day hospitalization program which provides a remarkably intensive, multifaceted therapeutic experience. The patient and his family are offered a variety of therapeutic interventions, comparable to what transpires in a period of weeks (or even months) in the traditional psychiatric hospital. Upon admission, the therapy team immediately formulates a treatment plan which it proceeds to implement with individual, group, conjoint, family, and multiple-family sessions, rapidly involving all key members of the patient's family constellation. Expectations are a key factor: The staff expects to operate on multiple therapeutic levels guided by immediately determined treatment goals; they expect the patient to assume an active role in mobilizing strengths to cope with his problem and they carefully avoid anything that will reinforce his sense of inadequacy. The treatment program is continued for thirty days following the patient's discharge from the hospital. Results are comparable to those of longer-term hospitalization.

REFERENCES

1. Langsley, D. G., Pittman, F. S., Machotka, P., & Flomenhaft, K. Family crisis therapy—results and implications. *Family Process*, 1968, **7**, 145-158.
2. Langsley, D. G., Flomenhaft, K., & Machotka, P. Followup evaluation of family crisis therapy. *American Journal of Orthopsychiatry*, 1969, **39**, 753-759.

Chapter 20

Short-Term Group Psychotherapy
in a Psychiatric Walk in Clinic

Benjamin Sadock, M D , Lenore Newman, A.C.S.W., and
William C. Normand, M.D.

A short-term group psychotherapy project was carried out in
the psychiatric walk-in clinic at the New York Medical College-
Metropolitan Hospital Center, serving mainly a socio-
economically deprived population. Methods of short-term individual and family treatment have been utilized in this setting, and it was hoped that short-term group psychotherapy
might also be applicable. This paper will present our findings.

The organization of the walk-in clinic has been described
previously (3, 4). In brief, the clinic, located near the emergency
room of the hospital, enables the patient to "walk in" and see a
psychiatrist and social worker. Therapy is limited to six visits,
although referral for long-term therapy, individual and group,
supportive and analytic, is also available.

The therapeutic approach is ameliorative rather than curative
and takes into account the severe socioeconomic deprivation
found in our patient population, from the East Harlem area of
New York City. The major emphasis is on understanding the
patient's presenting problem and providing as much relief as
possible in the limited time available. Often, treatment tactics
focus on environmental modification, although interpersonal
and intrapsychic events are also considered.

Several workers have reported on the use of groups in active
outpatient departments as a diagnostic and intake vehicle (6, 8).
In the project reported upon in this paper, the group was used
solely as a treatment method.

Reprinted from *American Journal of Orthopsychiatry*, 1968, **38**, 724-732, by permission of the publisher and the authors. Dr. Sadock is Assistant Professor of
Psychiatry and Director of Group Psychotherapy Training at New York Medical College. Miss Newman is Assistant Instructor in Psychiatry and Psychiatric Social Work Supervisor and Dr. Normand is Associate Professor of Psychiatry and Director, Psychiatric Outpatient Service, New York Medical College—
Metropolitan Hospital Center.

ORGANIZATION OF THE PROGRAM

Short-term group psychotherapy is a fairly well documented technique (9). Its application to the walk-in clinic, however, presented certain unique problems. First, the population of the clinic is characterized by a rapid turnover of patients and it was to be expected that the membership of the group would also be changing rapidly. Short-term group techniques are most effective when the group population is as stable as possible [although one of us reported on the successful outcome of a rapid turnover group in another setting (7)]. Second, in order to fit the group project into the framework of the clinic as it was already functioning, it was necessary to limit the number of sessions the patient was allowed to attend. And third, although short-term individual and family psychotherapy had been found to be applicable to this clinic, short-term group psychotherapy had not been applied previously.

A patient was referred for group psychotherapy after an initial evaluation had been made in an individual session by a member of the walk-in clinic staff. Guidelines regarding the type of patient to be included were broad. No specific diagnostic category was excluded except for those extremely paranoid patients who might incorporate the group into their paranoid ideation. Patients strongly opposed to group therapy were not referred to the program, although resistances to this modality were explored by the intake worker if group psychotherapy was believed to be the treatment of choice. In general, the decision as to which patients would be referred was left up to the various clinic staff members on the basis of their evaluations.

The group was conducted by co-therapists, one a psychiatrist and the other a psychiatric social worker, who had their first contact with the patient at the group session. The diagnostic model formulated by the intake worker was available and utilized although, as the patient proceeded in treatment, this model was subject to constant review and modification as indicated. A limit of ten sessions as the maximum number each patient was allowed to attend was set to approximate the limits already placed upon the patient in individual psychotherapy; the patient was so advised by the intake worker prior to being placed in the group. The patient was also told that if his problems could not be resolved within that time, arrangements could be made for long-term treatment. Sessions were held on a weekly basis and lasted approximately one hour. Both therapists were available for any emergency consultation that might be required. The number of patients in the group at any one time was to be limited to eight. However, as soon as a member left the group, a new member was admitted to take his place.

RESULTS

The program reported on consisted of 40 group sessions extending over a 10-month period.

During this time, a total of 29 patients were referred by the walk-in staff for short-term group therapy. Of this number, 28 patients (96% of those referred) attended their first group session.

As was expected, there was great variability in the number of sessions attended by a patient and the number of patients at any one session. The number of sessions attended by a patient ranged from one session to ten, the latter figure being the maximum allowed. The average number of sessions attended by a patient was five. Attendance at any particular session varied from two patients to the maximum number of eight, with the group being made up, generally, of at least five members.

The diagnostic breakdown of the 28 patients who participated was as follows: schizophrenic reaction, 15; psychoneurosis, 4; passive-agressive personality, 4; passive-dependent personality, 5. There were 13 women and 15 men in the total group population. Eleven patients were white, 7 were Puerto Rican, and 10 were Negro. The distribution of patients in terms of diagnosis, sex, and race closely approximated that of the walk-in clinic in general.

Twenty-one patients were Catholic, 3 Jewish, 4 Protestant. Twelve patients were single, 3 were separated, 6 were married, and 7 were divorced. One patient was a widow and another a widower. Ages ranged from 20 to 60 years. Most patients referred were in the 30-to 35-year-old group.

The average educational level reached was twelfth grade, with a range from fourth grade to one year postgraduate college.

Fifteen patients were unemployed, 3 considered themselves housewives, and the remaining 10 worked only intermittently.

The reasons the patient presented himself to the walk-in clinic for treatment varied considerably, ranging from intrapsychic disequilibrium as seen in the decompensating schizophrenic to environmental disequilibrium as seen in the sudden and unexpected loss of a job. Two patients had made recent suicide attempts. Several presented with the symptom of excessive alcohol intake.

In only one case was a patient not accepted for group therapy, and then after he had attended one session. In this instance, the patient was observed to be in the midst of a severe paranoid psychosis which could not be managed in the group setting.

*

EFFICACY OF TREATMENT

Of the total group population of 28 patients, 10 patients (35%) attended the maximum number of ten sessions. All these patients were rated by the therapists as having improved as a result of their group experience.

Improvement was judged to have occurred on the basis of clinical examination if one of the following criteria were met: (1) the patient's presenting problem had been ameliorated; (2) work inhibitions had been removed; (3) family relationships were more stable; (4) intragroup and extragroup interpersonal relationships had improved. In addition, the patient had to report subjective improvement to independent examiners in follow-up interviews.

Eighteen of the 28 patients (65%) terminated treatment prior to the tenth group session and have been designated group therapy dropouts.

At the time a patient dropped out of the group, the therapists attempted to determine whether or not improvement had occurred. Of the 18 patients who left, 8 patients (44% of the dropouts) were rated as improved as a result of their limited group experience. Five of these patients were available for follow-up evaluation by independent examiners and 4 were rated as improved by them. The significance of this group will be discussed.

TREATMENT TECHNIQUE

The limited number of group sessions the patient was allowed to attend and the rapid turnover of patients required modification in both therapist technique and orientation.

A patient who completed the maximum number of sessions allowed was discharged from the group at that time. In the last session, a segment of the group was devoted to his departure. The patient was asked to evaluate his course of treatment in terms of goals expected at the beginning of treatment and goals achieved by the end of treatment. This evaluation was then examined by the other members and by the therapists.

In an ideal situation, the following might occur: goals at the beginning of treatment were well defined and realistic; they could be and were achieved in the limited time available; and the patient in question, the other group members, and the therapists concurred in the evaluation. In a particular case, the deviations from this ideal were quite variable. Goals for treatment were often vague or, if definable in certain cases, impossible to achieve in a short-term program. Expectations of certain patients were sometimes magical with no therapeutic effort able to fulfill them.

Also, any group member or all of the members might, on occasion, disagree with the formulation and so might the therapists, either separately or together.

Within this framework, then, it behooved the therapists to conceptualize the individual patient's problem in as concrete a way as possible, and the early meetings were directed towards this end. Upon entering the group, the new member was introduced and was asked to give a biography with particular emphasis on current problems that brought him to treatment. Other group members were encouraged to verbalize uncertainties, to ask questions, and to express reactions about the new member's situation. Attempts were made in the beginning sessions to formulate goals for treatment. In the remaining sessions, both therapist and group activity was geared to realizing these goals. The culmination of this group work occurred in the final session of a particular member, by which time, hopefully, the goals had been achieved for him. In the interim between a patient's first and last session, several new members might have entered the group, and each time the introductory, goal-seeking process was repeated with the new member as focus. As a result, the new member was accepted readily by the rest of the group.

Interaction between the various group members was encouraged and processes unique to group psychotherapy were observed within the confines of a single group session. Patients would identify with one another and provide mutual support and stimulation. For some, the group was a corrective emotional experience, as in the case of a young woman who, having been raised in a hostile and coercive family setting, saw the group initially in the same way. As she progressed in treatment, however, she became aware of the group as the giving and protective unit it was. Her feelings of being rejected by the members were replaced by the more reality-oriented feelings of being accepted.

Member activity outside of the regularly scheduled group therapy sessions was also encouraged. In one case, for example, a patient actively found employment for another and accompanied him to the job. In another, a patient who was severely depressed was given support and encouragement by another patient in her home.

Attempts were made to foster a therapeutic atmosphere by emphasizing the need for each member to express his thoughts and feelings as openly as possible. Where a hostile interchange between patients occurred, and these were rare, it was interpreted and support for the member under attack was provided. In general, the therapists attempted to convey a feeling of optimism, emphasizing the need for concerted group work if problems were to be solved in the limited time available. When a patient used the limited number of sessions in the service of resistance, claiming that more time was required to work out problems, the reality of his being able to continue in long-term therapy was presented and the resistance to using the present experience constructively was examined.

CASE REPORTS

The case reports will illustrate how member activity and therapist activity effect therapeutic change. Where indicated, community agency contact was made. In general, these contacts were used to alter the environment of the patient when it was believed that aspects of the environment were contributing significantly to pathological functioning.

Case 1

Lisa is a 27-year-old Negro widow, mother of four, who came to the walk-in clinic with complaints of insomnia, severe headaches, and inability to care for her children. Her difficulties began three years previously when she witnessed her husband murder her mother and then kill himself with a shotgun. Shortly thereafter the patient's younger brother was killed in a gang war in the housing project in which she lived.

Following these episodes, the patient attempted to move to another housing project in a different neighborhood in an effort to blot out the memories of these tragedies, but at the time of her visit to the walk-in clinic she had been unsuccessful in effecting this change.

The patient had sought psychiatric treatment before at another clinic but she kept appointments sporadically and was described as not motivated for psychotherapy.

In the screening interview, Lisa emphasized her need for re-housing and, although preoccupied with the deaths of her mother, husband, and brother, was unwilling to examine the possible effects of these events on her personality functioning. She maintained that a new apartment would solve her problems.

When Lisa attended her first group session and was asked to describe her situation, she told of the murders and of her need to move from the neighborhood where they happened. The group was as one in reacting with sympathy and understanding. They agreed with the patient that a move was necessary and expressed anger that it had not been effected immediately after it had been requested. Some of the members began to give Lisa advice as to how to put "pressure" on the Housing Authority; suggestions ranged from enlisting the aid of congressmen to using "Black Power." When the therapists were asked their opinion, they concurred that relocation would alleviate some of the stress Lisa was under but emphasized that, in addition, exploration of her feelings about these incidents was important.

Therapist activity then took the form of a discussion between psychiatrist and social worker as to how relocation could be effected in the shortest time. In open interchange before the group, the therapists concluded that a letter emphasizing the psychiatric indications for re-housing be sent to the Housing Authority. Both therapists expressed optimism that such a request would be granted, and Lisa and the other members appeared pleased at the course of action to be taken.

In Lisa's second group session, one of the members reported that he had been upset during the previous week. He admitted to having murderous fantasies towards his mother-in-law and identified with Lisa's husband. Lisa questioned him closely about the reasons for his thoughts, to which he replied that, in part, he resented his wife's attachment to her mother. One member suggested that perhaps Lisa had the same kind of relationship with her mother and that her husband committed the murder out of resentment. Another member associated to the death of his father and the guilt he subsequently experienced. He suggested that Lisa's husband committed suicide to punish himself.

What was apparent in this session was Lisa's interest in the experiences and questions brought up by the other members. While there was still concern about the outcome of the request for relocation, she was willing to participate in the group and made tentative steps towards examining her feelings pending an answer from the Housing Authority.

One month after the request was made, during Lisa's fourth group session, the therapists reported that relocation had been approved. The group members identified with her happiness over this news. Several gained strength from this concrete sign that change was possible.

Lisa returned to her fifth group session and continued to attend until the maximum number of ten sessions allowed was reached. She became interested in and involved with the other patients and offered suggestions as to how they could cope with their problems more effectively. She began to talk more openly during this period and examined her feelings about the murders, the relationship she had with her family, and her current relationships with her children.

In her tenth and final session, Lisa evaluated her brief course of treatment. She described herself as much improved. She was sleeping well, her headaches had disappeared, and she was more confident about her ability to cope with her children. In addition, she was more optimistic about her relationship with a man she had been dating.

In a follow-up interview, she reported that she had moved into a new apartment and was doing well.

Case 2

Angelina is a 20-year-old single Puerto Rican girl, employed as a secretary, who came to the walk-in clinic with fears that she was a lesbian. She denied any homosexual activity but questioned her femininity and her sexual impulses, if any, towards women.

Her symptoms began two years previously when she was accused by her stepmother of being a homosexual because of the close relationship that then existed between Angelina and her stepsister. There was, in fact, no basis for the accusation but Angelina was extremely upset about being called a lesbian. She began then to withdraw from her sister in an effort to ward off further accusations.

At that time also, the patient's father became involved in a voodoo cult and accused her of being "possessed by spirits." He attempted to prohibit her from going out on dates and insisted that she stay at home except to go to work.

Angelina attended a mental hygiene clinic for help with these problems shortly after they began; but continued pressure from both parents to stop psychiatric treatment eventually succeeded.

In the screening interview, the patient was overtly depressed. She described herself as suicidal at times. Her parents did not know about her coming to the clinic and she feared her father's reaction if he were to find out. He had been known to become physically assaultive, especially after he had drunk excessively. She saw her present clinic contact as a final effort to obtain help with her homosexual fears and the destructive home situation.

In the first session that Angelina attended she made no mention of her homosexual preoccupation, nor did the therapist encourage her to talk about this. Instead, she focused on her family situation and how she was rejected by her stepmother, who openly preferred the stepsister, and how she was abused by her father. To questions from the other group members, she admitted to being an out-of-wedlock child, deserted at birth by her mother about whom she knew little. She had heard that her real mother was a "tramp" and her father often said that she was going to grow up like her. She denied that this would ever happen.

The group members showed interest in her situation and were sympathetic with the disordered family setting she described. One member, a woman in her fifties, told of how she had run away from home when she was Angelina's age to get away from her parents. She advised Angelina to do the same. Another member, a man with a 15-year-old daughter, agreed that Angelina might do better out of the home but suggested a residence for girls instead.

The idea of moving away from the family appealed to the patient, but she felt that her father would "kill" her if he found out that she wanted to move. Another member doubted this and described how her 18-year-old son moved to his own apartment with the result that although worried about him, she was relieved at no longer having the responsibility of caring for him.

Most of the members believed Angelina should take immediate steps to leave the home, and while the therapists agreed there were more constructive environments for her, it was apparent that Angelina was poorly prepared emotionally to manage by herself and that such a move was premature. In the light of the group pressure being exerted, a statement by the therapists reassuring Angelina that she did not have to move in the immediate future was necessary. Angelina's position was then better understood. One member commented that Angelina would move when she was ready and others agreed that it was difficult to make changes in one's life, particularly that of moving away from home for the first time.

In the fifth session Angelina attended, a new group member reported on his feelings that people at work thought him to be a homosexual. When this theme was explored, Angelina mentioned her homosexual fears for the first time and described how they developed after her mother's accusation. One of the members then commented on how "feminine" Angelina was and several others mentioned her attractiveness in an effort so they thought to reassure her. When asked by the therapists about her sexual experiences, she reported that she was a virgin. She admitted to having sexual impulses towards boys and described how she had enjoyed "necking" experiences. These feelings, however, only added to her confusion when her stepmother accused her of being a lesbian.

As Angelina continued to attend the group sessions, she became more able to talk about her sexual impulses. In her eighth session, for example, she mentioned that when nine years old, she had sex play with an older male cousin. She felt extremely guilty about this incident and had never told anyone about it before. Her story elicited accounts of childhood sexual activity from several other group members, much to Angelina's surprise.

In her final session, Angelina described herself as feeling much happier. She was less concerned about her homosexual fears although they still troubled her at times. Long-term psychotherapy was recommended and the patient was able to recognize this as necessary if she were to gain further understanding of herself.

Angelina is currently in combined individual and group psychotherapy in the mental hygiene clinic. She recently went on vacation to Mexico with some friends and has been dating regularly. Her parents know of her psychiatric treatment.

CONCLUSIONS

Of the patients referred into this program, none had previous experience in group psychotherapy and most would be categorized as both socially and economically deprived. In the treatment of such patients, the availability of peers in the group setting may be the decisive factor in therapeutic progress. Peers provide support for the patient who, because of unfortunate, if not unavoidable, experiences with bureaucratic agencies, sees the therapist as a punitive authority figure. Where the patient may feel misunderstood or threatened by the therapist because of the differences in their status, he may feel understood by a fellow group member. There is much about the community of the poor that is difficult for those not part of it to understand fully, and it was not uncommon for the therapists to learn new things about the community from the group. When this did occur, it was mutually beneficial.

Experience with psychotherapy with the socially deprived has shown that the patient may need some immediate kind of relief before becoming involved in treatment (2, 3, 5). The group approach may allow for some modification in that the patient may be willing to delay gratification after observing that other patients have been helped as a result of treatment. In addition, patients can be motivated for psychotherapy, as the experience of a significant number of patients in our project wanting to go on to long-term therapy appears to indicate.

The overlapping of the professional skills of psychiatrist and psychiatric social worker as group co-therapists had several advantages. First, the group setting was able to provide total care for the patient, including medication and community agency referral. Second, the psychiatrist, with his tendency to focus on intrapsychic and interpersonal activity might not have been aware of realistic environmental stresses acting upon the patient or, if he was, might not have been fully aware of the ways in which these stresses could be modified. The psychiatric social worker, on the other hand, familiar with community resources, was often in a position to better evaluate the possibilities for change.

Male and female therapists in this project also contributed to the therapeutic process. Patients were able, in certain instances, to use the harmonious interaction of the therapists as a model against which to evaluate either current or past marital or parental strife. It was not uncommon for a group member to direct remarks only to one of the therapists. When this occurred it could be traced, usually, to a traumatic experience with an important figure in the patient's life, represented by the sex of the therapist who was avoided.

The significance of those patients who terminated the group experience prematurely is of interest. Reports of group therapy dropouts are available and, in general most studies look at the dropout as a therapeutic failure (10). In the short-term group, however, such a designation may be misleading. The patient may have dropped out of the group because he was feeling better or because the situation that brought him to the clinic initially had been resolved to his satisfaction. A 23-year-old man, for example, left the group after four sessions. He came to the clinic depressed over recent academic failure. In a follow-up interview he reported that he had reapplied to college and saw no need for further treatment. His depression had lifted. A 33-year-old man, on the other hand, reported that he left the group after three sessions because he felt it to be of no use and was "not interested in the other members." He still had the same symptoms in follow-up examination. It is therefore necessary to determine whether a patient drops out of the group because his objectives have been achieved or because he is resistant to therapeutic efforts.

Our sample, although small, does allow for the possibility that the patient who drops out of this type of short-term psychotherapy group may have benefited from the contact even though he did not complete the entire series of ten sessions allowed.

In the community mental health center, newer approaches must be used to provide for the ever-increasing treatment needs of the community. As a result of the project reported in this paper, the walk-in clinic is planning to make further use of this modality to provide both increased and more effective services to our patient population.

REFERENCES

1. Christmas, J. Sociopsychiatric treatment of disadvantaged psychotic adults. *Amer. J. of Orthopsychiat.*, 1967, **37**, 93.
2. Christmas, J. & Davis, E., Group therapy programs with the socially deprived in community psychiatry. *Int. J. of Group Psychother.*, 1965, **15**, 464.
3. Normand, W., et al. The acceptance of the psychiatric walk-in clinic in a highly deprived community. *Amer. J. of Psychiat.*, 1963, **120**, (6), 533.
4. Normand, W. et al. A systematic approach to brief therapy for patients from a low socio-economic community. Paper read at annual meeting of Amer. Orthopsychiat. Assn., 1966.
5. Overall, B., & Aronson, H. Expectations of psychotherapy in patients of lower socio-economic class, *Amer. J. of Orthopsychiat.*, 1963, **33**, 421.
6. Peck, H. An application of group therapy to the intake process. *Int. J. of Group Psychother.*, 1953, **23**, 338.
7. Sadock, B., & Gould, R. A preliminary report on short-term group psychotherapy on an acute adolescent male service. *Int. J. of Group Psychother.*, 1964, **14**, 465.
8. Stone, A., et al. The use of diagnostic groups in a group therapy program. *Int. J. of Group Psychother.*, 1954, **4**, 274.
9. Wolf, A. Short-term group psychotherapy. In L. Wolberg (Ed.). *Short-term psychotherapy*. New York, Grune and Stratton, 1965.
10. Yalom, I. A study of group therapy dropouts. *Arch. of Psychiat.*, 1966, **14**, 393.

Chapter 21

Experience with Multifamily, Time-Limited, Outpatient Groups at a Community Psychiatric Clinic

Jane Donner, Ph.D., and Anita Gamson, B.S.

A new short-term treatment, combining group and family therapy, has been added to the program of our outpatient community psychiatric clinic. We shall present here our experience in treating 30 adolescents and their families in eight groups. This treatment model combines the rationales of family therapy and group therapy: that a person's emotional problems are in a broader sense a family problem, requiring a study of the family interaction; and that people can explore and work through some aspects of their problems to advantage in a group setting. Our objectives are: (1) to provide a setting in which all members of the group can be involved in an exploration of what is going on in the families that contributes to the problems of the adolescents; (2) to help the families search for new and better solutions to the problems that are revealed; (3) to utilize the insights gained as a supplementary diagnostic tool in recommending further therapy if indicated.

Family therapy grew out of the recognition that the family often behaves as if it were a psychological unit. Family therapy is based on the premise that it is not the person but the family that is the problem when trouble arises with a family member, and its goals are to change the structure and functions of the family group (2).

Reprinted from *Psychiatry*, 1968, 31, 126-137, by special permission of The William Alanson White Psychiatric Foundation, Inc., and the authors. Copyright 1968, The William Alanson White Psychiatric Foundation. Dr. Donner is a Group Counselor at the University of Maryland Counseling Center, College Park, Maryland, and a Psychotherapist at the Community Psychiatric Clinic, Bethesda, Maryland. Mrs. Gamson is a Psychotherapist at the Community Psychiatric Clinic, Bethesda, Maryland.

Group therapy proceeds from the idea that many emotional problems arise from people's distortions of their relationships with others and can therefore best be examined and worked through in a group setting which reproduces on a small scale the situation in which the problems exist.

The adolescent has the task of making the transition from his family unit to the larger world outside as he approaches maturity, gradually achieving ego autonomy for himself so that he can function as an independent person. The family unit must be flexible enough to accommodate to his growth needs. Whatever the reason may be for referral of adolescents to a psychiatric clinic, they are often caught in some way in the conflicting value systems of family, peer group, and society in general.

The theory underlying the treatment model discussed in this paper is as follows: If the family is a unit, perhaps it can be combined with other units in the manner of group therapy and thus add to the benefits achieved in group therapy, such as peer support, the stimulation of conflicting value systems, encouragement to verbalization through the example set by others, and the opportunity for reality testing.

Harry Stack Sullivan in the 1930's and 1940's led the movement to examine the influence of interpersonal experiences. In the same period there occurred a development in the theory and practice of analytically oriented group psychotherapy (3, 15). Sociologists and social psychologists were at the same time conducting research into small group process (4, 10). Today many therapists make sophisticated use of the resulting new understanding of group dynamics in combination with psychoanalytic concepts (17).

In the early 1950's the significance of the family as a psychological unit began to be recognized (17). Jackson spoke of family homeostasis in 1954 and said that "emphasis on family interaction is but a logical development in the natural history of psychiatry" (6). From the mid-fifties on, many significant studies have appeared concerning the theory and practice of family-centered therapy, leading to a much better understanding of family dynamics (1, 12, 19).

Parloff in 1961 delineated four stages in psychiatric thinking regarding the family (11): (1) outright avoidance of the family altogether while treating the individual, as in classical psychoanalysis; (2) focus on the parent "as the noxious agent" and treating him (or usually her) simultaneously, though separately and by a different therapist; (3) treatment of the relationship, with the different therapists of family members conferring about the family, or with one therapist treating members of the same family but apart from one another; (4)

finally, family-centered therapy, going directly to the relationship existing between the patient and his family, with the idea that the patient could be understood best as part of the family system.

The practice of treating several families together in one therapy group is a relatively recent development. Groups of marital couples are now no rarity, and other combinations of family members from several families have been reported. During the sixties there have been several reports of groups of adolescents and their parents in hospital settings; these have dealt with severely ill inpatients.

We have learned of only three reports of outpatient multifamily groups of adolescents and their parents: Davies and her co-workers reported on an experience with groups of families in a psychiatric day center (5). Kimbro and his co-workers have described a study of several outpatient groups of carefully selected, underachieving eleventh-grade boys and their parents (8). Leichter and Schulman have reported an experience with an ongoing group of three families which had run for over a year (9). We offer here what we think is the first report on an attempt in a community psychiatric clinic to engage randomly selected teen-agers of both sexes with their parents in short-term outpatient groups.

PROCEDURE

Format

Eight groups have been conducted thus far at this community psychiatric clinic, seven with both of us functioning as co-therapists, one run by one therapist alone. The groups were composed of three or four teen-agers, together with their parents. In the last five groups, some teen-aged siblings were included. Each group met for an hour and a half once a week, with sessions scheduled in the evenings to make it easier for fathers to attend. Five groups ran for sixteen sessions, one for ten. The seventh group became the eighth, in that two families elected to continue and new families were added. We experimented here with an open-ended situation, with families leaving and entering at different times, in a total of 30 sessions.

An initial intake interview of an hour or two, with one or both of the therapists, included both parents and the adolescent, and sometimes a sibling as well. A history was taken, the nature of the group was explained, and questions were answered. Therapy was begun as soon as a new group was formed.

The young people, ranging in age from 13 to 17, were referred to the clinic by schools, courts, private psychiatrists, and parents for a variety of reasons, such as truancy, gross underachieving, promiscuity, shoplifting, despondency, and so on. The groups consisted of boys only, girls only, or two boys and two girls. Aside from ruling out obvious psychosis and gross mental retardation in the teen-ager who was the initial patient, we have not made any further efforts to be selective.

Some families selected themselves out. Several families invited to join a group were so resistant to the idea that it did not seem useful to try further persuasion. Other families who were hesitant at first were eventually willing to commit themselves to the 16 sessions. As we gained experience we were able to present the recommendation with confidence and most families responded by accepting it.

There was some staff discussion about the wisdom of including youngsters who engaged in extreme acting out, who might be disruptive to the group. In our experience, however, this was not an important factor in the selection. Two teen-agers ran away and one attempted suicide during the course of the groups, but in each case the young person returned to the group and his actions became part of the group material.

We had mixed reasons initially for choosing the 16-week period: (1) We were uneasy at first about trying this kind of group and decided to make it time-limited in case we found it unworkable or too difficult either for ourselves or for the group members. (2) We thought we would stand a better chance of involving the fathers if we could present the group as occupying a definite time bloc. (3) We had just heard William Lordi report the gratifying results of his time-limited therapy groups at the Memorial Guidance Clinic in Richmond, Va. *

Initial Phase

At the first session of such groups, we repeat essentially what was said in the intake interview, approximately as follows: When a young person gets into difficulties it is not something that involves him alone, but the whole family. We do not think in terms of one person being "the bad one" or "the sick one." We feel that when trouble arises there is something going on in the family circle which people do not understand. It has been our experience that when a family explores what might really be going on, it is better equipped to deal with whatever the

* Report to the Mid-Atlantic Group Psychotherapy Society in Baltimore in 1964. In his program Lordi had latency-age boys in one group and parents in another, run simultaneously.

difficulty may be. Therefore, that will be our focus in this time-limited group. All of us together will try to understand what is going on in the different families that contributes toward the young people's difficulties, and each can make contributions to the others. A person may have a blind spot for what is going on in his own family since it is so close, but he may be able to see something in another family's interaction that helps clarify his own situation. Again, people have different ways of dealing with family problems. By observing other families in action, people can get new ideas and perhaps try them out if they seem appropriate. Feelings arising in the session which relate to any of the group members can be communicated, discussed, and understood. In this way new insights are gained that can apply to one's own family.

We then list the simple ground rules: First and most important, all three members of each family involved—or all four or five if siblings are included—must attend every session. Next, there are no restrictions on subject matter during the sessions. Third, no one is to be punished at home for anything he says during a group meeting. We wish to achieve as free and open communication as possible, reaching a level of honesty that goes beyond the normal manner of functioning in the outside world. Fourth, the raw materials we will deal with are of two sorts: the things which group members wish to report from their family experience outside the clinic, and the feelings and observations they have in this room here and now. In this manner we will all of us together try to understand what is going on in each family and thus enable them to make changes. A fifth ground rule that we have found useful asks families not to socialize outside the clinic during the life of the group, since that may affect their freedom to interact within the group. We then remain silent and allow the members to take over.

Three Stages of Group Experience

The young people are often sullen, timid, or insolent at the beginning of the group sessions. Typically the initial sessions are dominated by the parents, who complain about their children's conduct, particularly about their children's unwillingness to assume responsibility. The parents are usually angry, unhappy, even despairing about what has gone wrong. They feel that they have tried everything, that nothing works, and that they have failed in their job as parents. They are also often frightened at the thought that their child may be mentally ill, and feel hampered in dealing with him on that account.

In the second stage, the young people generally become better able to join the group interaction. They, too, are angry, hurt, and despairing. We often experience violent confrontations by members of the same family and by members of different families as well, who take sides and express empathy or hostility as the case may be. Even those who are relatively quiet during the session are reported by other members to be involved in heated discussions concerning their problems or those of the other families on the way home or during the week between sessions. The young people both support and criticize one another, and so do the parents.

In the third stage—and we find this stage better defined as we have increased our competence in dealing with these groups—the fact of one's role as parent or child diminishes in importance, as when a father expresses sympathy to a child of another family, and relates his own similar experiences as a boy. Thus the participants often relate as fellow human beings able to resonate with one another across the lines of generation or sex or family. There seems to develop something of a good-natured tone, despite the frequent vehemence of the interaction. Some quieter intervals of mutual understanding occur. In other words, the families often appear to have adjusted to the idea that it is all right to bring out strong feelings, and that perhaps something productive can come of it. They begin to realize that warmth is not excluded by doing so—and, in fact, that quite the opposite may be the case: They can experience more warmth as a result of their new freedom. Some shifts in family relationships may begin to take place.

The progression of these three stages is demonstrated in one family's experience in this type of group therapy. The 17-year-old son, Jim, in his fury and despair made a suicide attempt between the third and fourth sessions. The early sessions were full of harsh mutual accusations and frightening threats by Jim that he would leave forever. But in the tenth session, the atmosphere in the room changed and softened. The concern of the whole group for him and his parents' anxiety and love for him finally seemed to come through to Jim. The father, a very busy man who had largely left the care of the children to his wife had now stopped deferring to his wife in order to keep peace and had taken the initiative of negotiating with the school authorities himself in a way supportive to both son and wife. This in turn had helped the mother to give up some of her nagging behavior. Another mother had pointed out to Jim's father that he spoke to Jim in a school-teacherish manner. He pondered between sessions about this remark, and then admitted its validity, asking her if she recognized this quality in him because she saw it in herself as well. She confessed laughingly that this was indeed so. Two other fathers told about the difficulties they had had in school. In this session, Jim no longer appeared as the furious

rebel against parents and all society, but rather seemed to be a
tired and sad boy wanting help. He referred to himself as a mixed-
up kid and mentioned a school where he thought he could
function. The remaining sessions consolidated these gains. Jim
was sent to the school he referred to and has been doing well there
for several months. *

We were dissatisfied with our attempt at an open-ended
group—the seventh group, which became the eighth. Some
members had wanted to continue, while others did not, so we
decided to try to keep the group at four families at any given
time, allowing them to move in or out without adhering to the
time limitation. The results did not appear as satisfactory as in
the closed groups. A major drawback appeared to be that the
families were deprived of the three stages of group experience
described above, and thus of an important part of the therapy.
Relevant to our experience is a comment by Whitman in
discussing T-group theory: "It is worth noting that the group
and its individuals are able to do and discuss things only because
the end is in sight. Opportunities for learning are maximized
because reactive fears of criticism are mitigated by the
diminishing time element" (18).

We recall a moving scene in the last session of one group: A
girl who had been referred to the clinic for depression
culminating in attempted suicide suddenly confronted her father
with her belief that he did not love her. Through sobs, she said
this was her last chance because it was the last session, and she
had to say it now or never. The father was dumfounded and
responded haltingly that he cared for her very much. The wall
between them was breached. This encounter certainly appeared
to contain elements of a corrective emotional experience.

RESULTS

Evolution of Techniques

Initially each of these groups was composed of three or four

---

* It is interesting to note that the three stages here defined appear to parallel
the typical stages of a T-group on the National Training Laboratories model
[see Bradford, (4)], or a study group of the Tavistock Institute of Human
Relations. One of the authors (J. D.) has participated in several such groups.
In December, 1966, she was in one group of a small two-group laboratory, with her young adult son in the other. Both felt this to be a valuable
contribution to mutual understanding. There are instances of T-groups for
marital couples, but we are not aware of any which include two generations
of the same family. The ramifications of such a powerful experience were it to
involve the most important persons in one's life rather than a group of strangers deserve further exploration.

teen-agers who were the referred patients, plus their parents. Our reason for omitting siblings at first was that we did not want to make the groups too unwieldy, and we did not at that time realize their importance in the family problem. As we proceeded we found that other teen-agers in the families were frequently mentioned and appeared to be playing important roles. Beginning with the third of the eight groups, we began inviting these siblings to join the group and found their presence useful. In several cases, the siblings themselves asked to join. It often became evident that the referred patient was by no means the person in the most trouble; including the siblings meant bringing an unknown variable into the realm of the known. There have been seven siblings so involved up to now. No children under the age of twelve have participated; we felt that they might find it too difficult to hold their own verbally in such a group.

From the start we worked from the conviction that it is invaluable to involve the fathers in the therapy of their children. We have become even more sure of this as time goes on. We have become stricter about insisting on the fathers' participation, and we regard most excuses for their absence as resistance. The excuses by no means always come from the fathers. Often the mothers represent their husbands as unwilling to involve themselves, whereas we find in talking with the fathers that they are quite willing and interested. They make a major contribution and their presence is absolutely essential to this sort of therapy. For the teen-agers it is often greatly reassuring to see that their fathers care enough about them to devote this time and effort to trying to work on the family problems. For the mothers, it means that their husbands are with them at a crucial time. For the fathers, it is a demonstration of how they are needed and valued as much more than breadwinners. Further, only when the father is present is it possible to observe and illuminate difficulties in the parental relationship which are affecting the young people.

In our first groups, we therapists maintained a too passive role. We regarded it as our function to hold the focus to family interaction, helping people articulate their feelings, and watching for verbal and nonverbal cues. Group members had the burden of introducing subjects for discussion and working out their own answers to questions that they had first directed to the therapists as "the experts." Significant insights may have been lost for lack of recognition and emphasis. As the groups progressed, the members developed some facility for pursuing their explorations relatively unaided, but the most consistent complaint at the close of the sessions was that time was wasted for lack of guidance.

In later sessions, we experimented with a more active role,

inviting comments from the reticent and checking the domination of the more aggressive. As we have become more accustomed to the stresses of this sort of group, we find ourselves able to be generally freer in interacting with the group members and with one another during the sessions, becoming more truly participant observers. At the same time, we continue to try not to allow ourselves to be lured into the tempting role of advice-givers. Our basic premise remains that when these families can bring into consciousness what is happening within them on the unconscious level, they can work out their own solutions.

We are more than ever convinced of the value of keeping everyone focused on the basic objective: namely, to discern what is going on in the family that appears to be hampering the best development of the young person. Whenever the discussion slides off onto the shortcomings of the schools, society, and so on, we say, yes, these things may have a bearing on the problem but we can't do anything about that here. What we have to work with is ourselves, right here in this room, and what we can observe about one another, and the conclusions we can draw here about the family situation. We find that the families respond to this sort of direction, and they often surprise and delight us with their cogent observations.

We had some difficulty forming our first groups; we began interviewing in September, 1964, and it was not until December and January that the first two groups were formed. This was partially because of our own insecurity in presenting this recommendation to the families concerned. Now that we have gained confidence in our ability to cope with this potentially explosive group experience, we find we are better able to involve families. We feel now that it is useful if the intake interview is done by one therapist, or both if possible, with the patient and parents present from the outset. Any psychological testing or psychiatric evaluations that appear advisable can be scheduled during the course of the group experience; a complete social history is not initially necessary because it develops out of the material brought into the group, and the family is involved in an exploration of its difficulties as soon as it undergoes its initial interview experience at the clinic.

One technique we developed for the later groups is a discussion of family systems and how the group members would define their own. We introduce some examples, as shown in the accompanying chart, starting with a model of the "ideal" family, with free communications all around. Then we sketch in on a blackboard other possible models, such as the four presented in the illustration, encouraging the families to consider where they and the others present might fit. Occasionally they suggest other models as more appropriate. The families find this an intriguing

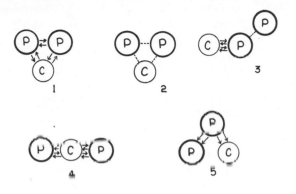

Figure 1. Models of some family systems. P = parent; C = child. 1. Communications free-flowing among all members of the family. 2. Communications completely inadequate. 3. Communications free-flowing between one parent and child, but other parent left out. 4. Communications free-flowing between child and each parent, but child, in middle, blocks communication between parents. 5. One-way communications by one parent with child and other parent.

exercise and the various members usually participate with much interest. It helps them to gain a more objective view of their interaction and to consider alternatives if they find their own models deficient. The device offers an additional parameter, but is only incidental to the whole group experience. Much depends on when and how it is used.

Achievement of Goals

We believe that the objectives of this program as stated in the introduction are achieved.

(1) The families are able to make use of the setting provided to explore what is going on within the family that interferes with the best development of the young person initially referred. The more obvious learning occurs on the level of simple observation of how other families do things. Families who have found themselves immobilized over issues such as chores, finances, allowances, bedtime hours, dating rules, and the like, have been able to compare their expectations with those of other families. By recognizing that other people are able to maintain different patterns, they have often found a way to compromise, to establish a few ground rules that help contain quarrels, and to begin to look at the feelings behind the impasse.

(2) The second objective is that of helping families search for

better ways to solve the problems that emerge. As the process of communicating with other families develops, there also develops a freer interchange among members of the same family, so that they say many things to one another for the first time. This fact in itself often makes it possible to achieve a better definition of the problem area on the basis of more information than was available before. With more data, the family is better equipped to search for solutions.

The B family illustrates this point.

Mike, aged 14, was referred to the clinic for underachievement at school and agressiveness with school authorities. His father complained in the group that his children were uncooperative. It emerged that during Easter vacation Mr. B, to help Mike learn writing and public speaking, had assigned him the topic "Onions," on which he was to write a composition and give an oral report to the family. Then he was to grow this crop in the garden, a chore that the boy hated. The other families found the onion project funny, and did not hesitate to criticize it, especially when they learned that all the children in the family were regularly assigned similar projects which they liked as little but dared not protest. The topic was discussed for part of two sessions and then Mr. B decided to drop the Easter project, saying ruefully that perhaps imposing it on his family hadn't been a very good idea. Mike, who had hung his head during the initial sessions and refused to look anyone in the eye, became freer and more direct in the later sessions. Toward the end, he reported happily that his father had *asked* him what time he wanted to be picked up from the Youth Center rather than dictating the time. Mrs. B., whose role at the start had been that of a frightened peacemaker trying to stand between an irascible husband and a sullen son, was able after several sessions to talk about her fear of quarrels and her need to placate her husband. He in turn spoke of the stresses and frustrations of his life, which contributed to his short temper, and his hopes of helping his children to an education better than his, which would place them in a more favorable position as adults to earn a decent living. The recommendation at the end of the 16 sessions was that the family take a vacation from therapy and see how they could work with the insights they had gained. They were encouraged to return to the clinic for consultations in case of future difficulties.

(3) The third objective is that of using the groups as a supplementary diagnostic tool in order to recommend further therapy, as appropriate. This group experience provides a clearer picture of the family dynamics than would otherwise be possible. Tensions existing between the parents, to which the young person is reacting, can be brought into the open. Ways in which the young people are acting out their parents' unconscious conflicts can be explored. The question of what happens to the family equilibrium if one member makes a change can be asked, and sometimes a hint of an answer appears as the families are observed in action. The families involve themselves in a process

in which they are approached as intelligent and feeling human beings rather than as patients or culprits, and this sometimes enables them to see the logic of referrals which they might not have been able to accept at all at the outset, when the teen-ager was defined as "the sick one." The S family provides an illustration:

The father in the S family and 15-year-old John would vie for the swivel chair during the group sessions, the son taking it whenever he could and being ordered out of it by Mr. S. Their fight for the seat of authority became obvious to the group. On one occasion a therapist was called out of the room for an emergency and returned later to find that John had usurped her chair. The parents *looked* their disapproval but they *said* nothing. The group discussed the situation and the parents' fear of commenting on the boy's inappropriate action, and also his desire to take over an adult's chair. This boy brought some fresh acting-out incident to the group meeting each week—cigarette stealing, suspension from school, and the like. Many meetings began with John sitting close to his protective mother while his father berated him from across the room. Within five sessions it became clear to everyone that the boy was manipulating both parents and in turn was being used in the fight between them. It became evident in the group that Mr. and Mrs. S were no longer functioning as mates except in the sense of maintaining a household and keeping up appearances. A major function of John's difficult behavior was to provide a focus around which the parents could unite, which they were unable to do in other areas.

In the past such a boy might have been placed in individual therapy or perhaps a boys' group, and the mother or both parents might have had concomitant sessions with a social worker. In this case the therapy experience in the group appeared to be sufficient for the boy. He recognized the part he was playing in the family triangle, and how destructive it was to himself. He stopped his acting out quite dramatically, he settled down at school, and his grades improved. That was a year ago and he has not been in trouble since. The parents, on the other hand, who in the past might have been only peripherally involved in therapy, were then able to confront one another directly instead of through John; they recognized the problem in their marriage, and entered a couples' therapy group where they have been working on their marital relationship. Considering that there are four other children in the family, two with problems severe enough to require referral to the clinic, this outcome was gratifying on several levels.

Aside from the achievement of these specific objectives, the efficacy of the therapy, as always, is difficult to assess. Eight of the families in our first three groups were interviewed by a social work student several months after the conclusion of the sessions. Seven of the eight reported that communications between family members had improved as a result of their group participation. Members of six families thought they had gained a better understanding of the other members of their families in these groups. Three of the families reported improvement in relationships between parents and adolescents. Four families said that they had arrived at a clearer understanding of the causes of their problems through this group experience. Three of these parental couples saw more clearly their own contribution to the problem.

There is negative feedback as well: In the eight families interviewed, several family members expressed disappointment in their group experience, though in two cases these same individuals said they would recommend such groups to their friends. Out of the 30 families in this study, three families dropped out of their groups, one after only one session.

The D's, who dropped out of our second group, had expressed great reluctance to join, and the son had vowed not to say a word in the group. The family sat silently during the first hour and a quarter of the first meeting, and then suddenly the father made a violent, 15-minute attack on all the youngsters present, calling them "boils on the face of the earth that should be eradicated." The next day Mrs. D called to apologize and to say they could not return. We talked with the parents several times after that but they refused to return to the group. We think that now with our present level of experience we might be able to anticipate and avoid such a traumatic explosion at this point in the group life.

In the case of the other two dropout families, one moved out of town and the other never really got involved. All four family members never came together to a group meeting; they came only in different combinations of two, and then only to five sessions. The mother came only once. This was a family of lower than average intelligence. They never seemed to grasp what we were trying to do in the group or the importance of weekly attendance by all members. We now require each individual family member to accept explicitly the commitment to attend every session.

There was symptomatic improvement in 20 of the 30 adolescents who were the referred patients. Fifteen of the 30 families left the clinic after the scheduled sessions were over. Eleven of these 15 families said they felt that relationships had improved because of their group membership. We later had five calls from schools and one from the juvenile court regarding adolescents who were former group members. In five of these cases we had strongly recommended further therapy but the families had not followed through.

For the other 15 families our groups were preliminary to more extensive therapy. One mother sought individual therapy for herself. Two families went into conjoint family therapy, bringing in other siblings. Two families have asked the clinic for an occasional consultative hour. Three sets of parents continued in married couples' groups to work on their own relationship, while their children continued in adolescents' groups. Two other couples continued in couples' groups without further involvement of their children. One 17-year-old boy chose to continue therapy in an adolescent group, paying his own way, and one boy continued therapy privately outside the clinic.

Overall, we and other clinic staff members feel the results of these groups to be very positive. On the basis of this experience, the Community Psychiatric Clinic in Bethesda, Maryland, has made such groups a part of its regular, community-oriented program, with several other staff members involved as multifamily group therapists. We believe that this therapy model is a valuable contribution to group and family therapy concepts and methodology.

DISCUSSION

In this 16 session combined family and group therapy, we try to help the group members talk freely about the stresses and strains to which they feel subject and which they often appear to be putting into words for the first time in this group experience. As these feelings emerge, often with great vehemence, we attempt to provide an atmosphere in which hurts can be aired, needs can be articulated, and each person can feel increasingly free to express whatever he has to say with the assurance that the entire group will hear him with respect. People get practice in making their feelings clear to one another. In these hurting families it is almost universally the case that each family member feels unappreciated, not respected, and not valued for himself. To the extent that these feelings can be brought into the open they can be dealt with. The people who really count most for each individual are right there in the room and are *hearing* what is being said to them, perhaps for the first time.

The theoretical base from which we operate is analytic, and thus excludes techniques such as those used in activity groups and inspirational groups. Within this broad definition, however, we have attempted to test and utilize whatever appears to us as potentially useful, and we have not felt bound by theoretical concepts in so doing.

Analytically oriented therapy in general, both individual and group, uses as prime tools the analysis of transferences and resistances and the uncovering of unconscious material. Even in these 16-session experiences there is some possibility of utilizing these tools—for example, in clarifying a mother's irrational identification of her son with an errant uncle, or a father's resentment of his wife as being overbearing like his mother.

Any analytically oriented therapy, whether group, or individual, must provide: (1) support; (2) a nonjudgmental atmosphere with tolerance and acceptance; (3) stimulation—pathological ideas should be expressed in the therapy situation; (4) encouragement to verbalization, with the possibility of abreaction and catharsis; and (5) the opportunity for reality testing. *

How do these conditions apply to the family groups under discussion? The families lose their feeling of having something wrong about them which isolates them from others. They are taken seriously, not only by the paid therapists but by their peers as well. They are not rejected by the group for revealing and exploring the family unhappiness—rather they are respected for their honesty. They come to play a vital role as active helpers of one another. As they articulate the thoughts and feelings that have long remained unspoken, they can feel the accompanying emotions and begin to work them through. The families can test out on themselves and with one another the insights they have gained and the changes they are making, with immediate feedback in the group.

Frequently illustrated in these groups are several concepts developed over the past two decades by researchers in family dynamics: for example, Johnson's recognition that the child tends to act out a parent's unconscious conflicts (7) the double-bind theory of Weakland and co-workers (16) according to which the child receives from the parents two related but contradictory and incongruous messages and is thus immobilized; Satir's finding that the child's symptom is very often a signal of trouble between the parents, who are focusing on their children because they dare not focus on each other (13); and Shapiro's concept of "parental delineation," according to which a child becomes boxed into a certain role—"Joe is a bum, wants to be a bum, always will be a bum"—and remains caught in it (14).

As such dynamics emerge in the group, the families get a feeling for what they can profitably work on even after the group experience is over. At the very least, they have been introduced to a new way of looking at their family relationships. Further therapy recommendations make more sense and become, at least in part, less threatening.

Economy was part of our motivation in trying these groups,

* Taken from a discussion in a seminar conducted by Morris B. Parloff as part of the Group Psychotherapy Training Program of the Washington School of Psychiatry, October 20, 1965.

both in terms of therapist time and in terms of duration of treatment. The groups turned out to be economical to some extent in terms of therapist time. We much prefer to work as co-therapists, however, finding that our own discussions before and after sessions and our combined observations are very useful to our work with the groups, and also help us to tolerate the high levels of tension generated in these groups. Our collaboration therefore doubles the amount of therapist time needed for such a group, but we feel that measured against the gain this is not an extravagance.

The economy this type of treatment presents is more in the direction of community mental health. Therapy can be offered to more people—an important factor, especially in clinics. But equally important, relationships within a particular family are eased, the other children benefit, and the people in the groups hopefully become somewhat more tolerant and more competent in their human relationships across the board. Some of the stigma and sting surrounding emotional illness is eased. Conceivably this sort of service could become an accepted community resource to which families could routinely turn, just as they go to the dentist or physician when something hurts them physically.

We are reminded of a remark made by Irving Schneider, Director of the Arlington Mental Health Center in Arlington, Virginia, in a meeting some time ago, to the effect that most clinics do long-term brief therapy. * These group sessions may be regarded as a way to do short-term brief therapy.

* In a meeting of the Washington Psychiatric Society on October 29, 1965.

REFERENCES

1. Ackerman, N. W. *The psychodynamics of family life: Diagnosis and treatment of family relationships.* New York: Basic Books, 1958.
2. Bell, J. E. A theoretical position for family group therapy. *Family Process,* 1963, **2**, 1-14.
3. Bion, W. R. *Experiences in groups and other papers.* London: Tavistock Publications, 1961.
4. Bradford, L. P., Gibb, J. R., & Benne, K. P. I—*Group theory and laboratory method.* New York: Wiley, 1964.
5. Davis, I. J., Ellenson, G., & Young, R. Therapy with a group of families in a psychiatric day center. *American Journal of Orthopsychiatry,* 1966, **36**, 134-146.
6. Jackson, D. D. The question of family homeostasis. *Psychiatric Quarterly Supplement,* 1957, **31**, 79-90. First presented at the annual convention of the American Psychological Assn., St. Louis, 1954.

7. Johnson, A. M., & Szurek, S. A. Etiology of antisocial behavior in delinquents and psychopaths. *Journal of the American Medical Association,* 1954, **154,** 814-817.
8. Kimbro, E. L., Jr., et al. A multiple family group approach to some problems of adolescence. *International Journal of Group Psychotherapy,* 1967, **17,** 18-24.
9. Leichter, E., & Schulman, G. L. Emerging phenomena in multi-family group treatment. Paper given at annual conference of the American Group Psychotherapy Assn., New York, January, 1967.
10. Lewin, K. *Resolving social conflict.* New York: Harper, 1948.
11. Parloff, M. B. The family in psychotherapy. *Archives of General Psychiatry,* 1961, 4, 445-451.
12. Ryckoff, I., Day, J., & Wynne, L. C. Maintenance of stereotyped roles in the families of schizophrenics. *Archives General Psychiatry,* 1959, 1, 93-98.
13. Satir, V. M. *Conjoint family therapy: A guide to theory and techniques.* Palo Alto: Science and Behavior Books, 1964.
14. Shapiro, R. L. The origin of adolescent disturbances in the family: Some considerations in theory and implications for therapy. In. G. H. Zuk and I. Boszormenyi-Nagy, *Family therapy and disturbed families.* Palo Alto: Science and Behavior Books, 1967.
15. Slavson, S. R. *Analytic group psychotherapy with children, adolescents, and adults.* New York: Columbia University Press, 1950.
16. Weakland, J. H. The "double-bind" hypothesis of schizophrenia and three-party interaction. In D. D. Jackson (Ed.), *The etiology of schizophrenia.* New York: Basic Books, 1960, pp. 373-388.
17. Whitaker, D. S., & Lieberman, M. A. *Psychotherapy through the group process.* New York: Atherton, 1964.
18. Whitman, R. M. Psychodynamic principles underlying T-group processes. In L. P. Bradford, J. R. Gibb, and K. P. Benne (Eds.), *T-group theory and laboratory method.* New York, Wiley, 1964.
19. Wynne, L. C. Some indications and contra-indications for exploratory family therapy. In I. Boszormenyi-Nagy and J. L. Framo (Eds.), *Intensive family therapy: Theoretical and practical aspects, with special reference to schizophrenia.* New York: Harper and Row, 1965.

Chapter 22

Crisis Family Therapy

Frank S. Pittman, III, M.D., Carol DeYoung, M.S., Kalman
Flomenhaft, M.S.W., David M. Kaplan, Ph.D., and Donald
G. Langsley, M.D.

There has been a recent upsurge of interest in finding
alternatives to psychiatric hospitalization. If for no other reason,
this interest is due to the often-made observation (3, 4) that
psychiatric hospitalization is unavoidably regressive and may
have far-reaching destructive consequences on the patient's self-
esteem, his relationship to his family, and his relationship
to society. The discharged psychiatric patient too often becomes a second class citizen with no sanctuary from his
iatrogenic stigmata except the highly addicting hospital.

Acute decompensation does not begin or continue or end in
an interactional vacuum. There is an ever-increasing focus on the
role of the family in precipitating, maintaining, or reversing
symptomatology. However, the patient's relationship with his
family is usually seen in one of two ways: (1) The patient should
be protected from his destructive family, or (2) the family should
be protected from the destructive patient. Both points of view fail
to consider the ongoing family relationship before, during, and
after the hospitalization. As Querido (12) states, "Any removal of
a mentally disturbed patient from his social background implies
the sidestepping of the nucleus of the problem."

Acknowledgement of these and other disadvantages of
hospitalization has led to the establishment of Psychiatric
Emergency Clinics, Suicide Prevention Centers, Day-Night
Wards, and such productive work as the Worthing Experiment in

Reprinted from *Current Psychiatric Therapies*, Vol. 6, J. H. Masserman
(Ed.). New York, Grune and Stratton, 1966, pp. 187-196, by permission of the
publisher and the authors. Dr. Pittman is Director of Psychiatric Services,
Grady Memorial Hospital, Atlanta, Georgia. Miss DeYoung is a Psychiatric
Public Health Nurse with the Family Treatment Unit, Denver. Mr. Flomen-
haft is a Doctoral Student of Social Work at the University of Denver. Dr. Kaplan
is Director of Social Work, Stanford University, Palo Alto, California. Dr.
Langsley is Professor and Chairman, Department of Psychiatry, University of
California School of Medicine, Davis, California.

England (2), the Amsterdam Home Service (9) and the Community Extension Service in Boston (6). These experiences have demonstrated that large numbers of severely emotionally ill patients can be treated outside the mental hospital with individual and community oriented treatment and services. The Family Treatment Unit at Colorado Psychopathic Hospital has set out to test the hypothesis that family oriented crisis therapy has advantages over either hospitalization or out-patient individually oriented crisis therapy.

Colorado Psychopathic Hospital is an 80 bed acute treatment facility serving the entire state. One thousand patients a year are hospitalized there for an average stay of 25 days. These are all voluntary patients who come through a 24-hour Emergency Psychiatric Clinic where 75 per cent of the applicants are treated as outpatients and only 25 per cent hospitalized or referred to the Family Treatment Unit. In the first year of its operation, the latter treated 50 families, each including at least one member who would have been hospitalized on an emergency basis.

The Family Treatment Unit is manned by a team which consists of a psychiatrist, a psychiatric social worker, and a psychiatric public health nurse. The research team of a psychologist and a research assistant obtain a variety of measures of family and individual functioning which can be repeated at six month intervals by independent raters and compared with control cases which were not seen by the Family Treatment Unit but hospitalized instead. The Family Treatment Unit is called, 24 hours a day, on all cases which are considered candidates for immediate voluntary hospitalization at Colorado Psychopathic Hospital, who live within an hour's drive of the hospital, and who have some adult relative living under the same roof. By a random selection system, we take 25 per cent of these cases, about one new family each week.

In most of our cases, we have seen a series of events which have led to the request for hospitalization. Initially, there is a change in the family equilibrium. This may be due to a change in family composition (e.g., birth of a child, visit of an in-law), a change in role performance of some member (e.g., physical illness, sexual maturation), or a change in circumstances which requires a new role (e.g., everyone is unemployed; the family moves to an unfamiliar community). Such changes require a reshuffling of the family's role assignments. This is a process which families undergo from time to time. A family crisis occurs when an important role is not being filled. If there is no agreement about who should fill the role or if the designated member cannot or will not undergo the proposed role change, family pressure builds. A susceptible member may escape the tension through psychotic symptoms, seemingly irrational behavior, suicide attempts, or requests for sanctuary in the hospital. His refusal to undergo a role change in itself may be enough to make the family demand hospitalization for him.

This process may be dramatic and acute or it may be so gradual and insidious that the precipitating factors and sequence of events have been buried under years of struggling over the chronic family impasse. Our crisis intervention has the goal of restoring the individual and the family to functioning. Often a functional status quo can be quickly restored while the family copes with or prevents the changes with which it is faced. In families in which the dysfunction is chronic, our goal is to reduce the immediate pressure and institute a temporary set of workable family rules and role assignments which will allow functioning until satisfactory permanent agreements can be reached. As Semrad (13) describes it, "Before we attempt to study the characterological underpinnings which led to decompensation, we first assist the patient (and the family) to recompensate."

TECHNIQUES

Our therapy, therefore, begins by attempting to prevent the requested designation of one family member as "the patient," the one who must be removed and/or changed. Our first step is to evaluate the family immediately, calling the absent relatives from school or work. We challenge the theory that the patient is responsible for the family problems, and replace this with our view that the family is in a crisis to which all are reacting. The patient's psychotic ramblings or suicide gestures are interpreted as attempts at communication. They are made to appear much more logical than they seemed before. The patient is instructed to communicate in more acceptable fashion and usually does. Eliciting the history of family role changes leading to the crisis, demonstrates the involvement of all members. If there is lack of cooperation on the part of any family member, his anxiety about facing or revealing his guilt and responsibility must be appreciated and explored. Occasionally considerable firmness is required. So far, in only two cases has the family been so totally unwilling to accept this responsibility at the initial contact that hospitalization occurred that day. In both cases, the spouse cited opinions from previous psychiatrists that he was totally uninvolved in the mate's illness.

Most often, the family is already aware of its role and quite guilty about it. They are desperate and open to our suggestions. We demonstrate their involvement, outline their responsibility, elicit an agreement to try our approach, explain our around-the-clock availability, schedule a home visit within 24 hours, and then assign tasks to each family member. There is much emphasis on responsibility, similar to that outlined by Glasser (5).

We challenge the patient and his family with the immediate stand that the presenting symptoms are a means of escape from responsibility, that insistence upon hospitalization is a further attempt to escape responsibility, and that the crisis can be resolved responsibly by a willingness to examine and modify family roles and rules. This latter is both a challenge and a promise to the family.

Therefore, the assignment of tasks is important and delicate. It demonstrates our expectations that the family members function, it clarifies our evaluation of role expectations, it puts us in the temporary position of making role assignments, and it tests the cooperation of the family. Tasks have included such things as cleaning the kitchen, applying for a job, writing a letter, discussing or not discussing some issue, fixing the washing machine, getting married, going out to dinner, going to the zoo, taking or not taking certain medications. Usually each member is given some task. The task is often one for the whole family. Invariably it involves a higher degree of functioning and is family oriented. If the task is performed, the functional paralysis is ended, and the patient and the family look much improved. If not, we know we are not getting cooperation and must determine why. On occasion, one of the team may assist in the performance of the task, as sitting in the kitchen directing a housewife in preparing a meal or taking a phobic child to school.

Many patients and family members receive psychotropic medications. If the patient is so uncontrollably psychotic that he cannot immediately go home, he is heavily sedated and sent home after a few hours of rest or a night in the emergency room. In all of our cases to date we have seen marked improvement upon awaking.

Any social agencies already involved with the family are contacted immediately and if possible are involved in the planning. Ministers, general practitioners, parole officers, as well as psychiatrists, social workers, and particularly public health nurses have been involved, not just for history taking and as referral sources but even in the therapy sessions. At times the crisis has been precipitated by changes in the relationship with such helping sources.

The next step is a home visit. Querido (12) has observed that an emergency psychiatric treatment program "cannot be carried out behind a desk or from a chair. It must be an on-the-spot service, ready to go where the conflict comes out into the open." In the home we see relationships in vivo. This is particularly important in observing parent-child interaction. The home visit furnishes considerable amounts of information, but equally important is its effect on the therapeutic relationship. In the office we focus on dysfunction, but in the home we see evidence of good and bad functioning from past and present. Families know we have seen this evidence of their healthier role performance too. Therefore, the relationship is based not just on sickness but also on health.

Through these techniques we gain an entry into the family within the first 24 hours, place the responsibility for the patient's symptoms in the family, and relieve tensions sufficiently to proceed with our major task of renegotiating the family role assignments. Everyone is involved in therapy who is involved in the family, in the crisis, or in the decision-making hierarchy of the family (which often includes distant relatives). In this stage of therapy the family is seen daily, as it attempts to find a set of rules and role assignments which will allow it to advance from the present impasse to a new and better level of family and individual functioning or, if this is not possible, to return to the premorbid level of acceptable functioning. A set of compromises, in family roles, rules, and expectations, in what Don Jackson (8) describes as the quid pro quo, is attempted in the crucial conflict areas.

At this point in therapy, each family member is made acutely aware of his responsibility to the family as a whole. He sees that his actions in fulfilling his own needs have considerable effect upon the ability of others to fulfill their needs and their willingness to assist him in fulfilling his. The team has obtained some idea of each member's unmet expectations of the others, his involvement in the family as a major source of gratification, his ability to give and take, and his range of flexibility. We have discovered, as the family has rediscovered, the ways in which the family met its members' needs in more successful times and often have gained some idea of the ways in which the members have interacted more successfully with the people outside the marriage.

The focus has shifted from the symptomatic member as the "patient," to the family as the "patient," and then if necessary to the one family member least able and willing to compromise. This may be the patient, his spouse, or even a mother-in-law miles away. Pressure, direct or indirect, is exerted on this person to accept his responsibility and to change. If he is not the patient, which is more frequent since the patient is usually in more pain and therefore more motivated for change, the very act of our recognizing his role in the patient's symptoms may be sufficiently encouraging to the patient for him to give up his symptoms as an unnecessary weapon. If the stubborn member is a nonresidential member of the extended family, the nuclear family can disentangle themselves from him or threaten to. If the patient himself is unwilling to change, then we must reevaluate the covert reasons for seeking therapy and clarify this to the family and the patient. Frequently, husbands and wives will find they can function symptom free in their legitimate roles as breadwinner, housekeeper, and even sex partner, when their failure to do so would bring divorce rather than a sympathetic psychiatrist's ear.

We must specifically discourage, from the very beginning, attempts to avoid the responsibility of compromise. Family members who refuse to meet with us can be contacted at their jobs or found at their homes at night.

More commonly, the method of escape from responsibility is through the technique described by Eric Berne (1) as the game of "Wooden Leg." In this maneuver, the patient asks how we can expect her to clean house or have sex or be pleasant when she is crazy or depressed or immature. She then cites previous professional opinion to support her inabilities, and the family often supports her. Alternately, her husband may ask how we can expect him to work when she is so unpleasant and makes him so nervous. A common remark is "Why should I cooperate with him? I don't love him anymore." Family members who attempt such maneuvers are confronted with their irresponsibility.

Sometimes there is an unwieldy backlog of anger over chronic conflicts and past failures. In some families, no one wants to give an inch, and retaliation seems more important than improvement. Such families usually involve two passive-aggressives, a chronically depressed and frigid wife with a sociopathic, severely passive, or infantile husband, either of whom may be the patient. The two have never communicated, cannot compromise, relate sado-masochistically, and require repeated crises to function. If the present crisis also involves some changeable person, as a mother-in-law or adolescent child, the couple may be returned easily to its precrisis level of inadequate functioning, or hopefully, may use the crisis to set some changes in motion. If we can work only with the rigid couple, there is less hope of change. Our power tactics produce only power struggles. Compromise is impossible. If either partner has any pride, the challenging tactics of Jay Haley (7) are sometimes helpful. Without the presence of pride, we may suggest the couple separate. This has the effect of producing an alliance of the couple against the team. This alliance may end therapy, but it may also bring about temporary changes which allow improvement in the present symptoms and a lull in the longstanding battle.

A case in point was the Elder family. Mrs. Elder, age 60, was given a diagnosis of acute paranoid schizophrenia and was to be hospitalized. Confusion, bizarre remarks, delusions and hallucinations of persecution by her husband and other relatives had developed within the past two weeks while the couple was living in California. The marriage was an unrewarding one. Mr. Elder's alcoholism had brought Mrs. Elder closer to their only child, Mrs. Middle, near whom the couple had always lived. When the granddaughter, Mrs. Young, entered an ill-advised early marriage the year before, Mrs. Elder and Mrs. Middle both began ruminating guiltily about their own similar first marriages. Mr. Elder decided to move with his wife to California, where Mrs. Elder had a brother. Mr. Elder found a good job, but Mrs. Elder was unhappy there because of her husband's neglect, her inability to get along with her brother's new wife (who told Mrs. Elder she had had an affair with Mr. Elder), and because Mrs. Middle wrote depressed letters about Mrs. Young's plight. Mrs. Elder begged her husband to return to Denver. He refused. She became anxious, depressed, and finally impetuous. He became frightened and drove her back to Denver with the intention of hospitalizing her here while he returned to California.

This history was obtained in the first interview with Mr. and Mrs. Elder and Mrs. Middle. Mrs. Middle had served as her parent's marriage counselor through the years and was retained in this role for this interview. She decided her mother's delusions were largely true, that her father was largely wrong, and that she would block the hospitalization. All three were placed on medications and given the task of clarifying the plight of Mrs. Young. The home visit was postponed until Mr. Middle could return from a business trip.

The second day all three looked rested. Mrs. Elder was directed to communicate sensibly, rather than through symptoms. She did so. Mr. Elder was encouraged to call California, quit his job there, and get a job here. Mrs. Middle again was left as arbitrator.

On the third day Mrs. Young also came in. She assured everyone of her ability to run her life by herself and was therefore directed to do so and to leave her parents and grandparents alone. Mrs. Middle then sobbingly told of her own marital unhappiness and her need to lean on her mother. Mrs. Elder responded by demonstrating strength. Mr. Elder continued to ignore his wife's health and exaggerate her symptoms. He was confronted with this pattern and again encouraged to go to work. The fourth day involved a home visit and our first contact with Mr. Middle, who was pleased to have the Elders there since it buffered his interaction with his wife. Mrs. Elder talked of going to work. The fifth day we saw the Elders alone. Mr. Elder had found a job. Mrs. Elder was rational. They discussed their future. After four more visits in the next two weeks, we terminated with the family. Mrs. Elder's continued medication was to be handled by their family doctor. No further referral was felt necessary. At six month and twelve month follow-ups, the family was functioning as it had during the previous 40 years.

The Martin family presented many similarities. Mrs. Martin, age 40, had had three previous psychiatric hospitalizations for depression and catatonia, one following the birth of each of her last three children. Each of these three deliveries coincided with a separation from her husband or increased drinking and woman-chasing on his part. After the last hospitalization, which lasted eight months, the family moved from another state to Denver. For six years Mr. Martin was faithful and Mrs. Martin symptom free. Then, Mr. Martin quit his job and announced his plan to return to the other state, become a private detective, and have more affairs. Mrs. Martin refused to go. Mr. Martin spent four months without looking for a job. He then announced that he was leaving. Within two days, Mrs. Martin was catatonic. He refused to consider our suggested alternative to hospitalization. For six weeks, she made no improvement in the hospital, her course marked by angry outbursts at her husband. He refused to seek work, insisted his behavior had no influence on his wife, and tearfully protested that it wasn't fair of his wife to impede his freedom. Finally, she was discharged, unimproved, with the suggestion that he either get a job or commit her. Her family applied pressure against commitment. He reluctantly got a job. The next day she was symptom free. Unfortunately, the hospitalization merely reinforced the myth that the hospital somehow helped the situation.

RESULTS

Hospitalization was avoided completely in 42 of these 50 cases. Only three patients were hospitalized with acute conditions. Three other patients returned with subsequent crises and were hospitalized three to six months later. These six patients hospitalized at Colorado Psychopathic Hospital were there from two days to six weeks, the average being 17 days. Two other cases were referred to another hospital for long-term hospitalization after the crisis was resolved.

Of the 84 percent receiving no psychiatric hospitalization at all, there was an average of six home or office visits per family. Some member of 75 per cent of the families was referred to another agency for long-term outpatient services or therapy.

Ten of the 50 families called us over a month after the last visit about a subsequent crisis. Most of these were handled over the telephone. Several required one or two office visits, usually to arrange more appropriate referrals.

An obvious objection to not hospitalizing patients is the danger of suicide. Fourteen of our patients had attempted suicide, 20 had threatened suicide, and 10 presented some recognized danger of physical violence, usually child beating or assault. Of the other six, two were catatonic and four severely paranoid and presented an unstated danger of violence. The approach to the suicide danger was similar to that outlined by Offenkrantz, Church, and Elliot (11). We declared each person responsible for his own actions and clarified that neither we nor anyone else could stop them from killing themselves if they really wanted to. We encouraged the family to avoid being blackmailed by threats of suicide and encouraged the patients to express their needs verbally. Two patients with suicidal histories made minor gestures while angry with us for terminating contact with them. Two others made more serious attempts and were referred for long-term hospitalization, during which they made further attempts.

We doubt that hospitalization and rigid suicide precautions prevent many suicides. On the contrary, these precautions may provide a challenge to the suicidal patient who has constant reminders of the danger. We feel the appropriate response should be toward the effort at communication contained in the suicide attempt, rather than to the attempt itself.

CONCLUSION

We have demonstrated that at least 84 per cent of our referred psychiatric patients do not need psychiatric hospitalization. We know from our work and that of Werner Mendel (10), Freeman and Simmons (4), and others that a major effect of psychiatric hospitalization is psychiatric rehospitalization. We must now attempt to discover if it has any other effects.

We do not delude ourselves into believing that our method of crisis family therapy produces any personality pattern changes in the patient or even any permanent changes in the family. We hope we are discouraging chronicity, blunting some of the weapon value of symptoms, and demonstrating to families that they can resolve crises more economically and function more gratifyingly. The few cases with whom we have failed have been those with whom hospitalization has failed previously and subsequently. We feel we are presenting an effective alternative to psychiatric hospitalization.

REFERENCES

1. Berne, E. *Games people play*. New York: Grove Press, 1964.
2. Carse, J., et al. A district mental health service: the Worthing experiment. *Lancet*, 1958, **2**, 39-41.
3. Fisch, R. Resistance to change in the psychiatric community. *Arch. Gen. Psychiat.*, 1956, **113**, 359.
4. Freeman, H. E., & Simmons, O. G. *The mental patient comes home*. New York: John Wiley & Sons, 1963.
5. Glasser, W. *Reality Therapy*. New York: Harper & Row, 1965.
6. Greenblatt, M., et al. *The prevention of hospitalization: Treatment without admission for psychiatric patients*. New York: Grune & Stratton, 1963.
7. Haley, J. Marriage therapy. *Arch. Gen. Psychiat.*, 1963, **8**, 213.
8. Jackson, D. D. Family rules-marital quid pro quo. *Arch. Gen. Psychiat.* 1965, **12**, 589.
9. Lemkau, P. V., & Crocetti, G. M. The Amsterdam municipal psychiatric service: A psychiatric sociological review. *Amer. J. Psychiat.*, 1961, **117**, 779-83.
10. Mendel, W. Effect of length of hospitalization on rate and quality of

remission from acute psychotic episodes. *J. Nerv. Ment. Dis.*, 1966, 143, 226-233.

11. Offenkrantz, W. C. E., & Elliott, R. Psychiatric management of suicide problems in military service. *Amer. J. Psychiat.*, 1957, 114, 33.

12. Querido, A. *Early diagnosis and treatment services. Elements of a community mental health program.* New York: Milbank Memorial Fund, 1956.

13. Semrad, E. V., & Zaslow, S. L. Assisting psychotic patients to recompensate. *Ment. Hosp.*, 1964, 15, 361.

Chapter 23

Three-Day Hospitalization—A Model for Intensive Intervention

Gilbert Weisman, M.D., Alan Feirstein, Ph.D., and
Claudewell Thomas, M.D.

A previous paper (13) has described the theoretical rationale and planning for the development of an inpatient Emergency Treatment Unit (ETU) at the Connecticut Mental Health Center (CMHC). The ETU is designed to investigate the use of brief (three-day) intensive hospitalization as a model for providing inpatient care which is especially tailored to the type of problems presented by lower socioeconomic class patients. Such patients often present themselves at the emergency room of large city hospitals as being in the midst of an emotional crisis with which they cannot deal effectively. ETU admits such patients from the Yale-New Haven Hospital emergency room with the goal of helping the person focus on current life struggles in order to facilitate the individual's return to the level of functioning that preceded the disruption and crisis that led to his seeking hospitalization. Following discharge from the three-day hospitalization, a one-month outpatient follow-up helps provide continued focus on present adaptive tasks and also provides referrals for longer-term outpatient treatment where appropriate. It was hoped that by utilizing crisis-intervention concepts in a brief inpatient setting, it would be possible to avoid having an individual pushed further into the role of being a patient by institutional and social factors which often seem to operate within state hospital systems or longer-term treatment wards.

The present paper will describe the techniques of treatment employed on ETU, the structure of the unit, the population served, and the nature of the treatment given. Data will also be presented assessing the success of the ETU in averting longer-

Reprinted from *Archives of General Psychiatry*, 1969, **21**, 620-629, by permission of the publisher and the authors. Dr. Weisman is Supervising Psychiatrist, Mission Mental Health Center, San Francisco, California. Dr. Feinstein and Dr. Thomas are at the Connecticut Mental Health Center and the Department of Psychiatry, Yale University Medical School, New Haven, Connecticut.

term hospitalization, and some attempt will be made to describe demographic variables that were found to relate to rehospitalization rates.

TECHNIQUES

The following techniques are employed to facilitate adaptive resolution of crises and early return of the patient to his precrisis level of functioning.

Time-Limited Contracts

Before patients enter ETU an agreement is made that ETU will provide three days of inpatient treatment and then 30 days of outpatient follow-up. The hope here is that by making the contract for inpatient care a limited one, both patient and staff will not be encouraged to view the patient as a hopelessly sick individual who must be nurtured, fed, and totally protected by the institution.

This time-limited type of therapeutic alliance has only been recently introduced in several outpatient clinics (7, 9) in the form of a six-visit limit, but has rarely been formally introduced into inpatient settings as a therapeutic tool. Many hospitals have informal limitations, but these usually do not become integral parts of the therapeutic contract. Indeed, time limits are perceived in many institutions as hindrances to therapy rather than therapeutic tools. One effect of the time-limited contract is to establish a "set" which promotes rapid identification of problem areas and requires patients to begin quickly developing new modes of dealing with these problems. By limiting the time allotted, the patient is given both clear guidelines by which to gauge how rapidly he must present his problem and also some idea of how much work must be accomplished in each day. This also transmits the staff's expectation that the patient will be able to function within three days and leave the hospital. Patients requiring further hospitalization after three days are transferred to longer-term treatment facilities. One of the research questions to which this report will direct itself is how many patients can be discharged after just three days of inpatient treatment. What kind of people cannot be discharged rapidly?

Intensive Intervention through
Multiple-Therapist Teams

The patient is seen each day by several staff members (mostly nurses and aides) each of whom has scheduled interviews with the patient and shares responsibility for his treatment. The goal here was to minimize dependency upon a single god-like figure (the "doctor") upon whom the patient is implicitly encouraged to be totally dependent.

In addition, the nursing staffing pattern is constructed to give a wide spectrum of social, racial, and educational backgrounds. This variety of people and varying styles of therapeutic intervention resulting from differing background or training maximizes the efficacy of the team and makes it probable that at least one member of the team will be able to break through barriers the patient erects to those outside his age, racial, or ethnic background. It was hoped that the patient could, through interplay with ward staff, re-establish who he is and where he is going. Team members also interact with patients in several types of daily group therapy and in family therapy. Through this intensive interaction with staff it was also hoped that the patient would become open to the redefinitions of his situation implied in the philosophy and structure of the unit (i.e., that outpatient treatment after three days would be feasible and desirable).

Intensive involvement with ETU also facilitates rapid discharge in another way. The hospitalization is structured as a 33-day contract with an inpatient and outpatient phase so that discharge after three days is not the termination of an intensive involvement but a continuation of it. This fact motivates patients to choose outpatient care rather than further hospitalization since the latter would necessitate termination with people who have become important and are perceived as effective helping agents.

Maximization of Autonomy

The milieu and therapy are so designed as to minimize implications that the patient is helpless, and maximize those factors which promoted autonomous functioning. Self-reliance is reinforced by focusing on the patient's responsibility for his life, in particular for discharge plans and for what is to happen to him once he leaves. Most patients upon admission have an intense need to be taken care of which is closely related to feelings of being overwhelmed and helpless. This dependency is seen as a symptom of crisis rather than exclusively a symptom of the basic psychiatric disorder. Rapid reintegration is facilitated by having the patients participate actively in decision making (e.g., in decisions about whether they needed further hospitalization). Dependency needs are met through a sense of concern and interest, but at the same time the staff avoids doing things for the patient which he can be encouraged to do himself. Another part of the effort to maximize autonomy includes a minimization of institutional restrictions upon the patient's activities. Doors are not locked and patients are free to be in the lobby of the Mental Health Center which is open to the outside through the main door.

Adaptive Focus in Therapy

In brief therapy, emphasis is placed on dealing with recent problems which have overwhelmed the patient, with the goal of helping the patient evolve adequate, adaptive strengths to begin again to cope with his problems (7). These include not only intrapsychic and interpersonal conflict, but also many life stresses which are primarily environmental (e.g., work, finances, care of children). The latter are likely to be particularly overwhelming in the lower socioeconomic classes. By helping the patient to begin to deal with these immediate problems, the level of stress is reduced and the sense of being overwhelmed by life's multiple problems diminishes. The patient also receives relief from his sense of being overwhelmed and helpless by feeling that he has formed a therapeutic alliance with individuals that will give him help with the immediate problems facing him. Since, as Gill (4) has pointed out, the recent problems facing the psychiatric patient are "derivative conflicts" directly related to the more basic underlying problems, a focus on recent conflicts in no way avoids dealing with core conflicts, but rather deals with them in a way which is highly relevant to the patient—in the here-and-now. Therapy which focuses on immediate problems involves not only clarification of the problems, catharsis, interpretation, etc., but also an adaptive orientation related to helping the patient examine alternative methods of dealing with these problems once he leaves the unit. The adaptive issues such as making plans, arranging for outpatient treatment, and appropriate relations with the family or community agencies, occupy an increasingly large proportion of each day as the patient's stay progresses. There is a movement from the past to the future, from "what was upsetting you" to "what are you going to do." It was hoped that this shift would facilitate change from a regressive dependent posture to an adaptive active mode of behavior and thinking.

Other Techniques

Other techniques employed include the use of psychotropic agents aimed at diminishing target symptoms, early intensive family involvement, and the use of a structured day to minimize regressive rumination. Group techniques used include a patient-staff meeting, an interactional group run by the nursing staff and a leaderless group.

DESCRIPTION OF UNIT AND STAFF

The ETU is a small seven-bed unit which uses five of its beds for three day intervention and the other two for briefer functions such as 24-hour care and disposition problems for emergency room patients. The unit has 450 admissions yearly, with 350 for 72-hour intervention (most of these are referrals coming from the emergency room of Yale-New Haven Hospital). The physical plant is compact, smaller than an average ward in a general hospital. In addition to the beds there is a dayroom for meetings, activities, and meals. The unit is open to the main lobby of the CMHC, and patients can mix with whoever is sitting in the lobby. The openness of the unit seems to diminish the tendency to perceive oneself as a "mental patient" in need of confinement.

The ETU has a very high staff-patient ratio. The large staff is required to provide the intensity of interaction necessary for maximal effect in a brief period, as well as providing the manpower to interview family, contact social agencies, and make dispositions rapidly and effectively. The day shift consists of two nurses, two aides, and a social worker. The psychiatric coverage is provided by the service chief, and two second-year residents who rotate through the service on a half-time basis for two months.

As mentioned earlier, central to the unit's approach is a team concept which de-emphasizes traditional role definitions and leads to the expansion of functions of nursing personnel. Nurses and aides are trained to do certain functions normally assumed to be the exclusive domain of doctors and social workers such as interviewing and therapy, both with patients and their families. Effective training and supervision of such personnel is a major task of the unit. Training includes didactic lectures as well as experience in "sensitivity groups." Staff members are also individually supervised on a weekly basis by a member of the senior staff. After four to eight months of experience, nurses and aides are assigned to individual patients as "team leaders" which gives them responsibility for the major portion of the nonmedical aspects of the patient's treatment. Assignments are tailored to individual capacities, experience, and training, and close daily review of each case by the entire team led by a psychiatrist provides an essential backdrop.

The high degree of responsibility given to the nursing staff leads to a high group elan, an eagerness to act responsibly and professionally, and rapid professional and individual growth. The various team members relate to an individual patient in several different therapeutic settings. The major therapeutic encounter occurs within the context of scheduled individual interviews which each patient has daily with various members of his team. Team members report their interactions with patients to a daily team meeting led by a psychiatrist where all their impressions are collated and integrated with other information gathered (e.g., interviews of family members, information from social agencies). In these meetings the patient's problems are discussed and formulated, the hospital care is structured, and planning for discharge and outpatient care is discussed.

Family members are also involved as rapidly as possible. Usually, within 24 hours team members have interviewed the most significant family members. When these results are reported to the team meeting, plans are made for further family contact, couples' therapy, or family therapy. Such treatment is initiated prior to the patient's leaving the hospital. Couples' or family therapy is usually done by the social worker with a nurse or aide as co-therapist. Families are further involved in a twice-weekly family group meeting which is structured around the showing of a movie regarding family problems and is followed by an open discussion. The overall goal is a rapid assessment of family problems, rapid involvement of family members, and the initiation of appropriate family treatment when indicated.

Psychoactive drugs are used in two-thirds of the cases. The goal of drug utilization is to facilitate rapid reintegrations and to relieve symptoms which disrupt the patient's functioning. The use of electroconvulsive therapy (ECT) has not proved necessary.

THE PATIENT POPULATION

Over the first two years of operation the majority of patients (66%) treated on ETU were referred from the Yale-New Haven Hospital emergency room, and 4% from other hospital emergency rooms. An additional 11% were unscheduled patients who walked in the CMHC asking for treatment. The remaining 19% were patients being seen in the CMHC outpatient clinic. Demographic factors related to this population are listed in Table 1. They were predominantly lower socioeconomic class patients, 76% of whom belonged to Hollingshead's Class IV and V. To keep the unit oriented toward these patients, we kept the emergency room as the main portal of entry and made no effort to reach out to the elements of the community which traditionally provide referral to psychiatric inpatient services such as other psychiatrists, physicians, or certain social agencies. Such sources of referral, we felt, would change the population to a middle- and upper-class one. Almost two thirds of the patients were female and most (80%) were white.

Of our patients, 39% had previous hospitalizations and 48% had an admitting diagnosis of psychosis or borderline psychosis (Table 2). By and large, we found ourselves treating individuals with marked chronic psychopathology.

Attempted suicide was a major problem in many of our patients. Fifty per cent of the patients were suicidal to some extent at the time of admission; 7% had made an attempt; 13% had made a suicidal gesture; and 20% had suicidal ideation. Many of these were women between the ages of 20 and 40 with a diagnosis of psychoneurotic depression. The problem of adequately evaluating the suicidal potential of these individuals within three days was a major clinical task facing the staff. Following discharge the availability of the unit around the clock appeared to be an important therapeutic resource of which these patients could make use. They no longer found themselves in a position where they felt there was no way out other than suicide.

A variety of other categories of patients and problems were identified. Some 18% of the admissions were adolescents, many of whom were embroiled in family problems or had begun using drugs and had joined a "hippie" subculture. The unit seemed to serve a stabilizing function for these patients and their families and at times led to further family or individual therapy or an effective break with the family. A major clinical function of the unit was in the treatment of adolescents and young adults who had been abusing drugs. With the increasing use of amphetamines, lysergic acid diethylamide (LSD), and "mind expanders" of various sorts, increasingly large numbers of patients come to the emergency room on "bad trips." The unit had a great number of acute and chronic drug users and toxic drug reactions (14% of admissions).

The treatment of schizophrenics on the unit was something which we set out to do in an exploratory fashion with no clear idea of what degree of success we would have. The schizophrenics were of two types. Initially, we treated individuals with first or, at least, fairly acute episodes. Later we decided, on the basis of Pasamanick et al.'s (11) findings, to treat chronic schizophrenics as well, frequently using a home treatment orientation.

Another distinct group was the geriatric group. These were primarily patients with some recent worsening of an arteriosclerotic condition and concomitant social or environmental disruption leading to the development of organic and psychiatric problems. For them, and certain other highly confused patients, the multiple therapist approach was suspended in order to avoid adding to their confusion.

TABLE 1   Demographic Factors

	Factors	Admissions (%)
Sex	Male	37
	Female	63
Race	White	80
	Negro	17
	Puerto Rican	2
	Miscellaneous	1
Marital status	Single	40
	Married	34
	Separated	13
	Divorced	11
	Widowed	2
Age	14-20	19
	21-30	41
	31-40	20
	41-55	13
	56-	7
Social class	I	4
(Hollingshead	II	6
2-factor scale)	III	15
	IV	39
	V	37

TABLE 2   Diagnosis

Diagnosis	Admissions (%)
Schizophrenia	32
Psychotic depression	6
Borderline psychosis	10
Neurotic depression	24
Neurosis (other)	4
Alcoholism and addiction	7
Organic brain syndrome	6
Adjustment reaction of adolescence	5
Character disorder	5

REPORT OF CASES

The following clinical examples illustrate typical cases. The first represents a nonpsychotic case, the second an example of treatment of a schizophrenic patient.

Case 1

This woman is a 24-year-old Catholic, a factory worker's wife, who was admitted to the ETU from the emergency room of the Yale-New Haven Hospital, following ingestion of 30 antidepressants. She had been put on antidepressants by her family doctor due to a two-month history of depression with weight loss and sleep disturbance. The suicide gesture was the culmination of two years of marital turmoil that had been progressively worsening. The marriage had gone well until the birth of their only child, 9 months of age. At this point her husband began spending less time at home, frequently drinking with his friends. Arguments increased and several hours before her gesture he had beaten her and gone out drinking. She took the pills and an hour later called her mother and told her what had happened. She was brought to the emergency room and seemed relieved when told she was going to be hospitalized. She talked to staff members quite freely, discussing her marital difficulties and other problems relating to her relationship to her mother who had disapproved of the marriage. At the end of her second day on the unit the patient and her husband were seen together. They began to verbalize many feelings about the marriage, which had been building up for months. The husband seemed interested in working out the marital difficulties. By the next morning, the patient's depression had dramatically lessened. Plans were made for her mother to stay with her during the day for a week. The patient was discharged on antidepressants and arrangements were made for her to be seen individually once per week and in family therapy with her husband weekly. By the end of the 30-day follow-up, the patient was asymptomatic and the marriage had stabilized and was improving. When asked if she felt a need for continuing treatment, she decided to try handling things on her own, promising that if they did not go well she would call back to arrange for further treatment.

Case 2

This man is a 55-year-old unmarried stock clerk with a history of two previous hospital admissions for schizophrenia. He had been asymptomatic for the past four years but on the day of admission he was picked up on the street by the police because he was "wandering around with a dazed expression, putting money on his head, and making strange howling noises." The patient's mother had died one year before and two months prior to admission the patient was informed by his brother that the house in which the patient had lived all his life with his mother would have to be sold. When the patient and his family did not discuss the sale of the house in great detail it was at this point that the patient's behavior started changing. He had difficulty sleeping and began to feel people at work were tape-recording everything he said in order to get evidence to fire him. Following admission to ETU the patient and his family were seen together to discuss the impending sale of the house and feelings about that sale. A plan was worked out for the patient to live with his brother until other arrangements could be made. This talking through plus the use of phenothiazines seemed to markedly improve the patient's condition, and after three days he was discharged from the inpatient unit and returned to his job. He was followed in our outpatient clinic twice a week for four weeks, showed progressive improvement, and was referred to the outpatient department for medication maintenance.

RESULTS

Follow-up Study

In an attempt to check on rehospitalization rates after patients leave treatment on ETU, we telephoned or made home visits to our first 100 patients one year after they left the hospital unit. Two of the first 100 patients could not be contacted, and were, therefore, replaced in our check by patients 101 and 102.

Table 3 shows rehospitalization rates (includes transfers and discharged patients who were rehospitalized) for the ETU and also, for comparison, for private or university affiliated hospitals treating similar patient populations. Looking first at the ETU data, 18% of the patients were transferred for longer term inpatient care immediately after their three-day ETU stay, with another 19% becoming rehospitalized within one year of ETU discharge. Of interest is that, of those ETU patients hospitalized in the first year, 84% were rehospitalized within six months past discharge point. At the one-year follow-up, 63% of admissions had not been rehospitalized or transferred after their three-day ETU treatment.

Table 3 also includes data obtained from published reports of other hospital outcome studies. Comparisons between outcome studies must take into account the following factors:

(1) Does the study include outcome on all admitted patients or only on discharged patients? Many studies exclude admitted patients who are not discharged but are either transferred elsewhere or remain as chronic patients.

(2) Hospitals differ from each other on criteria for admission. ETU excluded violent patients who could not be quieted with phenothiazines, and limited the number of alcoholics and addicts. Referrals tended to be biased toward patients with acute symptoms, but this was not strictly adhered to. Other treatment centers exclude patients for varying reasons such as the lack of cooperative family, or the unavailability of a disposition.

(3) Populations differ from study to study in terms of diagnosis and demographic data.

(4) Hospitals differ in quality of facilities and staff.

(5) Rehospitalization often excludes brief readmissions. This varies from study to study. ETU readmissions are defined as rehospitalization for over 72 hours. Three percent of our sample were admitted for up to 72 hours with "boarder" status during periods of crisis and then returned to the community.

TABLE 3 Rehospitalization Rates

Source	Average hospital duration	Transferred for longer-term treatment (%)	Discharged but rehospitalized by: (%)			Admissions not transferred or rehospitalized (%)		
			0-6 Mo.	6 Mo.-1 Yr.	1-2 Yr.	1 Yr.	2 Yr.
ETU	3 days	18	16	3	6*	63	57*
Wilder (14)	3 weeks	6†				59‡	48
Levenstein et al (8)	8 months	0				72	53
Friedman et al. (3)	4 months	14	19	11	12	56	34

* Projection based on rate of rehospitalization in the last six months studied.
† Never discharged.
‡ Data estimated by present authors.

Keeping in mind these difficulties in making comparisons between different hospital treatment outcomes, one can still get a rough idea of rehospitalization rates by comparing different studies. All studies included here come from comparable treatment facilities, either private or university-affiliated hospitals. Looking at these data, ETU had a slightly lower rehospitalization rate at one year than two other studies (3, 14) and a slightly higher rate than that reported for Hillside Hospital in Levenstein's (8) study (which had an average duration of inpatient stay of eight months). Clearly, then, rehospitalization rates for former ETU patients is not strikingly different from those reported for longer-term units. Keeping in mind the differences in patients, resources, and type of treatment, one can conclude that the ETU treatment modality results in an acceptable outcome in terms of rehospitalization rates.

An attempt was made to investigate patient variables that might be related to rehospitalization rates—these variables include demographic factors, factors related to psychopathology, and factors related to family organization.

The results in Table 4 indicate that men were rehospitalized significantly more than women. Perhaps to have come to a hospital asking for help represents a greater and more complete breakdown in social roles for men than for women, and hence the draw to longer-term hospitalization is less easily reversed in men than in women.

Table 5 indicates that younger patients tended to be more likely to be rehospitalized than older patients, but this trend was not statistically significant.

Psychopathology

Not surprisingly, patients with schizophrenic diagnoses (Table 6) were much more likely to be hospitalized than other groups. Also, number of previous hospitalizations (Table 7) was strongly related to rehospitalization rates—73% of patients with three or more previous hospitalizations were rehospitalized within one year of their ETU stay. This suggests that ETU did not serve as an effective deterrent to later hospitalization in patients who had probably previously become acclimated to hospital living. It should be noted, of course, that the variables being explored here are not mutually independent—number of previous hospitalizations is related to diagnosis. These data indicating higher rehospitalization rates for schizophrenics and people with multiple hospitalizations are not unique to the ETU population—Wilder et al. (14) and Guy et al. (6) report similar relationships in other hospital settings.

TABLE 4   Rehospitalization and Sex

Sex	Total no.	% Rehospitalized
Male	33	57
Female	67	27

$$\chi^2 = 11.8, P < 0.001$$

TABLE 5   Rehospitalization and Age

Age	Total no.	% Rehospitalized
11-19	14	36
20-29	35	46
30-39	23	40
40-49	14	21
50-59	9	22
60-	5	20

$$\chi^2 = 4.8, P = \text{Not significant.}$$

TABLE 6   Rehospitalization and Diagnosis

Diagnosis	Total no.	% Rehospitalized
Schizophrenia	32	50
Depression	26	31
Character disorder	15	33
Other	27	29

$$\chi^2 = 3.0, P = < 0.02.$$

TABLE 7   Rehospitalization and Previous Hospitalization

No. previous rehospitalizations	Total no.	% Rehospitalized
0	48	27
1	23	25
2	15	53
3	14	73

$$\chi^2 = 10.4, P < 0.02$$

Family Organization

Tables 8 and 9 show relationships between variables of family organization to rehospitalization rates. Table 8 reflects a tendency for single people to be rehospitalized relatively more often than other groups. The data in Table 9 shed some more light on these data by showing a statistically significant relationship between

TABLE 8   Rehospitalization and Marital Status

Marital Status	Total no.	% Rehospitalized
Married	43	30
Separated or divorced	27	33
Widowed	3	0
Single	27	55

$$\chi^2 = 6.5, P < 0.10.$$

TABLE 9   Rehospitalization and Residential Arrangements

Lives With	Total no.	% Rehospitalized
Self	8	37
Parents (under 21)	10	50
Parents (over 21)	10	90
Spouse	43	30
Other	29	24

$$\chi^2 = 8.0, P < 0.02.$$

place of residence and rehospitalization rates. Most striking is the finding that 90% of the adult patients who reside with their parents were rehospitalized within one year after their ETU treatment. This suggests that people who have not achieved an adequate adult role at some point in their lives prior to ETU hospitalization (i.e., were not able to or interested in moving out of the parental house or both) were very likely to be rehospitalized in the course of the year. Achievement of some degree of autonomous living prior to ETU admission is probably very important in determining outcome after hospitalization. Again, similar relationships to rehospitalization were found in other outcome studies (6).

COMMENT

This report presented a crisis-intervention model for inpatient hospitalization which provides an alternative to longer-term inpatient hospitalization for many psychiatric patients. A wide variety of psychiatric disorders which are usually treated in longer-term treatment settings seemed to respond well to a three-day hospitalization contact with a 30-day outpatient follow-up. Thus, the ETU provided brief inpatient treatment to many patients who would normally be sent directly to longer-term units, allowing utilization of other inpatient units within the CMHC only for those patients who absolutely required long-term care. This permitted the CMHC to treat a number of patients previously sent to large state hospitals, while at the same time avoiding a situation where the center itself became a large, overcrowded, and understaffed institution.

The development of the techniques used on the ETU stems from two conceptual movements in the field of mental health—first, the emphasis on crisis theory exemplified in the works of Caplan (1) and Erikson (2); and second, the emphasis on the mental hospital as a social system as emphasized in the discussions of "disculturation" or "institutionalism" by Goffman (5), Wing (15), and Stanton and Schwartz (12).

Concerning crisis theory, Caplan (1) states that, "The essential factor influencing the occurrence of crisis is an imbalance between the difficulty and importance of a problem and the resources immediately available to deal with it." Most of the patients admitted to ETU come experiencing such an imbalance. Patterns of interpersonal relations have been disrupted, role obligations have gone unmet, feelings of incipient loss of control are experienced—all of these would seem to be indicators of at least temporary disruption in the person's capacity to deal effectively with a problem. The consequence of this state involves a sense of being overwhelmed and a weakening in the individual's ability to act autonomously and effectively. A sense of identity diffusion (the individual's lack of a sense of who he is and where he is going) is often experienced and the person becomes especially amenable to external influence.

It is at this point that concepts of the mental hospital as a social system become relevant. With the disruption in usual styles of coping that accompany crisis, the person becomes extremely susceptible in many hospital systems to learning the role of the helpless "mental patient" for whom an outside agency must assume executive ego functions. Goffman's powerful portrayal of the mental hospital, *Asylums*, (5) describes the mechanics of the disculturation process. According to Goffman, in the total institution a small staff will be expected to control and provide care for a large unit of patients. The staff, in order to deal with this responsibility, institutes a social control system in which routine, compliant behavior is rewarded. The operating assumption is that the patient is incapable of a normal level of instrumental functioning without causing harm to himself or others. The staff may retain total control to all physical necessities, with a result that the patient finds a whole class of unknown people wielding complete control over him. The staff attempts to control patient behavior through a series of privileges and punishments which "are largely known in the inmate's home world as something applied to animals and children." He is, in short, being treated like a child.

It is our belief that such a disculturation process occurs not only in large state institutions, but is also a phenomenon implicitly encouraged in many better-staffed psychiatric facilities which equate treatment with depth psychotherapy. Often, in such institutions, the patient is traditionally encouraged to see the causes of his present plight in previous failures of adaptation, which in turn, are seen as a result of underlying pathology. In such a system the patient is told that there is something basically wrong with him, that it has been wrong for a long time, and that something must change radically if he is ever to improve. He is further asked to commit himself to investigate this underlying pathology, for such "insight" will be a major index of his improvement. Rapid symptomatic improvement is considered a defensive maneuver and often discouraged. Such approaches are often useful but simultaneously may undermine adaptive strengths and solidify pathologic roles such as that of being a "psychiatric casualty."

This traditional patient role thus demands a high degree of dependent behavior upon an outside person's ideas of health which in itself can involve a disruption in the person's sense of himself. Using a Parsonian (10) model, autonomous need dispositions would find no facilitation for their expressions, while dependent strivings would be rewarded. In Erikson's (2) terms, the individual would be seen as having lost the social and environmental supports and the continuity that serve as the cornerstones of personal integration and clear ego identity.

In contrast, the ETU established as a working assumption that the patient, although temporarily disrupted, will be shortly capable of returning to the community. In addition, the patient is seen as capable of problem-solving behavior and autonomy while hospitalized. Decisions are not made unilaterally by the staff; the patient and family are very much involved in this process. Also, rather than disrupting the patient's past network of relationships, the ETU attempts to involve the family to help reinforce this network. In summary, the three-day inpatient stay, multiple-therapist approach, stress on patient autonomy, and emphasis on current modes of adaptation are all techniques designed to discourage adoption of the patient role. This is done by establishing a treatment environment in which neither total dependency nor identity discontinuity would be "built-in" aspects of treatment expectations.

It must be noted that the data on rehospitalization presented in this report give only a very rough assessment of treatment outcome. Some patients may be discharged and stay out of the hospital but still perform very poorly in their home environment and social roles. In order to obtain further data on the outcome of

ETU treatment, a group of patients are being followed with home interviews at two months and again at one year after their ETU admission. These patients are being compared with a "control" group of patients who are referred to ETU, deemed acceptable for admission, but then randomly turned down for research purposes. This "control" group of patients may then be referred by the emergency room resident to any other available clinical setting—long-term inpatient, day hospital, outpatient, etc. This allows comparison of ETU outcome with the outcome obtained with the range of treatment facilities which were available prior to the development of ETU. We hope that such a comparison study will give a more complete picture of ETU outcome, not just in terms of rehospitalization rates but also in terms of symptomatology, social functioning, employment, and cognitive efficiency. In addition, an open-ended interview is being given which allows us to assess the degree to which the individual experiences himself as an intact, functioning, capable person.

Further research is also being planned to study the process of treatment on ETU. Of particular interest is a comparison of the impact of the multiple-therapist team as compared with a single therapist, and also a comparison of the three day limit on inpatient stay as compared with an open-ended contract.

SUMMARY

The Emergency Treatment Unit (ETU) was established to develop a model for brief intensive intervention as an alternative to longer-term hospitalization. The unit, located in the Connecticut Mental Health Center, provides three to five days of hospital care followed by 30 days of outpatient care. It treats primarily lower socioeconomic class patients admitted from the emergency room of the Yale-New Haven Hospital. Specific techniques which promote rapid reintegration include the use of time-limited contracts, intensive daily involvement with multiple therapists, maximization of autonomy, and an emphasis on adaptive issues. In addition, extensive use is made of tranquilizers, individual dyadic therapy, milieu therapy, and family or marital therapy where indicated. Of those admitted 82% are able to return to the community after a three-day inpatient stay while 18% required transfer to longer-term treatment settings. A follow-up study found an additional 19% of admissions were readmitted for longer-term care within a year of discharge. Thus, 63% of admissions were neither transferred for longer-term care nor rehospitalized. This compared favorably with other recent follow-up studies. These data suggest that brief intensive hospital care provides an effective alternative to longer-term hospitalization for a wide variety of psychiatric disorders.

REFERENCES

1. Caplan, G. *Principles of preventive psychiatry.* New York: Basic Books, Inc., 1964.
2. Erikson, E. *Childhood and society.* New York: W. W. Norton & Company, Inc., 1950.
3. Friedman, I., von Mering, O., & Hinko, E. N. Intermittent Patienthood. *Arch. Gen. Psychiat.*, 1966, **14**, 386-392.
4. Gill, M. Psychoanalysis and exploratory psychotherapy. *J. Amer. Psychoanal. Assoc.*, 1954, **2**, 771-797.
5. Goffman, E. *Asylums.* Garden City: Anchor, 1961.
6. Guy, W., et al. A controlled evaluation of day hospital effectiveness. *Arch. Gen. Psychiat.*, 1969, **20**, 329-338.
7. Jacobson, G. F. Crisis theory and treatment strategy: Some sociocultural and psychodynamic considerations. *J. Nerv. Ment. Dis.*, 1965, **141**, 209-218.
8. Levenstein, S., Klein. D. F., & Pollack, M. Follow-up study of formerly hospitalized voluntary psychiatric patients: The first two years. *Amer. J. Psychiat.*, 1966, **122**, 1102-1109.
9. MacLeod, J. A., & Tinnen, L. W. Special service project. *Arch. Gen. Psychiat.*, 1966, **15**, 190-197.
10. Parsons, T. *Social structure and personality.* New York: The Free Press of Glencoe, Inc., 1964.
11. Pasamanick, B., Scarpitti, F., & Dinitz, S. *Schizophrenics in the community.* New York: Appleton-Century-Crofts, 1967.
12. Stanton, A., & Schwartz, M. *The mental hospital.* New York: Basic Books, Inc., 1954.
13. Thomas, C. S., & Weisman, G. K. Emergency planning: The practical and theoretical backdrop to the emergency treatment unit. *Int. J. Soc. Psychiat.*, to be published.
14. Wilder, J. F., Levin, G., & Zwerling, I. A two-year follow-up evaluation of acute psychotic patients treated in a day hospital. *Amer. J. Psychiat.*, 1966, **122**, 1095-1101.
15. Wing, J. K. Institutionalism in Mental Hospitals. In T. Scheff, (Ed.), *Mental illness and social process.* New York Harper & Row, 1967.

V. Contemporary Perspectives of Psychotherapy

Much has been written about the nature of psychotherapy. Two recent papers have been included which are particularly germane to brief therapy because of their conceptualizations of disturbed behavior and its correction. When possible, a basic objective of brief therapy is to interrupt vicious circles. Wender's discussion of deviation amplifying feedback depicts how small changes in systems can magnify into positive or negative consequences of major proportions. Wender reminds us that maladaptive behavior patterns, while initiated by past events, are perpetuated by present forces. Small therapeutic interventions sometimes bring about realignment of these forces which can lead to profound behavioral change.

Strupp's paper is not about brief psychotherapy, but it was selected as appropriate ballast to provide a larger perspective of the complexities involved in examining psychotherapy. Strupp, who has made outstanding contributions in the field of research on psychotherapy, discusses some recent attempts to describe psychotherapy in terms of learning theory, as well as taking note of some of the other frameworks which have been applied. Some of the goals outlined by Strupp clearly require the long-term psychotherapeutic techniques which he considers and favors, particularly for patients with severe neuroses and character disorders. To reiterate what was stated at the beginning of this book, there exists a multiplicity of therapeutic objectives ranging from those which are circumscribed to those which require complex, multi-layered learning processes. When necessary and feasible, the latter clearly take precedence over the limitations of short-term therapy. On the other hand, since more circumscribed forms of learning are sometimes the only possibility or all the patient wants or even the treatment of choice, "lessons" such as those enumerated by Strupp should be ordered on a continuum ranging from those of a relatively modest scope to those which encompass the total fabric of the personality. Strupp's article reminds us of more ambitious psychotherapeutic options, while at the same time making us wonder which of the "lessons" of therapy he specifies can be imparted by short-term techniques. Strupp urges increased knowledge of the mechanisms of therapeutic learning to define this range of applicability.

Chapter 24

Vicious and Virtuous Circles:

The Role of Deviation Amplifying Feedback in the Origin and Perpetuation of Behavior

Paul H. Wender, M.D.

It is the purpose of this paper to call attention to a mechanism which has been used by behavioral scientists in a variety of fields—as well as by the man in the street—to explain the origin and continuance of much human behavior. This explanatory mechanism is usually introduced ad hoc so that its generality and applicability are not recognized. It is most commonly identified in its pathological form, the vicious circle, although the similar mechanism, with beneficent effects, has been noted and called the virtuous circle. Both vicious and virtuous circles are examples of what is called, in cybernetic terms, positive feedback, or what Maruyama has called "deviation amplifying feedback" (DAF). *

In the past, many of those concerned with the relevance of cybernetics to behavior have focused on the mechanism of negative feedback, in which feedback serves as a stabilizing principle. Common examples of negative feedback are the linking of a furnace and a thermostat to maintain constant temperature, or the various homeostatic mechanisms in the mammalian body—for example, those maintaining the constancy of glucose level in the blood.

The mechanism of deviation amplifying feedback (DAF) has been less clearly explicated despite the fact that this mecha-

Reprinted from *Psychiatry*, 1968, **31**, 309-311, 317-324, by special permission of The William Alanson White Psychiatric Foundation, Inc. Abridged by permission of the author. Dr. Wender is a Research Psychiatrist at the Laboratory of Psychology, National Institute of Mental Health, Bethesda, Maryland.

* Magoroh Maruyama, (12). Common parlance recognizes DAF as "snowballing," the military as "escalation."

nism is operative in many biological and social systems. An understanding of it permits a better understanding of the genesis and perpetuation of behavior and suggests methods for the alteration of such behavior. Simply stated, DAF is a mechanism which explains how small variations in a system can (or must) become associated with large effects—how small perturbations can generate chains of events that can result in gross alterations. It is a process in which the output of the system is fed back (either directly or indirectly) into that system in a manner such that output continues to increase or decrease. This last statement may seem quite abstract and general, but a few concrete examples should show that this is not the case.

Consider (as Maruyama does) the fate of a boulder in a temperate climate. The process of DAF acts to increase the probability that such a boulder will eventually be replaced by gravel. This is so because if a random perturbation—a crack—appears, the process of DAF will act to increase the probability that further cracks will develop. Let a minor nick be introduced. With the succession of seasons rain will fall, freeze, and expand and further enlarge the crack into a fissure. With successive cycles the fissure grows and new ones are formed. It becomes increasingly probable then that organic material or plant seeds will find their way into the interstices, grow, further enlarge the cracks, cause new ones to form, and so forth. The first small nick does not shatter the rock, but given the specific properties of the environment (rain, freezing temperatures, the fact that water expands when it freezes, the presence of plant life), the occurrence of a minor deviation results in a major effect. Given a different environment, say a dry cave, the initial crack would not produce this sequence of events. It is important to note that without a knowledge of the specific properties of the system one would not know that this mechanism would operate in it.

Another simple physical example of the operation of DAF would be an amplification system in which a fraction of the output is fed back and added to the initial stimulus. This effect often occurs in public address systems or in hearing aids when they are not being worn. Random electronic noise is generated, amplified, and fed back to the microphone and reamplified. As a result, a small hum rapidly increases to a howl or a roar. Other natural examples of the operation of DAF are shown in the formation of meanders in rivers (9) and ripples in dunes, and in the development of "moguls" on ski slopes. A striking and important biological example is the evolution of new species of life. Random mutations which are better suited to a given ecological niche than the existing species have an increased probability of survival. Continued selection of such mutations is favored until optimal adaptability is achieved.

Two pathological physiological instances of DAF may be seen in congestive heart failure and hypertension. In heart failure, the heart's inability to pump sufficiently vigorously activates mechanisms which result in increased sodium and fluid retention. Increased fluid retention increases circulatory volume, which increases venous pressure, which *reduces* the heart's pumping capacity. In some forms of hypertension, diminished renal blood flow releases substances which elevate blood pressure (a homeostatic mechanism whose function is to increase renal blood flow). Elevated blood pressure—if prolonged—produces vascular changes which narrow the lumina of arteries and decrease renal blood flow. Continued operation of the DAF mechanism can produce irreversible hyptertension and renal damage.

Note that in the examples given above the DAF process proceeds to a certain magnitude and then levels off. This effect is that of "dampening." In the case of the amplification system, dampening occurs because the physical properties of the components are such that they cannot amplify signals above a certain strength; when the input is increased to that level no further amplification occurs. In biological evolution, dampening occurs for a variety of reasons: For example, further amplification may lessen survival value—the Brontosaurus apparently exceeded a size capable of dealing with a fluctuating environment. It should be noted that the causes of dampening are as specific as those of the DAF process itself—that they, too, cannot be predicted without a detailed knowledge of the individual components of the system.

At this point it would be useful to define and list some properties of DAF systems: *

(1) An event (A) may be positively linked with a succeeding event (B) so that a change in A is followed by a change in B in the same direction. (If A increases, B increases; if A decreases, B decreases.) This linkage will be indicated by a "+." Or,

(2) An event (A) may be negatively linked with a succeeding event (B) so that a change in A is followed by a change in B in the *opposite* direction. (If A increases, B decreases; if A decreases, B increases.) This linkage, seen in homeostatic systems of negative feedback, will be indicated by a "—."

(3) Consequently, if a system contains no negative links or an even number of negative links the system will manifest DAF. If there are an odd number of negative links, the system will show negative feedback and tend to be stable.

* This notation is Maruyama's.

(4) A given event may participate in more than one cycle so that several cycles can be linked together.

(5) The overall effects of such linked cycles will depend on then relative strengths. This last assertion is a statement of ignorance. Whereas in the case of a single loop (e.g., the amplifier example), the direction of change could be predicted by Proposition 3, in more complex systems prediction can be made only with a detailed knowledge of the component events.

(6) The DAF process may lead into one in which negative feedback exists so that the deviation which has occurred will then be stabilized. (Consider, for example, the case of the Brontosaurus. Presumably mutant Brontosauri who were larger were selected against and their size, which presumably had increased through DAF, was stabilized.) *

To illustrate the use of this notation, let us examine an ecological system (quasi-Australian) incolving predators (wolves), their prey (rabbits), the rabbits' food source, and a virus disease that attacks rabbits. As Figure 1 indicates, given a system consisting only of wolves, rabbits, and rabbit food, a stable equilibrium can be predicted although the numbers of animals and amounts of forage at equilibrium cannot be predicted *a priori*. However, when the virus is introduced into the system the outcome can only be predicted probabilistically. This is so because a new equilibrium would be achieved only if mutant rabbits immune to the virus appeared, and this change can only be assessed probabilistically.

I shall now turn to the role of DAF in human behavior. It will be seen that as a consequence of DAF.

(1) It is often the case that an arrangement of events that are unstable exists between individuals or within an individual.

(2) When such unstable conditions exist, change will occur. This change will often be large and result in the establishment of a new and stable equilibrium.

(3) Unstable equilibria can often be generated by small shifts from the stable condition.

PSYCHOPATHOLOGICAL DEVELOPMENT

The Interpersonal Context of Depression

As is commonly recognized, but not formally explicated,

---

* I feel a bit reluctant to introduce this kind of notation and the accompanying diagrams as both often serve a pretentious pseudoscientific role in psychology. They should be taken as visual aids and not the author's illusion of the logical precision of the scheme.

DAF frequently operates to aggravate and perpetuate depressive states. Using the model that hypothesizes that depression is due to anger unexpressed or turned inward, consider the fate of an individual who is angry at another and unable to express that anger, and whose values do not permit him to perceive himself as weak or succorant. As may be seen in Figure 2, several loops operate to increase the probability that unexpressed anger and concurrent depression will increase.

(1) Depression leads to decreased coping ability, which leads to negative self-evaluation. The latter may lead to increased anger, increased depression, or both.

(2) Decreased coping ability "forces" others in the environment to provide assistance. The patient's perception of himself as one who requires aid may generate anger and/or a decreased self-evaluation, both of which will probably lead to increased depression.

The "Shut-in" Personality and the Schizophrenic Reaction Type

Adolf Meyer proposed that the etiology of the schizophrenic syndromes might well be psychological (13). He argued that this reaction type could be understood as that of a socially unskilled person's response to stress. This social incompetence was—he felt—more easily understood in terms of an individual's psychological evolution than as an organic brain disease. The individual likely to manifest these reactions, Meyer felt, was the "shut-in personality. Formation of this personality was, in turn, explained by a vicious circle in which initial mild social incompetence led to protective withdrawal, which in turn led to inexperience and greater social incompetence. The model is analogous to that of the school failure, as is the proposed solution: For the shut-in, gradual acquisition of greater social skills, and a greater feeling of competence; for the school failure, graduated education, and a diminished feeling of ignorance.

The Psychiatric Breakdown Syndrome

Gruenberg argues that many "psychiatric breakdowns" are not the product of an illness (either psychological or biological) but are rather the product of a vicious cycle produced by the interaction of a transient disturbance with certain cultural prescriptions (6). He argues that otherwise transient periods of psychological turmoil are apt to become chronic because such factors as definition of the sick role and treatment arrangements act to amplify deviations that might well be short-lived.

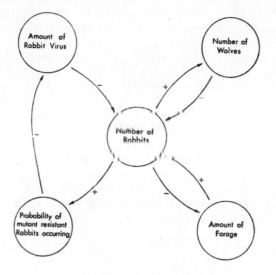

Figure 1. The operation of DAF in a hypothetical ecological system.

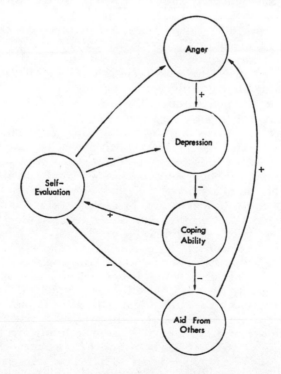

Figure 2. Some operations of DAF in depression.

This is an explication of a principle of social psychiatry: The "illness" is largely a product of how it is handled. The further implication, obviously, is that modification of these outward influences greatly reduces both the severity of the deviation and its length.

It should be obvious that the DAF mechanisms operative in normal development can, when gone awry, provide a mechanism for abnormal development. Loops which operate to generate increasing feelings of competence, appropriate assertiveness, and so forth, can likewise operate to generate increased feelings of *in*competence or *in*appropriate *non*-assertiveness. Without additional counteracting forces (negative feedback loops) which tend to favor movement in one direction (e.g., toward competence rather than *in*competence), these mechanisms are as apt to promote movement in one direction as another.

PSYCHOTHERAPY

The Rambunctious Child and the Inconsistent Mother

Maurice Rosenthal describes a pattern of mother-child interaction, characterized by DAF, which is frequently seen in child guidance clinics: the limit-testing child and the inconsistent mother (15). This cycle begins when the mother is lax in setting limits. This laxity may be prompted by guilt toward the child, perception of the child as special or weak, or confusion of consistency with severity. DAF proceeds as follows: Laxity leads to increased limit testing; increased limit testing leads sooner or later to excessive punitiveness (as in one blast the mother releases her pent-up antagonism). The mother than feels guilty because of her outburst and resolves to be more patient—that is, to restrict the child less. Further limit-testing behavior by the child is generated by this process and is sustained because he receives intermittent (variable) reinforcement for such behavior (he "gets away with it" unpredictably). Such a schedule of reinforcement is, of course, particularly effective in engendering habits that are resistant to extinction.

The method of therapy which Rosenthal proposes, and which he claims is effective, is that of interrupting the cycle. By relieving the mother's guilt (primarily by emphasizing that "strictness" is not synonymous with severity or rejection) and supporting her efforts to set firm legitimate limits, the therapist helps to bring the child's behavior under control in a very short time. It should be emphasized that such therapy is directed at the mother's behavior and not at her motivations. Her motivations become relevant *only* when—and this, Rosenthal states, is apparently the exception—they are so strong as to preclude voluntary change. Otherwise alteration of the feedback loop is sufficient to promote marked behavioral change. *

The Corrective Emotional Experience

In their discussion of brief psychotherapy Alexander and French attribute particular efficacy to the "corrective emotional experience" (1). The authors assert that long-term beneficial effects may result from a few contacts with a therapist whose behavior and responses invalidate the patient's expectations or assumptions about others. For example, an hysteric who views all men as seductive may have these views (unconscious fantasies, transference feelings, etc.) profoundly revised on the basis of an intense short contact with a therapist whose behavior demonstrates that "all men are not after the same thing." As a prototype of such a radical revision of personality on the basis of brief contact, the authors cite the experience of Jean val Jean in *Les Miserables;* Hugo expects his readers to believe that his protagonist's lifelong attitudes are completely altered when the bishop gives val Jean the silver candlesticks which val Jean had stolen.

Alexander and French do not propose that such immediate radical conversion is the rule, but they do *imply* that such alterations *can* lead to a DAF chain whose effect is both beneficial and long lasting.

The Mutative Interpretation

James Strachey, operating within a psychoanalytic model of therapy, uses the mechanism of DAF to account for the working through of the transference neurosis. The proposed mechanism is as follows: The analytic situation permits the release of some repressed material which manifests itself as transference. The recognition of the discrepancy between the analyst and the patient's projection diminishes the anxiety with which the repressed material is perceived. The corrected view is introjected, anxiety is decreased, and more repressed impulses may emerge in the transference to the analyst. The mutative interpretation—the pointing out of the discrepancy between projection and the real figure—facilitates the initiation of the cycle. It should be noted that this model is based upon the

* See, for example, Levy's experience with overprotective mothers. Alterations of their behavior or that of their children was, in general, impossible. Effective behavioral change did occur, however, when the fathers of the children became motivated to intervene in the DAF loop between mother and child. (10).

Kleinian model for the generation of difficulties. The author states (16, pp. 137-138):

> . . . the pathological obstacle to the neurotic individual's further growth is in the nature of a vicious circle . . . and, if a breach could somehow or other be made in the vicious circle, the processes of development would proceed upon their normal course. If, for instance, the patient could be made less frightened of his super-ego or introjected object, he would project less terrifying images onto the outer object and would therefore have less need to feel hostility towards it; the object which he then introjected would in turn be less savage in its pressure upon the id-impulses, which would be able to lose something of their primitive ferocity. In short, a benign circle would be set up. . . .

Strachey's model also resembles that of Alexander and French, although he emphasizes the cognitive perception of discrepancy and Alexander and French emphasize the emotional perception. *

"Rational Psychotherapy"

Ellis propounds the interesting thesis that the persistence of maladaptive and inappropriate behaviors and emotions is the product of semantic irrationality and self-indoctrination (5). The fixity of psychopathology, he argues, is generally not the product of a repetition compulsion (which is after all a name, not an explanation), but is the result, in effect, of autosuggestion. The patient tells himself, for example, that it would be "terrible" if not everyone loved him unconditionally. Disappointment is, of course, guaranteed and this disappointment leads to further strengthening of the initial and fallacious premise. Ellis' evidence for the operation of this process is not compelling, but he does present clinical anecdotes to illustrate that persistence of values can be countered by autosuggestion (actually by the patient's challenging his own premises). If the patient can be brought to acknowledge the absurdity of the tactit premise, he will be able to act in a way which will further weaken its hold. Ellis' clinical material supports the view that neurotic patterns can be altered by the creation of a virtuous circle, although his evidence is not convincing that such patterns have been maintained by the particular vicious circles that he describes.

---

* Other differences exist as well: First, Alexander and French propose that the therapist role-play a person discrepant with the patient's expectations; second, they suggest that one experience—carrying the conviction of a conversion experience—is often efficacious, while Strachey argues the need for repeated small experiences, i.e., "working through."

Berne's Interpersonal Games

Eric Berne has described stereotyped sequences of interpersonal transactions, which he has called "games" (4). What is important, he states, is not only that an individual plays a role in such a game, but that he has a "script"—that is, he is capable of behaving and does behave in such a manner that he is able unconsciously to dictate the parts of the other actors in his little drama. Such compelling behavior acts in a manner similar to that by which expectations operate in a self-fulfilling prophecy. As with the self-fulfilling prophecy, not all B's are compliant and willing to enter into A's DAF chain. The proposed therapy consists, initially, of identifying the sequence of transactions and helping the participants to recognize them. Presumably, in many instances, such recognition is sufficient to alter one behavioral link and so to disrupt the chain (as with Rosenthal's therapy for the limit-testing child and inconsistent mother).

DISCUSSION

The concept of Deviation Amplifying Feedback will be described in three contexts: (1) explanatory usefulness; (2) relevance to psychotherapy; (3) human adaptation.

Explanatory Usefulness

The mechanism of DAF explains how small causes can become associated with large effects—how small, perhaps chance, variations in experience can generate chains of events which culminate in gross alterations.

One of the reasons it is difficult to understand the evolution of personality is that often major causal events cannot be found which can account for major differences in personality. This is exemplified in developmental studies in which the correlations between early and later personality attributes are often no higher than .3 and .5. Why? Some attempts to explain the low correlations point out that the measures employed are crude and "really only approximate" Platonic attributes that would remain constant over time, that not enough relevant variables can be specified, and that there may be a massive accumulation of undiscoverable small events all pointing in the same direction. Other explanations for this unhappy state of affairs are: unconscious forces, unspecifiable biological variations, or major events that occurred but were not well documented or reported. (An alternative explanation—that of psychological *in*determinism—is avoided at all costs.) Without denying the importance of the above classes of events, one should realize that they alone will never account for all observed variations. I would add that predictability is low because "error" variance must, in general, be large: because small variations in experience often produce large effects. It is inevitable that the process of DAF and happenstance will produce variations. To the novelist this is "old-hat" but to the scientific psychologist it is unsettling. Teachers, friends, spouses, and others met by chance often produce profound and lifelong changes in one's values and direction, changes that survive a brief contact, and, seemingly, are of much greater intensity than the initial events seemed to warrant (8). Furthermore, memory of such contacts—"random perturbations"—may later seem to have disappeared, not because of repression but because of the initial apparent triviality of the contact; thus discovery may be impossible.

The obvious needs recognition. It is easy to conceptualize human relations in terms of actors and reactors, of forces and substrates. Clinical "examples" abound: the schizophrenogenic mother and her schizophrenic child; the alcoholic's wife and her alcoholic husband. With characteristic cultural lag it is only now being recognized in *print* (3) that interaction is what the word says: It is a two-way street and there are psychological consequences to having a schizophrenic in the household or an alcoholic for a husband. What seems not to be *formally* recognized that this formulation is also too simple and that the actor's reaction to the "reactee" affect the latter, and so on. Repeated actions and reactions do not fit a unidirectional causal model, are difficult to describe—except historically—and do not lend themselves to simple generalizations pretty to exposit. This realization is apparently not lost on people who deal with conflicting people: Marriage counselors, parents of small children, and other mediators recognize that it is difficult—if not impossible—to determine "who started it." (Although those authors concerned with "transactions"—e.g., Berne—have focused on what is going on rather than how it was initiated.) It is unfortunate, perhaps, but it seems that in many respects history provides a better model for psychology than does physics. That assignment of discrete primary causation may be irrelevant to treatment will be discussed in the next section.

Relevance to Psychotherapy

The mechanism of DAF is relevant to some problems of psychotherapy and other efforts at behavioral change. To begin with, its existence may supply an explanation for the phenomenon of profound change produced by apparently small therapeutic interventions. The explanations usually proposed for such change include such statements as: "The patient was ready to get better," "He really was not sick," "It's only a transference cure." Although several authors recognize the virtuous cycle (for example, Horney, Alexander, French, Rosenthal), it is generally perceived as an unusual rather than a fairly common *modus operandi.*

Next, the recognition of DAF leads to the implication that fixed behavior patterns may be sustained by present—not past—forces. This does not deny the existence and importance of "inertia" of attitudes, values, or habits, nor the role of unconscious motivation. It raises the useful question of whether or not persistent behavior is due to these factors—that is, whether behaviors are rigid because they were learned at an early developmental stage, imprinted, or acquired in a hypnoid state, or because *present circumstances continue to support them.* *

An initial deviation may, because of conditions existing at that time, lead to a DAF chain. For example, a fat and pimply adolescent may withdraw in embarrassment and fail to acquire social skills; in adulthood, acne and obesity may have disappeared but low self-esteem, withdrawal, and social ineptitude may remain (17). Social withdrawal and low self-esteem are apt to stay fixed because the DAF chain *now* operates: social ineptitude leads to rejection, which leads to lowered self-esteem, greater withdrawal, less social experience, and greater ineptitude. *What has initiated the problem is no longer sustaining it.* A knowledge of the problem's origin would not be expected to alter the *currently operative* loop unless such insight served to motivate behavioral change. Presumably, albeit somewhat paradoxically, only such change could produce changed behavior. Finding the initial event (acne and obesity) may have less usefulness than understanding the current sustaining feedback mechanism. Furthermore, in some instances the initial event may have left no traces of its existence and may be undiscoverable.

Finally, these mechanisms are relevant to the problem of the resistance of behavior to change. DAF generally does not continue indefinitely: Equilibria are generally reached from which it is difficult to induce change. Why? As postulated earlier,

---

* One psychoanalytic theoretician who considers the role of current forces in the maintenance of psychic structure is David Rapaport, who cites as an example the dependence of the conscious superego on a familiar and stable setting (what might be referred to as the traveling salesman phenomenon). Likewise Rapaport notes that certain ego structures (e.g., values and attitudes) are sustained by group involvement. What he does not discuss is the role of DAF in such maintenance. An individual seeks a group which favors his attitude, which in turn strengthens his attitude, and so forth. See Ref. (14).

some behaviors may play a role in several feedback loops, having a different role in each. If some roles have negative feedback the stability will be enhanced. A physical example of the stability produced by negative feedback is seen in the furnace-thermostat model. Introduction of an electric heater, less powerful than the furnace, will not alter the stable temperature of the house—the furnace will simply go off, and if the conductance of the heat from the house is great enough, the temperature will never rise above that set by the thermostat. The concept of symptom substitution fits this model. According to the usual paradigm, anxiety leads to the formation of symptoms, which in turn reduce anxiety. If the symtoms are removed, anxiety will tend to increase and these or other symptoms will reappear. This is the mechanism which accounts for symptom stability in the psychoanalytic model. *

Human Adaptation

Given the existence of exploratory (epistemic) drives and the fact that competence seems to be reinforcing (18), a human is apt to develop a wide variety of behaviors. The operation of DAF together with this behavioral variation allows an organism (here man) to develop maximum adaptational ability for his given ecological niche: The operation of DAF allows individual evolution to best fit the condition of life. It is very nearly identical with the mechanism of mutation in biological selection in the evolution of species. If the DAF mechanism did not operate, behavioral variations would be dampened and disappear. Teleologically speaking, it is useful that this operation occurs because the possibilities of behavioral variation and adaptation are maximally enhanced. Any designer of a "successful universe" would be wise to incorporate the principle of DAF.

The principle of DAF also insures the unhappiness of the tough-minded (James) and the simple-minded (Whitehead), † who will have to accept the possibility that large variations in outcome may not derive from equally large antecedent causes. It is understandably disconcerting to have to acknowledge that a few simple rules will not suffice to explain many biological and social events, and that, also, some deterministic chains may have to remain forever unknown. It may perhaps be a slight solace to the simple-minded—among whom the author numbers

---

* Freud's well-known recommendation that at some stages the phobic patient should be exposed to the phobic object is a recognition of the fact that something other than unconscious displacement of anxiety is maintaining the phobia. What this "something other" is, is not clear.

† Versus the tender-minded and the muddle-headed, respectively.

himself—to be able to substitute this general principle for a few simple laws and to be able to maintain a belief in determinism, which experience seems only too often to deny.

One penultimate point. Why, if the principle of DAF is as important and generally applicable as I have proposed (even allowing for the tendency of authors to overvalue their own theses), has it been overlooked so long? It is difficult enough to trace the origin of ideas, harder still to explain their failure to appear. I would venturesomely propose that it has been neglected because of its clarity and obviousness. For some reason, many seem to prefer explanations that are murky and unclear to those that are transparent. Perhaps it is pride in understanding what the uninitiated cannot; perhaps it is a fear that one has no special mysterious knowledge. It has always seemed to me that there is a tendency to label the murky as profound (because the profound is often difficult to grasp), and to regard the lucid as superficial. Hume has been called superficial, Hegel has been called profound. *

In this regard it is interesting to note the comparatively late development in dynamic psychiatry of concern with the etiological role of contemporaneous manifest behaviors. It was only in 1949 that Johnson proposed that some forms of acting out in children were the direct result of their parents' current and quite visible manifest actions (7). Likewise, only in recent years has there been interest and focus on behavior within couples and families, which manifest behavior has been judged most relevant to an understanding of the participant's feelings and actions. I do not wish in the least to propose the unimportance of unconscious forces but only to suggest that interest in the concealed has resulted in a neglect of the patent. Why only now this "blinding glimpse of the obvious"? I have no answer other than that given in the previous paragraph, but I would opine that the recognition of the role of DAF falls into the same category.

Finally, DAF supplies a name for a commonly understood chain of causality—one which is so commonsensical that scientists (behavioral or otherwise) are apt to advance it only with embarrassment. † Supplying this principle with a formal name may allow its explanatory use in totally respectable circles.

---

* Or, to quote Lucretius, who is somewhat stronger, "For fools admire and like all things the more which they perceive to be concealed under involved language. . . ." (11).

† Asher aptly observes that named disease syndromes are "recognized" when not present, while a "condition without [a name] has far less chance of clinical recognition. A rose without a name may smell as sweet, but it has a far less chance of being smelt" (2, p. 359).

REFERENCES

1. Alexander, F., & French, T. M. *Psychoanalytic therapy.* New York: Grove Press, 1961.
2. Asher, R. Making sense. *Lancet,* 1959, Part 2: 359-365.
3. Bell, R. Q. A reinterpretation of the direction of effects in studies of socialization. *Psychol. Review,* 1968, **75,** 81-95.
4. Berne, E. *Transactional analysis in psychotherapy.* New York: Grove Press, 1961.
5. Ellis, A. *Reason and emotion in psychotherapy.* New York: Lyle Stuart, 1962.
6. Gruenberg, E. M. The social breakdown syndrome—some origins. *American Journal of Psychiatry,* 1967, **123,** 1481-1489.
7. Johnson, A. M. Sanctions for superego lacunae of adolescents. In K. R. Eissler, (Ed.), *Searchlights on Delinquency.* New York: International Universities Press, 1949.
8. Kanner, L. *Child Psychiatry.* Springfield, Ill.: Thomas, 1962.
9. Leopold, L. B., & Langbein, W. B. River meanders, *Scientific American,* 1966, **214,** 60-73.
10. Levy, D. M. *Maternal overprotection.* New York: Columbia University Press, 1943.
11. Lucretius, De rerum natura. Book I. In *The stoic and Epicurean philosophers.* New York: Modern Library, 1957, 641-642.
12. Maruyama, M. The second cybernetics: Deviation amplifying mutual causative processes. *American Scientist,* 1963, **51,** 164-179.
13. Meyer, A. What do histories of insanity teach us concerning preventive mental hygiene during the years of school life? (1908) In A. Lief (Ed.), *The commonsense psychiatry of Dr. Adolf Meyer,* New York: McGraw-Hill, 1948.
14. Rapaport, D. The theory of ego autonomy: A generalization. *Bulletin of the Menninger Clinic,* 1958, **22,** 13-35.
15. Rosenthal, M. J. The syndrome of the inconsistent mother. *American Journal of Orthopsychiatry,* 1962, **32,** 637-644.
16. Stratchey, J. The nature of the therapeutic action of psycho-analysis. *International Journal of Psychoanalysis,* 1934, **15,** 127-159.
17. Stunkard, A., & Burt, V. Obesity and the body image: II. Age at the onset of disturbances in the body image. *American Journal of Psychiatry,* 1967, **123,** 1443-1447.
18. White, R. W. Ego and reality in psychoanalytic theory. *Psychological Issues,* 1964, **3,** (3, Whole No. 11).

Chapter 25

Toward a Specification of Teaching and Learning in Psychotherapy

Hans H. Strupp, Ph.D.

In one of his last papers, Alexander (1) commented on the remarkable fact that very few changes in the intricate procedure of psychoanalytic therapy have occurred since its guiding principles were formulated by Freud between 1912 and 1915. He asked: "Is it due to the perfection of the standard procedure which because of its excellence does not require reevaluation and improvement, or does it have some other cultural rather than scientific reason?" Alexander's career as a psychotherapist and his contributions to the problem of therapeutic technique bear eloquent testimony that any formulations cannot possibly be the final word in science; to act as if they were can only result in stultification of progress. While admitting that "Almost all statements concerning technique could be legitimately only highly tentative," Alexander noted that the essential psychodynamic principles of analytic therapy rest on solid observational foundations, which he summarized as follows (condensed quotation):

1. During therapy, unconscious (repressed) material becomes conscious. This increases the action radius of the conscious ego and permits greater ego control of previously repressed impulses and tendencies.

2. The mobilization of unconscious material is achieved mainly by two basic therapeutic factors: (a) interpretation of material emerging from free association and (b) the patient's emotional interpersonal experiences in the therapeutic situation (transference). The therapist's relatively objective, nonevaluative, impersonal attitude is the principal factor in mobilizing unconscious material.

Reprinted from *Archives of General Psychiatry*, 1969, **21**, 203-213, by permission of the publisher and the author. Dr. Strupp is Professor of Psychology and Director of Clinical Training, Department of Psychology, Vanderbilt University, Nashville, Tennessee.

3. The patient shows resistance against recognizing unconscious content. Overcoming this resistance is one of the primary technical problems in therapy.

4. The patient will sooner or later direct his typical neurotic attitudes toward the therapist. He develops a transference which is the repetition of interpersonal attitudes, mostly the feelings of the child to his parents. The resolution of the "transference neurosis" becomes the aim of therapy (1).

Most analytic therapists will agree with Alexander's succinct summary of the process, but few have followed his quest to explore what therapists actually do in the therapeutic situation. It became clear to Alexander, as it did to Glover in the 1930's, and to a host of researchers since about 1940, that general formulations can serve onlyas the barest scaffolding for the transactions between therapist and patient. There must be a continuing search to identify and refine the principles underlying the therapist's actual operations. Glover's pioneering survey of British psychoanalysts was the first step in exploding the myth, since then articulately elaborated by Kiesler (9), that there is a standard therapeutic technique and that the therapist's behavior in therapy is uniform even if he shares with his colleagues a set of common theoretical assumptions. Psychotherapy is an immensely complicated process, and any system which attempts to reduce it to a single or a few general statements cannot escape the charge of oversimplification. Realizing this, Alexander was firmly convinced that psychotherapy must be studied "from the ground up," that is, through painstaking observation of the process. Acting on this conviction, he initiated the program at Mount Sinai Hospital to study the therapeutic process as objectively as possible. Unfortunately, he did not live to see the completion of this project, but even on the basis of the preliminary results he arrived at two important conclusions:

The traditional descriptions of the therapeutic process do not adequately reflect the immensely complex interaction between therapist and patient. The patient's reactions cannot be described fully as transference reactions. The patient reacts to the therapist as a concrete person and not only as a representative of parental figures. The therapist's reactions also far exceed what is usually called countertransference. They include, in addition to this, interventions based on conscious deliberations and also his spontaneous idiosyncratic attitudes. Moreover, his own values are conveyed to the patient even if he consistently tries to protect his incognito. The patient reacts to the therapist's overt but also to his nonverbal hidden intentions and the therapist reacts to the patient's reaction to him. It is truly a transactional process.

The therapeutic process can best be understood in terms of learning theory. In particular, the principle of reward and punishment and also the influence of repetitive experience can be clearly recognized. In psychotherapy, the reward consists in less conflicting, more harmonious interpersonal relations, which the patient achieves first by adequately relating to his therapist, then to his environment, and eventually to his own ego ideal (1).

Alexander's statement concerning the transactional character of the therapeutic relationship and his prophecy of a fruitful integration between the theory of psychoanalytic therapy and learning theory are of the utmost importance for the future of psychotherapy. Both assertions of course have been made before, but none of the earlier authors has been so thoroughly immersed in, and identified with, the evolution of analytic theory and practice. I believe it is evidence of the "cultural lag" and the encapsulation of psychoanalytic theory, to which Alexander alluded, that these reformulations are only now finding gradual acceptance within psychoanalysis. For the same reason, Alexander's conceptions of "learning theory" fail to reflect developments which have occurred during the last two or three decades in that area. It is also questionable whether the advancement of technique in psychotherapy is best assured, as Alexander believed, by closer naturalistic observation of the process. The latter approach assumes that it is possible to make observations in a complex field without theoretical presuppositions, a difficult problem whose implications are beyond the scope of this paper.

It is one thing to describe psychotherapy (including psychoanalysis) in terms of learning principles; it is quite another to take seriously the implications of this position. Apart from the fact that there is at present nothing resembling a unified learning theory, research findings obtained in laboratory settings cannot readily be applied to the psychotherapy situation. In this paper I have set myself the task of compiling, in a very preliminary way, an inventory of some important things the patient learns in dynamic psychotherapy. In this way I propose to extend somewhat the statements made by Alexander and others on this subject. My purpose is to move closer to an understanding of the technical operations designed to reach these goals. It will become clear, I trust, that psychotherapy mediates different forms of learning and that these learnings follow different principles. To the dynamic therapist I wish to emphasize that psychotherapy is indeed a learning process and that "analysis of resistances" and "interpretations" are only two facets of the therapeutic influence albeit important milestones on the road to therapeutic learning. To the critics of dynamic psychotherapy, I hope to present more concrete examples which may indicate that "reconstructing the past," "analyzing the transference," or providing "emotional insight" into the patient's motivations are not ends in themselves in dynamic psychotherapy, as is frequently alleged.

First, however, it seems apropos to advance some observations to show that (1) mere translation of one theory into the language of another does not seem to contribute substantively to the advancement of either; and (2) in psychotherapy, as an applied art or science, theoretical formulations follow, rather than precede, technical modifications. Hence, advances in psychotherapy are not likely to come from theoreticians or researchers but from therapists engaged in clinical pursuits.

Relative to the first point, it seems profitable to briefly revisit the first major systematic attempt to cast psychotherapy in terms of the principles of learning theory (4). This work rests on the fundamental assumption that neurotic behavior is learned behavior; this being the case it should be unlearned by the same principles by which it was taught. Dollard and Miller assert that the laws of learning promulgated by Pavlov, Thorndike, Hull, and their students should be of material help in this effort, although they concede that principles and laws which are as yet unknown may play an important part. Of major significance in this book are the principle of reinforcement; repression viewed "as the inhibition of the cue-producing responses which mediate thinking and reasoning"; a reformulation of transference as a special case of the wider concept of generalization; and an elaboration of the dynamics of conflict from more basic principles. The bulk of their work is devoted to a recasting of Freudian theory in terms of these principles.

As Bandura (2) correctly observed, Dollard and Miller's massive effort had remarkably little impact upon therapeutic practice, nor has it inspired a great deal of research along the lines implied by the authors. In part, the reason may be found in the general decline of all molar theories in contemporary psychology; to a larger extent, however, I am inclined to believe that Dollard and Miller provided merely a translation of psychoanalytic principles into learning theory terms. That is, they tended to accept as more or less established and immutable the technical procedures and formulations of the psychoanalytic theory of psychotherapy without raising questions about their range of applicability and a host of issues which recently have been brought to the fore (8). Dollard and Miller, for example, recognized and stressed that "the therapist (in traditional dyadic psychotherapy in an office setting) does not control the important primary rewards and punishments in the patient's life" (4, p. 394). However, they failed to raise such incisive questions as did Goldstein et al. (8): Under what conditions does therapeutic learning become generalized to real life situations? Are there better techniques for insuring such generalizations than trusting to luck that somehow the patient will work out more adaptive solutions in the outside world? How can the therapist's influence be maximized, etc.?

In addition—and perhaps more important—is the fact, already alluded to, that theories of psychotherapy are very loosely articulated to technical procedures. Psychoanalytic theory provides a general, but vague, underpinning to therapeutic operations, and the same criticism applies to the theories developed by Rogers, Wolpe, and others. The evolution of the major theories of psychotherapy clearly shows that therapists first experimented with techniques, often in purely empirical fashion, and subsequently constructed a theory to fit their technical procedures. Ford and Urban (5) observed that the major theories of psychotherapy are considerably more explicit about therapeutic goals than they are about the procedures by which these goals are to be reached. If this is true—and I believe it is—it follows that translations of one theory into the language of another remain a sterile exercise unless such translations become a prelude to innovations in practice whose viability can be corroborated in clinical work, and perhaps documented by controlled research. Research per se, however, seems to have precious little effect on clinical practice.

This statement may sound odd coming as it does from an author who has invested a good many years in efforts to elucidate the process of psychotherapy through objective research. While objective research in psychotherapy has shown a stupendous growth during the past two decades, there is hardly a study which the average clinician (or researcher, for that matter) could cite as having significantly affected therapeutic techniques. One would expect that the substantive yield of this work, which is by no means inconsequential, would have exerted at least some influence on practice, but the evidence is hard to find. Is this merely a demonstration of cultural lag or does it go deeper? It is true, however, that the research contributions have produced a certain attitude change in therapists, who have become more mindful of the requirement to adduce empirical evidence for their assertions. Personally, I am convinced that the major function of research in an area like psychotherapy (and probably in others similarly complex) is to document in more or less precise fashion what therapists are doing, to compare their operations, and to raise questions concerning the adequacy of their theoretical formulations. In and of itself research does not result in new insights which, in my judgment, are the creation of practitioners who have become dissatisfied with the current status of the art. The same judgment must be entered about theoretical refinements or reformulations.

The assertion that theoretical advances stem from clinical

innovations is well exemplified by the innovations introduced by Alexander and French. What created excitement in psycho-analytic circles in the 1940's and 1950's was the fact that these therapists began to experiment with changes in therapeutic procedures, such as planned interruptions, modifications of therapist behavior to provide a corrective emotional experience, and the like. The excitement and controversy were not primarily due to the theoretical reformulations but to the changes in technical operations which threatened time-honored practices. Consequently, the conclusion emerges that new departures in psychotherapy derive from changes in technical procedures, not from theoretical reformulations, however sophisticated the latter may appear. From the standpoint of the researcher, this conclusion suggests, from a different angle, that he needs to focus on the therapist's operations, that is, on empirical data of what he does rather than upon verbal descriptions of intentions, goals, and theories.

As a further example of this contention, Freud never wrote a systematic account of analytic technique, a point which has been noted repeatedly (11, 12). From all accounts it is clear that as a therapist he never adhered closely to what later came to be termed the "classical model" technique; rather he experimented extensively with variations in technique and permitted himself considerable latitude in departing from what he espoused in writing. The formalization and the seeming imperviousness to change of the classical model technique is clearly a creation of his followers. The implications of this observation are that the institutionalization of a set of techniques from which no departures are permitted (except through such procedures as Eissler's "parameters," whose stipulations are probably unrealistic and unrealizable) can only lead to stagnation in the development of a science; and that, even if considered desirable by a professional organization, unwavering adherence to a technique is a virtual impossibility. Again, it may be noted that therapeutic practices change when perceptive practitioners begin to look at phenomena and accepted procedures in "unorthodox" ways and, to the chagrin of their mentors, tinker with sacrosanct practices. If the innovations work—and I believe the most creative therapists have been exceedingly pragmatic—the theory is modified to fit the changed practices.

PRODUCTS OF LEARNING IN PSYCHOTHERAPY

In this section, I shall enumerate a set of "lessons" the patient learns in analytically oriented therapy. The order in which they are presented is of no importance, nor is it contended that the items are independent; in fact, a good deal of overlap will be noted. Empirical support derives from a vast body of clinical experience as well as from retrospective accounts of former patients (13, 14). What the patient, in part, learns are new convictions or beliefs about himself and other people as well as new strategies for handling interpersonal experiences with the therapist, reinforced by subsequent reality testing. It is difficult to determine whether the new beliefs are the consequence of symptom relief or whether the acceptance of new beliefs results in the diminution of troublesome symptoms. With most therapists, I tend to believe the latter although I cannot prove it. It is interesting, however, that in the studies referred to patients after therapy typically talked much less about the symptoms that propelled them into therapy; that is, the place the symptoms played in their lives had changed or, stated otherwise, the experience of therapy had contributed to an emotional and cognitive restructuring of their view of themselves, others, and reality.

Typical "lessons" include:

(1) The world is not such a bad place after all. People are more reliable and trustworthy than had been previously experienced. In some respects they are "bad" (that is, not satisfying to the patient) but in others they are much more valuable than he had believed.

(2) One has to be less demanding of people; others resent and react negatively to exploitation. One has to scale down one's (infantile) demands and expectations if one wants to be "happier." This means he has to give up some things he always wanted (for example, praise, adulation, etc.), that is, one has to reduce one's narcissism, and accept limitations in oneself and others.

(3) If one achieves something or gets pleasure out of some activity or experience, one's own satisfaction must be sufficient. One cannot expect others to praise and applaud nor can one bask in the glory of reflected feelings. Otherwise, one will be continually disappointed, and this disappointment tends to breed hostility and resentment, which in turn set in motion vicious cycles.

(4) As a prime lesson, one learns to delay gratification. This learning is painful because often one cannot get what one wants in the form and at the time one wants it. He has to modify his wishes and desires, learn to accept "half a loaf," and in general get along with less (for instance, narcissistic supplies of all kinds). One also has to learn to endure tension, frustration, and privation—all of which is at first painful. (Compare Menninger's apt phrase that therapeutic gains are the products of the patient's frustrations and disappointments.)

(5) Separation is painful but it need not last forever. At least, one can hope (sometimes against great odds) that gratification will eventually be forthcoming. Stated otherwise, the gratification of interpersonal closeness need not be physical; it can be symbolic.

(6) If one wants to reach a goal one has to institute realistic action. Sitting back and wishing is not likely to produce results. A large part of the satisfaction in any achievement is commensurate with the invested effort. By the same token, some things are realistically unattainable; therefore, the wish has to be abandoned or modified. (This, of course, is Freud's well known distinction between passivity and activity, the former being a thoroughly infantile aim.)

(7) Tension, suffering, anxiety, depression, etc., are not quite so bad as one had considered them to be. The patient realizes that he has greater strength than he has given himself credit for. Phobic fears have to be endured and inevitably one gains greater strength and self-confidence in the process. Ultimately, it does not help to avoid painful, difficult, and anxiety-provoking situations; avoidance may provide temporary relief but essentially it is a pseudo (neurotic) solution which intensifies rather than solves the problem. One has to learn to stand one's ground.

(8) Certain interpersonal maneuvers do not work and are self-defeating. At the same time, they are not as dangerous as the patient had considered them to be, either when used by himself or others. Examples include: (a) Anger and hostile feelings in oneself and others are neither lethal nor dangerous. They will not destroy the other person or, via retaliation, oneself. Feelings, contrary to infantile beliefs, are not the same as acts and must not be confused with the latter. (b) Ingratiation typically does not work; for the most part it does not produce the approval one seeks, and when it does, it is at the cost of self-depreciation. (c) Negativism in adult interpersonal relations usually does not coerce the other person to do one's bidding. (d) Each person is an entity and ultimately has to stand on his own feet; therefore, attempts to "merge" with another person do not work. (e) The talion principle in interpersonal relations is self-defeating. For example, even if the other person has hurt one, nurturing a grudge against all people, or trying to "get even" with the aggressor results at least in wasteful effort and has other untoward consequences.

(9) In contrast to the foregoing, cooperation as a technique for getting along with others generally brings the greatest returns. One cannot "buy" others but one can cooperate with those who are willing to cooperate. Other people, of course, are not obligated to cooperate, nor are efforts to subjugate them likely to

"pay off." It is wise to avoid other persons whose exploitative tendencies have been identified. One is not beholden to others, nor are others likely to enjoy slavery (except for neurotic reasons of their own).

(10) Honesty about one's feelings and motives, no matter how unpleasant or "immoral" they may seem to oneself, is a good policy. This does not mean that one needs to broadcast one's less desirable tendencies—although they are universal—or wallow in an orgy of guilt or self-pity because one is not perfect. These feelings have to be accepted as part of man's primitive strivings which are present throughout life. At the same time, recognition of their existence is no justification for acting on them. In the end, man is judged by his actions, not by his fantasies. By recognizing one's motivations, one can often take more appropriate action. On the other hand, one is responsible for one's actions; they cannot be blamed on others, nor can the therapist absolve the patient from guilt. The patient has to forgive himself.

Mowrer's assertion, that the analytic therapist "forgives," "absolves," and encourages "immoral behavior" is not in accord with Freud's teachings nor is it accepted technique. To accept feelings as "data" without value judgment is a very different process from approving them. Mowrer, in contrast, would prefer to see them condemned.

Analytic therapy, however, is in complete accord with Mowrer, Glasser (7) and other contemporary authors in insisting on the importance of accepting responsibility for one's feelings, motives, and actions (see point 14).

(11) Every person has his rights, and one needs to learn to stand up for one's own. In this way one learns to respect others and oneself; often one can also gratify one's wishes more effectively in this manner.

(12) One needs to respect, accept, and subordinate oneself to higher authority. It is futile to try to topple persons in higher positions, aggress, compete with, or rebel against them, or defeat them in other ways. Their power is never complete, and ordinarily one has the choice of leaving the domain of oppressors to search for a more congenial climate.

(13) Accepting authority, however, does not entail abandoning one's freedom, a belief frequently held by patients. On the contrary, accepting authority frees the patient from struggles with others. As Fromm showed years ago, many people prefer an escape from freedom, which they see as threatening a symbiotic relationship.

(14) It is crucial to accept full responsibility for one's psychological processes and for one's actions. With regard to the former, they must be recognized as part of man's biological

heritage and of his past experience; the latter, insofar as they affect the lives of others, largely determine man's social worth. The past is irreversible, but man usually has considerable latitude in shaping the present. Blaming others for one's predicament is self-defeating and ineffectual. One of the most important findings from the accounts of former patients (13) pertains to this "lesson" as the touchstone of successful therapy. With considerable regularity former patients expressed a heightened sense of responsibility which in turn permitted them to take active steps in shaping their fate or coming to terms with limitations in themselves and others. Stated otherwise, they gained an increased sense of strength and mastery.

(15) Implicit in several preceding items is the process of achieving a clearer understanding of one's identity and role functions, whose central importance in personality development has long been recognized. The disastrous consequences of faulty identifications are most glaringly seen in homosexuality and certain forms of schizophrenia but are equally important in neuroses and personality disorders. Also, the concept of sex-typing appears too narrow to account for the kinds of learning under this rubric in psychotherapy. Concretely, the patient learns not only to see himself more clearly as an adult man (or woman), but he acquires greater flexibility, depending upon the circumstances, to function as an authority or as a subordinate, a person who in some conditions is dependent and in others independent, who can assert himself and submit, who can compete when it is appropriate or abstain when it is inappropriate, who can be a parent as well as a son or daughter, etc.

The above inventory is illustrative of significant learnings which occur in psychotherapy but is in no way exhaustive; nor is there anything original about it. In fact, analytic therapists will regard the items as rather commonplace. My purpose in adducing these examples is to pave the way for a consideration of the techniques and procedures used by psychotherapists to mediate these cognitive and emotional reorientations. To elaborate:

Learning in psychotherapy occurs on a *broad* front; the patient learns a variety of strategies and techniques for relating to himself and others; the "insights" he gains in the therapeutic situation necessarily must be tested and applied in real-life situations.

Learning in psychotherapy, almost by definition, occurs within the context of an interpersonal relationship, in the course of which the patient typically becomes dependent on the therapist as an authority, teacher, and mentor. Through the imposition of the "fundamental rule" and similar devices, the therapist increases the patient's amenability to psychological influences and enhances the latter.

A variety of techniques are employed by the therapist in analytic therapy (as well as in other forms). The contention that analytic therapy solely employs interpretations is untenable (which, *mutatis mutandis,* is equally true of other schools). It is highly probable that different forms of psychotherapy employ techniques based on similar principles. However, the application is often haphazard and unsystematic, although the schools admittedly place different emphases on various techniques.

It is clear that analytic therapy employs such common techniques as those mentioned by Dollard and Miller (4): (1) suggesting, urging, commanding, and forbidding; (2) reward and punishment, disapproval and approval; (3) permissiveness; (4) sympathetic interest and understanding; (5) reassurance; (6) questions designed to raise doubts about par formulations entertained by the patient; and (7) interpretations which serve to label feelings, impulses, and patterns of behavior.

To a very significant extent learning in psychotherapy encompasses learning by imitation and identification. Throughout therapy the therapist serves as a model whose feelings, attitudes, values, and behavior (to the extent it can be observed in the therapeutic situation) the patient learns to accept, imitate, emulate, internalize, and respect. They become an integral part of his own view of the world and his system of values. While this process has long been recognized, beginning with Freud, it has generally been regarded as a "nonanalytic" influence. In contrast, learning by imitation and identification is probably the single most important aspect of the therapeutic influence and the fulcrum upon which the latter turns.

Whether one accepts Freud's (6) original concept of defensive identification or any of the more recent formulations which variously stress developmental aspects, role practice (10), learning through reinforcement by punishment and reward, imitation (3), an essential problem for psychotherapy with adult patients relates to the conditions, necessarily created by the therapist, which are instrumental in producing imitation, or identification, or both. To observe the occurrence of the process is but one step in specifying causal relationships. The recreation of a reasonable replica of the parent-child relationship in the transference situation is probably a highly important strategy in this regard. However, despite the sizeable literature on the topic, it seems that we possess as yet little systematic knowledge concerning the precise manner in which therapeutic techniques instrument this form of learning.

To cite some specific examples of therapist behavior: Throughout therapy he sets an example and portrays an ideal. When the patient is anxious, the therapist is calm; when the patient feels guilty about his feelings or past actions, the therapist through his attitude more than by any other means, disagrees with the patient's a priori assumptions and evaluations of his behavior; when the patient attempts to provoke the therapist, the latter does not participate in the maneuver, when the patient is horrified by the enormity of his demands and expectations of others, the therapist accepts the feelings as "scientific data," although he places them continually in the context of infantile wishes and questions their adaptive value; when the patient feels overpowered or helpless in the face of manipulations by significant others, the therapist displays a sense of mastery and competence and at times may suggest alternative courses of action; when the patient attempts to "act out" passivity, erotic longings, etc., with the therapist, the latter thwarts these wishes by nonparticipation; and so on. Thus, the patient's learning is to a large extent experiential but it is also cognitive. However, cognitive learning is seen as maximally effective when feelings have become mobilized, most notably feelings about the therapist and the patient therapist interaction.

Concomitant with the foregoing, the interpretation of unconscious fantasies is viewed as a part, but perhaps a less crucial part, of the therapeutic learning process. It would be foolhardy to follow the behaviorists in discarding the hard-won insights concerning these important internal determinants of attitudes and behavior. There can be no doubt that primitive fantasies influence the patient's feelings, attitudes toward others, and the quality of his interpersonal relations. Still it remains a moot question to what extent the process of making these fantasies conscious furthers in and of itself the therapeutic enterprise. Unquestionably, this process is part of the therapeutic process, but it may account for only a relatively minor portion of the therapeutic force and the change effected by it. On the other hand, I am convinced that interpretations of resistances, that is, those roadblocks which the patient erects to prevent a more open and closer relationship to the therapist, are of the greatest significance and tremendously important in facilitating the identificatory process.

For significant therapeutic learning to occur, the most important precondition is the patient's *openness* to the therapist's influence. Therefore, as I see it, the major effort in analytic therapy is devoted to creating a condition in the patient which permits the therapist to influence him through suggestions, interpretations, appeals to reason, and in general "imprinting" him. Thus, psychotherapy essentially consists first and foremost of social influence techniques or—if you will—behavior control. It is quite feasible to produce attitude and behavior change through the use of a variety of techniques, but, in my opinion, Freud will be conclusively upheld in his conviction that the analysis of transference phenomena is the single most effective technique for exerting a profound influence upon another person.

The transference paradigm, without question, is a highly ingenious design, unequaled by any other method yet created by psychologists (except perhaps through pharamacological agents and, more transiently, through hypnosis) for creating an almost incredibly intense state of openness, emotional arousal, or permeability in the patient. To be sure, this state is achieved only after a considerable amount of work has been accomplished, by means of interpretations of resistance and other techniques designed to break down the barriers impeding its development. Nor, as every therapist knows, does it typically last very long. However, the therapist works strenuously at creating and re-creating it. It is at those times when the therapist is sure of its existence that he injects the "corrective elements" considered most appropriate at that time. Similarly, it is this state of heightened influence or arousal which facilitates the patient's identification with the therapist: He has strong positive feelings toward the therapist, feels keenly dependent upon his love and approval, and "absorbs" his message in the deepest layers of his being.

In part the patient works consciously at following the basic rule—he becomes convinced that he does so in his own interest—but in an important sense he also complies to earn the therapist's approval which becomes an exceedingly crucial leverage. He goes through the agonizing process of subordinating himself to a powerful parent figure whom (following his past experiences) he never fully trusts, and he re-experiences a variety of painful feelings, ultimately out of love for the therapist and the rewards the latter dispenses. Likewise, he experiences consciously violent rage, disappointment, competitive strivings, envy, etc. Frequently, these wishes are thwarted once they are expressed, which again is painful.

Freud and his followers have amply described this process, familiar to all therapists and patients. What has long delayed research and further development are the excess baggage of the instinct theory and other esoteric concepts which have been invoked as explanatory principles. As time goes on, it will be necessary—and altogether possible—to conceptualize the process in terms of simpler psychological principles. This step, I am convinced, will revitalize the basic transference phenomena, whose importance for the understanding of the mechanisms operating in psychological influence is second to none.

Psychoanalysis hypothesizes that truly significant and basic therapeutic change is contingent upon the patient's undergoing the foregoing experience. While I am inclined to agree, the criterion of therapeutic effectiveness cannot be invoked to disprove the existence of the transference phenomena, as has often occurred, nor does it per se further our knowledge concerning them. It is conceivable that other technical procedures prove equally effective (which I consider unlikely) and it is quite possible that with many patients the "ideal" conditions for therapeutic change cannot be created. In other instances, the enormous expenditure of time and effort may not justify the utilization of the method. These questions are akin to engineering problems and essentially unrelated to the advancement of scientific knowledge.

The issue has been seriously confounded by analytic authors as well as proponents of other therapeutic approaches. Freud, perhaps unwittingly, started this unfortunate trend by asserting that in psychoanalysis research and therapy go hand in hand. Since Freud had come upon his important discoveries through his therapeutic efforts, his view is entirely understandable. Furthermore, to Freud research largely meant making observations and drawing inferences from data gathered within the framework of the analytic situation. As Alexander correctly observed, therapy is not research in any strict sense and the procedure of linking research with therapeutic effectiveness is indefensible and inevitably leads to an impasse. It goes almost without saying that a set of therapeutic operations may be effective for reasons quite apart from the theoretical assumptions; conversely, the effectiveness (or the lack) of particular therapeutic operations proves nothing about the adequacy or "correctness" of the theory. However, it is entirely legitimate to challenge the effectiveness of any set of therapeutic operations qua therapeutic operations and to insist on empirical demonstrations of their efficacy.

For example, it may turn out that behavior techniques are the most efficient ones, say, in simple phobias. There is no need for a big cannon to kill a mosquito; indeed, the procedure would be absurd. There may also be cases in which the elimination or alleviation of a disabling phobia or similar conditions may set in motion benign cycles which will produce far-reaching personality and behavior changes. Under other conditions it may be inexpedient, even in severe neuroses or behavior disorders, to use intensive and prolonged psychotherapy. But it seems highly unlikely, although it remains to be demonstrated, that behavioral techniques will prove very effective in producing significant improvements, however defined, in adults with severe neuroses or personality disorders of long standing. In fact, analytic exploration may provide important clues in such instances as to why this is so. The stumbling block is largely the criterion problem, that is, the difficulty of devising and agreeing on acceptable change measures. Unquestionably, changes resulting from all forms of psychotherapy are often not stupendous, which merely confirms the extraordinary difficulties in learning and unlearning. It is hard to believe that psychologists, who after all know a few things about learning, still expect miracles from psychotherapy. Such miracles are simply not to be expected. Realism, however, is not tantamount to nihilism nor should it induce a sense of complacency about existing knowledge or techniques.

SUMMARY

Psychotherapy is a learning process of considerable complexity. The illustrations which have been used to call attention to various kinds of learnings often discussed in terms of global mechanisms (e.g., reinforcement, modeling, etc.) leave little doubt that single principles do not adequately describe the learning process. Therapeutic learning always proceeds on a broad front even though divergent theories may stress one form of learning at the expense of others.

The therapist's operations are typically not very well articulated to the kinds of changes of learning to be effected. Rather, it seems that the therapist sets in motion a complex process whose consequences are predictable only in a very broad sense. The task of the future is to achieve greater specificity concerning the effects of particular kinds of interventions.

Therapeutic learning appears to be most effective when there exists a strong emotional tie between patient and therapist, which the therapist controls and manipulates in the interest of effecting therapeutic change. Therapeutic learning appears to be predominantly experiential, although the therapist's explanations (interpretations) of the patient's experience may aid the process. As Fromm-Reichmann put it: The patient needs an experience, not an explanation.

The kinds of learning occurring in psychoanalytic therapy are not intrinsically different from those in other forms of therapy, although the objectives in long-term intensive therapy are obviously different from, say, those in a case of snake phobia. The former aims at effecting significant changes in the patient's identifications, role perceptions, self-control, etc. Even under the best circumstances such efforts require long periods of time.

While the goal of therapeutic efficiency (in terms of time, effort, etc.) is important, in the long run increased knowledge concerning the mechanisms involved in therapeutic learning is predictably more important. Greater knowledge may lead to greater efficiency, if only by defining the range of applicability. The transference paradigm is considered an exceedingly fruitful vehicle for illuminating the processes at issue, but little progress has been made in exploring its potential.

REFERENCES

1. Alexander, F. The dynamics of psychotherapy in the light of learning theory. *Amer. J. Psychiat.*, 1963, **120**, 440-448.
2. Bandura, A. Psychotherapy as a learning process. *Psychol. Bull.*, 1961 **58**, 143-159.
3. Bandura, A., & Walters, R. H. *Social learning and personality development.* New York: Holt, Rinehart & Winston, 1963.
4. Dollard, J., & Miller, N. E. *Personality and psychotherapy.* New York: McGraw-Hill, 1950.
5. Ford, D. H., & Urban, H. B. *Systems of psychotherapy.* New York: John Wiley, 1963.
6. Freud, S. Group psychology and the analysis of the ego (1921). In Strachey, J. (Ed.), *Sigmund Freud.* London: The Hogarth Press, 1955.
7. Glasser, W. *Reality therapy.* New York: Harper & Row, 1965.
8. Goldstein, A. P., Heller, K., & Sechrest, L. B. *Psychotherapy and the psychology of behavior change.* New York: John Wiley, 1966.
9. Kiesler, D. J. Some myths of psychotherapy research and the search for a paradigm. *Psychol. Bull.*, 1966, **65**, 110-136.
10. Sears, R. R. Identification as a form of behavioral developments. In D. B. Harris, (Ed.), *The concept of development: An issue in the study of human behavior.* Minneapolis: University of Minnesota Press, 1957.
11. Strachey, J. The nature of the therapeutic action of psychoanalysis. *J. Psychoanal.*, 1934, **15**, 127-159.
12. Strupp, H. H., Overview and developments in psychoanalytic therapy: Individual treatment. In J. Marmor, (Ed.), *Modern psychoanalysis and perspectives.* New York: Basic Books., 1968.
13. Strupp, H. H., Fox, R. E. & Lessler, K. J. *Patients view their psychotherapy.* Baltimore: John Hopkins Press, 1969.
14. Strupp, H. H., Wallach, M. S., & Wogan, M. Psychotherapy experience in retrospect: Questionnaire survey of former patients and their therapists. *Psychol. Monog.*, 1964, **78**, (Whole No. 588).

Epilogue

Chapter 26

The Art of Being
a Failure as a Therapist

Jay Haley

What has been lacking in the field of therapy is a theory of failure. Many clinicians have merely assumed that any psychotherapist could fail if he wished. Recent studies of the outcome of therapy, however, indicate that spontaneous improvement of patients is far more extensive than was previously realized. There is a consistent finding that between 50 and 70 per cent of patients on waiting list control groups not only do not wish treatment after the waiting list period but have really recovered from their emotional problems—despite the previous theories which did not consider this possible. Assuming that these findings hold up in further studies, a therapist who is incompetent and does no more than sit in silence and scratch himself will have at least 50 per cent success rate with his patients. How then can a therapist be a failure?

The problem is not a hopeless one. We might merely accept the fact that a therapist will succeed with half his patients and do what we can to provide a theory which will help him fail consistently with the other half. However, we could also risk being more adventurous. Trends in the field suggest the problem can be approached in a deeper way by devising procedures for keeping those patients from improving who would ordinarily spontaneously do so. Obviously, merely doing nothing will not achieve this end. We must create a program with the proper ideological framework and provide systematic training over a period of years if we expect a therapist to fail consistently.

An outline will be offered here of a series of steps to increase the chance of failure of any therapist. This presentation is not meant to be comprehensive, but it includes the major factors

From *The Power Tactics of Jesus Christ and Other Essays,* New York, Grossman, 1969. Originally published in *American Journal of Orthopsychiatry,* 1969, **39**, 691-695. The author is Director, Family Research, Philadelphia Child Guidance Clinic.

which experience in the field has shown to be essential and which can be put into practice even by therapists who are not specially talented.

(1) The central pathway to failure is based upon a nucleus of ideas which, if used in combination, make success as a failure almost inevitable.

Step A: Insist that the problem which brings the patient into therapy is not important. Dismiss it as merely a "symptom" and shift the conversation elsewhere. In this way a therapist never learns to examine what is really distressing a patient.

Step B: Refuse to directly treat the presenting problem. Offer some rationale, such as the idea that symptoms have "roots," to avoid treating the problem the patient is paying his money to recover from. In this way the odds increase that the patient will not recover, and future generations of therapists can remain ignorant of the specific skills needed to get people over their problems.

Step C: Insist that if a presenting problem is relieved, something worse will develop. This myth makes it proper not to know what to do about symptoms and will even encourage patients to cooperate by developing a fear of recovery.

Given these three steps, it seems obvious that any psychotherapist will be incapacitated, whatever his natural talent. He will not take seriously the problem the patient brings, he will not try to change that, and he will fear that successful relief of the problem is disastrous.

One might think that this nucleus of ideas alone would make any therapist a failure, but the wiser heads in the field have recognized that other steps are necessary.

(2) It is particularly important to confuse diagnosis and therapy. A therapist can sound expert and be scientific without ever risking a success with treatment if he uses a diagnostic language which makes it impossible for him to think of therapeutic operations. For example, one can say that a patient is passive-aggressive, or that he has deep-seated dependency needs, or that he has a weak ego, or that he is impulse-ridden. No therapeutic interventions can be formulated with this kind of language. For more examples of how to phrase a diagnosis so that a therapist is incapacitated, the reader is referred to *The American Psychiatric Association Diagnostic Manual.*

(3) Put the emphasis upon a single method of treatment no matter how diverse the problems which enter the office. Patients who won't behave properly according to the method should be defined as untreatable and abandoned. Once a single method has proven consistently ineffective, it should never be given up. Those people who attempt variations must be sharply condemned as improperly trained and ignorant of the true nature

of the human personality and its disorders. If necessary, a person who attempts variations can be called a latent layman.

(4) Have no theory, or an ambiguous and untestable one, of what a therapist should do to bring about therapeutic change. However, make it clear that it is untherapeutic to give a patient directives for changing—he might follow them and change. Just imply that change happens spontaneously when therapists and patients behave according to the proper forms. As part of the general confusion that is necessary, it is helpful to define therapy as a procedure for finding out what is wrong with a person and how he got that way. With that emphasis, ideas about what to do to bring about change will not develop in an unpredictable manner. One should also insist that change be defined as a shift of something in the interior of a patient so that it remains outside the range of observation and is uninvestigable. With the focus upon the "underlying disorder" (which should be sharply distinguished from the "overlying disorder"), questions about the unsavory aspects of the relationship between therapist and patient need not arise, nor is it necessary to include unimportant people, such as the patient's intimates, in the question of change.

Should student therapists who are not yet properly trained insist upon some instruction about how to cause change, and if a frown about their unresolved problems does not quiet them, it might be necessary to offer some sort of ambiguous and general idea which is untestable. One can say, for example, that the therapeutic job is to bring the unconscious into consciousness. In this way, the therapy task is defined as transforming a hypothetical entity into another hypothetical entity and so there is no possibility that precision in therapeutic technique might develop. Part of this approach requires helping the patient "see" things about himself, particularly in relation to past traumas, and this involves no risk of change. The fundamental rule is to emphasize "insight" and "affect expression" to student therapists as causes of change so they can feel something is happening in the session without hazarding success. If some of the advanced students insist on more high-class technical knowledge about therapy, a cloudy discussion of "working through the transference" is useful. This not only provides young therapists with an intellectual catharsis but it gives them a chance to make transference interpretations and so have something to do.

(5) Insist that only years of therapy will really change a patient.

This step brings us to more specific things to do about those patients who might spontaneously recover without treatment. If they can be persuaded that they have not really recovered but have merely fled into health, it is possible to help them back to ill health by holding them in long-term treatment. (One can always claim that only long-term treatment can really cure a patient so that he will never ever have a problem the remainder of his life). Fortunately the field of therapy has no theory of over-dosage, and so a skillful therapist can keep a patient from improving for as long as ten years without protest from his colleagues, no matter how jealous. Those therapists who try for twenty years should be congratulated on their courage but thought of as foolhardy unless they live in New York.

(6) As a further step to restrain patients who might spontaneously improve, it is important to offer warnings about the fragile nature of people and insist they might suffer psychotic breaks or turn to drink if they improve. When "underlying pathology" becomes the most common term in every clinic and consulting room, everyone will avoid taking action to help patients recover and patients will even restrain themselves if they begin to make it on their own. Long-term treatment can then crystallize them into therapeutic failures. If patients seem to improve even in long-term therapy, they can be distracted by being put into group therapy.

(7) As a further step to restrain patients who might spontaneously improve, the therapist should focus upon the patient's past.

(8) As yet another step with that aim, the therapist should interpret what is most unsavory about the patient to arouse his guilt so that he will remain in treatment to resolve the guilt.

(9) Perhaps the most important rule is to ignore the real world that patients live in and publicize the vital importance of their infancy, inner dynamics, and fantasy life. This will effectively prevent either therapists or patients from attempting to make changes in their families, friends, schools, neighborhoods, or treatment milieus. Naturally they cannot recover if their situation does not change, and so one guarantees failure while being paid to listen to interesting fantasies. Talking about dreams is a good way to pass the time, and so is experimenting with responses to different kinds of pills.

(10) Avoid the poor because they will insist upon results and cannot be distracted with insightful conversations. Also avoid the schizophrenic unless he is well drugged and securely locked up in a psychiatric penitentiary. If a therapist deals with a schizophrenic at the interface of family and society, both therapist and patient risk recovery.

(11) A continuing refusal to define the goals of therapy is essential. If a therapist set goals, someone is likely to raise a question whether they have been achieved. At that point the idea of evaluating results arises in its most virulent form. If it becomes necessary to define a goal, the phrasing should be unclear,

ambiguous, and so esoteric that anyone who thinks about determining if the goal has been achieved will lose heart and turn to a less confused field of endeavor, like existentialism.

(12) Finally, it cannot be emphasized enough that it is absolutely necessary to avoid evaluating the results of therapy. If outcome is examined, there is a natural tendency for people not fully trained to discard approaches which are not effective and to elaborate those which are. Only by keeping results a mystery and avoiding any systematic follow-up of patients can one ensure that therapeutic technique will not improve and the writings of the past will not be questioned. To be human is to err, and inevitably a few deviant individuals in the profession will attempt evaluation studies. They should be promptly condemned and their character questioned. Such people should be called superficial in their understanding of what therapy really is, oversimple in their emphasis upon symptoms rather than depth personality problems, and artificial in their approach to human life. Routinely they should be eliminated from respectable institutions and cut off from research funds. As a last resort, they can be put in psychoanalytic treatment or shot.

This program of twelve steps to failure—sometimes called the daily dozen of the clinical field—is obviously not beyond the skill of the average well-trained psychotherapist. Nor would putting this program more fully into action require any major changes in the clinical ideology or practice taught in our better universities. The program would be helped if there was positive term to describe it, and the word "dynamic" is recommended because it has a swinging sound which should appeal to the younger generation. The program could be called the therapy which expresses the basic principles of dynamic psychiatry, dynamic psychology, and dynamic social work. On the wall of every institute training therapists, there can be a motto known as *The Five B's Which Guarantee Dynamic Failure:*

Be Passive
Be Inactive
Be Reflective
Be Silent
Beware